TROY AND HOMER

TROY AND HOMER

Towards a Solution of an Old Mystery

JOACHIM LATACZ

Translated from the German by

KEVIN WINDLE AND
ROSH IRELAND

OXFORD
UNIVERSITY PRESS

OXFORD
UNIVERSITY PRESS

Great Clarendon Street, Oxford OX2 6DP

Oxford University Press is a department of the University of Oxford.
It furthers the University's objective of excellence in research, scholarship,
and education by publishing worldwide in

Oxford New York

Auckland Cape Town Dar es Salaam Hong Kong Karachi Kuala Lumpur
Madrid Melbourne Mexico City Nairobi New Delhi Shanghai Taipei Toronto

With offices in

Argentina Austria Brazil Chile Czech Republic France Greece
Guatemala Hungary Italy Japan South Korea Poland Portugal
Singapore Switzerland Thailand Turkey Ukraine Vietnam

Oxford is a registered trade mark of Oxford University Press
in the UK and in certain other countries

Published in the United States
by Oxford University Press Inc., New York

First published in English 2004

Originally published under the title *Troia und Homer*

Translated from the 'Umgekürzte, überarbeitete Taschenbuchausgabe,
Piper Verlag GmbH, München 2003'.
Updated for the English version in December 2003.

British Library Cataloguing in Publication Data

Data available

Library of Congress Cataloging in Publication Data

Data available

ISBN 0–19–926308–6

1 3 5 7 9 10 8 6 4 2

Typeset by Kolam Information Services Pvt. Ltd, Pondicherry, India

Printed in the USA

Uxori optimae laborum sociae
et
amicis qui consilio operaque semper me iuvabant

TRANSLATORS' ACKNOWLEDGEMENTS

A number of friends and colleagues at the Australian National University have been generous in their assistance during our work on this project. We are particularly grateful to Elizabeth Minchin, who read the whole manuscript closely, offered many helpful suggestions, and supplied background information on Homeric and Trojan scholarship. Robert Barnes, Graeme Clarke, Marian Hill, Roger Hillman, and Gaby Schmidt also gave willing assistance at difficult points. The author, Joachim Latacz, followed the translation process closely, provided welcome encouragement, and was always ready to provide clarification when we needed it. Frank Starke kindly provided the English translations from the Hittite of the Manabatarḫunta and the Aleksandu Treaty.

Kevin Windle
Rosh Ireland
Canberra, September 2003

PREFACE

Troy has been a European myth for over three thousand years. For this it has the ancient Greek poet Homer to thank: in the eighth century BC he composed a long narrative in verse recounting a dramatic conflict between two outstanding Greek leaders engaged in a foreign military expedition. This expedition, which according to Homer took place many generations in the past, is enacted before the walls of Troy, a city of fabulous wealth on the eastern shore of the Hellespont, that is, the Dardanelles, in present-day Turkey (close to Çanakkale).

For nine years, according to Homer, a vast 'Achaian' (Greek) besieging force has stood before the gates of Troy, having crossed from Greece in 1,186 ships to seize the city on the coast of Anatolia. All previous attempts have failed. Troy is too strongly fortified and has powerful allies, who have rallied to its aid. Now the siege is entering its tenth year and Troy is still holding out. Then the besieging force is struck by a fearsome plague: men and beasts succumb in great numbers. A mood of resignation spreads through the army: clearly the gods wish to prevent the fall of the city. In this critical situation, with everyone on edge, the two most important leaders of the besieging Greek coalition clash violently—Agamemnon of Argos-Mycenae, the supreme commander, and Achilles of Thessaly, the commander of the most important fighting contingent. The quarrel—outwardly about women, just as the whole Trojan War itself was about the beautiful Helen of Troy—flares in a sharp exchange of words before the whole assembled army. It culminates when Achilles hurls everything in Agamemnon's face and withdraws from the battle with his troops. Agamemnon lets him depart in a rage, believing he can manage without him. This proves to be a serious error: the Greeks, weakened by Achilles' boycott, are driven by the Trojans right back to their ships. The first of the Greek ships is about to go up in flames. The danger is acute: if the ships are burned the entire Greek army will be lost.

Here Achilles rejoins the fray. With his men he pushes the Trojans back into the city, thus rescuing the Greeks for the moment, but Achilles has lost his closest friend and comrade-in-arms, Patroklos, in the battle, and Hektor, the chief defender of Troy and favourite son of old King Priam, has been killed. In order that Hektor can be buried, an eleven-day truce is negotiated. Then, on the twelfth day, the battle for Troy resumes...

Some time after Homer's day, a Greek supplied a title for this story, told in highly poetic language, dramatically composed in a total of 15,693 lines divided into twenty-four books, with many sub-plots, digressions, complications, flashbacks and flashes forward. The title is the 'Iliad', that is, the 'poem of Ilios' ('Ilios' being a second name in the poem for the besieged city). The *Iliad* is Europe's first work of literature—no other language of Europe possessed any literature at this early date—and to this day it is the only written work to tell at length of the 'Trojan War', that war which to the Greeks was never a myth but a factual event in their early history.

The *Iliad* has inspired countless poets, graphic artists, painters, and composers, as well as scholars, from the Greeks themselves, through the Romans and Byzantines, down to the modern age and most recent times, to produce great works of art and scholarship. It has also inspired great controversy. A substantial number of these artistic and scholarly works were displayed in Germany from March 2001 to April 2002, in a comprehensive exhibition entitled 'Troy—Dream and Reality'. Supported by the governments of the Federal Republic of Germany and the Republic of Turkey, and opened by Presidents Rau and Sezer in Stuttgart, the exhibition enchanted some 850,000 people at its three venues—Stuttgart, Braunschweig, and Bonn. A richly illustrated scholarly companion volume, 487 pages in length, set out the theme of the exhibition and the exhibits, but also situated the whole of the Troy story in its broader context—from the first settlement of the hilltop site at what is now Turkish Hisarlık, in about 3000 BC, through the time when it was abandoned in about 1000 BC, to the rediscovery of the ruins by Heinrich Schliemann in 1870, and on to the most recent scientific discoveries and theories of the latest excavations and research conducted since 1988 in and around Hisarlık, in the region of the

Troad, under the leadership of Manfred Korfmann, the Tübingen professor of prehistoric archaeology. The exhibition and the companion volume received extensive coverage in the mass media.

Thanks to this exhibition, Troy was again placed firmly in the European consciousness. A further contribution to this stemmed from a controversy which in summer and autumn 2001 enriched the feature pages of German-language newspapers great and small, as well as the cultural programmes of many radio and television stations. It was triggered by Frank Kolb, professor of ancient history at the University of Tübingen, who for many years had shared with Manfred Korfmann the running of a research training group on Anatolia, with the support of the German Research Foundation. Referring to the exhibition, for whose scientific management Korfmann was responsible, Kolb charged Korfmann in press articles with 'misleading the public' and even went so far as to call him a 'Däniken of archaeology'.[1] Troy, he asserted, had never had the importance claimed for it by the research team in their thirteen years of investigation and now upheld in the exhibition.

The immediate causes of this sudden attack remain unclear to this day. The Würzburg professor Gernot Wilhelm, the German Research Council's expert on the 'Troy Lower Town' project, wrote in *Die Zeit* on 16 August 2001 of 'personal and intra-university squabbles'. Be this as it may, a minor media battle erupted, culminating in a public scholarly symposium with the title 'The Importance of Troy in the Late Bronze Age', held in the Auditorium Maximum of Tübingen University on 15–16 February 2002. The Troy research team led by Korfmann there faced a small group of scholars from various disciplines assembled round Frank Kolb. The latter group, most of them lacking any archaeological let alone empirically based knowledge of Troy, questioned practically all the results and conclusions reached by the excavators and their collaborators from related fields. The contributions and the discussions, attended by hundreds of specialists and students, journalists and the interested public in the hall, as well as by a radio audience of thousands, did little to bring about a rapprochement. In retrospect, the director of the German Archaeological Institute in Athens, Professor Wolf-Dietrich Niemeier, who, as a neutral observer, had in his contribution evaluated Korfmann's Troy research as well founded and forward-looking, described the Tübingen symposium and the whole 'one-sided Tübingen battle for Troy' in the *Frankfurter Allgemeine Zeitung* on 16 March 2002 as a 'Swabian provincial farce, over which the international scientific community could only shake its head'. He then voiced the hope that 'the scholarly energy... would not be squandered in further confrontations with the "Kolbians"'.

In the six months that followed, Niemeier's hope was largely realized. In the 2002 digging season, the research team, strongly supported by the German Research Foundation and several German and foreign scientific institutions and reinforced in its work by high national and international academic honours for the team leader Manfred Korfmann, was able to get on with its work in peace and arrive at important insights. These insights will in due course, once the active participants have been won over by thorough interdisciplinary study of all the material discovered in fourteen years, provide further endorsement for the research path taken to date.

The presentation of this research path forms the content of the present book. It arose from my personal acquaintance with Manfred Korfmann since 1985, which later grew into friendship, and from following the work of the research team continuously from the time the first sod was turned at Hisarlık in 1988, leading to the joint publication in 1991 of a specialist yearbook *Studia Troica* (twelve issues so far in the period 1991–2002). The idea of writing a book about the new research at Troy, which had developed in so many directions, arose from a combination of external impulses and a personal feeling that, given the fundamental turnabout in the research situation in Bronze Age history, which is to a large extent due to the new Troy research, a provisional appraisal of the facts and theories now to hand was needed and would probably be of value for further work in the various disciplines involved. This proved to be correct: both within the study of antiquity and beyond it the book has been received with great interest, and, as innumerable letters have shown, with gratitude. In a short period of time it has undergone several editions and is now being translated into several languages.

For this edition the entire text has been reviewed and at some points revised, updated, and expanded. It has been possible to include a new discovery, made in August 2003, which lends decisive support to the view set out here. The notes have been extended and the Bibliography brought as far up to date as possible. Extended discussion of the few opposing statements which have appeared since the first edition of March 2001, and which objectively had little new to contribute, seemed to me unnecessary for the present in view of the fact that the extensive material evaluated here (from archaeological, linguistic, Egyptological, Hittite, and Hellenistic studies) appeared to have been less than fully assimilated as yet by the respondents. This position seems to me to be fully supported by the thoroughgoing dismissal—on grounds of both archaeology and Hittite studies—of the 'Kolbian' counter-'argument' by the internationally renowned British experts D. F. Easton, J. D. Hawkins, A. G. Sherratt, and E. S. Sherratt in a recent issue of the specialist journal *Anatolian Studies*.[2] This work was unfortunately not taken into consideration by the representatives of the opposing position writing in *Der neue Streit um Troia* (Ulf 2003) (see p. 296, n. 121). It concludes with the statement, 'Consequently we think that the criticisms raised against Professor Korfmann are unjustified.'

It is impossible to name all those who have helped to make this book possible. I have forgotten none of them. The dedication attempts to state this in succinct form. However, special mention must be made of some of them.

This venture would never have even started but for the determined and unerring persuasive powers of Michael Siebler (Frankfurt). The first drafts met with the approval of Manfred and Katja Korfmann, who read the manuscript pages reaching them almost daily by fax in Troy during the 1999 dig and made numerous corrections to them. The book has the collaboration of Manfred Korfmann (which has since become considerably more intensive) and his wide-ranging connections in the relevant parts of the international research community to thank for many and varied suggestions from the most diverse quarters and perspectives of science. In vital questions of Hittite, Frank Starke (Tübingen) afforded selfless and loyal assistance; Günter Neumann (Würzburg) protected me from many an exaggeration. In the field of classical archaeology, I owe a special debt of gratitude to Wolf-Dietrich Niemeier

CONTENTS

PART II. *Homer*

LIST OF FIGURES

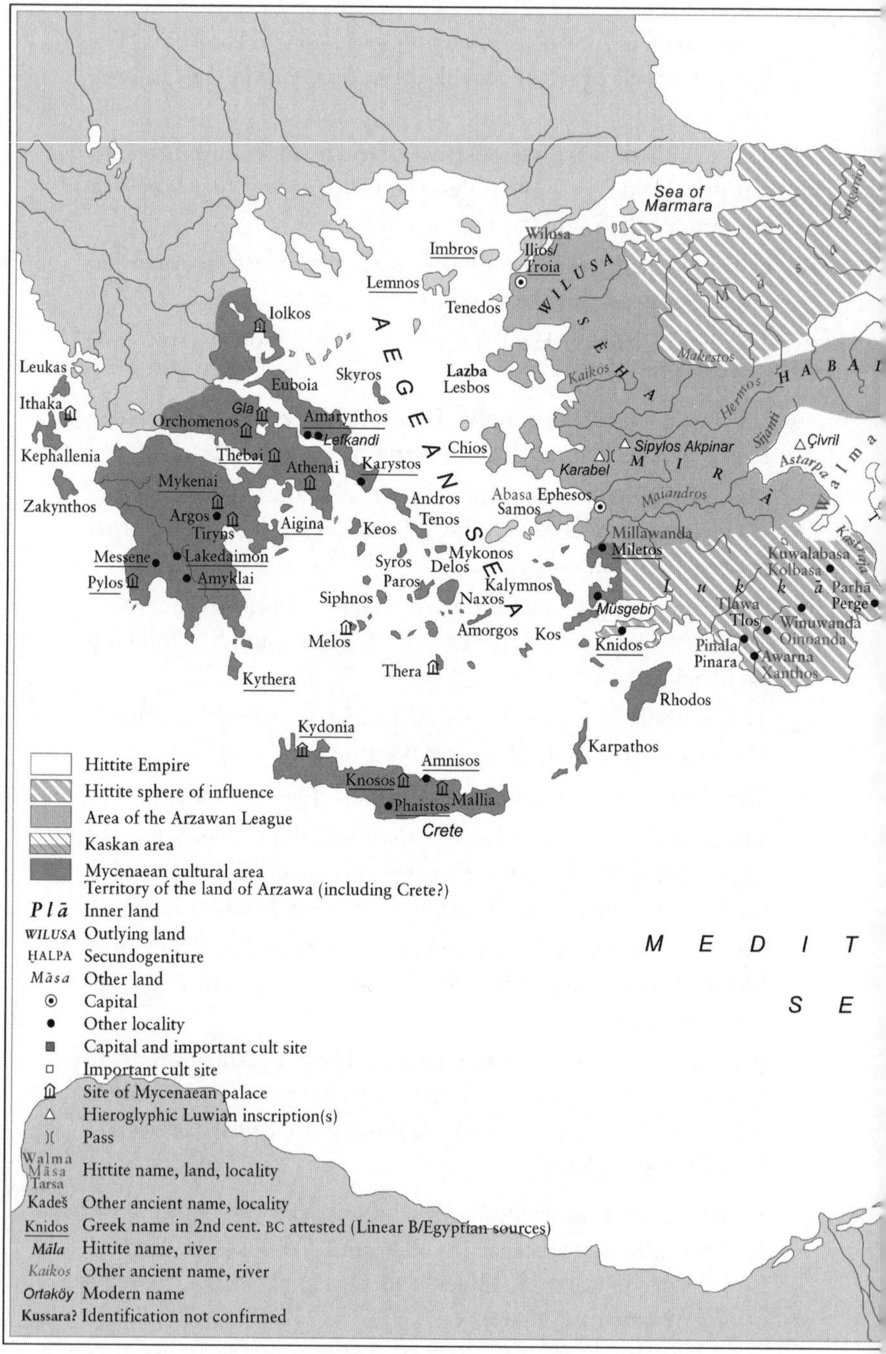
Sea of Marmara
Sangarios
Wilusa
Ilios/
Troia
WILUSA
Imbros
Lemnos
Tenedos
Māsa
Makestos
SĒHA
Kaikos
Iolkos
AEGEAN SEA
Skyros
Lazba
Lesbos
HAPALLA
Hermos
Siyanti
Leukas
Ithaka
Euboia
Gla
Orchomenos
Amarynthos
Lefkandi
Kephallenia
Thebai
Athenai
Karystos
Chios
Sipylos Akpinar
Karabel
MIRĀ
Çivril
Astarpa
Walma
Zakynthos
Mykenai
Argos
Tiryns
Andros
Tenos
Abasa
Samos
Ephesos
Maiandros
Aigina
Keos
Millawanda
Miletos
Kastraja
Messene
Lakedaimon
Pylos
Amyklai
Syros
Paros
Mykonos
Delos
Kalymnos
Kuwalabasa
Kolbasa
Lukkā
Parhā
Perge
Siphnos
Naxos
Müsgebi
Tlawa
Tlos
Winuwanda
Oinoanda
Melos
Amorgos
Kos
Knidos
Pinala
Pinara
Awarna
Xanthos
Thera
Kythera
Rhodos
Kydonia
Karpathos
Amnisos
Knosos
Phaistos
Mallia
Crete
MEDIT
SE
Hittite Empire
Hittite sphere of influence
Area of the Arzawan League
Kaskan area
Mycenaean cultural area
Territory of the land of Arzawa (including Crete?)
Plā Inner land
WILUSA Outlying land
ḪALPA Secundogeniture
Māsa Other land
Capital
Other locality
Capital and important cult site
Important cult site
Site of Mycenaean palace
Hieroglyphic Luwian inscription(s)
Pass
Walma Māsa Tarsa Hittite name, land, locality
Kadeš Other ancient name, locality
Knidos Greek name in 2nd cent. BC attested (Linear B/Egyptian sources)
Māla Hittite name, river
Kaikos Other ancient name, river
Ortaköy Modern name
Kussara? Identification not confirmed

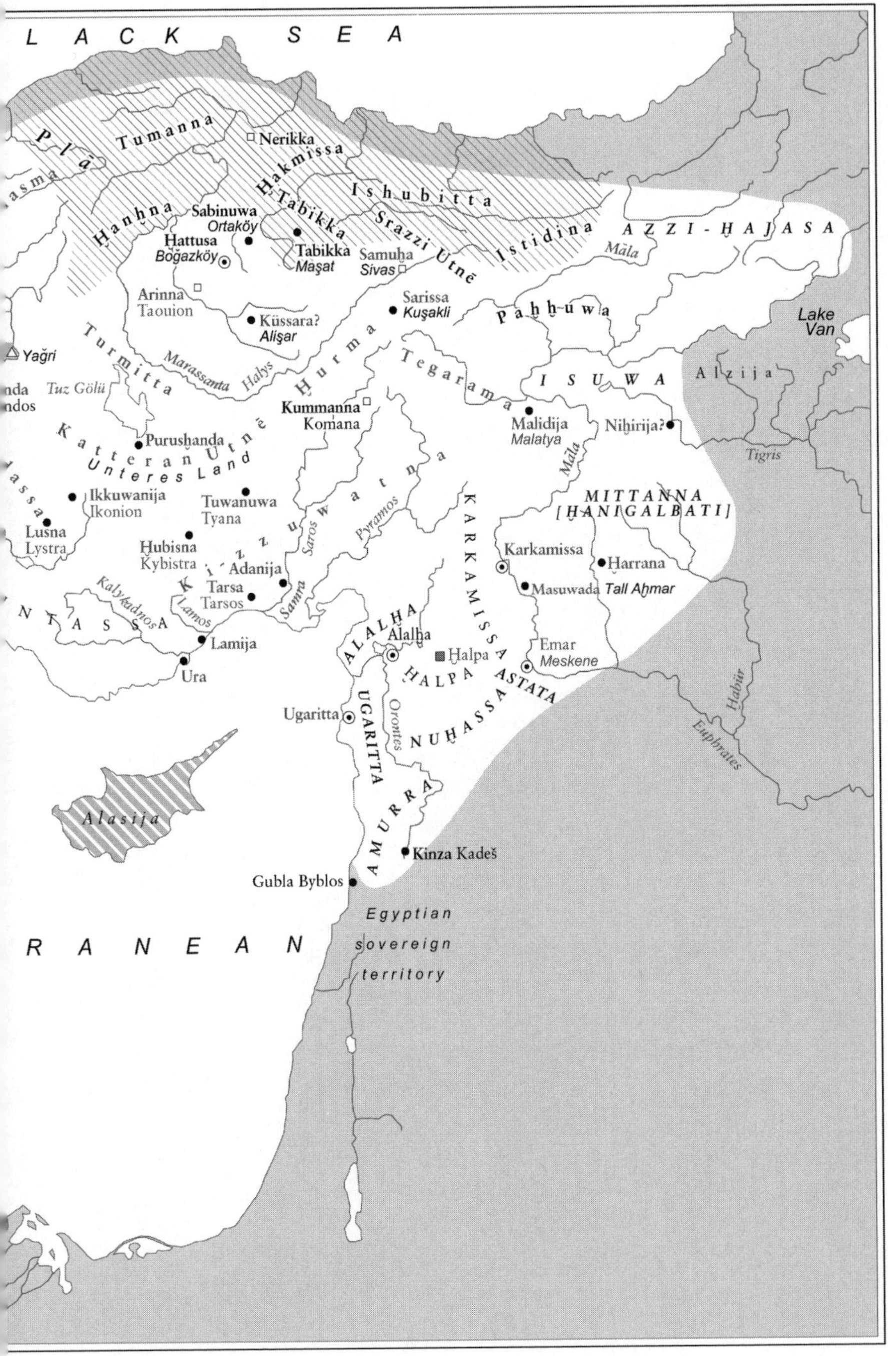

LACK SEA
Plā
Tumanna
Nerikka
Ḫakmissa
asma
Ishubitta
Ḫanḫna
Sabinuwa
Ortaköy
Tabikka
Ḫattusa
Boğazköy
Tabikka
Maşat
Samuḫa
Sivas
Srazzi Utnē
Istidina
AZZI-ḪAJASA
Māla
Arinna
Taouion
Küssara?
Alişar
Sarissa
Kuşakli
Paḫḫuwa
Lake Van
Turmitta
Marassanta
Halys
Ḫurma
Tegarama
Yağri
Tuz Gölü
nda
ndos
Kummanna
Komana
ISUWA
Alzija
Malidija
Malatya
Niḫirija?
Katteran Utnē
Unteres Land
Purusḫanda
Tigris
Māla
Kizzuwatna
Ikkuwanija
Ikonion
Tuwanuwa
Tyana
Pyramos
Saros
KARKAMISSA
MITTANNA
[ḪANIGALBATI]
Lusna
Lystra
Ḫubisna
Kybistra
Adanija
Karkamissa
Ḫarrana
Tarsa
Tarsos
Samra
Masuwada
Tall Aḫmar
Kalykadnos
Lamos
NTASSA
Lamija
ALALḪA
Alalḫa
Ḫalpa
ḪALPA
ASTATA
Emar
Meskene
Ura
Ugaritta
UGARITTA
Orontes
NUḪASSA
Ḫabur
Euphrates
Alasija
AMURRA
Kinza Kadeš
Gubla Byblos
Egyptian sovereign territory
RANEAN

Introduction

In recent years the theme of Troy has been appearing with increasing frequency in the newspapers, magazines, radio, television, and film. There are several reasons for the fascination that continues to adhere to the name and to everything to do with Troy (the Trojan War, the Trojan horse). One of these is certainly the fact that to many people Troy is synonymous with archaeology, with the excitement of a journey into the past, with the search for mysterious buried treasures, in other words, with the rediscovery of what is lost. For many people, another reason may lie in the fact that Troy marks the beginning of the science of modern excavation, and this beginning is inseparably linked with the name of Heinrich Schliemann, to whom many myths are attached. Among these is the 'treasure of Priam', which Schliemann discovered in 1873 and brought to Berlin, and which reappeared a few years ago in the Pushkin Museum in Moscow. Michael Siebler gave a riveting account of this incredible story in 1994 in a special issue of the journal *Antike Welt*: 'A New Odyssey: From an Air-Raid Shelter to the Pushkin Museum' ('Eine andere Odyssee: Vom Flak-Bunker zum Puschkin-Museum'). A third reason is very likely a feeling of satisfaction at the fact that the site of Troy and the problem of Troy have again been under intensive study since 1988 by an international research team, after a gap of fifty years, and that this work with its often sensational discoveries continues year after year to remind us of the significance of Schliemann's achievement.

Behind all these reasons, however, lies something else and something deeper: Troy is one of those great rich human cultures which exemplifies the historical law of the rise and fall of empires as self-contained processes: Sumer, Babylon, the Cretan kingdom of Minos, the Hittite empire of Asia Minor, the first Greek high culture in Mycenae-Tiryns-Pylos, the Assyrian empire, the empire of

Alexander the Great, and many other empires, reaching down to the Soviet empire in the twentieth century. Among these cultural and power systems, Troy occupies a special position: about the rise and fall of this particular centre, which lasted for two thousand years, we know very little. Was it really destroyed by the 'Trojan War' and consigned to the flames? After ten years of unsuccessful siege by the Greeks, was the means of destruction really the Trojan horse, that ingenious creation of the prototypical engineer and inventor, Odysseus? And what has Homer to do with it—the Greek poet, who in his *Iliad* tells of the fall of Troy centuries after the event and seems to know so much about this wealthy city? These are the main questions which continue to stimulate fresh interest and trouble the deep-seated human passion for solving riddles.

In Troy and on the problem of Troy, science—which after all is nothing more than systematized riddle-solving—has achieved outstanding successes in the last ten to fifteen years. It is the purpose of this book to tell of these to readers who are unable to participate in the adventure of science. It is intended for a broad readership, but this does not exclude the possibility that colleagues in the numerous disciplines of the study of antiquity as well as students and teachers may also find it useful. Since it is aimed primarily at non-specialists rather than specialists, every effort has been made to avoid as far as possible the professional jargon of works of this kind, to provide explanations, which the specialist will not need but should regard with friendly tolerance, and to translate all foreign-language material and generally present this in the clearest possible way.[1] This is sometimes difficult when one has dealt with a subject for decades, and no doubt the attempt has been less than fully successful. But it is hoped that the effort will be visible.

It should not be expected that all the problems connected with Troy will be treated. That would mean building up such a mass of material that there would be no apparent connecting theme. Instead this book is about a particular problem which stands at the heart of the whole question of Troy. Those who have become familiar with this central problem will then find it easier to understand all the other problems surrounding Troy.

The question at the heart of Trojan studies may be divided into four parts: (1) Is the hill on the Dardanelles, where excavations have been going on for 130 years, to be identified with the 'Troy' that Homer takes as the setting for his *Iliad*? (2) If so, what was the historical Troy like before it went up in flames? (3) How could the knowledge of this historical Troy and its fall have reached the Greek poet Homer 450 years later? (4) If this was possible, and if the progress of the transmission of this knowledge may be reconstructed, to what extent can we use Homer's *Iliad* as a source of information on the historical Troy?

These four questions all add up to the single question of the relation between Troy and Homer. Accordingly, 'Troy and Homer' is the title of this book. This does not mean that all questions relating to Troy and Homer will be answered in it. It merely indicates that the preconditions need to be created so that these questions may be approached from a sound basis. For no question having to do with Troy and Homer can be resolved in any satisfactory way without previously clarifying what the relation is between Troy and Homer. The sole primary source of information about the Trojan War and the Trojan horse—and on many related matters—remains, as before, Homer. All other references are of later provenance and derive from him.

However, before we can begin to tackle these questions, some essential information must be set forth or recalled to mind. The following section attempts to do this as concisely as possible—too concisely, perhaps, for some. Readers who seek further or more precise details may refer to the bibliography at the end of this volume. One of the author's modest hopes is that the content will whet readers' appetites and entice them into the great adventure of the study of Troy. But those who are already infected will find their way forward without help.

Troy,[2] also known as 'Ilios',[3] provides the setting for a poem composed in about 700 BC in ancient Greek by the poet Hómēros, known to us as Homer. The poem is a long *epos*, a narrative poem of almost 16,000 lines; each line is a hexameter (Greek: 'six-measure'), which means a long line of six elements. (The poetic form will be examined in more detail later on.) The story is set in the distant past: the narrator informs his audience at the very start, and keeps repeating, 'The story I am telling here is far in the past.' The title of the epic is 'Ilias', which is the feminine form of an adjective meaning 'pertaining to Ilios', and a Greek listener hearing this would automatically supply a noun such as *poíēsis* (poem) and understand 'Ilias' as 'a poem about [the city of] Ilios'. The title was not provided by the poet, but was added later to a poem which originally had none, to distinguish it from others of a similar nature, such as the *Odýsseia*, also attributed to Homer (over 12,000 hexameter lines), which, however, does not take place before Ilios but at many different Mediterranean sites, and was therefore best named not after its setting but after its main protagonist, Odysseus. The *Iliad*, like its sister-epic the *Odyssey*, was copied and recopied over many centuries, first under the Greeks, then under the Romans, since the educated classes read and spoke Greek as their first foreign language, and later in the Byzantine empire and in the Christian monasteries. Finally, when printing began in Europe in about 1450, it was printed in book form.

The *Iliad* is Europe's oldest literary monument. We know this because only a few decades lie between the time it was set down in writing and the earlier creation by the Greeks of the *alphabet* (*c.*800 BC) which, in its Latin form, we still use today. For centuries before this, the Greeks, having no writing, had been unable to write down anything.

Homer's Troy/Ilios was identified by his contemporaries, as well as later generations in Greece and Rome right down to the sixth century AD, with the ruins of a citadel in the Troad, that is, in that part of Asia Minor in present-day Turkey close to the narrow straits separating the Mediterranean from the Black Sea. We know these straits as 'the Dardanelles' (after Dardanos, the ancestor of the Trojans named in the *Iliad*). The Greeks called the same straits 'the Helles-póntos' (sea of Helle), Helle being a figure from Greek mythology. The whole area of the Troad had been settled by Greeks since about 800 BC. The ruined citadel itself, however, as we now know, remained unoccupied and largely undisturbed. There was probably only a temple there, to which the population repaired on feast days to offer up sacrifices. In the *Iliad*—the text by which Greek children were taught to read—Homer, whom the Greeks continued to revere as their national poet, had celebrated a great victory by the united European Greeks over Asiatic Troy. As a result, Troy came to be treated as a site of national triumph and pilgrimage. Alexander the Great paid homage to the shrine when he crossed into Asia in 334 BC. This may have been a sign: in about 300 BC the Greeks built a new, modern city, the so-called Hellenistic city of *Ilion*, over the entire hill and its gently sloping approaches. Large temples were constructed, often over remnants of much older walls, and to do this the whole of the ridge-top plateau was levelled. After Greece and Asia Minor had fallen under *Roman* domination, from the time of Gaius Julius Caesar onward (the first century BC), a new phase of construction began under the Caesars: the site was once more built over and Roman *Ilium* arose. Greeks and Romans alike were fond of visiting the new cities of Ilion or Ilium respectively, and honouring them as historical sites.

In the sixth century AD the site fell into disuse. In the course of the following centuries the Greek and Roman buildings collapsed and gradually became overgrown. The area returned to heath, pasture, arable and fallow land. Here and there the remains of buildings could be seen, but the people of the region did not know whether they were of ancient or comparatively recent origin. When the whole region came under Turkish rule (Constantinople fell in 1453), the hill on which the citadel and the towns had once stood came to be known by the Turkish name of Hisarlık, on account of the still recognizable ruins.[4]

Outwardly the hill looked like many others in the region. The precise topographical situation of Ilion/Ilium, and thus of Troy/Ilios, was forgotten. But since Homer's *Iliad* continued to be read—especially in eighteenth- and nineteenth-century Europe, in the classically-oriented grammar schools of the period—efforts were made to rediscover the site. Travellers frequently proposed possible new sites, including Hisarlık, but since there was no excavation none of the suggestions could be followed up.

Troy was rediscovered and excavated by two men: Frank Calvert, the British and American consul, an amateur archaeologist and long-time resident of the Dardanelles, was convinced that Hisarlık must be the site of Troy and began to excavate the hill of Hisarlık in 1863. His efforts were on a modest scale, however, as he lacked the financial resources for a really systematic investigation. At this point Heinrich Schliemann entered the picture. The son of a Protestant clergyman from Mecklenburg (born in Neubukow in 1822, died in

Naples in 1890), he had amassed a vast fortune as a merchant in St Petersburg, mostly during the Crimean War of 1853–6. Since 1864, however, he had largely withdrawn from business ventures and devoted himself to the study of various subjects: languages, literature, the study of antiquity (at the Sorbonne), and to endless travel. Relying on information from Frank Calvert and with Homer's *Iliad* as his guide, he began his excavations in Hisarlık in April 1870 and then pursued these on a grand scale from 1871 to 1873, and in 1878–9 and 1890, accompanied by the Berlin professor of medicine, politician, anthropologist, and archaeologist Rudolf Virchow and the architect and researcher of architecture Wilhelm Dörpfeld.

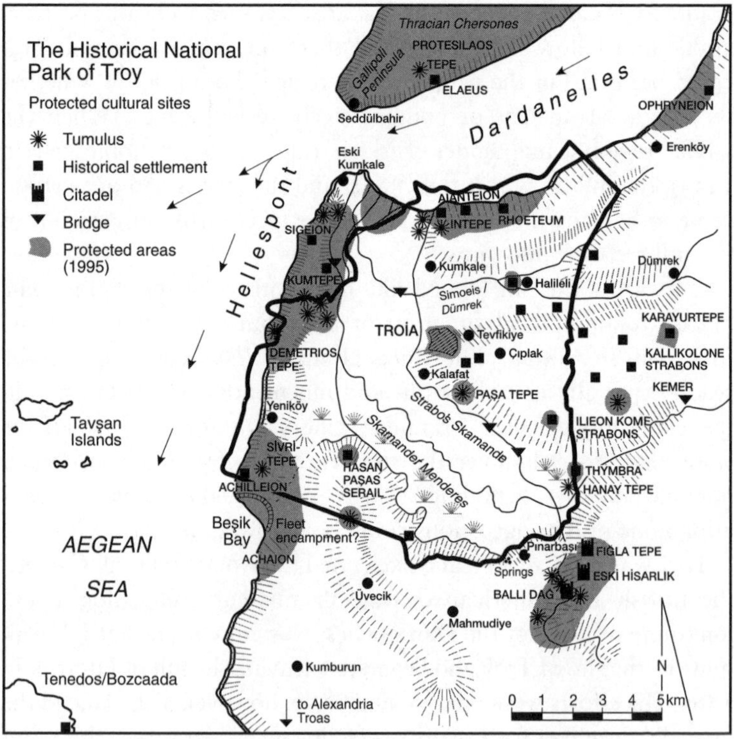

FIG. 1. Troy and its environs today. The black line shows the boundaries of the National Park.

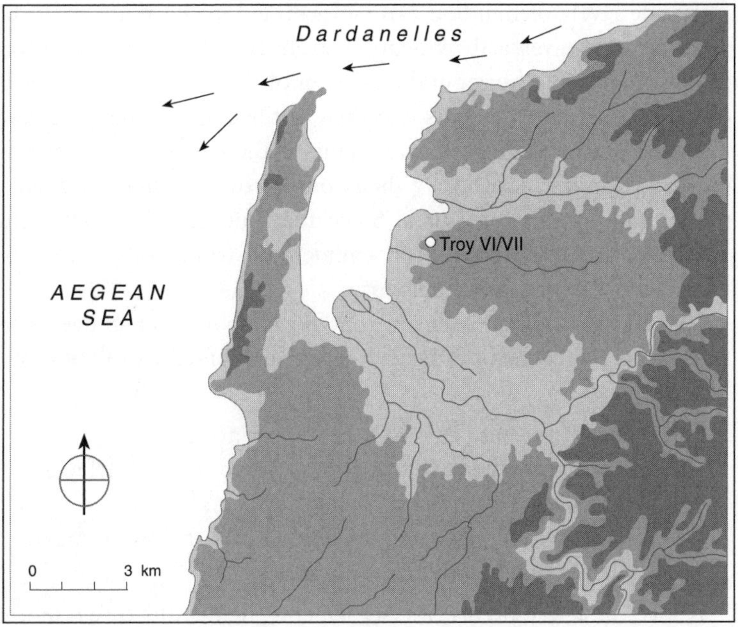

FIG. 2. Troy and its environs in the second millennium BC.

His finds—including the so-called treasure of Priam, which was first kept in Berlin but is now mostly in Moscow and St Petersburg—and his discoveries (not only at Troy but also in Greece: Mycenae, Tiryns, and Orchomenos) brought him world fame.[5]

The hill of Hisarlık, which measures 150 by 200 metres in area and now stands about 37 metres high, forms a spur-like projection of a limestone plateau, 6 kilometres east of the Aegean coast and 4.5 kilometres south of the Dardanelles (Figs. 1 and 2). As we now know from archaeological investigations, as early as prehistoric times, from *c.*3000 to *c.*1000 BC, it was occupied continuously and fortified. As dried mud bricks were the main building material, and these have a limited life, every forty or fifty years on average renovation of large parts of the settlement was called for. The old structures were then levelled, which meant that the new ones stood at a higher level than their predecessors. In this way, on the natural rock of the hill a second, man-made mound arose, about 16 metres in height. If vertical shafts are bored into the ground, a total of forty-one levels of building can be identified in the shaft walls. In addition to the vertical renovation, from time to time population growth required a horizontal extension of the area occupied. Each of the expanded settlements was then fortified again, that is, a new defensive wall was built. The remnants of these walls can be distinguished from one another by their construction methods and technique, and by other features. Since the time of Schliemann and Dörpfeld the levels have been enumerated from bottom to top, from the oldest city to the newest.

Schliemann at first believed that he had discovered five such forts from the prehistoric period. These he named as follows (see Fig. 3a):

(I) First settlement (16–10 m. below surface);
(II) Second settlement, 'burnt city' (10–7 m. below surface);
(III) Third settlement (7–4 m. below surface);
(IV) Fourth settlement, 'wooden city' (4–2 m. below surface);
(V) 'Alien people' (2 m. below surface).

Above these five prehistoric settlements, he identified two more, from the historical period:

(VI) Greek Ilion (1 m. below surface);
(VII) Roman Ilion (1–0 m. below surface).

As Fig. 3a shows, this division was maintained, with some deviations, by the American excavation of 1932–8. In the meantime the terminology 'first settlement' etc. was replaced, thanks to Dörpfeld's influence, in 1882 by 'Troy I', 'Troy II', and so on up to 'Troy IX'.

The fortress which Schliemann until shortly before his death had taken to be the setting for the *Iliad* became in the new terminology, after his death, 'Troy II', a stage in the history of the citadel between *c.*2600 and *c.*2300 BC.[6] At this point the Greeks had not yet moved into the south of the Balkan peninsula, so could not possibly have launched their assault on Troy from strongholds in Greece, as described in the *Iliad*, at this period. A period in which such an assault is conceivable is, at the earliest, the peak of the first Greek high culture, usually called Mycenaean after its capital city, *c.*1250–1150 BC. In Troy this corresponds, as Fig. 3b shows, to the last phase of Troy VI (the fortress walls of which Dörpfeld had first discovered in 1893–4), and the beginning of Troy VII. For this reason this phase in the history of Troy is commonly known as 'the Homeric city'. For the sake of brevity this designation is also adopted here, with the proviso, however, that it is merely a convention and in no way a historical statement. Whether the Mycenaeans, that is, the Greeks of the Mycenaean era, really attacked Troy, and did so in a single operation, and whether the 'Trojan War' between the Greeks and the Trojans, which Homer in the *Iliad* takes for granted, is a fact of history or a Greek, perhaps even a Homeric, invention is still less than fully clear. The intention here is to bring a solution closer.

This period of the 'Homeric city'—together with the 'Trojan War', which, if it happened anywhere, happened here—is the focus of the present book.

On the hill of Hisarlık—if we disregard Frank Calvert's modest exploratory efforts beginning in 1863 (Fig. 4)—there have so far been excavations by four investigators and their teams:

(Frank Calvert	1863–9)
Heinrich Schliemann	1870
	1871
	1872
	1873
	1878
	1879
Heinrich Schliemann (+ Wilhelm Dörpfeld)	1882
	1890
Wilhelm Dörpfeld	1893
	1894
Carl Blegen (Cincinnati)	1932–8
Manfred Korfmann	1988–2002

Korfmann's excavation is the longest continuous study of Troy to date. It is financed by state and private funding. It is conducted every summer for about three months. Between fifty and ninety specialists, technicians, and students of many nationalities and many branches of the study of antiquity take part every season, together with natural scientists and computer specialists. The finds remain in Troy, or in nearby Çanakkale, while the results are

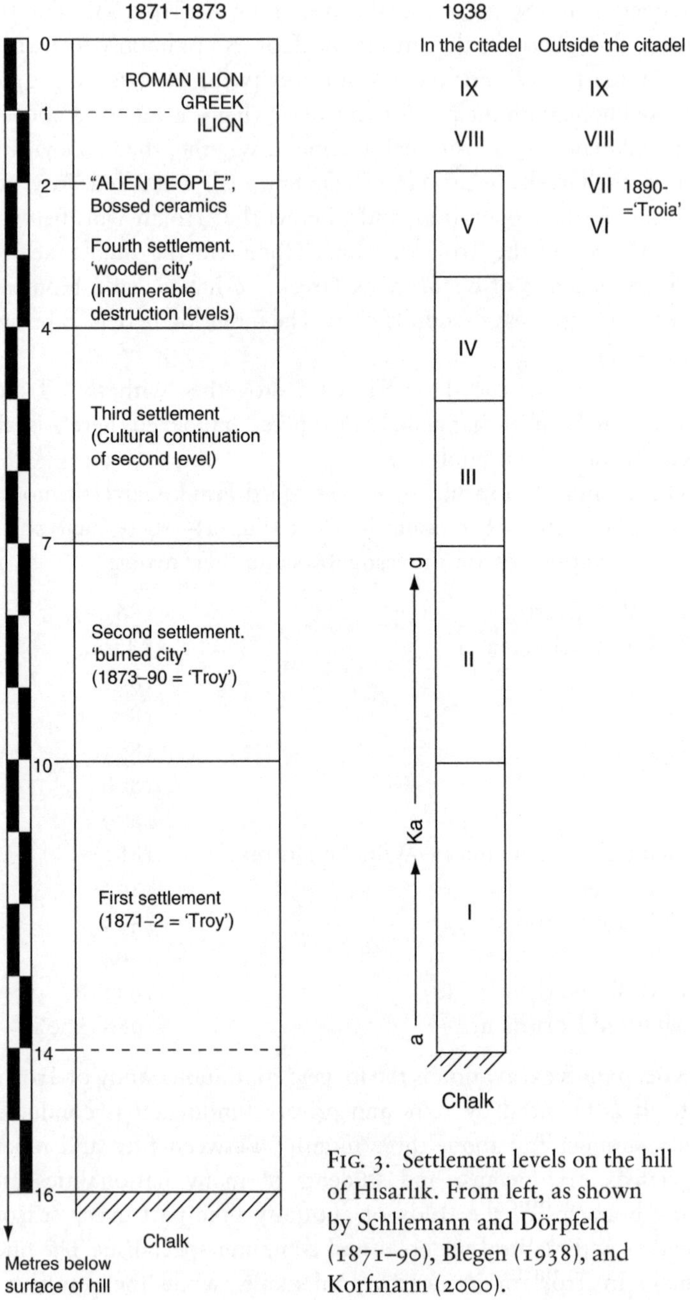

FIG. 3. Settlement levels on the hill of Hisarlık. From left, as shown by Schliemann and Dörpfeld (1871–90), Blegen (1938), and Korfmann (2000).

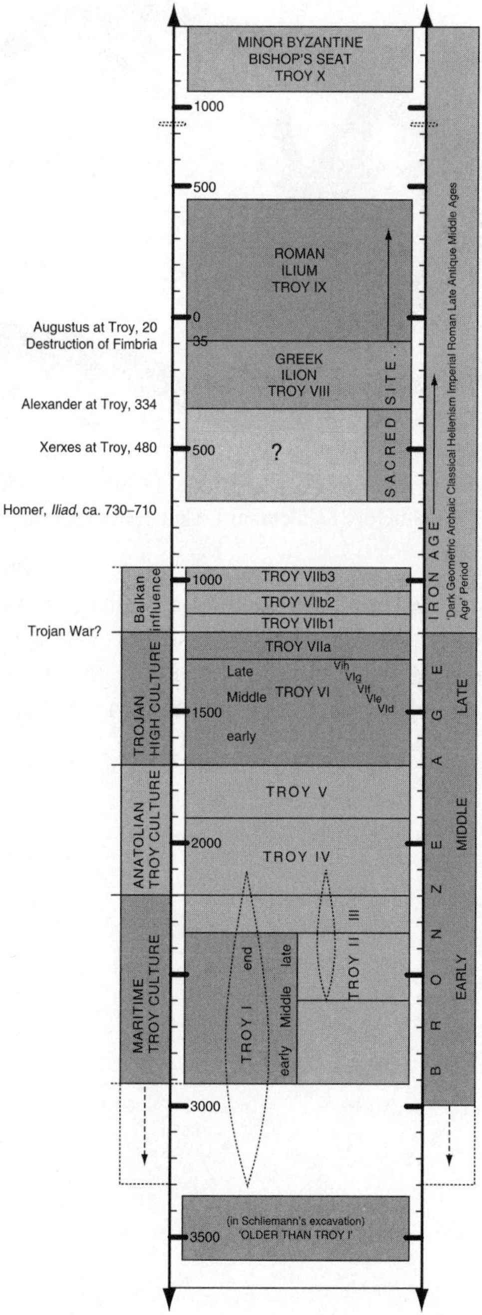
MINOR BYZANTINE
BISHOP'S SEAT
TROY X
1000
500
ROMAN
ILIUM
TROY IX
Augustus at Troy, 20
Destruction of Fimbria
0
35
GREEK
ILION
TROY VIII
Alexander at Troy, 334
Xerxes at Troy, 480
500
?
SACRED SITE..
Homer, Iliad, ca. 730–710
Balkan influence
1000
TROY VIIb3
TROY VIIb2
TROY VIIb1
Trojan War?
TROY VIIa
TROJAN HIGH CULTURE
Late
Middle
TROY VI
VIh
VIg
VIf
VIe
VId
1500
early
ANATOLIAN TROY CULTURE
TROY V
2000
TROY IV
MARITIME TROY CULTURE
III
TROY II
TROY I
end
late
Middle
early
3000
(in Schliemann's excavation)
'OLDER THAN TROY I'
3500
IRON AGE
'Dark Geometric Archaic Classical Hellenism Imperial Roman Late Antique Middle Ages Age' Period
BRONZE AGE
LATE
MIDDLE
EARLY

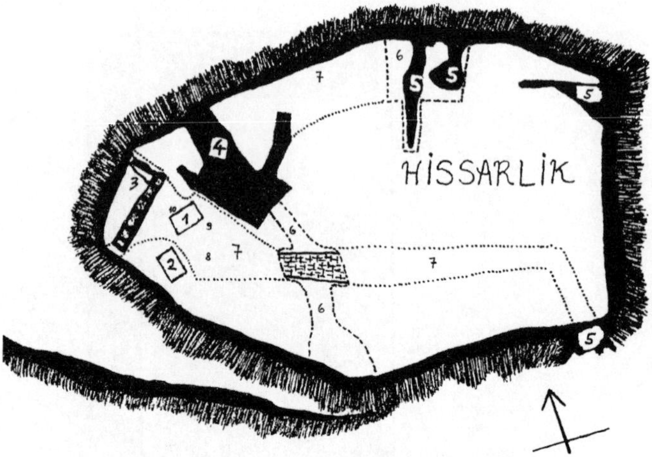

FIG. 4. The first excavations on the hill of Hisarlık
(Nos. 5 and 6 before Schliemann). Sketch by Adolphe Laurent.

processed and evaluated during the remaining part of the year as part of 'Project Troy' at the University of Tübingen. The most significant results are published annually in the specialist journal *Studia Troica*, of which twelve issues (1991–2002) have so far appeared.

PART I

Troy

The Old Sources: A Lack of Authenticity

Troy existed as a citadel, city, and trading centre for close to two millennia, from *c.*3000 to almost 1000 BC. This has been established by the recent excavations led by Manfred Korfmann, the Tübingen prehistorian and archaeologist, since 1988. This time-span is four times the duration of the entire 'modern age' (counting from the invention of printing in 1450, or the discovery of America in 1492). This long history notwithstanding, the world would have known little more of Troy after its destruction in about 1200 BC—and nothing at all of the 'Trojan War', which remains to this day the subject of heated scholarly debate—if a Greek living some 450 years after the fall of the fortress-city and far from the scene of the action had not composed a dramatic story against the backdrop of this site: we refer to Homer and his *Iliad*.

This situation is difficult to grasp: throughout its history this city was, as we know, surrounded by cultures of writing in various languages and writing systems (cuneiform, hieroglyphs), and the notion that only in this precise place nothing at all was written may be dismissed, but so far not a single piece of written evidence that definitely originates in Troy has come to light.[1] Troy itself remains mute. There is not so much as one mention of its name. Of course, this will not necessarily remain the case forever. There are many places in the ancient world which have given up their written legacy with much delay—in the east, in Egypt, Greece, and Crete. It is therefore quite possible that some day Troy itself will speak to us in its own language. Until recently, however, only one voice has spoken at length of the power of Troy and its fall, and this voice speaks to us in Greek, from the mouth of a poet. No wonder, then, that only one scholarly discipline has concerned itself with Troy: the study of classical antiquity (with classical archaeology as a branch of it), which deals with the history and culture of the Greeks and Romans. How inappropriate this was may easily be seen: it was rather as if Moscow had long lain in ruins and we had no evidence of the glorious history of Moscow in Russian, and nothing resembling historical writing in other languages; and instead of such documents we had only a French novel about Napoleon's Russian campaign and learned of the existence of Napoleon and of France at this period exclusively from that book. The result would be that, first, Moscow would seem to us above all the setting for a novel—and therefore very 'romantic'—with Napoleon as its hero, and second, that the discipline of Romance languages, with Romance archaeology, would feel that it held exclusive rights to the pile of ruins known as Moscow. The image of Moscow, to say nothing of the image of France, produced by such a narrow focus on a single source of dubious value would be indistinct and could hardly be taken very seriously. Researchers would come forward to explain that the novel was the product of the purest fantasy and declare that there had never been such a person as Napoleon and that the Moscow of the novel was not to be confused with the Russian ruins.

The extreme one-sidedness of the written source material came to an end in 1996. It was one-sided because there was no domestic source from the Trojan perspective, and only a single foreign source; and this foreign source has not the remotest resemblance to either a body of inscriptions or a chronicle, or to anything resembling history, scholarship, or systematic research. That source is nothing more than a poem, a poem, moreover, which came into being some 450 years after the fall of the city and is concerned with something other than depicting the site, with its human inhabitants and its wars. Before tracing the course of these events, step by step, to see how the situation has changed, we shall once more recall the problem which was thus solved.

The Fundamental Problem: Was Hisarlık Really Once Troia/Ilios?

By 1996 there had been twenty-five excavation campaigns in five series under four expedition leaders at the Turkish hill of Hisarlık on the Dardanelles (see the table on p. 11). In the course of these excavations, the history of the occupation of the citadel on the hill, and also, since 1988 and more particularly since 1993, the occupation of the lower town, has been steadily clarified. However, none of the excavators knew the contemporary name of the settlement being brought to light. All of them knew, or thought they knew, only that the site of their excavations was the same as the place which a Greek poet of the eighth century BC called Homer had called Troy or Ilios in his poem. This was the name they adopted, just as the world had done before, since the *Iliad* was written. But how Homer could have come to call these ruins in the north-western corner of Asia Minor, however impressive they were, Troy or Ilios nobody knew. The uncertainty lay even deeper: had there ever been a Troy or an Ilios at all? Might not Homer, being a poet, have simply invented the name, and with it the whole story of Troy, including the 'Trojan War', while sitting on a block of stone contemplating the ruined walls, which lent wings to his imagination and inspired him to poetry? Against this there was the double name. What poet would invent not one name but two for the scene of a work of fiction? Was this dual appellation not clear evidence of an ancient tradition—whatever might be the explanation of the duality. Yet this idea was not fully convincing either. Heinrich Schliemann himself, the pioneer of Trojan studies, was troubled by doubts in dark hours.[1] Nor would any of those who came later be completely spared. Archaeology as such, without any written discoveries on the site, can never deliver the name of a settlement being excavated. In such cases, one must always have recourse to identification through external sources. As regards the archaeological study of Troy, thirty-five years ago this fact brought an influential sceptic, the then professor of prehistory and ancient history at Saarbrücken, Rolf Hachmann, unerringly to the following conclusion:

If neither the epic itself *nor any other sources* provide any indication that Troy may be identified with one of the settlements on the hill of Hisarlık, this means there is no evidence at all, since archaeology possesses absolutely no evidence. Furthermore, if the authenticity of the city of Troy and the Trojan War cannot be confirmed in the epic itself *or on the basis of other evidence*, this means that the question of the historical authenticity of the city and the war is a false one, since there is no possibility of proof from archaeology.[2]

Almost thirty years later, in 1992, the situation remained the same: Donald F. Easton, who in his three-volume thesis, published in 1989, took issue with Schliemann's excavations of 1871 and 1873 in the most thoroughgoing manner, again declared:

Archaeology cannot give proof of the Trojan War if we are not sure that this was the site of Troy. So far nothing has proved this. We have no late Bronze Age written evidence, no cuneiform or Linear B tablets,[3] no stones inscribed with hieroglyphs, nothing that might really say to us, 'Here lies Troy.' Nor is there anything relevant in the Linear B texts from other sites.[4]

These statements were correct and Hachmann's conclusion was logical. The condition he laid down for identifying Hisarlık with Homer's Troy/Ilios—proof either *from the epic itself* or *from other sources*—remained unmet, in spite of all efforts, until 1996. It is true that 'the epic itself', combined with increasing precision in the evaluation of the archaeological results and thus a narrowing of the gap between these and the textual information, pointed to their being one and the same, and doubts about this were steadily diminishing.[5] But the fundamental uncertainty remained for those who wished for cast-iron proof rather than indications, and the 'other sources', the dot on the 'i' demanded by Hachmann, had still to be found. Where else might such proof come from? It would be ideal, of course, if there were a discovery of an unmistakable Trojan palace archive on the site, bearing the title 'archive of Troy/Ilios', in one of the contemporary Mediterranean languages, like the clay tablet texts of Knossos or Pylos. This of course remains the dream of every excavator of Troy, a dream which, as we shall see, thanks to Korfmann's investigations, now has increasingly realistic chances of coming to fruition.

Evidence of another kind, though less than ideal, would constitute proof enough: texts in any language from the time of Troy, originating outside Troy, providing unmistakable geographical identification of the exact site of the excavations and naming this site 'Troy' and/or 'Ilios'. The direction the search should most probably take, according to such texts, was stated thus in 1983 by another eminent sceptic, Justus Cobet, the ancient historian from Essen, taking up old hypotheses and some suggestions (new at the time) offered by the Asia Minor specialists Kurt Bittel and Hans Gustav Güterbock: 'I do not wish to exclude the possibility that... Troy VI/VII...was really called Troy or Ilios', and he added in a footnote, 'It is possible that *Hittite texts* will yield the proof...'.[6]

Staging Posts in a Search: What was Hisarlık Called in the Bronze Age?

A NEW EASTWARD GLANCE

Five years later, in 1988, Manfred Korfmann began digging at Hisarlık. From that moment the chances of Cobet's prophecy proving true began an upward leap, since for the first time in about 120 years of the study of Troy an archaeologist and prehistorian, not a classical scholar, had come to Hisarlık. This signified a fundamental change: from the time of the Greeks themselves, and later the Romans, right down to Korfmann's predecessor Blegen, Troy had always been viewed from the west, from Greece, and always with Homer in mind. This meant that the perception was not only automatically Greece-centred, but also text-centred. The site was always seen only in connection with Homer's *Iliad* and not as an entity in its own right. With Korfmann, who came to Troy from the east, having worked for many years at the German Archaeological Institute in Istanbul and later conducted excavations in central Anatolia, the perspective was radically altered.[1] Korfmann came to the Dardanelles in 1982 not to verify the *Iliad*, but to study the effects of the ancient cultural region surrounding Troy on movement, trade, the 'world economy', and power structures, at the point where Asia and Europe come closest to each other, at the dawn of both continents, long before the flowering of Graeco-Roman culture. For the first time in the history of the influence of Troy, interest in the archaeological monument of Troy as a whole did not derive from its function as setting for a foreign snapshot in verse, the Greek *Iliad*, but from its importance in its own right as a place of settlement and hub of trade. In this way the compulsion to associate Homer automatically with Troy was removed.

For the study of Troy this proved a liberating break. At last researchers could turn their full attention to the areas which for two millennia had formed Troy's natural hinterland—to the north and south, but above all to the east. After all, by the time the Greeks migrated into the south of the Balkan peninsula from the north in about 2000 BC, Troy had already existed at the same location for over a thousand years. Is it likely that in those thousand years no traditions could have developed which came from the east, the dominant cultural area in that period? The fact that this question had hardly ever been asked had much to do, as Korfmann once put it, with 'the fascination which Homer and his poem exert as "Greek archetypes", and which envelops the site in myth, not to say mist'.[2] Thus a change of perspective seemed to be strongly called for. Manfred Korfmann took this up.

TROY'S LOWER TOWN DISCOVERED

> I can now state most categorically that it is impossible that Priam's city could have extended in any direction from the citadel over the ancient hilltop...
>
> Heinrich Schliemann, 1874

Hypotheses

The first fruit of this changed perspective was the discovery of a lower city—of a clearly Anatolian type—outside the citadel. This discovery had a long prehistory. Schliemann himself, despite his original 'most categorical' statement, had on other grounds (Homer!) expressed doubt 'concerning the extent of the city' in 1884. That is, he doubted whether Troy could have consisted only of the hilltop fortress, which was simply too small. There must, he suspected, have been a larger lower town.[3] His plans for the 1891 digging season included 'exposing the lower city of Troy'.[4] His death in Naples on 26 December 1890 pre-empted this.

When Dörpfeld resumed the excavations in 1893–4, he pursued the matter of the lower city further: although he first exposed the outer fortress walls of Troy VI, instead of the lower city as had long been expected, he instructed the prehistorians Max Weigel and Alfred Götze to take soundings on the ridge running south and south-west of the fortress for up to 500 metres. The results led Alfred Brückner, Dörpfeld's collaborator, to the conclusion that the fortress of Troy VI—the most extensive settlement at Troy and the one whose fall the *Iliad* describes, in the view of the excavators of that time—must have had a lower city with an area of at least 80,000 square metres.[5] Since there were no excavations in the following years, the search for the lower city could go no further. When Dörpfeld published his comprehensive excavation report in 1902, he deeply regretted this shortcoming: he did not wish to conclude the section on the history of the excavations without expressing the hope that 'a substantial part of the lower city would soon be discovered'.[6]

Unfortunately the American excavation under Blegen in 1932–8 did not take up the challenge. When in 1934 a cemetery was discovered from Settlement Stage VI—that is, the level at which the hilltop fortress reached its greatest extent—some 500 metres south of the southern gate in the fortress wall,[7] there was no attempt to investigate the logical question: was it likely that the inhabitants of the fortress, every time there was a death, carried the body for half a kilometre over unoccupied ground and after the burial covered the same distance in reverse? Or was it more likely that the cemetery marked the perimeter of the settlement, as in other settlements of the period, which means there must have been residences—that is, a lower city—built between the fortress wall and the cemetery?[8]

Discoveries

Beneath Ilion lies Troy VI

Korfmann proceeded quite differently. In 1988, in the first year of the new excavations, he took up the 'lower city' thread as Dörpfeld had wanted to do.[9] The use of a new technique, (geo-)magnetic imaging, a form of X-ray photography which made it possible to obtain an extensive picture of the lower strata without disturbing the surface strata, and thus pave the way quickly and efficiently for time-consuming probes and core samples, yielded discoveries in the first year of excavation that far exceeded everything obtained previously. Of course, Schliemann and those who came after him knew that to the south of the fortifications, in the Graeco-Hellenic period (from about 300 BC) and in the Roman period, especially under Caesar and later Roman emperors, an extended town of Ilion had been built (in the terminology of the profession, Troy VIII, or Hellenic Troy, and Troy IX, or Roman Troy), and in 1893–4 Dörpfeld had uncovered the 'bouleuterion' (town hall) and part of the 'odeion' (small theatre) of this town just outside the fortress walls. However, hardly anybody had examined the terrain further down, with the exception of some isolated chance finds.

With the aid of the new technique, Korfmann's expedition was able to establish in the very first year of excavation that from the beginning the Hellenistic and Roman town of Ilion had been laid out in accordance with a large-scale urban design (the streets and house-fronts following an east–west and north–south alignment); that it must have had 'every appearance of being a big city'[10] (wide streets with kerbstones; large buildings; substantial public amenities, such as theatres and baths; an excellent water-supply system, with pipes made of clay, and efficient sewage disposal); and that it extended over a considerably wider area than had been supposed hitherto. But there was another much more exciting discovery: wherever probes could be bored deeper within the limits of the Graeco-Roman area of development, directly beneath the lowest Hellenistic stratum one reached the Troy VI stratum, or the 'Homeric' level. Since in one case a probe was bored at a distance of 170 metres south-east of the south gate of the Troy VI fortress wall, this pointed to a 'possible lower settlement of Troy VI',[11] and Brückner's hypothesis that Troy VI could have had a lower town no smaller than Graeco-Roman Ilion already appeared thoroughly realistic in 1988, the very first digging season.

As more evidence came to light in subsequent excavations, in 1992 Korfmann gathered together in a special study all the arguments then to hand for the existence of an extensive lower town, planned from the very beginning, in Troy VI. The arguments included the almost total absence of arrowheads in the citadel proper: an adjoining residential area would explain this, as it would absorb such projectiles and thus, besides its economic function, serve militarily as a buffer zone for the citadel. On the basis of various other considerations, Korfmann concluded that 'this outer settlement was surrounded by a wall'. To resolve this important question, further excavations were essential.[12]

The wall?

Success in this single-minded search for the lower town was not long in coming. In the 1992 excavation season, using a more sensitive caesium magnetometer than the previous one, Helmut Becker, Jörg Fassbinder, and Hans Günter Jansen discovered a 'burnt mudbrick wall' about 400 metres south of the Troy VI fortress wall at a depth of two to three metres beneath all the other ancient structures. They located this wall, which was up to 6 metres thick and could be followed for about 120 metres, at what was apparently its most southerly point, just before a gate which must have been the south gate of the settlement. The investigators were in no doubt that they had found 'the lost Bronze Age wall of Troy VI/VII', in other words the 'Homeric city wall'.[13]

This discovery radically altered the accepted picture of Troy. Account now had to be taken of the fact that, as Brückner had concluded in 1894, to the known built-up area of some 20,000 square metres within the citadel a further area of *at least* 80,000 square metres in the lower town had to be added. Thus Troy VI/VII, at the moment of its greatest extent in about 1200 BC, covered at least 100,000 square metres. As we shall see, this estimate was still far too low. According to Korfmann's well-founded earlier calculations, this city must have had more than 6,000 inhabitants.[14]

First inferences

The change that even this signified in the perception of 'Homer's Troy'—and later excavations increased the dimensions yet further—has largely escaped the notice not only of the broader public, but also of the research community, except those studying Troy, and not only in the year of the publication of these discoveries but also since then. As we have seen, it was not only Heinrich Schliemann, the first excavator, who thought Troy 'too small'. The minds of many experts who were accustomed to ancient settlements of different dimensions from those proposed by Schliemann, Dörpfeld, and Blegen were haunted by a vision of Troy as a 'nest of brigands and pirates', of greater or lesser importance. One of the best specialists in ancient cities and urban design, Frank Kolb, had said of Troy VI/VIIa in his standard work *Die Stadt im Altertum* (The City in Antiquity), published in 1984: 'Troy VI and VIIa, which might be considered a chronological match for Homer's Troy, were wretched little settlements which could make no serious claim to the title of city.'[15] The new discoveries showed this appraisal to be false.[16] They suggested quite different comparisons: as Korfmann argued in 1993, Troy VI/VIIa in its entirety could now be seen to take its place in a series of known Anatolian fortresses, usually with fortified settlements adjoining them, which belonged to 'the old Near Eastern type of "royal seat and trading town"'. These included, among many other such towns, which naturally were larger, 'the Hittite capital, Boğazköy-Hattuša'.[17] At this point, attention was turned firmly eastwards. The excavation results of subsequent years in the lower town would now be awaited even more eagerly.

The ditch

The very next year of excavation, 1993, yielded the fundamental confirmation, though in not quite the form expected: three test excavations under the local leadership of Peter Jablonka in the area of the 'wall' discovered by geo-magnetic imaging in the previous year, about 400 metres south of the citadel, brought a result which the excavator rightly described as 'spectacular'.[18] What emerged was not a wall, as had been mistakenly assumed on the basis of the 'X-rays' of the year before, but a ditch, cleanly hewn out of the rock, 3.2 metres wide on its floor, up to 4 metres wide at its top, with almost vertical walls. These walls were one metre high on the south side, looking towards the plain, and on the north side, the inside, taking advantage of a natural step in the rock, up to 2.2 metres. At the point excavated the ditch ran east–west. Geomagnetic imaging, which naturally could now plot its further course from both ends of the excavated section with greater confidence, was able to trace it for a distance of 320 metres. If one reconstructed the complete course, relying on the lie of the terrain, a length of about 2 kilometres resulted. This meant a total enclosed area for Troy VI/VIIa, with the citadel, of about 200,000 square metres.[19] Any doubt that the ditch was part of a defensive system could be ruled out, and it was also clear now why the Troy VI cemetery, which Blegen had discovered, but, as we have seen, not explained, was situated so far from the citadel wall: the area in between was occupied.[20] Naturally this defensive system must originally have included a wall as well: a ditch as an obstacle has a purpose only if it slows the impetus of the attackers so much that, as they negotiate it and perhaps succeed in crossing it in scattered groups, they are confronted by the next obstacle, the wall, from which they can be dealt with. Jablonka observed, 'The existence of a wall north of the ditch [that is, on the side of the town] must be assumed as almost definite.'[21] We shall see how this forecast proved correct.

The defensive ditch could be precisely dated to the time of Troy VI, certainly to an earlier period of this stratum than the 'Homeric period', by which time it had evidently been filled in and abandoned. The reason for this will become apparent. Troy therefore had obviously spectacular fortifications even before its great flowering in about 1200 BC—defences which could not remain unknown in the eastern Mediterranean. Maritime trade would see to that.

Jablonka's conclusion at one stroke put an end to earlier false estimates of the area of Troy:

> Now for the first time the limits of the lower settlement could be established ... We may now posit an area of over 170,000 square metres for the lower town of Troy VI, plus 23,000 square metres for the citadel, a total, therefore, of some 200,000 square metres.... Moreover, the population figure of 6,000 to 7,000, arrived at by Korfmann, seems plausible.... If we take the totality of the citadel and fortified lower town, it appears, as Korfmann has ascertained, that it has closer analogues in Anatolia than in the Mycenaean region; it is probable that Troy belongs among the contemporary 'royal seats and trading centres' of the eastern Mediterranean and the ancient east.[22]

In the following excavation season, 1994, further confirmation was found: in addition to more precise clarification at the three known points along the ditch and two new ones, another new cross-section was dug 300 metres west of the easternmost point. This yielded a continuation of the ditch along the line already plotted by the magnetometer, and in exactly the same form and the same dimensions as in the three sections known from the previous year. This meant that the east–west ditch-line was clearly established for 300 metres. (Naturally one does not expose such features over their full length: the cost would be far too high, and present-day agricultural work would be disrupted. Proof is considered furnished when the lie of an earthwork plotted by geo-magnetic imaging or by logic is confirmed by digging at certain significant points.) The east–west course exploited a natural east–west contour in the rock. To east and west of the ditch-line, the contour turns north. The ditch had therefore been discovered at its 'southern bow'. This meant, first, that it must run on to the north from both the east and the west of the slope until it met the citadel's fortifications, and secondly that, given the gentle decline towards the south, somewhere in its 300-metre east–west course it must logically have been possible for humans, animals, and carts to cross it somehow to ensure access for traffic and supplies, by a bridge, a causeway, or something of this nature. At one point in the course of the ditch the geo-magnetic imaging had already indicated an interruption. Had there been a crossing there? And where had the city wall stood, the wall which—as we knew from the history of city fortification—could not be far behind the ditch?[23]

The gate

The major turnabout in the history of the study of Troy came in 1995. Manfred Korfmann began his excavation report for 1995, which appeared in 1996, with the following sentence: 'The excavations of 1995 were, from the perspective of the chief investigator, the most successful to date.'[24] What followed in the first three pages of the report, recorded in his usual tiny handwriting and laconic businesslike prose, was enough to wrench any specialist in the archaeology and the centuries-old discussion of Troy and Homer literally out of his chair. Unfortunately these excavation reports are read regularly and attentively by relatively few experts, and—contrary to the view of almost all non-specialists—even by relatively few archaeologists. Archaeology has become a greatly diversified discipline in which only a fortunate few researchers can maintain an overview of even their own special field. There is no time left for the broader view: a specialist keeps up by reading general journals in the discipline, which can report only the most salient facts, at conferences, and through personal contacts. Those who work in Greece, Italy, North Africa, Egypt, Israel, Syria, or in any other country usually have neither the time nor the energy to follow in detail the progress of the excavations of their colleagues elsewhere. A large-format journal like *Studia Troica*, comprising some 500 pages annually, with its innumerable diagrams, plans, and graphs, and its extraordinarily varied subject matter, especially in the natural sciences which form part of archaeology (archaeological botany and zoology, scientific measuring techniques, computer statistics, and many others), cannot hope to be impatiently awaited by all professionals and devoured as soon as it appears. But Volume 6, 1996, would have deserved this more than all earlier volumes.

The series of discoveries made in 1995 began on the ditch. At the point in the ditch long identified as an 'interruption', a crossing in the form of a causeway was uncovered. The causeway had been fashioned by leaving the rock in place for about 10 metres while digging on either side of it. To left and right of this point the ditch was dug deeper than elsewhere—understandably, in view of the ever-present and special danger of intruders breaking through at access points. (We may note in passing that among the refuse deposited at this section of the ditch, along with numerous horse bones, the lower jaw of a lion was found; it is possible that a knacker's yard disposed of its waste here, and that this included the remains of wild animals killed by hunting.) Some three and a half metres from this rock causeway, a smaller ditch running parallel to the ditch, on its city side, was exposed, just 50 centimetres wide and 30 centimetres deep. Like the larger ditch, it was interrupted, but by a passage not of 10 metres but only 5.2 metres. In the middle of the passage, post-holes had been sunk. The interpretation was plain: the ditch had been the footing of a palisade, in which a double wooden gate had been set (with post-holes in the middle of the gateway). (Fig. 5)

It thus became clear that this was one of the gateways through the fortifications of the lower town of Troy VI, apparently the south

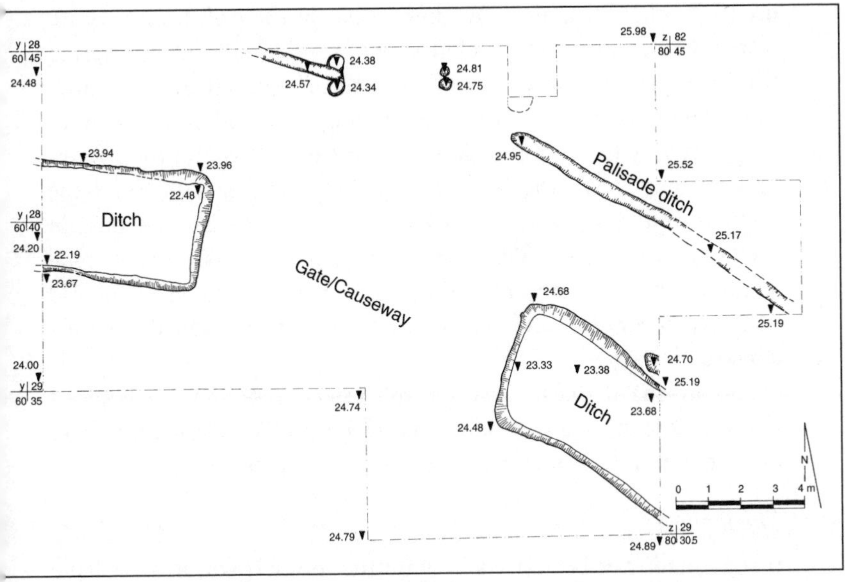

FIG. 5. The site of the gate in the perimeter wall of the lower town of Troy VI, excavated in 1995.

gate. 'In this way the passage of enemy chariots, for example, could be prevented, and access to the lower town and citadel of Troy/Ilios controlled.'[25] What still remained unclear, of course, was the question of the existence and location of the actual wall. The palisade and wooden gateway, after all, merely reinforced the security of the passage over the ditch. The causeway could certainly be controlled from the palisade, but could this have been the full extent of the impediments? As would become clear later, the palisade was restricted to the area of the causeway.[26] The gateway through the fence could hardly have been the actual city gate. It was far too flimsy for the purpose. It must have served as part of the entrance to the city, as an outer gateway. But where was the real city gate? And where was the wall? The fact that at first there was no trace of it to be found following the line of the causeway and the gate can be explained: a ditch, once cut in the rock, may be filled in, but it remains a permanent part of the landscape. Excavators may expose it at any time, as happened here. A wall, however, is built at least partly of stone, which for some people is a valued raw material. As soon as the wall ceases to serve its purpose, the stone is removed and used for other structures. We know that in the eighth century BC several Greek towns on the Hellespont experienced a new flowering (for example, Sigeion and Achilleion on the Aegean coast). If anything remained of a wall at that period, it would certainly have found its way to these towns. For others old walls and their foundations may be in the way. To anyone who bears in mind the immense building works, proven by Korfmann's excavations, in the lower town in the Hellenistic and Roman periods, it will come as no surprise that anything that might have remained of the old wall disappeared completely when the site was levelled for new construction.

Should one therefore give up and utterly renounce all hope of finding evidence of a wall surrounding Troy VI/VIIa? Or were there other possibilities? Imaginative thinking was called for.

The wall

If there had ever been a wall round the lower town, it must have protected the entire residential area. It could only do this if its course was uninterrupted. It must therefore have joined the fortress wall, which ringed the crest of the hill, at the highest point of the lower town. Since the slope there is particularly steep, and since at these points there had been the most intensive building on the site of old buildings, on account of the confined space (which also made it particularly dangerous to break away stone), there seemed to be most hope of finding remains of the wall precisely here.

The search for the needle in this haystack did in fact lead to success, first on the north-east side of the citadel. Here even today the north-east bastion (in the Korfmann and Mannsperger official *Guide to Troy*, Bastion No. 3) is impressive. With foundations measuring 18 metres by 18 metres, this imposing tower still rises to a height of 7 metres, and was originally 2 metres higher. These measurements alone show that the bastion was particularly important. It had multiple functions: as could now, in 1995, be seen, at this exposed point, it protected not only the citadel (and a 10-metre-deep water reservoir within it) but also the town. The wall of the lower town meets the south wall of the citadel where the latter is indented (Fig. 6). The meeting point could be recognized beyond doubt by its typical Troy VI stone foundations, of large stones on

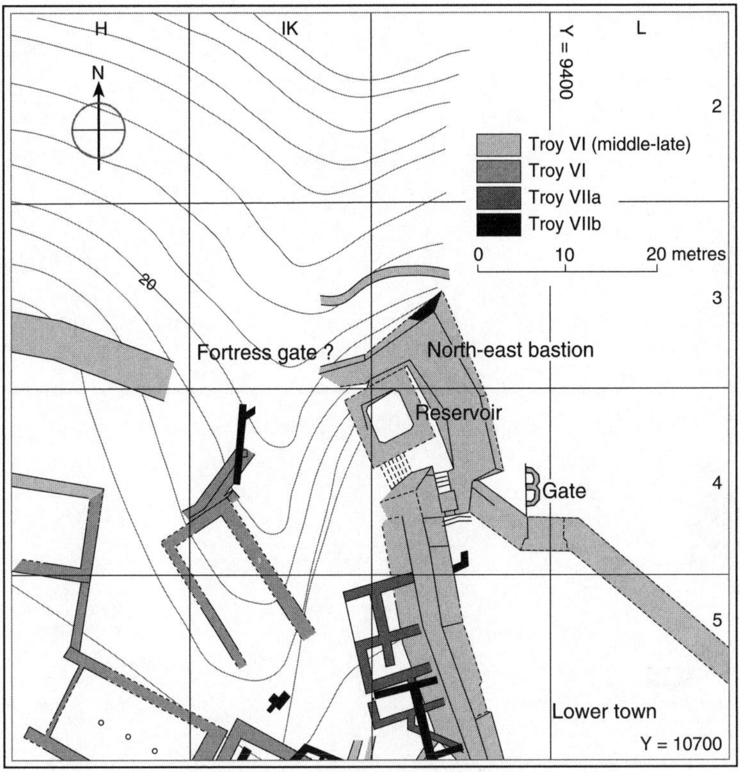

FIG. 6. The north-east bastion of Troy. The meeting point of the fortress wall and lower town wall.

the inner side, often conically shaped, and by potsherds from Troy VI/middle period. On the stone foundations lay a large quantity of mud bricks. 'We are dealing with a mud-brick wall rather than a stone wall.'[27] This immediately explained why (up to this moment, at least) no trace of a wall had been found in the lower town: the mud-brick structure, as the evidence of the lower town showed, had been allowed to erode and crumble, while the stone of the foundations had been removed and reused elsewhere. Yet all hope of discovering some remnant of the wall in the lower town was not completely lost. However, the pleasure of finding the foundations of the city wall at the *western* corner of the fortress wall, matching the junction in the east, eluded the investigators in the 1999 and 2000

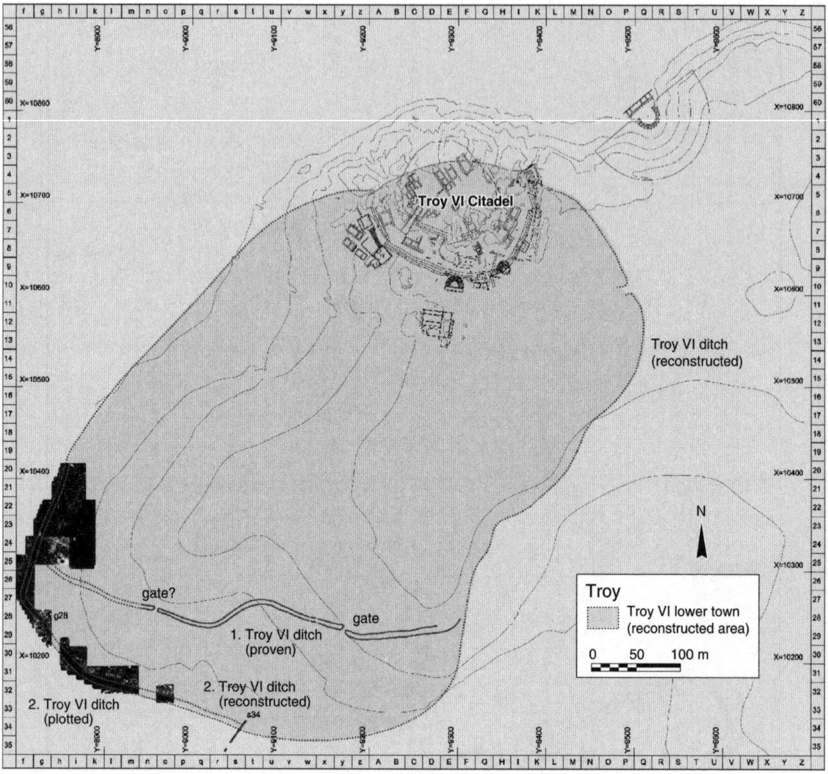

FIG. 7. The extent of Troy VI, with fortifications.

seasons.[28] At the angle in question, the lower town wall of Troy VI had been completely dismantled during construction of the Hellenistic town wall and the surrounding wall of a Hellenistic temple.[29]

With this knowledge to hand, it is now possible to reconstruct the appearance of the whole city in the period of Troy VI/VIIa, first as a ground-plan (Fig. 7), and then as an artist's impression (Fig. 8). The perimeter wall of the lower town should be imagined as being an arrow's flight from the ditch, that is, by Korfmann's estimate, 'roughly 90–120 metres from the ditch and the gateway through the palisade. At the time when Trojan culture was at its zenith (Troy VI/VIIa), such a wall must have formed a most imposing monument

FIG. 8. Model of Troy VI.

in the landscape. But even later, in a state of gradual collapse, when Balkan influences were making themselves felt in Troy (Troy $VIIb_1$, Troy $VIIb_2$, Troy $VIIb_3$, and Troy $VIIb_4$?), it must still have had a certain significance. Then came the stage in which the remains of the structure became a topographical feature. As a ruined wall, at some stage it became a hindrance, certainly when work began on the planning and substantial rebuilding of Troy/Ilion (Troy VIII and Troy IX).'[30] In this short history of the city wall of Troy VI/VII, one sentence is of particular importance for the larger question which occupies us in this book: 'Then came the stage in which the remains of the structure became a topographical feature.' When could this stage have begun? How long did it last, and how much of this 'feature' remained to be seen at different periods of history? And from this another question follows: What remained to be seen of a ditch at different periods of history? The answer to this is important in judging the relation between the real Troy and the image of it in literary works which have Troy as their backdrop. We shall have occasion to return briefly to this question when we consider Homer and the *Iliad*.

The second ditch

This would prove to be all the more urgent when in 1995 a second rock ditch was discovered, more than a hundred metres south of the ditch previously found. This ditch was approximately 3 metres wide and at least 2 metres deep on the town side, and apparently ran roughly parallel to the first. At this point we are a good 500 metres from the fortress wall and already at the foot of the hill, though not yet on the plain. The great Hellenistic and Roman lower city never reached as far as this. The matter of greatest interest was the date of this ditch. Could it be prehistoric? In fact Peter Jablonka, the excavator who had exposed the first ditch, was able to date this ditch too to the period of Troy VI, on the basis of the material used to fill it in ('exclusively from the time of Troy VI/VIIa'). He did, however, consider it 'possible that this ditch could be dated somewhat later than the inner ditch'.

This immediately poses the question of the function of this second ditch. Was it a second line of defence (a 'phased array of concentric obstacles')? But since this ditch seemed more recent than the inner one, it could, as Jablonka proposed, be taken to have 'something to do with a chronological sequence of ditches with the same purpose. Its position would point to a growth in the area of the settlement.' The nature of the filling material also supported this: fragments of household pottery (cups, bowls, and pitchers) and animal bones. 'If we assume that refuse and waste was not transported all the way from the settlement for the sole purpose of filling the ditch, we can only conclude, on the basis of the content of the filling material, that the area in the immediate vicinity of the ditch was occupied. This would mean that late Bronze Age Troy was even larger than had previously been supposed. In the south, the settled area would have extended beyond the limits of the Hellenistic-Roman city. At the end of the Troy VI period, even land outside the fortifications of the lower city would have been at least partly built on.'[31]

Korfmann himself, however, gave preference to an interpretation of the ditch as a 'second contemporary obstacle'. The decisive factor here was his view that both ditches must have been designed as obstacles 'against the approach of battering rams, but most particularly of war chariots'. He arrived at this view having been influenced by a work by Brigitte Mannsperger,[32] who 'had pronounced the last word on the subject of "ditches and chariots", having in mind the *Iliad* as a source'.[33] Korfmann subsequently developed his picture of chariot warfare using the descriptions in the *Iliad*.

These two interpretations need not be in any way mutually exclusive. By the end of the Troy VI period, the very summit of the city's cultural development, the population may have grown so large that settlement had extended even beyond the fortifications (the ditch and the wall). There may have been a wish to secure the outer development in the same manner as the older inner city. A new ditch, similar to the existing one, was therefore dug. (Whether there was also another wall is thus far unknown, but on balance improbable.) The inner city thus acquired redoubled security. It is possible that the ditches were designed specially to repel chariot attacks.

However, at this point, it is not yet appropriate to voice a more definite opinion, as we are still at the stage of exploring whether the *Iliad* may be regarded as a source at all. Only when this is demonstrated will it be possible to discuss what and how much of the evidence in the *Iliad* can properly be used in the interpretation of the archaeological findings. The application of the evidence thus becomes the third step. For the time being we shall content ourselves with simply stating the facts: Troy VI/VII clearly had two defensive ditches in front of its (apparently single) city wall. The first ditch was 400 metres from the citadel, the second a hundred metres beyond the first, at the very bottom of the hill. The area protected would have been the largest in the entire history of Troy before the Hellenistic reconstruction. We leave open for the moment the question of the possible purpose of the ditches.

The west gate and the wagon road

The visitor to Troy today invariably approaches the ruins of the citadel from the east, that is, from the landward side. After branching off the main Çanakkale–Edremit road, on the narrow side road which leads to the ruins of Troy, shortly after passing the village of Tevfikiye, one comes to the entrance to the excavation site. It is entirely possible that from this direction too in prehistoric times an important access road led to the citadel: the largest gateway of the Troy II citadel (*c.*2500 BC) stands in the south-east. The main entrance to the Troy VI citadel, however, lay in the west, on the seaward side. This was not realized until 1995. In 1995, to the west of the great temple from the Hellenistic-Roman period, familiar to all visitors (No. 10 in the *Guide to Troy*), beneath a great mass of Hellenistic-Roman rubble and detritus, a broad paved road from the Troy VI period was uncovered. It led gently uphill to the fortress wall and ended at a gate (Gate VI U on the archaeological site-plan). This gate into the citadel was sealed shortly before the end of Troy VI or at the beginning of Troy VIIa—we shall return later to the possible reasons for this. In 1997 Korfmann definitively established that this gate, 'with an internal width of 3.6 to 4 metres', was 'the largest gate in the Troy VI fortress wall'.[34] Even allowing for the fact that at this point a natural declivity makes access to the citadel from the side of the Skamander Plain particularly easy—which is why there were access points to the gateways at even earlier periods, like that to the imposing ramp from Troy II (No. 8 in the *Guide to Troy*)—this is a highly informative discovery. It means that for the rulers of the Troy VI period the direct connection between the fortress and the coast was of primary importance. In 1997 Korfmann went on to say, 'From this gate a road led south-west onto the Skamander Plain. The fortress hill and the plateau of the lower town slope gently away here, affording the easiest route down to the plain . . . But at the same time, this is the most dangerous point.'

Why dangerous? At the very start of our journey into the history of the exploration of the lower town, we pointed out that the existence of such a town had to be assumed as it would have had an additional defensive function for the citadel. This defensive function is naturally best served where the fortifications of the lower town are at their furthest from those of the citadel. In Troy the terrain ensures this to the south of the citadel. And where the fortifications of the lower town come closer to those of the citadel and the distance between the town wall and the fortress wall is less, the defensive potential of the lower town is also reduced. Owing to the position of the citadel on the hilltop (not, for example, in the middle of the lower town), the city wall had to rise upwards in two places to meet the fortress wall: in the east and in the west. In both cases, there would necessarily have been increasingly narrow wedges between the town walls and fortress walls. In the east this was less dangerous, as the slope rose sharply. But in the west the gentler climb meant that the advantage of this—the opportunity to build a road into the citadel—brought with it an immense disadvantage: the distance between the town and fortress walls was very short at precisely this point. From the city gate to the fortress gate, through which the road led, was only about 80 metres, precisely the flight of an arrow. Korfmann commented in 1998, 'For this reason this point was particularly favoured by attacking forces, and must have been a vulnerable point.'[35] Korfmann links this archaeologically demonstrable feature of the topography of Troy with certain moments in the *Iliad*. On methodological grounds, we shall deliberately refrain, for the time being, from making such connections, and for this reason confine ourselves to emphasizing only the following sentences, to return to this point later: 'From this spot [from the fortress wall] one had a clear view over the plain as far as Tenedos, ... over the ground which the attackers must have crossed, and over their natural approach route. There was ... only one point in the fortress where ... the attackers ... were close enough to the citadel fortifications ... to be identified.' It is desirable that we keep these archaeological facts, confirmed by the discovery of the lower town, firmly in mind.

The result: Troy VI/VIIa—an Anatolian royal seat and trading centre

A royal seat?

The mere proof that Troy VI/VIIa consisted of more than the citadel—a kind of cliff-top eyrie with the function of a 'knight's castle'—and actually combined a citadel with a town at least five times its size had led to its being reclassified as an 'old near-eastern royal seat and trading centre'.[36] The discovery of the system of fortifications of the lower town meant that there could no longer be any doubt about this, for, while this system showed some structural similarities to Mycenaean sites,[37] it bore much stronger resemblances to Anatolian and North Syrian urban construction of the second millennium BC: (1) defensive ditches do not form part of Mycenaean urban sites,[38] but are typical of Anatolian towns, for example Boğazköy, Karkemiş/Jerablus, and Tell Halaf;[39]

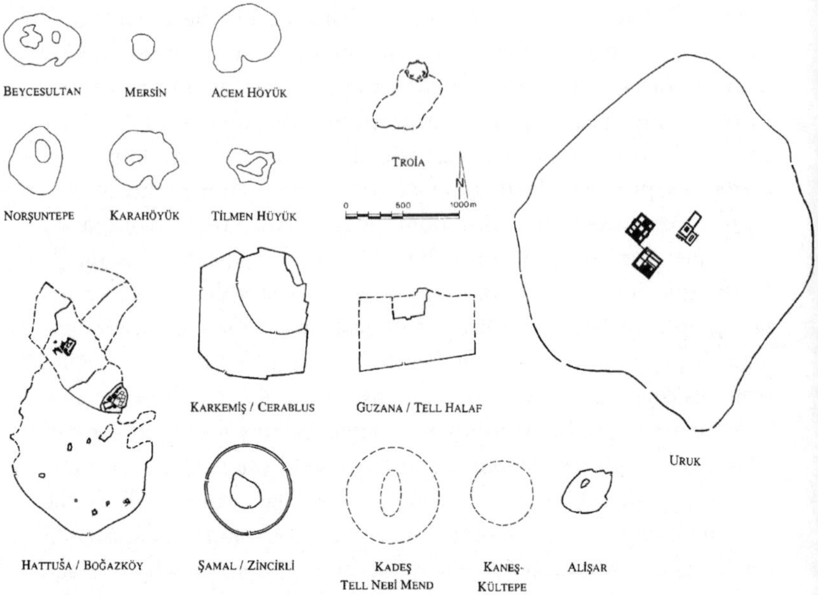

FIG. 9. Anatolian towns: comparative size.

(2) Mycenaean perimeter walls appear to have had hardly any superstructure of mudbrick,[40] which is characteristic of Anatolian sites; (3) in Anatolia, in the period of Hittite domination, towers are a fundamental component of perimeter walls;[41] in Troy VI they form the backbone of the citadel wall.

We can dispense with the enumeration of further matching details which specialists in architecture have brought out. A glance at Fig. 9, in which early oriental and Anatolian town- and fortress-plans are set side by side, should make clear that Troy VI belongs to this type.

The architectural argument is backed by the argument of scale: once the limits of the lower town were established, it became clear that Troy VI/VIIa was at least ten times larger than earlier excavators—and thus the broader public—had supposed. With an area of 200,000 square metres or more, and between five and ten thousand inhabitants, by Korfmann's estimate, Troy VI/VIIa was by the standards of its day a large and important city.[42]

Of course, such states do not grow of their own accord. They possess their own ruling stratum, which organizes and manages matters such as the planning and development of the fortifications. The élite of this ruling stratum is formed by the citadel rulers, comprising one hierarchically structured clan. At its apex stands the monarch/patriarch (king/prince, or whatever may be his title), who claims direct descent from a god; the citadel is the seat of that clan. These dynasties are usually hereditary and identified by name. The names of the rulers are widely known; we find them in various items of epigraphic evidence, such as correspondence and inscriptions. This applies in Boğazköy/Ḫattuşa, just as in Karkemiş or Ugarit, and it continued to apply subsequently in manifold forms in Europe, as long as the nobility played a leading role. It not only can but must be assumed that the same applied in the citadel of Troy VI/VIIa. If, then, the names of rulers from a Trojan dynasty were to appear in some language in the documentary evidence from the second millennium BC, this would not be at all surprising. It would be natural.

Besides these connections in matters of town-planning, demography, and political dynasties, further coincidences between Troy and Anatolia intrude and should be at least listed here.

1. During excavations at Troy, large quantities of potsherds are turned up every day. The majority of these are so-called grey Minyan ware, practical vessels made of grey clay, such as plates, cups, bowls, mugs, pitchers—objects used in the kitchen and dining-hall. As early as 1992 Donald F. Easton, another researcher on the new Troy project, pointed out that, by its form as well as the technique of manufacture, all this tableware was patterned not, as Blegen had assumed, on Greek models, but on Anatolian models, and had been since at least Troy V.[43] After the eight digging seasons from 1988 to 1995, this assertion received emphatic confirmation: after it had become clear that all this pottery production was indeed Anatolian, and that there was only one per cent of Mycenaean pottery (and most of it imitation made in Troy) to many tons of this grey tableware, 'grey Minyan ware' was finally renamed 'Anatolian grey pottery'.[44] All of Troy's domestic pottery production displays Anatolian techniques and forms; Greek (Mycenaean) pottery was imported, and no doubt highly prized, or it would not have been imitated, but it was none the less foreign to Troy.

2. Funerary practices (house-shaped tombs, storage vessels as urns, cremation instead of burial), as well as at least some cult features, are Anatolian. In the 1995 digging season, in a house from the Troy VIIa level, a stone pedestal topped with clay was discovered in the corner of a room. Since a bronze effigy of a god was found on the floor in front of this structure, apparently having fallen from it, the pedestal was almost certainly a place of domestic worship. The figure represented an Anatolian deity. Figures of the same type are found in the Hittite area, as well as in Syria and Palestine. Citizens of Troy were still worshipping Anatolian gods in about 1200 BC.[45]

3. An Anatolian characteristic well established among the Hittites—and also in the written Hittite records—is the stone cult. Gods and spirits were thought to reside in large stones, and their protection was invoked by placing stones, often the height of a man, carved and decorated in many ways (*stelai*), before entrances: at the doors of houses, streets, cemeteries, and especially at city gates. In Troy seventeen such *stelai* have so far been found, all of them before or right beside the fortress gates. Earlier excavators, with their Western outlook, had paid virtually no attention to these. Korfmann paid particular attention to them and, like many historians of religion before him, linked them with an Anatolian god who was clearly the object of special reverence in Troy VI, Ap(p)aliunas. Korfmann, like some of his predecessors, believed that there was more than a phonetic relation between this god and the Greek Apollon.[46] This has not so far been confirmed,[47] but there can be no doubt as to the connection between the gateway *stelai* of Troy VI and the Anatolian gate-stone cult.

A trading centre

That Troy VI/VIIa belonged to the Anatolian cultural area of the second millennium BC may thus be regarded as proven. This means that all kinds of cultural relations must have existed between Troy and other Anatolian towns, both on the Aegean coast and in the interior of Anatolia. These relations naturally included trade. For an understanding of the significance of Troy in prehistoric times, and thus its permanent vulnerability, this is perhaps the most important thing. If Troy had been no more than a regional centre of agriculture and cattle markets, its continuous growth to far-reaching supra-regional magnitude in the Troy VI period would be utterly inexplicable. For this, much more economic and financial power, intellectual superiority, especially technological know-how, and certainly a military deterrent capacity without equal in the region, at least, were an essential prerequisite. Where did the resources for these stem from?

Troy lay by the sea. Before Korfmann began excavating the hill itself, he had thoroughly explored the Bay of Beşik to the south-west of Troy, some 8 kilometres from the citadel, on the Aegean coast (1982–7). Numerous finds had clearly established that this bay had long been part of Troy. This was Troy's harbour.[48] In all logic and probability, this harbour provided the foundations for the rise of the city. In the straits of the Dardanelles quite exceptional shipping conditions prevail: at the height of the season (May to October) a strong north-easterly blows in the face of vessels wishing to enter the straits. Furthermore, a powerful current sweeps down from the Sea of Marmora to the Aegean. The wind and the current together often condemned oared and sailing vessels, in a time when the art of tacking into the wind was still in its infancy, to long periods of waiting. The Bay of Beşik was the 'last petrol station before the motorway'.[49] Here ships could wait out bad weather in comparative safety. Of course they could also load and unload cargo. Lastly, they could take on fresh water and victuals. It would fly in the face of reason to suppose that all of this was to be had for the asking. The strongly fortified and populous city of Troy stood high over the coast and watched over everything that happened. Without its approval, there could be no activity in the harbour.

Of course, we do not know in any detail how this control was exercised. For this we would need to have had the regulations of the port authority handed down, and this is something not to be expected. Experience and analogies from later times should be sufficient in a case like this to suggest that income was earned not only by victualling the ships, but also by port tariffs.[50] The services of pilots, with their intimate knowledge of all counter-currents which might eventuate and of the channels through the straits, should also be borne in mind. Ferry services between the Asian and European shores of the Dardanelles must also be added. At the same time, the involuntary port-stays offered ample opportunities for the exchange of produce and accumulated goods for foreign products, and thus for trade to develop as a professional activity. This is so self-evident, in view of the unchanging commercial life of seaports, ancient and modern, that one hardly dares to emphasize it. We may add that the colossal proportions of many buildings in the citadel of Troy from the time of Troy I undoubtedly did not serve merely for prestige. It has long been supposed that these structures were mostly warehouses, used for secure storage. Since nothing of the kind has been found on the coast itself, this hypothesis remains highly plausible. All of this comes as a consequence of trade.

For a long time consideration of the question of the importance of trade for Troy took second place to excavation work. Certainly it has always been realized that from the very beginning Troy must have maintained extended trading links in every possible direction. This is evidenced by more than twenty 'treasure hoards' discovered in the burned debris of the Troy IIg level (*c.*2450 BC), including what Schliemann called 'the treasure of Priam', which in reality has nothing to do with Homer's Priam. These hoards contain materials not found in the city or its immediate and more distant hinterland, so these must have been obtained by long-distance trade.[51] Above all the liberal use of bronze, with other materials essential for the manufacture of weapons, pointed to extensive trading links, since the raw material, tin, needed for making bronze had to be imported from Central Asia or Bohemia. Troy was also apparently the first place in the Aegean region to use the fast-turning potter's wheel. However, this technical innovation was invented in Mesopotamia, and therefore had to be imported from there, also by way of inland Anatolian contacts, as has emerged more and more clearly in recent times.

There was thus an ancient trading tradition here. The continuous growth of the city and the steady refinement of its fortifications, into which we have gained some insight, show that for centuries this tradition of trade and accompanying cultural exchange not only went on uninterrupted, but must have steadily expanded. We can see the result in Troy VI: a large and prosperous city with stone foundations and large buildings, two storeys high in the citadel area; major construction projects executed with outstanding planning and craftsmanship—the Troy VI fortress wall is a model of extraordinary precision in its detail as well as its larger features; and a clearly flourishing manufacture of all forms of pottery and metalwork. Our knowledge of the lower town is being extended year by year and yielding growing quantities of information. We now know, for example, something of the commercial activity in the Troy VI lower town. The excavation reports make increasingly frequent mention of metal-working shops and dyeing works; in the 1996 and 1997 seasons, in a confined space beside a building from the middle of the Troy VI period, more than 10 kilograms of shells of purple shellfish were found.[52] Besides these, there are immense quantities of horse bones from the later phase of Troy VI. Previously little notice was taken of these bones. The Korfmann excavation, involving a range of different disciplines, such as zoological archaeology, the study of fauna remains, has endeavoured to examine *all* types of finds, to analyse them separately and turn the results to account in building up a complete picture of the life of the period.

As for the horse bones, it has long been known that the second millennium BC was the 'age of chariots'. Throughout the Near East, especially for the Hittites, chariots constituted, as it were, the 'tank corps' of the day. As they naturally relied on 'horse power', in the literal sense of the term, the demand for horses must have been enormous. There were wild horses in inland Anatolia and the steppe regions north of the Black Sea. They had first, of course, to be trained for their task. The Hittites have left us entire manuals of horsemastership.[53] In view of the bone finds, one must wonder whether Troy also served as a market in the horse trade, perhaps even as a breeding and training centre.

These are questions that for the time being we can only ask. The answers must await further excavations. In the meantime, however, we can put forward theories. It would be wrong to baulk at the word 'theory'. Theories often guide our searches, which would otherwise of necessity be blind. In the sixth century BC the Greek thinker Heraclitus pointed the way for the whole of European science when he formulated one of his cryptic aphorisms: 'He who does not expect will not find out the unexpected, for it is trackless and unexplored.'[54] It is in precisely this spirit that in recent times Manfred Korfmann, the leading excavator of Troy, has proposed a theory of the importance of trade for the city, a theory which merits the most serious attention.[55]

Given the size and geographical situation of Troy, trade can only mean long-distance trade. In the greater Mediterranean area, since the third millennium BC at the latest, such trade was conducted among three main cultural areas: Mesopotamia (Babylon, Assyria); Egypt, Arabia, and the great Phoenician Levantine ports, such as Byblos, Beruta (Beirut), Siduna (Sidon), and Tyre; and thence further distribution proceeded by sea to the west—Crete, Greece, Italy, Spain, North Africa, and north to western Anatolia and Thrace. Between the corners of this triangle, conforming with the topographical conditions, trade routes had been established for caravans of donkeys, and these did much to lay the foundations for present-day roads. At the beginning of the second millennium BC the Assyrians dominated this network, with chains of trading settlements, the so-called *Kārum*-settlements. Feeder routes to this triangular network came from all regions which could provide the desired products. One of these routes ran from the southern coast of the Black Sea, whence access could be gained to the Caucasus region with its rich mineral deposits, including gold, through central Anatolia to the triangle. Since the eighteenth century BC, however, in central Anatolia the Hittites had risen to become the leading political and military power. If the old trade routes to the Black Sea were to remain open, they had to rely on the protection of the Hittites. But the Hittites could no longer permit this route (the reasons need not be discussed here). This did not, of course, mean that trade with the Black Sea region became impossible. It simply had to be diverted to new routes.

Against this background, it can scarcely be a coincidence that at precisely this time, 1700 BC, Troy's Black Sea maritime trade begins to flourish, with the start of the city's rise to its cultural heyday (that is, Troy VI). All the indications are that the old trading partners switched their routes from land to sea at this time. The long-distance routes to and from Mesopotamia and the other two cultural areas on the Mediterranean coast remained unaffected, but transport to and from the Black Sea region was transferred to ships.[56] The upsurge in maritime trade along the east coast of the Mediterranean in the second half of the second millennium BC has recently emerged clearly in the cargoes of sunken ships, which have been intensively studied and evaluated by underwater archaeologists in recent decades.[57] Sea transport was immeasurably more profitable, as a single vessel had the carrying capacity of approximately 200 donkeys, and, moreover, could make delivery considerably faster. The rate of turnover was thereby increased, and profits multiplied. With the shift of Black Sea trade to the sea-lanes, Troy as the natural controlling authority over these routes must have acquired increased and predominant importance.

Long-distance trade was mainly organized by central institutions. As a rule these were supra-regional and regional rulers, with their 'palaces'. In these and other comparable contexts (political, military, or religious), 'palace' is to be understood not as an edifice constructed for personal prestige, but as a centre of administration, of government. The 'palaces' protected trade, as trade served their interests (import and export of raw materials for the production of weaponry, trade in luxury goods, interest collected from profits, and so forth). The main instrument of protection was the treaty, but military intervention (trade wars), when necessary, was not excluded. The practical implementation was entrusted to agents. In order to ensure continuity, trading posts were fostered and protected. These relied mainly on existing settlements, but constituted separate localities within them or on the fringes of them. Among the traders' families, which may well have included personages of high social status such as diplomats and army officers, carefully cultivated relations were maintained, often reinforced by intermarriage. Trade thus formed a second horizontal plane, parallel to the political plane of the palace dynasties. Both planes worked together to their mutual advantage.

If we consider Troy's immediate and less immediate environs—the Troad to the east and north, with both shores of the Dardanelles and those of the Sea of Marmora, then the southern coast of the Black Sea; the west coast of Asia Minor to the south, with the offshore islands of Imbros, Tenedos, and Lesbos down as far south as Abasa (later the Greek Ephesos) and Millawanda (later the Greek Miletos: on this toponym, see pp. 124–5); and the north coast of the Aegean (Thrace) to the west, with the Balkans beyond it—we see that in all of this vast area there is no power centre and no

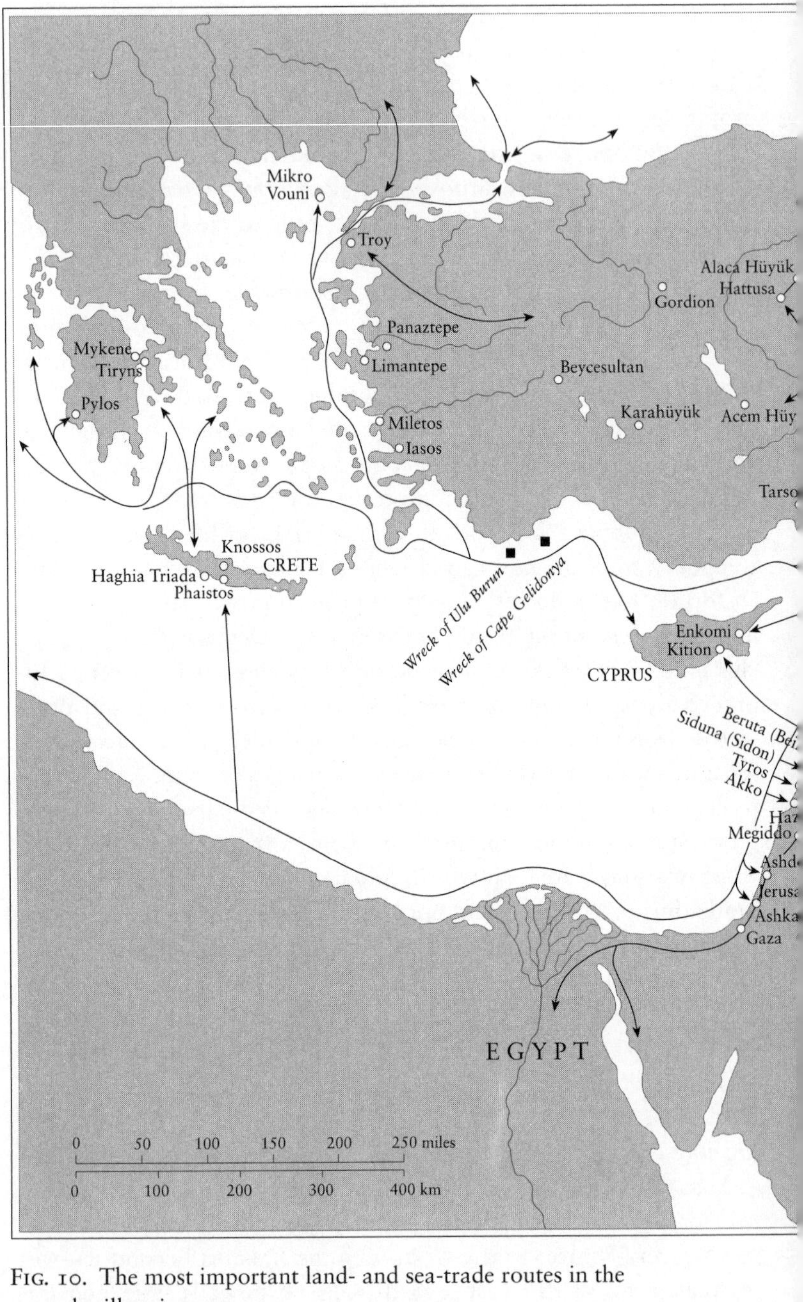

FIG. 10. The most important land- and sea-trade routes in the second millennium BC.

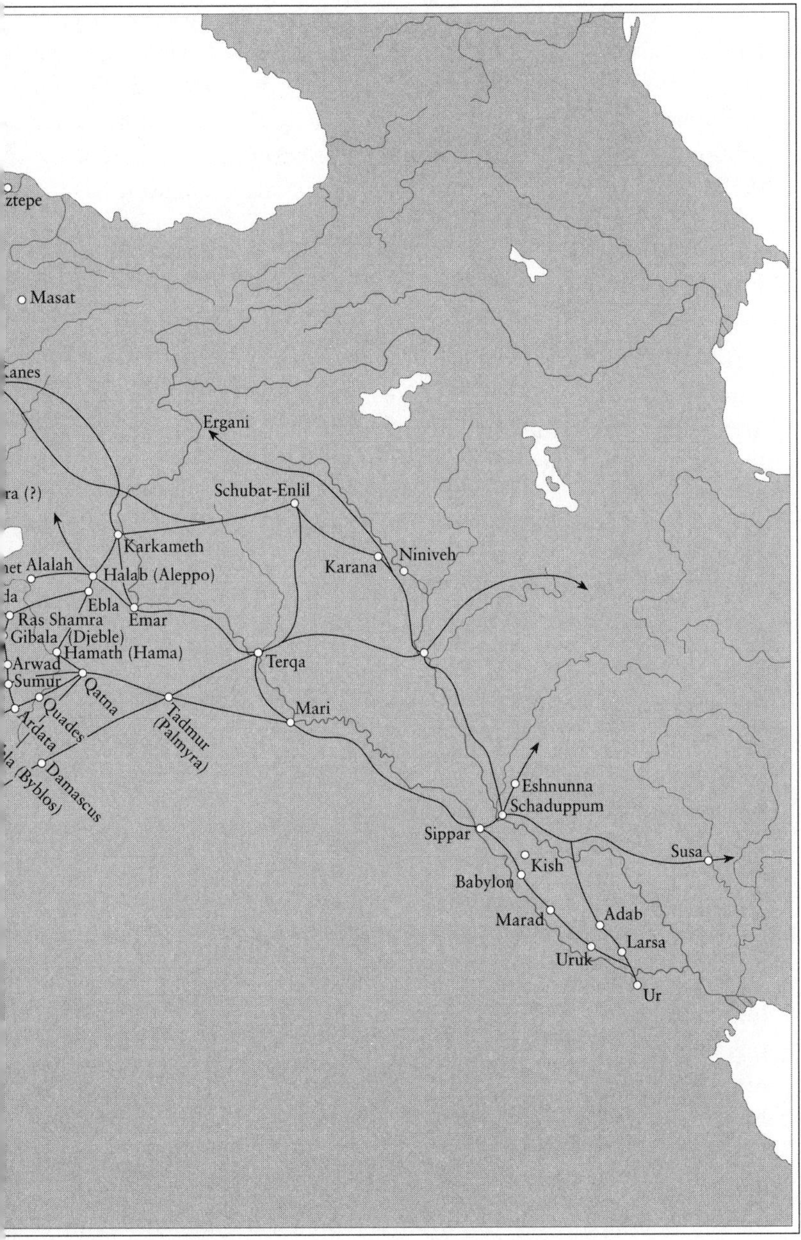
ztepe
Masat
Kanes
Ergani
ra (?)
Schubat-Enlil
Karkameth
Niniveh
Karana
net Alalah
Halab (Aleppo)
da
Ebla
Emar
Ras Shamra
Gibala (Djeble)
Hamath (Hama)
Terqa
Arwad
Sumur
Qatna
Quades
Ardata
Tadmur (Palmyra)
Mari
la (Byblos)
Damascus
Eshnunna
Schaduppum
Sippar
Susa
Kish
Babylon
Marad
Adab
Larsa
Uruk
Ur

economy which might offer Troy any competition. In short, if Troy had not existed, one would have had to establish it. One is obliged to conclude that all these regions, with their own small and medium-sized centres, had outposts in Troy and maintained their trading agencies and representatives there, protected by treaty. Troy, the purchasing, collecting, and organizing centre, functioned as the capital of this 'Union of the Three Seas' (Aegean, Sea of Marmora, and Black Sea), and as an entrepôt, whose unimpeded operation was in the interests of all.

In consequence of this, from an early date, the ruling family in the citadel of Troy could have depended less on expansionist armies or navies than on the steady growth of the commercial significance and increasing indispensability of the city. The self-perception of the Phoenician city states and later, from about 600 BC, of Greek Miletos, was of essentially the same nature. This would also explain the defensive character of Troy, which was clear from the very beginning of the excavations, manifested in its extraordinarily massive fortifications. The geographical situation of the city allowed it to be a 'spider in a web', towards which everything gravitates of itself, as long as the web is maintained. In this case, storekeeping, property administration, the safeguarding of merchandise, organization of trade and control of shipping take up all its strength and consume all its energies. In such circumstances there is neither need nor time for expansionist endeavours.

If Troy—especially Troy VI/VIIa—were therefore to be correctly classified and described, it would have to be as a leading member of a kind of Hanseatic league. This would also explain why Troy was relatively independent of the great powers of the time: the Hittites, Egyptians, and Mycenaeans. Since these powers had an interest in long-distance trade with Troy's catchment area and the Black Sea region beyond it, Troy, in its role as a well-organized entrepôt, and a kind of northern outpost which itself posed no military threat, could bring them nothing but good. At the same time, however, its monopoly status and hence blocking capability, together with its constant accumulation of capital, could have become a thorn in the side to many. To dismiss such historical common sense as fantasy, as is often the case in discussions of Troy, would be to let one's sense of *Realpolitik* be clouded by irrelevant emotions, most of which arise from an aversion to what many regard as a debate that is already 'played out' about Troy and Homer. But after the varied discoveries of recent years in many relevant fields, it now looks as if this debate is not only not 'played out' but only now beginning to be responsible in its methods. This should very soon become even clearer.

All organizational and trading activity on the scale proposed was, of course, dependent on a particular instrument, the deployment of which established order and with it oversight for the first time: writing. Scenarios such as that sketched above could easily be dismissed as speculation, as long as there was no evidence of writing in Troy. The year 1995 brought with it change in this area too.

A WRITTEN TEXT SURFACES

Since Schliemann's time all excavators of Troy have had the foresight to leave certain areas here and there on the hilltop completely undisturbed, in order to facilitate later comparisons. One of these untouched points, the so-called 'pinnacles', which show the original level before the start of Schliemann's excavation, lies on the south side of the hilltop, west of the 'Pillar House', and reaches up as far as the Troy VI fortress wall (square E 8/9 in the general plan of the *Guide to Troy*). During the new excavations in 1995, when the southern crest of this pinnacle (in E9) was investigated, the footings of several one-room houses came to light, positioned between the fortress wall and an inner street running parallel to it, with access from this street. In one of these houses, among the potsherds, bones, and detritus of all kinds in the Early Troy $VIIb_2$ level—that is, in round figures, the second half of the twelfth century BC[58]—an item was discovered which electrified not only the excavation team. In the account of the finds, published a year later in *Studia Troica*,[59] this was described as 'the first attested prehistoric inscription from Troy'. It is a small round bronze seal, convex on both sides ('biconvex') (Fig. 11).

In itself, in the earliest settlements of Asia Minor, but also of Greece and other Mediterranean lands, a seal is nothing out of the ordinary. Seals are the earliest form of property marking. To this day, containers, documents, letters—in short, everything that

FIG. 11. The seal (original and sketch).

should pass unopened between sender and intended recipient—is 'sealed', as are official papers, as a mark of their authenticity and dependability. Just as before, our documents (certificates of birth and marriage, contracts, etc.) need to be validated by an official seal. The seal is usually kept under lock and key and may be used only by individuals who have the permission of higher authorities. Authorization by seal is therefore a mark of official power. To this day, document seals, in the form of rubber stamps, are usually round.

The earliest known seals are of stone and the shape—not yet standardized—might be square, rectangular, oval, or round, often displaying a single incised mark. In the course of time, seals came to show greater uniformity, tending to be round, and their content more expressive. They contained succinct details in written form concerning ownership, status, or the sender, just as our stamps do today. Biconvex seals form a separate category. Their defining char-

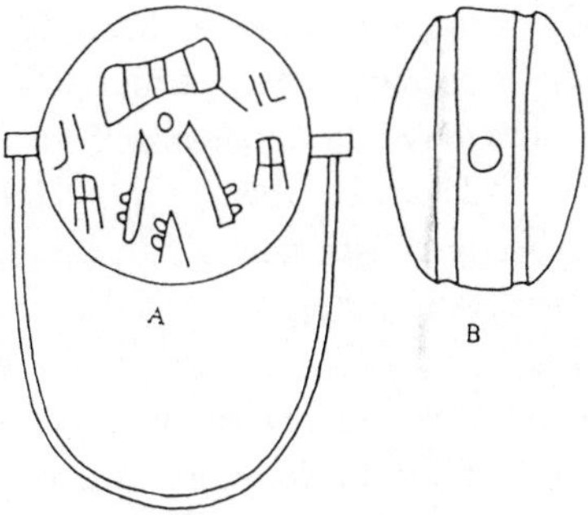

FIG. 12. Diagram of an Anatolian reversible seal.

acteristic is that they usually bear inscriptions on both sides; for maximum efficiency, these seals have a hole bored horizontally through them from edge to edge at their widest point. A metal shank is pushed through the hole and fastened at each end to a long stirrup-shaped metal loop (Fig. 12). This means that the seal may be quickly reversed.[60] As each side bore a different name—on one side usually the name of an official and on the other that of his wife—a document could be stamped twice by one and the same person with one and the same seal, apparently for greater prestige and authority. The need to have two seals and two individuals present at the same time was thus obviated.[61]

The bronze seal found in Troy was of this latter reversible type. In 1996 Korfmann offered the following description: 'Since seals are almost always cut from stone, this one stands out by the mere fact of being metal. In addition, this find is special in having inscriptions on both sides. We have always assumed, like some others, that the Trojans could read and write.'[62] After everything we have seen, in the end it became necessary not merely to posit this as a supposition, but to deduce it logically from the body of evidence. But in which language did the Trojans read and write?

Luwian: the language of the seals

If Schliemann, Dörpfeld, and Blegen had been able to see the seal inscription, they would not have been able to answer this question, as at that time the script had not yet been deciphered and the language set down in the script was either unknown (in Schliemann's and Dörpfeld's day), or reconstruction had barely begun (in Blegen's day). In order to be able to appreciate adequately the significance of the discovery of this seal, an excursion is called for into the history of the deciphering of the script and the reconstruction of the language.[63]

Writing as a means of leaving a permanent record of spoken facts and rendering them communicable, independent of place and time, was invented, as far as we can tell, by the Sumerians in Mesopotamia, between the Tigris and the Euphrates in present-day Iraq, and by the ancient Egyptians on the Nile, perhaps not independently of each other in the fundamental concept, in about 3000 BC. At first both the Sumerians and the Egyptians used purely pictorial signs which signified nothing more than the objects depicted: a painted sun meant 'the sun'; a wavy line, 'water'; an eye, 'eye', and so on. These absolutely unambiguous signs are termed 'logograms'. The next stage was the use of these signs for related concepts: a picture of the sun could also stand for 'light', 'day', 'bright', and 'hot'. Signs which have this function are known as 'ideograms'. Up to this point this proto-writing system is independent of the language of the people who may see it, just like our modern pictograms (picture writing): at an airport, a stylized woman bending over a stylized child on a stylized table denotes, in any language, a mothers' and babies' room; a curving line on a road sign means 'Beware! Bend in Road', whatever the language. Inscriptions restricted to signs of this kind are thus independent of particular languages and may be understood and used by members of the most varied speech communities: they are 'inter-national'. Inscriptions such as this are therefore well suited to communication within multicultural societies, which are at the same time multilingual societies. They are ill-suited, however, to the expression of more than elementary concepts.

The next stage is the use of the picture of the sun in a particular language in such a way that it represents only the first syllable of the word for 'sun' in that language (in German, the first syllable 'so-' or 'son-' of 'Sonne'). The last stage is the use of the sun for no more than the initial sound (in German 's') of the word.

In both the latter stages, as can easily be seen, the script, termed 'acrophonic' (from the Greek, meaning 'initial sound'), is now bound exclusively to the language on which these stages were based. If in our example our readers were not German speakers but Greeks, for example, they would be unable to read the picture of the sun as *so-*, *son-*, or 's', according to the acrophonic principle, because in their language 'sun' is phonetically represented not by 'Sonne' but by 'hēlios'; they would therefore read the symbol not as *so-, son-*or 's', but as *hē-/hēl* or 'h'.

Pictographic writing is unsuitable, then, for direct international communication if anything that is not elementary is required. Nevertheless it forms the basis for our own script. With frequent use the pictorial signs gradually become simplified, stylized, and abbreviated, as a result of a wish to save time in setting down the sign for each picture. If one day they become so greatly simplified and stylized that, instead of the original pictures, only signs remain, no longer clearly pictorial, but clearly distinguishable as signs, each one indicating a distinct sound, then this inventory of signs may be passed from one speech community to another. At this point the teacher has to pass on to the student only the sound value of each sign.

Since the time of the Greeks, Europe has taken the path of adopting essentially unchanged a developed system of representation, with the result that all European languages and many non-European languages are written today in the Greek alphabet, mostly in its Latinized form. The shift to this form of writing, the most advanced so far developed, with its principle of 'one sound—one symbol', took place in about 800 BC. All scripts developed and used before this time were more or less imperfect combinations of pictographic, syllabic, and phonetic systems. Of the materials on which writing was recorded—stone, clay tablets, and others—many have come down to us over the centuries and millennia, for example on stones that were reused again and again in house-building, in rock inscriptions, which have remained legible over long periods of time, on monuments such as the Egyptian obelisks, and lastly on archaeological finds unearthed in recent excavations, including seals. However, since there are no longer any speakers of the languages in which these texts were written, all these inscriptions have had to be laboriously deciphered, and in some cases this has not yet been achieved. Bilingual or trilingual texts, that is, the same text—mostly government decrees—appearing in two or three languages (and scripts), at least one of which is known, are of much assistance. But even in this situation, deciphering the unknown script and then reconstructing the unknown language is one of the greatest challenges the human intellect can face, and the history of this deciphering and reconstruction forms one of the most thrilling adventure stories that science can tell.

The beginning of this ongoing story is marked by the deciphering of the Ancient Egyptian writing system, the hieroglyphs—as the Greeks, who ruled Egypt from the time of Alexander the Great (332 BC), called these pictograms. (The Greek word means literally 'sacred inscriptions'; we recognize the first element from the word 'hierarchy' or 'ruling order', and the second from 'glyph' or 'carved character'.) After innumerable attempts by innumerable scholars, this script was at last deciphered in 1822. Jean François Champollion, the Frenchman who achieved this, is regarded as the father of modern cryptography.

The second great feat of cryptanalysis concerns Old Persian cuneiform, known since 1684 from rock inscriptions at Persepolis, 60 kilometres north-east of present-day Shiraz in Iran. With this the names of Carsten Niebuhr, Georg Friedrich Grotefend, and Henry Creswicke Rawlinson, in particular, are linked. The deciphering was mostly completed by about 1850.

The third decryption—of Mesopotamian cuneiform, and thus of Sumerian, Elamite, and Babylonian Assyrian, or Akkadian—was dramatic. Rawlinson, who had also puzzled over this script, wrote in 1850, 'I frankly confess, indeed, that... I have been tempted, on more occasions than one to abandon the study [of the Assyrian inscriptions] altogether, in utter despair of arriving at any satisfactory result.'[64] In the same year, 1850, after countless attempts, partial successes and failures by numerous scholars, the Irishman Edward Hincks came to the path-breaking realization that the script was syllabic. Each symbol stood for one syllable: consonant + vowel, vowel + consonant, or consonant + vowel + consonant. But in addition, one and the same symbol could have multiple values: it could represent a word, a syllable, or be added to certain groups of symbols denoting a certain class of objects to form a generic term, or determinative, such as 'man', 'woman', 'country', 'wood'. However, when it emerged that even this was not the full extent of the possible readings, but that a single sign could have multiple sound values, all decryption work done up to that point fell into disrepute.

In this seemingly hopeless situation, in 1857 the Royal Asiatic Society in London set four eminent Assyriologists, who had long been working on Mesopotamian cuneiform, another decoding problem. Rawlinson, Hincks, Fox Talbot, and Oppert were each independently to translate a newly discovered inscription, which none of the four could know, and submit their solution. At a ceremonial meeting of the Society the four sealed envelopes were opened: in all essentials the four translations matched. From that moment the decipherment of Babylonian Assyrian (Akkadian) has been considered complete.

Thus the three most important writing systems of the ancient Near East were deciphered: Egyptian hieroglyphs, Old Persian cuneiform, and Babylonian Assyrian (Akkadian) cuneiform with its predecessor, old Sumerian cuneiform. One puzzle, however, still awaited a solution, and it would be more than a hundred years in coming: the writing system and the language of the Hittites. That there had once been such a people, and that they must have played a significant role in Asia Minor in the second millennium BC, was known from the Bible. At numerous points the Bible speaks of the 'sons of Heth' and the Hittites,[65] for example in Genesis 23: 1 ff. One of these points is particularly stimulating to the imagination: 2 Kings 7: 6 runs: 'The Lord had caused the Arameans to hear the sound of chariots and horses and a great army, so that they said to one another, "Look, the king of Israel has hired the Hittite and Egyptian kings to attack us!"'

The 'Hittite kings' allied with the 'Egyptian kings' would signify the predominant power of the age: this could only mean that these Hittites were a people of great importance. But this was all that could be said about them. There was no monument, no ruined settlement, no epigraphic evidence—only the Bible to proclaim their existence. If such evidence had ever existed—in the nineteenth century the Bible was looked upon by historians as a dubious source—it was now lost.

When epigraphic evidence did emerge, the discoverer unfortunately failed to realize that the document referred to them. In 1812 Johann Ludwig Burckhardt ('Sheikh Ibrahim'), the scion of a patrician Basel family and representative of the Royal African Society and the East India Company, was visiting the Syrian town of Hama (the biblical Hamath, later Greek Epiphaneia on the Orontes). There in the bazaar he noticed a stone marked with figures and signs that reminded him of Egyptian hieroglyphs, yet were fundamentally different. Unfortunately his observations passed unnoticed. The reports of other travellers concerning the same stone fared no better. Only in 1872 was this stone sent, with four similar ones, by the Governor of Syria to Constantinople, and plaster-casts went to the British Museum. European and American orientalists soon agreed that this must represent the language and writing system of the Hittites. This was confirmed by numerous similar inscriptions found since 1876 by British excavators at Jerablus on the Euphrates (now close to the Turkish–Syrian border post of Carablus, near Gaziantep). When excavated, the town proved to be the former Hittite centre of Karkame (also Karkemiş, Karkamiş—other forms are also known), familiar from Egyptian and Akkadian sources. Further inscriptions of this kind emerged in connection with the monumental rock sculptures in the Turkish village of Boğazköy, 150 kilometres east of Ankara, which was later found to be the former Hittite capital of Ḫattusa, and at the Karabel Pass, 30 kilometres east of Izmir (see p. 87–8 for more detail), and other sites. At first, however, nobody could read these texts.

Archibald Henry Sayce, a Welshman who later became Professor of Assyriology at Oxford, took a significant step in 1880, on the basis of a seal. This seal (Fig. 13) was a small silver disc, which eight years earlier had been described in a specialist journal by the German orientalist Mordtmann.[66] In Smyrna (Izmir) it had come into the possession of a numismatist, Alexander Jovanoff, who had offered to sell it to the British Museum. The Museum directors had taken it to be a forgery and declined to buy it, but had had the foresight to get a copy made. This foresight would pay dividends not only in 1880, but, as we shall see, in very recent times, in quite sensational fashion in 1997, and this in direct connection with the Trojan question. But we should not run ahead of our story. At that

FIG. 13. The so-called Tarkondemos seal, known since the nineteenth century.

time, in 1880, Sayce studied the copy of the seal at the British Museum. In a narrow outer band it bore a cuneiform inscription, and the middle showed a richly attired, well-armed warrior—as Mordtmann described it. He added, 'On each side are various symbols.' Mordtmann had already made an attempt at reading the cuneiform text in the outer ring and, with the aid of the determinatives in it, arrived at the rough interpretation: 'XY (= indecipherable name), king of the land of XY (= indecipherable name).' He had then interpreted the name of the king as 'Tarkudimmi', which appears frequently in Cilicia, and compared this with the name 'Tarkondemos', which occurs in the writings of the Greek writer Plutarch (second century AD). The seal has been known to Hittite scholars ever since as the 'Tarkondemos Seal'. The correct pronunciation did not emerge until 1997.

Except for the reading of the name itself, Mordtmann's interpretation of the cuneiform text was correct, but he had not taken the step which would prove decisive for the entire future of the decipherment of Hittite. This was left to Sayce. Mordtmann had paid no further attention to the pictorial signs on each side of the warrior, dismissing them as 'symbols'. Sayce realized that these were not mere decoration, but pictograms. He also realized that the designs in the middle of the disc must express the same meaning as the cuneiform characters in the outer ring. This was a milestone in the progress of research, as it meant that the seal represented the first bilingual Hittite text. But at the time nothing more could be done with it, since both the language represented by the cuneiform in the outer ring and that of the inner pictograms were unknown. It was rather as if we had a text before us today in Latin script, and another in Greek script, but on assembling words out of the letters, whose phonetic values are known, we found that the words were neither Latin nor Greek. The lexemes appear completely meaningless, as not only are they neither Latin nor Greek, but come from no known language. The text can be read but it cannot be understood.

This was a frustrating situation, made even more so in 1888 by a discovery at El Amarna in Upper Egypt. This was an archive of clay tablets bearing extensive remnants of correspondence between the Egyptian Pharaohs Amenophis III and Amenophis IV (Akhenaten) and some Near Eastern kings. Among the letters, written in fully intelligible Akkadian, were two from the 'Kings of Ḫatti', that is, from the Hittite kings. The Bible was right after all! One of the letters came from a king by the name of Suppiluliuma, congratulating Akhenaten on his accession to the throne. Other letters yielded valuable information about Hittite wars and expeditions in the south of Asia Minor (Syria). The historians were jubilant. At last a people and an empire once as unknown as the Hittites had emerged into the light of history! But the linguists had less cause for jubilation, as this was a repetition of the situation which had led them to despair over the Tarkondemos Seal: two of the clay tablet letters were written in Akkadian cuneiform script, but in a language which was completely unknown. They were addressed to a recipient in the 'land of Arzawa'—this much could be made out. But the 'land of Arzawa' was not known to anybody, and the text was incomprehensible. How these 'Arzawa letters' might be related to the Tarkondemos Seal did not emerge until 1997. When they were made public in 1902, they caused great controversy. The publishers, Knudzton, Bugge, and Torp, had ventured the theory that the unknown language was Hittite, and that Hittite belonged to a completely different language group from the other languages written in cuneiform. While those other languages were Semitic, Hittite, they claimed, was Indo-European, which meant that the Arzawa letters therefore constituted the oldest epigraphic evidence of Indo-European. At the time this was an unheard-of hypothesis. The Indo-Europeanists rejected it, and the publishers recanted. The question of the language of these letters remained unresolved.

More frustrations were to come. In 1905 the German Assyriologist Hugo Winckler, commissioned by the German Oriental Society and Kaiser Wilhelm II, excavated a large temple at Boğazköy with his team and found in it an archive of clay tablets with over ten thousand fragments. Many of the documents were very well preserved. Those that were written in Akkadian—the language of diplomacy in the Near East at the period—Winckler could read immediately. He realized at once that he was in the erstwhile capital of the Hittites, in Ḫattusa! Twenty days after starting to dig, on 20 August 1905, Winckler held in his hand a letter from the Egyptian Pharaoh Ramses II to the Hittite king Ḫattusili III concerning a peace treaty between Egypt and the Ḫatti empire, from the year 1269 BC. This treaty was already known in its Egyptian version from the hieroglyphs on the temple wall at Karnak, the ancient city of Thebes, on the Nile. More documents and letters of all sorts soon followed. In a second campaign in 1911–12, the amount of material multiplied again and the history of the Hittites began to take shape. But not all texts were in Akkadian. Many were in the same exasperating language as the Arzawa letters, which many took to be 'Caucasian'. Exactly forty years had now passed since this language had been found in the cuneiform legend on the Tarkondemos Seal, and still nobody could understand it...

The solution came three years later, thanks to Bedřich (later Friedrich) Hrozný, (born in 1879), the son of a priest from Bohemia. Hrozný had studied Semitology and Assyriology in Vienna and Berlin, and at 24 had been appointed to a chair at the University of Vienna. In 1914 the German Oriental Society sent him to Constantinople to copy the Boğazköy texts which were held in the museum there. Hrozný made the crucial discovery that in the incomprehensible Hittite text the same cuneiform letter groups appeared with different terminations, which must represent grammatical endings. This meant that Hittite must share features of Indo-European, that its words were inflected, declined, conjugated. Illumination came to the then 35-year-old professor when he had teased out the sentence:

nu BREAD-an e-iz-za-at-te-ni wa-at-tar-ma e-ku-ut-te-ni

The sign for 'bread' was an ideogram known from Akkadian, but here it had an ending, *-an*. When the third word was read according to the rules of cuneiform writing, it sounded as *ezzāteni*. The root of this could hardly be anything but the Indo-European *ed-*, which is seen, for example, in the Greek *ēdein*, Latin *édere*, and German *essen*. The fourth word, in its phonetic form, looked like *wātar (-ma)*, which could only be related to *water*. This line must therefore have to do with 'eating bread' and 'drinking water'. At this point everything fell into place and Hrozný arrived at the sentence, 'Now you are eating bread but drinking water.'

The conclusion was inescapable: Hittite was an Indo-European language. On 15 November 1915 Hrozný announced this result to the Near Eastern Society in Berlin. In the world of scholarship, this was a sensation. In 1917 he published his book on the subject, *Die Sprache der Hethiter, ihr Bau und ihre Zugehörigkeit zum indogermanischen Sprachstamm* (The Language of the Hittites, its Structure and Derivation from Proto-Indo-European). There could be no argument about the key findings. Cuneiform Hittite had been deciphered.

However, 'pictographic' or 'hieroglyphic Hittite' had not yet been deciphered. Since the discovery of the Tarkondemos Seal in 1872 and Sayce's realization in 1880 that the pictorial signs in the middle part of the seal must contain the same meaning as the cuneiform legend in the outer ring, there had been hardly any progress towards decipherment. A theory which would later prove correct and important, however, had gained ground (and this is fundamental to the question of the Trojan seal): the pictographic script appeared to reflect a language related to that written in cuneiform, but not the same. In the cuneiform Hittite texts there were points at which words and phrases from two closely related languages were signalled by *luwili* or *palaumnili*, which could only mean 'in Luwian' and 'in Palaic'. This suggested that the pictographic script recorded one of these two 'dialects', Luwian or Palaic. This hypothesis assumed firmer and more precise shape when further study of cuneiform Hittite texts revealed that, in the later course of Hittite history (the fourteenth or thirteenth century BC), Luwian exerted increasing influence on 'metropolitan' Hittite.

The Luwians, a people closely related to the Hittites, formed part of the Hittite empire from earliest times. The influence of their language on 'High Hittite' was particularly apparent in the word-stock. Gradually, within the empire the Luwian language apparently became a kind of demotic, through which many loan-words from contemporary Mediterranean languages, including Mycenaean Greek, found their way into Hittite texts.[67] After the fall of the Hittite empire in about 1175 BC, it was Luwian that lived on in the small new successor states and principalities, especially in the Syrian region, the 'Luwian southern belt' of Asia Minor, but also extending northward. Many Anatolian languages known from the first millennium BC, such as Cilician, Cappadocian, and Lycian, are now termed 'late Luwian', 'neo-Luwian', or 'Luvoid' languages, because of the evident continuity.[68]

As studies of language distribution in the Hittite empire have shown, Luwian was spoken especially in the south and west of the empire, but pictographic texts, as we have seen, had been found mainly in these areas: Hama and Karkemiş in Syria, and at Karabel near Smyrna (Izmir), where the Tarkondemos Seal originated. It thus became steadily clearer that 'hieroglyphic Hittite', a complex pictographic script, was used for Luwian. But, as before, nobody could read it.

The decipherment of this script, unlike some other cases, was not the achievement of a single individual at a single point in time. Rather it came as the result of a prolonged search and exchange by several scholars from different countries, especially in the period between 1928 and 1946, but even today it is not quite complete. Among these researchers, the following deserve particular mention: the Italian Piero Meriggi, the Polish-born American Ignace J. Gelb, the Swiss Emil Forrer, and the German Helmuth Theodor Bossert. At the end of World War II some fifty pictograms could be read as syllables of the type 'consonant + vowel'. In 1947 it became apparent that these efforts were on the right track. In that year Bossert found a bilingual Phoenician–Hittite hieroglyphic text in Cilicia, at Karatepe, the 'black hill', north-east of the modern Turkish town of Adana. The work previously done was confirmed in all essentials by this text, in which a petty king named Asitawatas gives an account of his own deeds.

In the years that followed, research into hieroglyphic Hittite was carried forward chiefly by the Frenchman Emile Laroche, as well as by the British scholars J. D. Hawkins and Anna Morpurgo Davies in close collaboration with the German Günter Neumann. In 1973 these three researchers were able, in a joint work, to publish their findings: hieroglyphic Hittite was closely related to Luwian. (In 1996 Hawkins reaffirmed this in his article in *The Oxford Classical Dictionary*, in which he described hieroglyphic Hittite as a 'Luwian dialect'.) In 1992 in his wide-ranging article entitled 'System und Ausbau der hethitischen Hieroglyphenschrift' (The System and Structure of the Hittite Hieroglyphic Script) Neumann formulated the widely accepted conclusion that there were 'indications that the Hittite hieroglyphic script was *designed* primarily for the *Luwian* language'.[69] As we have seen in all pre-Greek scripts as a principle, this system combines logograms, ideograms, and determinatives with unambiguous acrophonic syllabic signs: a donkey's head, for example, may stand simply for a donkey, but it may also represent the first open syllable of the Luwian word for 'donkey', *targasna*, *ta-*.

In this article Neumann also answers the question which occurs to everybody who has ever followed this story: Why? Why should a part of the great Hittite empire, the Luwians, go to the trouble of inventing a second writing system to add to the Hittite cuneiform which they already had? Neumann's answer takes us back to our starting point, the biconvex bronze seal found in Troy in 1995. Armed with this background knowledge of the origins and structure of early writing systems, we can now better appreciate the significance of this find for the whole of the Trojan question.

We proceed from the conclusion which became possible after Hrozný's decipherment, on the basis of intensive study of the Hittite cuneiform, that today one thing above all is clear: the Hittites and their cousins the Luwians and Palaites were an Indo-European people who in the third millennium BC migrated from the north, probably from the regions north of the Black Sea, to Anatolia, and there gradually developed and expanded from small beginnings to become a great power. In its heyday this power dominated large areas of Asia Minor, possibly even all of Asia Minor, from the Black Sea to the Levant in the south-west and the Aegean in the west. For a clearer understanding of the following outline of Hittite history, a chronological overview in the form of a graph is appended, with a list of the Hittite kings and queens, as far as these are known (Figs. 14 and 15).[70]

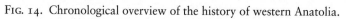

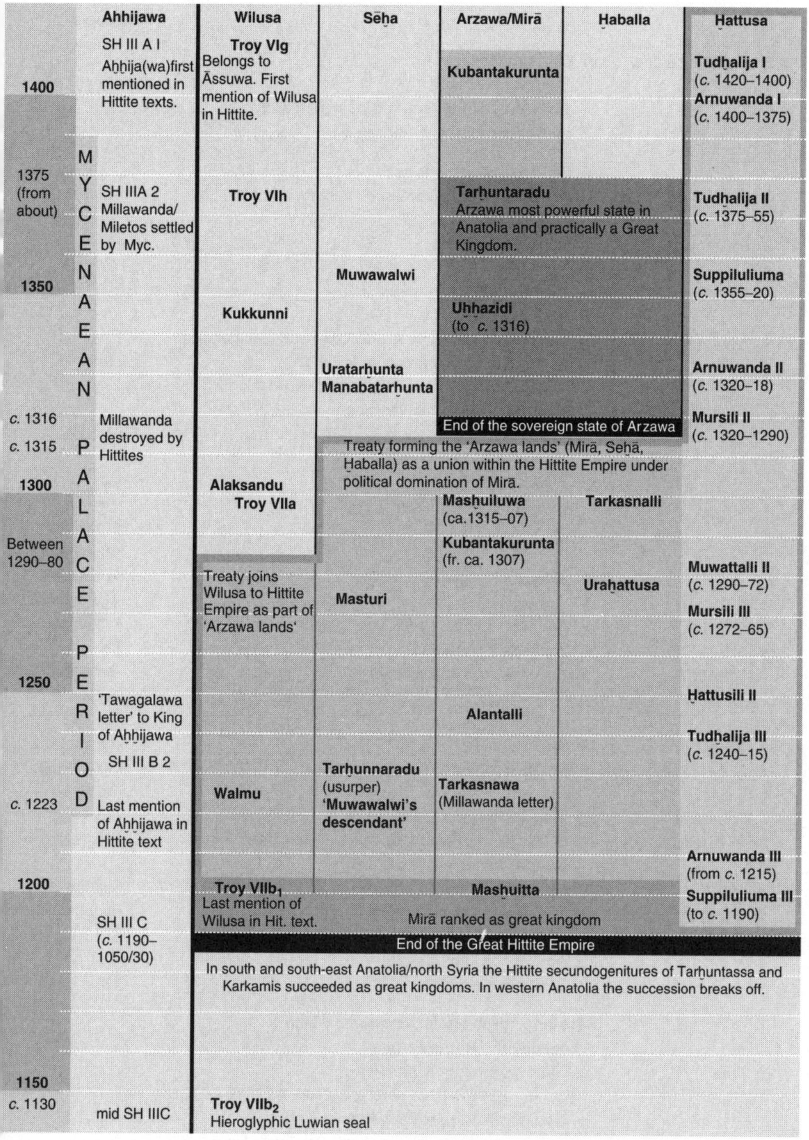
Ahhijawa
Wilusa
Seḫa
Arzawa/Mirā
Ḫaballa
Ḫattusa
1400
SH III A I
Aḫḫija(wa)first mentioned in Hittite texts.
Troy VIg
Belongs to Āssuwa. First mention of Wilusa in Hittite.
Kubantakurunta
Tudḫalija I (c. 1420–1400)
Arnuwanda I (c. 1400–1375)
M Y C E N A E A N
1375 (from about)
SH IIIA 2
Millawanda/ Miletos settled by Myc.
Troy VIh
Tarḫuntaradu
Arzawa most powerful state in Anatolia and practically a Great Kingdom.
Tudḫalija II (c. 1375–55)
1350
Muwawalwi
Suppiluliuma (c. 1355–20)
Kukkunni
Uhhazidi (to c. 1316)
Uratarḫunta
Manabatarḫunta
Arnuwanda II (c. 1320–18)
c. 1316
c. 1315
Millawanda destroyed by Hittites
End of the sovereign state of Arzawa
Mursili II (c. 1320–1290)
P A L A C E
Treaty forming the 'Arzawa lands' (Mirā, Seḫā, Ḫaballa) as a union within the Hittite Empire under political domination of Mirā.
1300
Alaksandu
Troy VIIa
Masḫuiluwa (ca.1315–07)
Tarkasnalli
Between 1290–80
Kubantakurunta (fr. ca. 1307)
Treaty joins Wilusa to Hittite Empire as part of 'Arzawa lands'
Masturi
Uraḫattusa
Muwattalli II (c. 1290–72)
Mursili III (c. 1272–65)
P E R I O D
1250
'Tawagalawa letter' to King of Aḫḫijawa
Ḫattusili II
Alantalli
Tudḫalija III (c. 1240–15)
SH III B 2
Tarḫunnaradu (usurper) 'Muwawalwi's descendant'
Walmu
Tarkasnawa (Millawanda letter)
c. 1223
Last mention of Aḫḫijawa in Hittite text
Arnuwanda III (from c. 1215)
1200
Troy VIIb₁
Last mention of Wilusa in Hit. text.
Masḫuitta
Mirā ranked as great kingdom
Suppiluliuma III (to c. 1190)
SH III C (c. 1190–1050/30)
End of the Great Hittite Empire
In south and south-east Anatolia/north Syria the Hittite secundogenitures of Tarḫuntassa and Karkamis succeeded as great kingdoms. In western Anatolia the succession breaks off.
1150
c. 1130
mid SH IIIC
Troy VIIb₂
Hieroglyphic Luwian seal

FIG. 14. Chronological overview of the history of western Anatolia.

Date	Kings	Queens
End of 18th century	**(a) Kings of Nēsa**	
	Pitḫāna of Kussara	
	Anitta (son of Pitḫāna), great king (break in succession lasting **c.**130 years)	
	(b) Great kings of Ḫattusa	
*c.*1565–1540	1. Ḫattusili I ['the Kussavaite'?? 'nephew of the *tauannanna*']	Kaddusi
*c.*1540–1530	2. Mursili I [son of 1]	Kali
*c.*1530–	3. Ḫantili I [brother-in-law of 2]	Ḫarapsegi
	4. Zidanta I [son-in-law of 3]	?
	5. Ammuna [son of 4]	?
	6. Ḫuzzika I [relationship to previous incumbent not clear]	?
*c.*1500–	7. Telibinu [son of 5? brother-in-law of 6]	Istabarija
	8. Taḫurwaili [8th position uncertain; relationship to previous incumbent not clear]	
	9. Alluwamna [son-in-law of 7]	Ḫarapsili
	10. Ḫantili II [probably son of 9]	?
	11. Zidanta II [probably son of 10]	Ijaja
	12. Ḫuzzija II [probably son of 11]	Summiri
		Kattesḫabi
		Kattesḫabi?
	13. Muwattalli I [son/brother of 12?]	Kattesḫabi?
*c.*1420–1400	14. Tudḫalija I [son of 12]	Nigalmadi
*c.*1400–1375	15. Arnuwanda I [son-in-law and adopted son of 14]	Asmunigal
*c.*1375–1355	16. Tudḫalija II [son of 15]	Taduḫeba
*c.*1355–1320	17. Suppiluliuma I [son of 16]	Taduḫeba
		Ḫenti
		Malnigal
*c.*1320–1318	18. Arnuwanda II [son of 17]	Malnigal
*c.*1318–1290	19. Mursili II [son of 17]	Gassulawija
		Taduḫeba
*c.*1290–1272	20. Muwattalli II [son of 19]	Taduḫeba
*c.*1272–1265	21. Mursili III – Urḫitesub [son of 20; recorded as being in Aegean exile in 1245]	Taduḫeba
*c.*1265–1240	22. Ḫattusili II (formerly 'III'!) [son of 19]	Puduḫeba
*c.*1240–1215	23. Tudḫalija III (formerly 'IV'!) [son of 22]	Puduḫeba
*c.*1220–?	24. Kurunta of Tarḫuntassa [son of 20]	?
after *c.*1215	25. Arnuwanda III [son of 23]	?
	26. Suppiluliuma II [son of 23]	?
	First kings of the great kingdoms which succeeded the Hittite empire	
*c.*1200	a. *Secundogeniture of Karkamis*: Kuzitesub [great-great-great grandson of 17]. Great king.	
	b. *Secundogeniture of Tarḫuntassa*: Ḫartapu [son of Mursili—probably 21]. Great king.	
	c. *Vassal state of Mirā*: Masḫuitta [great-great grandson of Masḫuiluwa of Arzawa/Mirā and the daughter of 17]. Great king.	

FIG. 15. The Hittite rulers.

After an initial period of expansion, involving the defeat of three native petty kingdoms, King Anitta founded the first great Hittite kingdom, with its capital at Nēsa. This was followed by the period of the so-called Old Empire, with the new capital of Ḫattusa (1650–1500 BC). In this period a policy of expansion was directed particularly towards western Asia Minor—the so-called Arzawa lands—and against Syria; in 1531 BC Babylon was also overrun. As a result of internal power struggles within dynasties, however, all these gains were lost until the so-called Middle Empire began with King Telibinu in about 1500 BC, when the previous policy of purely military conquest was complemented by one of forming alliances. The headquarters in Ḫattusa now installed vassal kings in many areas of Anatolia which had been conquered or turned into dependencies, and bound them to it by treaty. At the same time Syria was reconquered and in the west the empire again moved against Arzawa.

From about 1400 BC the rise began of the great empire of Ḫattusa, which eventually came to be the third great power of the period, ranking equally with Babylon and Egypt. At its highest point (the fourteenth and thirteenth centuries BC), all the petty states between the capital and the Levant belonged to the empire, while Arzawa, with its capital Abasa (Ephesos), had been conquered and reduced to the vassal states of Mirā, Ḫaballa, and Sēḫa, so that the empire reached to the Aegean coast, including offshore islands such as Lazba (Lesbos). Here the area of Troy was also firmly bound to Ḫattusa. To this we shall return. At the battle of Kadesh in 1275, the northward thrust of Egypt under Ramses II was halted.

In 1175 BC the empire collapsed. The reasons for this are many and their interplay is not yet fully clear. However, numerous great and petty kingdoms, which had previously been allied to the empire, survived after its collapse as autonomous princedoms. Here much of the Hittite or Luwian culture, with its language and writing system, survived. It was not until the eighth and seventh centuries BC that these Hittite successor states, also known as 'secundogenitures', merged into new units such as Lycia, Caria, and Lydia. The language, Luwian in particular, survived in some areas of Asia Minor until the fourth and third centuries BC—in the Roman provinces of Isauria and Lycaonia (roughly the triangle Antalya–

Konya–Adana in modern Turkey), and some personal names survived into the sixth century AD.[71]

From this brief survey of Hittite history it will be clear that the empire in its entirety was never the property of any single nationality. The territories of the empire included many non-Hittite regions and petty states, and others were linked by treaty. The empire of the Hittites, especially at the period of its greatest geographical extent, thus appears as a multi-ethnic and multilingual state. Here Günter Neumann offers his explanation for the use of a second writing system, hieroglyphic Hittite, in the empire, side by side with the traditional cuneiform (following recent discoveries, and to avoid confusion with Egyptian hieroglyphs, it might be better to call the Hittite script 'Luwoglyphic' or 'hieroglyphic Luwian'):[72]

> The new script created in Asia Minor had the advantage that many of its symbols were pictorial and naturalistic, and told the contemporary reader directly what they meant, no matter what language that reader spoke or understood. In this they were distinct from the highly abstract cuneiform. In the second millennium BC the individual characters of the latter consisted purely of lines and angles, which could be read only by those who had studied them and, moreover, had a command of the language of the text. Even the format of the cuneiform tablets suggests that each was intended for only a single reader.
>
> In the creation of hieroglyphs, therefore, a wish to speak directly to a wider public in a multilingual country may have played a part, using a new medium, in which everybody, not only the educated, could immediately understand at least some of the signs. Both the monumental inscription of Nişantaş, inside the capital Ḫattusa, and the rock monument of Karabel, for example, beside a major road . . . and many others are clearly accessible documents. Like large hoardings they address passers-by in a way in which nobody in Asia Minor attempted with cuneiform. At Nişantaş we can see that Suppiluliuma II, one of the last kings of the high imperial period, announced his own majesty with extremely detailed honorifics, and other old rock inscriptions show that there were rulers who arranged to have these made as a means of self-expression.

Neumann then transfers this illuminating hypothesis to the 'Luwoglyphic' seals:

> The oldest sure evidence of this Hittite hieroglyphic script, however, is the seals and their imprints. The symbols on them transmit mainly the names (and titles) of the ruler, in an artistic form that was intended to be seen, and

most likely was seen, as reflecting prestige and pomp. But besides the names and titles of kings (REX), princes and princesses (REX FILIUS, REX FILIA), the seals also bear the symbols for PRAECO (herald), AURIGA (charioteer), PINCERNA (cup-bearer), SCRIBA (master-scribe, apparently in at least three ranks), and MAGNUS DOMUS INFANS [...] (squire of the palace). All of these denote high officials. Later comes the symbol (L 372) for the title SACERDOS (priest). Thus the right (or the practice) of using seals had evidently been current in the royal court from an early date. (Each of these titles had its own distinct symbol, and these symbols clearly belonged to the central stock—and the oldest stock—of this writing system.) The seals sometimes bear hieroglyphs and cuneiform side by side. All in all the impression is created that the script was deemed suitable for the public expression of the power of the rulers and the might of the royal court.[73]

From this it follows that the Hittites possessed an 'official script', for use within the inner circle of government and administration, as well as in diplomatic communications: cuneiform. (Records of this constitute vast masses of text, which, because of the limited number of experts world-wide, remain largely untranslated.) But for prestige purposes and for demonstrations of authority over the peoples of the empire, the pictographic script was preferred, being more immediately intelligible and making a purely visual impression, and being understood by both ordinary people and officials.

Handwriting styles in the 'Luwoglyphic' script have one peculiarity which distinguishes them clearly from the hieroglyphs of Egypt. One specialist in Hittite, famous in her day, once described the difference as follows:

When an Egyptian writes, he creates. The product is pleasing to the eye, and this is far more important to the writer than the content, which is mostly formulaic. A Hittite, on the other hand, is garrulous. To modify the old saying, what the heart thinks, the hieroglyphs say. He writes for the sake of the content. The appearance of the writing matters little to him. The individual letters are not disposed according to a known conventional pattern... The symbols seem to float in space, rather than arrange themselves in lines. A specialist needs to have great experience simply to read them in the right order... Hittite writing runs literally all over the place, heedless of margins, round corners, onto the next slab [in rock inscriptions], over the bodies of animals depicted, wherever the writer pleases... What might a pedantically-minded Egyptian have thought of this floating script?

And of Hittite seals, she wrote:

The Hittite seals have none of that order in design, that intricate interlocking [which typifies Assyrian seals]. Either a figure stands alone and barely tolerates written symbols and attributes beside it, in a subordinate position, or, as in the writing, we find a surging spring, an unstoppable narrative urge, with no sense at all of orderly arrangement. This may be the main reason why the Hittites had no use for a reversible seal and continued to use their stamps. A cylinder seal forms right angles, requiring that some thought be given to vertical and horizontal lines, while their stamp was round, and therefore the ideal framework for the surge and drift of Hittite art, completely lost in empty space.[74]

In the light of this, it is hardly surprising that the text of a Luwian seal found in Troy in 1995 has still not been fully deciphered even by the leading specialists. It is made the more difficult by the poor state of preservation of the inscribed symbols. The seal had apparently been much used, so that the metal surfaces between the notches were sometimes completely worn away, like the tread of a motor tyre, and the notches themselves smoothed out.

FIG. 16. Specimens of Hittite stamps.

The meaning of the seals: Trojan scribes!

Fortunately this was not of crucial importance, as the legible part clearly showed the *type* of inscription: 'title + name'. The first thing that J. D. Hawkins, to whose care the find was at once entrusted, established in his report of 1996 was that 'Luwoglyphic' seals were commonly of this type: one side often showed a man's name and title, while the other bore a woman's name, presumably that of the man's wife.[75] As for the period when these seals were in use, Ronald L. Gorny concluded in his special study of 1993 that these seals were typical of the high imperial era (the fourteenth to thirteenth centuries BC), and were in most general use in the thirteenth century, that is, the late imperial era.

The Trojan seal is now most clearly and unmistakably legible at the very points which matter most for our present scientific interests: precisely where on the male side the title and on the reverse the word 'wife' can be seen. The personal names of the man and his wife are no longer clearly legible. We may see at once that it is a lucky chance for us that the inscriptions have survived in the way they have: if our descendants found a stamp from our time in which the names 'Richard' and 'Irene' could be made out in one part, while in the other, where the title and perhaps address of Richard and Irene might be expected to appear, nothing had been preserved, the information value of the find would be limited. But on the Trojan seal, on the man's side, it is the title that can be recognized: 'scribe', or, as Günter Neumann has it, 'master scribe', and on the reverse the word 'wife'. As usual, on both sides the personal information about the owners is framed by the symbol for 'good', to wish them good luck.

The title 'scribe' or 'master-scribe', on those seals that are more than simply stamps, is quite a common mark of status or profession. It testifies that the owner was not merely the proprietor or dispatcher of the sealed item—a merchant, for example—but a member of a superior caste, a person of education, able to read and write, and thus be counted an intellectual. Furthermore, the title is evidence that here 'speaks' an official with authority conferred upon him by the highest echelons of power. In 1993 Gorny defined the owners of such seals as holders of the highest positions in society, and concluded: 'If the use of these seals was reserved for some group of special officials, one might be able to make a case tying them to the Hittite king or a class of individuals connected to the crown.'[76] As we have seen, Günter Neumann had formed the same opinion in 1992, but in more categorical terms. And now such a seal had come to light in Troy! Are we to regard this as insignificant, as a matter of chance devoid of any meaning? Given the current state of research, it is difficult to assume that somebody wore on his neck a piece of antique jewellery whose meaning he was no longer able to understand, as an ornament, then one day tired of it and threw it away. And we can hardly be satisfied with the notion that perhaps a visitor to Troy lost a seal, failed to notice this, but when he did finally notice gave it no more thought. Would a senior government official who lost his diplomatic passport react with comparable unconcern today? Should we not draw other conclusions from the Trojan seal? First we need to consider where seals of this kind have been found in the ancient world, since only by this means can we properly classify this seal within its possible structural context.

The distribution of Luwian seals

In his first report on the discovery of the seal Korfmann pointed out that seals of this kind were not uncommon and had been found in over fifteen Anatolian towns.[77] This sounds like an underestimate. Gorny's special study, which appeared in 1993, of biconvex seals from Alişar Höyük, cited by Korfmann, had painted a much fuller picture. Gorny named and described biconvex seals of the same type from more than twenty Anatolian sites and demonstrated that their numbers ran into hundreds. He made it emphatically clear that in recent years the number of biconvex seals made public had risen 'dramatically'. He quoted a letter from Peter Neve, the excavator of Ḫattusa, dated 17 June 1990: 'We have hundreds of typically late biconvex seals or their stamps on bullas found in the Upper City... They all belong... to the latest Hittite period.'[78] In this communication from Neve, the 'stamps' and the indication of the time of origin are of particular interest. If one reviews the literature of recent years on Anatolian seal finds even superficially, on the one hand one is struck by the amount of supporting detail regarding innumerable concave seal impressions on documents. These of course can only have been made by convex seals. To the hundreds of biconvex 'Luwoglyphic' seals physically available, we must therefore add this 'negative' evidence. On the other hand, the high number is less surprising if we bear in mind the second point of general agreement in the reports: that the overwhelming majority of these seals and impressions date from the late period of the empire, roughly speaking the late thirteenth century and early twelfth century BC. These observations taken together form a familiar picture, of a highly developed society in which the administrative mentality has spun the web of bureaucracy over all aspects of life: there is no halting the advance of the stamps.

In view of this, there seems to be little to be gained by pointing out that seals of the same type have also been found in Greece. Korfmann himself mentions a biconvex seal of the same kind from a tomb in Perati in Attica, but adds at once that that seal served as part of a necklace: a girl had used it like a pearl. More seals of this kind had been found, as Neumann reports, in Thebes and Mycenae.[79] Scientific honesty demands, of course, that there should be no suppression of these or any future finds. It should, however, be clear that these can hardly be anything other than trophies. As the girl's necklace shows, the new owners had no idea what these objects were for. The finds in their totality allow us to state, without hesitation, that the actual 'professional' area of use of the Luwian seal lay not in Greece but in Anatolia.

Troy as a Hittite royal seat

What conclusions are we to draw from this? We should not of course leap straight to the conclusion that the Trojans spoke Luwian. In view of the city's probable role as a focal point in a trade network uniting the peoples of the Three Seas Region, we must in any case assume a degree of 'internationalism', which included multilingualism. What the first language of the native population was must remain open, even after these discoveries. But given all that we now know of the fundamentally Anatolian orientation of Troy, as shown in the foregoing sections, quite independent of the seal, there is nothing to dissuade us from accepting in essentials what Korfmann said immediately after the discovery of these seals, 'The place where they have been found is a Hittite sphere of activity and interest.'[80] He had thus already taken the next step, from the general geographical concept of 'Anatolia' to the political notion of the 'Hittite empire'.

In a new work, Günter Neumann has voiced a similar view, if somewhat more cautiously: 'This find indicates the existence of relations—economic or political—between Troy and the other parts of Anatolia . . . '.[81] Since 'the other parts of Anatolia' in the second millennium BC were overwhelmingly Hittite-dominated, this statement also implies that Troy must be counted as part of the Hittite empire.

The existing evidence and the previously cited conclusions drawn from it, all pointing in the same direction, should therefore now enable us to state the current position with greater confidence: since the research of recent years—particularly that of Günter Neumann—has demonstrated that 'the creation of the hieroglyphs may have reflected a wish to speak directly to broader strata of the population *in a multilingual country*', and that the 'Luwoglyphic' seals 'were perceived and intended to bespeak pomp and prestige',[82] the Trojan seal is the firmest link so far in the existing chain of evidence pointing to the inescapable conclusion that Troy was at least connected to the empire of the Hittites. How was it connected—as a royal seat, outpost, or satellite state? When, for how long? All these questions remain to be discussed, and the fact that the seal originates in the latter half of the twelfth century BC will be borne firmly in mind, since a short time before this, in about 1175 BC, the Hittite empire fell apart. If Luwian seals remained in use in Troy after this, as in the petty princedoms of the Luwians (Karkamis, Tarḫuntassa), which now called themselves 'great kingdoms', this would suggest an entirely new picture of Troy.

At this point we should take preliminary stock of the foregoing discussion of the seal, if only to state that the significance of this discovery has until now been greatly underrated. Appraisals of it have given too much weight to the quantitative argument that one swallow does not make a summer. However, what is critically important is not the number of finds which point to the Hittite empire, but the mere fact of their existence in Troy, a city 200 kilometres as the crow flies from the Karabel Pass, with its monumental Luwoglyphic reliefs. Another two, five, or ten biconvex Luwoglyphic seals, which may very well turn up soon in Troy, would not add to the strength of the argument either. What matters is that this seal, like a long-missing piece of a jigsaw puzzle, fits into the bigger picture which was already to hand.

'ILIOS' AND 'TROY': TWO NAMES REHABILITATED

All the evidence that Korfmann's excavation has produced for a relationship between Troy VI and the Hittite empire indicates that Troy—an Anatolian city with a built-up area of over 200,000 square metres, 7,000 to 10,000 permanent inhabitants, and a vital economic role—cannot have been an insignificant area to the Hittites at the time of their pre-eminence in Anatolia. During the period of the rise of their empire, as we have shown, the Hittite kings had at first relied on military expansion. In subsequent centuries this policy changed. There was now more reliance on incorporation of areas as yet unconquered by treaty. Their treaty partners were the local dynasties of the day. In the vast diplomatic correspondence of the Hittite kings, found in the clay tablet archive of Boğazköy, more and more names of rulers and their regions, over many centuries, continue to emerge—as is only to be expected, this being the nature of the archive. The work of ordering and classifying this correspondence and other documents by region—the compilation, as it were, of records for individual regions and states belonging to the empire or bound to it by treaty—is still in progress and will continue for some time, because of further acquisitions from new excavations. Research to date has naturally concentrated first on the larger individual states, such as Egypt, and the chronological development of relations between the Hittites and Egypt can clearly be seen, especially as the other side, Egypt, is represented by the relevant answering correspondence. But the records of the Hittite 'foreign ministry'—those catalogued to date—on relations with smaller and less important regional kingdoms and princedoms, though unfortunately incomplete, also show at least in outline the course of relations between 'provinces', foreign and incorporated states, and the 'centre'. Such is the case with Arzawa, which we have already encountered in the history of the decipherment of Hittite cuneiform.[83] Much the same may be said, though with gradually diminishing precision, of relations between Ḫattusa and regions and states like Isuwa, Alalḫa, Amurra, Lukkā, and many others.

Regrettably, no map of the empire of the Hittites has come down to us. Historians have therefore had the wearisome task of reconstructing the geography of the empire from the fragmentary records. While it is true that in letters and other documents references occur to certain areas and/or the names of their rulers, so that the existence of these places can at least be recorded as they appear in the bureaucratic terminology, most of these references—often intended only for 'insiders'—are much too fleeting and assume too much prior knowledge for present-day readers of the documents. This means that they often cannot be precisely categorized or pieced together to form a meaningful picture. We have the names of countries and rulers, references to events, pleas, petitions, instructions, records of state documents of all kinds, but this is not yet sufficient to reconstruct reliably the complete network of Hittite diplomacy and Anatolian history in the second millennium BC. Future readings and new finds of documents will no doubt cast more light into the partial darkness. But for the moment we must be satisfied with the meagre information we possess.

Among classical historians this necessarily incomplete picture is often misunderstood. The documents are frequently treated with suspicion or ignored. This is a mistake. The (temporary) gaps in the material should not be interpreted as meaning that the documents at our disposal should be deemed of little or no value in relation to any given question. This would be a methodologically incorrect approach. These documents do not represent anybody's private reflections from a worm's-eye view, but the official papers of an imperial administration. On many occasions we would be glad if in much more recent or historically better illuminated eras we had documents as eloquent as these, for example, in the field of relations between imperial Rome and certain of its allies or vassal states. The widespread mistrust, particularly on the part of classical historians, towards Hittite and oriental documents as a whole may be related on the one hand to the European bias against the East—from which they expect little more than tales from the *Arabian Nights*—and, on the other hand, to the fear which overcomes classicists schooled and well versed in Greek and Latin when confronted by texts in tongues as 'exotic' as Akkadian, Egyptian, Hittite, or Luwian, which they cannot read in the original and can apprehend only at second hand. The classicist of the future, along with the ancient historian, will take account of the immense broadening of our historical horizons achieved by the decipherment and hence the usability of these same documents, and will have to be above all a universal linguist to a degree scarcely imaginable today. The days when classical studies essentially meant the study of Greek and Roman antiquity are numbered.

'Ilios' is 'Wilusa'

Soon after cuneiform Hittite had been deciphered, a treaty concluded between King Muwattalli II (*c.*1290–1272 BC) and a certain Alaksandu of Wilusa came to light among the documents of the imperial archive in Ḫattusa. The treaty, the preamble to which is badly damaged, says among other things (in Frank Starke's translation):

> If some enemy arises for you, then I, my Majesty, will not abandon you, just as I have not now abandoned you, and I will kill the enemy on your behalf. If your brother or someone of your family withdraws political support from you, Alaksandu,—or accordingly someone withdraws political support from your son (and) your grandsons—and they seek the kingship of the land of Wilusa, I, My Majesty will absolutely not discard you, Alaksandu, that is, I will not accept that one. As he is your enemy, in exactly the same way he is My Majesty's enemy, and only you, Alaksandu, will I, My Majesty, recognize. I will certainly [not recognize] him.[84]

As early as 1924, in a notable essay entitled 'Alakšanduš, King of Viluša', the Indo-Europeanist Paul Kretschmer equated the toponym which appears here, 'Wilusa' (in the spelling most commonly used today), with the Greek toponym 'Ilios'.[85] 'Ilios' appears over a hundred times in Homer's *Iliad* as a second name, side by side with 'Troy', for the scene of the action, and provides the name of the whole epic. From the established phonetic laws of Greek, it was by then well known and beyond dispute that that original toponym in an earlier period, before Homer, was 'Wilios', with an initial 'w'. (This means, incidentally, that Greek poetry mentioned the town long before Homer's time; we shall return to this matter.) By the time when Homer was composing (the eighth century BC), in his Ionian dialect initial 'w' had completely disappeared everywhere, not only in this toponym. To equate the two therefore seemed fully logical. It appeared all the more attractive—though to many all the more fantastic—because the Hittite *Alakšandu* so unmistakably echoed the Greek *Aléxandros*, and Alexander (Paris) in the *Iliad* is the first-born prince of Troy. (Alexander is not killed in the *Iliad*, but as it were outlives the *Iliad*, later to kill Achilles, the arch-enemy of Troy, as foretold in the *Iliad*.) So was 'Wilusa' the same as 'Wilios'? (For the moment we shall leave aside the question of Alakšandu.)

Kretschmer's paper appeared at a time when cuneiform Hittite had just been deciphered (Hrozný's discovery had been published seven years earlier), and Hittite studies were still in their infancy. At the time Kretschmer's hypothesis must have looked more like sensation-mongering than scholarly reasoning. But the more Hittite studies advanced after Kretschmer, the more Hittite documents were found which mentioned the name of 'Wilusa'. What was to be done? Many were inclined to accept Kretschmer's view. Thus Oliver Robert Gurney, one of the doyens of Hittite studies, wrote, on the one hand, in his influential book *The Hittites* in 1952 (revised 1990):

> Phonetically none of these equations [we shall return later to the other equations to which Gurney refers] is altogether impossible... If it were certain, or even probable, on other grounds that the Hittites never penetrated as far to the west as the Troad, one would not hesitate to abandon the whole tissue of hypotheses. On the contrary, however, we have the evidence of the Egyptian text that the Drdny (Dardanians—no other similar name is known) fought as allies of the Hittites at the battle of Kadesh. Wilusa was certainly a western country and part of the confederacy of Arzawa.

But Gurney, like most other Hittite specialists and orientalists of his day, was not willing to accept the equation unreservedly. Why was this? 'But so long as the greater problem of *Hittite geography* remains unsolved, the arguments for the location of Wilusa cannot be regarded as conclusive.'[86] Since 1996 this objection has lost its validity. We now know for certain that 'Wilusa' and 'Wilios' are one and the same. The progress of research that led to this realization is of sufficient interest to be described in outline at least.

In the introduction to the treaty between the Hittite king Muwattalli II and Alakšandu of Wilusa, as is customary to this day in this kind of assurance of recognition and protection, a brief summary is provided of the political relations between the side offering recognition (Ḫattusa) and the side receiving it (Wilusa), up to the time the treaty is concluded. Here Muwattalli recalls this, among other things:

Formerly at one time the *labarna* (honorary title of the Hittite Great King), my ancestor, had made all of the land of Arzawa [and] all of the land of Wilussa (political) clients. Later the land of Arzawa waged war because of this; but since the event was long ago, I do not know from which king of the land of Ḫattusa the land of Wilusa defected. But (even) if the land of Wilussa defected from the land of Ḫattusa, they (the Royal Clan of Wilussa) remained on terms of friendship with the kings of the land of Ḫattusa from afar and regularly sent envoys to them.[87]

This is followed by a detailed description of the relations between the two countries from the time of the Hittite king Tudḫalija I (*c.*1420–1400 BC) to the time of writing (*c.*1290–1272 BC), roughly 150 years later. All of this section contains extremely important information for us. It tells us, first of all, that for at least 150 years (1420–1272 BC) friendly relations had existed between the Hittite capital and Wilusa; secondly, that politically these relations took the form of a kind of subordination of Wilusa to Ḫattusa (Wilusa never actually 'defected' from Ḫattusa!); thirdly, that in spite of this throughout this period Wilusa was never a 'province' of the Hittite empire, but an autonomous entity, which maintained contact with the court and the central administration by means of 'envoys'. This recalls relations such as those between the British crown and either India under one of the viceroys appointed by the crown, or Australia under a prime minister appointed with the authority of the crown. With regard to 'foreign policy', Wilusa therefore resembles a member state of the 'Hittite Commonwealth'. Given this structure, Wilusa slots easily into the imperial policy of the Hittite empire as described here. At the same time it emerges clearly that the diplomatic correspondence between the Hittite rulers and the dynasty in Wilusa was conducted in Hittite for at least 150 years. Wilusa must therefore have had a state chancellery which, as in other power centres linked with Ḫattusa, regularly processed incoming and outgoing communications. Against this background, we may further suppose that the 'envoys' mentioned in the treaty communicated with the Hittites of Ḫattusa in Hittite. In any event, the ruling stratum of Wilusa, at least, spoke and understood Hittite.

However, the Alakšandu treaty contains more information which is important to us: Wilusa had not always been a state politically linked with the Hittite empire. The quotation begins with a clear reminder, couched in a familiar diplomatic tone of friendliness with concealed menace, of the essential fact of the union of the two states—achieved by the military conquest of Wilusa by Ḫattusa! This event—a cause of less rejoicing for Wilusa—had taken place in a time long past, of which the present Great King of the Hittites apparently had absolutely no historical memory: 'under the *labarna*, my ancestor'. Starke has explained that, 'by the use of the term *labarna* alone to designate the ruler, reference is made to a time before 1600 BC, from which no (complete) archive material is available';[88] the title *labarna* without the name of the bearer may be taken to denote the founder of the state, Anitta.[89] The conquest of Wilusa by Ḫattusa therefore preceded the Muwattalli treaty by over 300 years, and in 1280 BC Wilusa had been an associated, 'corresponding member', one might say, of the Hittite state for this length of time.[90]

Equally deserving of note is another piece of information in the treaty: 'my ancestor... had made all of the land of Arzawa [and] *all of the land of Wilussa* (political) clients', and in particular: 'Later the land of Arzawa waged war because of this.' This indicates unambiguously that Wilusa was at first linked with Arzawa, possibly even allied to it, and that Arzawa, at first conquered with Wilusa, unlike Wilusa, would not come to terms with either its own subjugation or the defection of Wilusa, and for this reason took up arms against Ḫattusa.

The question that arises with growing insistency is: where were Arzawa and Wilusa?

At this point it is as well to emphasize that this question arises from the Hittite material itself: it is not possible to draft a definitive history of the Hittite empire without knowing the inner geography of that empire. From the very beginning this was the one motif in Hittite studies repeatedly taken up—the investigation of geography with an intensity which might at first seem off-putting to outsiders, rather than a wish to compare Hittite toponyms with those in other languages, in particular Greek, as non-specialists sometimes seem to assume.

Thirty years after the decipherment of cuneiform Hittite, efforts to clarify the geographical question led to a first major result and a highly impressive one: the first edition of *Der grosse historische Weltatlas* (Great Historical World Atlas), conceived in 1949 and published in 1953 by the Bavarian School Textbook Publishing House in Munich, in what was then a ground-breaking scholarly achievement of international note. It included the 'Ḫatti Empire' as Map 5, under the title 'The Time of the Great Migration of Peoples (Urnfield-Bronze Age). 1250–750 BC.' In essentials it remains accurate to this day. We shall refer from time to time to this map, which got things right almost half a century ago and was designed for grammar-school use, to counter any possible impression that the matter of Hittite geography might be a completely new achievement, or even something exotic, to be looked upon with mistrust.

In matters of detail, however, much remained to be done, in particular to confirm the geographical positions. As previously mentioned, Gurney in 1952 lamented the absence of a reliable overall picture of the geographical organization of the Hittite empire and its surroundings. Seven years later, in 1959, *The Geography of the Hittite Empire* appeared in London as a publication of the British Institute of Archaeology at Ankara, by the prehistorian John Garstang and edited by his nephew, the same O. R. Gurney. From as early as 1923, Garstang had worked to clarify the problem of geography in a long series of articles, but was always prevented from completing his analysis by other activities, above all excavations, such as those at the 8,000-year-old Stone Age settlement of Yümüktepe near Mersin in Cilicia. On the very last day of his life, in August 1956, his draft manuscript was finally ready. Gurney made some revisions, while leaving the basic design unchanged.

Garstang began his Foreword as follows:

> The imperial archives of the Hittite kings include numerous records of military adventure and achievement, of relations with friend and foe, and of recurring periods of danger to the throne and empire. These fascinating records, even when lucidly translated from the Hittite idiom, remain for the most part unintelligible, or at least deprived of their essential value, for want of a reliable map whereby the setting and scale of the episodes described may be appreciated....

> This state of affairs deprives would-be students of rich new material of the highest interest and historical significance; for the Hittite archives comprise not only records of military achievements, but many lost pages of ancient history that might fill the gap between the story of Syria in the Amarna period [*c.*1350 BC] and the pre-Homeric legend of the Troad.[91]

The result of this book is a map of the Hittite empire based on the most painstaking examination of all Hittite texts known at the time in which toponyms appear. For Arzawa and Wilusa, which are of interest to us, it produced a geographical location which was in its essentials accepted by subsequent scholarship for many years (Fig. 17), though never without reservation. For example, Heinrich Otten, one of the leading twentieth-century oriental historians, adopted Garstang's map in his excellent book, *Hethiter, Ḫurriter und Mitanni* (1966), but only as a complementary map beside an earlier one drawn up by the Hittite scholar A. Goetze as early as 1928.[92] Garstang had situated Arzawa in the region of what later became Lydia (from the Hermos valley to the Maeander valley) with its royal seat at Abasa (= Ephesos). To its north, in the area of the Kaïkos valley (the area of Pergamon), he placed the land of Sēḫa, and further north again he believed that Wilusa lay. For his Wilusa he had posited an enormous area, reaching from the river Sangarios (now Sakarya) down into the Troad. In this context his equation of *Wilusa* and *Wilios*, the eponymous capital which would then lie at the extreme western edge of the country, was not immediately clear.

The result of an extensive special analysis of the relevant sources, conducted almost twenty years later by Susanne Heinhold-Krahmer in her standard work *Arzawa*, in which the north-westerly situation of Wilusa is largely accepted, is equally vague: 'Wilusa could have occupied a north-westerly position within the Arzawa region. From Arzawa (in the narrower sense) and from Mirā it would then have been separated by the Sēḫa River land, and the latter should be seen as its southern, south-eastern or eastern neighbour.'[93] As a result, Heinhold-Krahmer had to leave the matter of the names and their equation unresolved: 'At the same time any identification of Wiluša with "Ilios", given our present state of knowledge, remains fraught with problems, from both a linguistic and a geographical perspec-

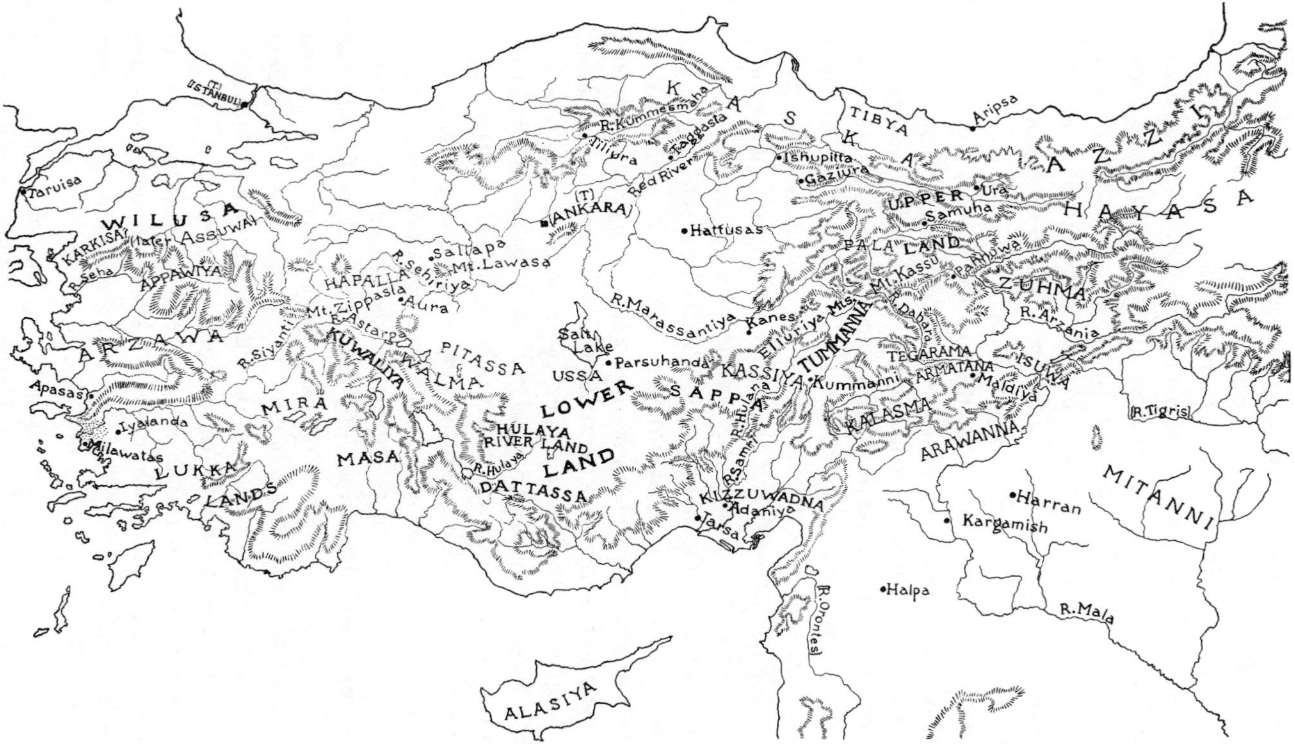

Fig. 17. The geography of the Hittite empire as known in 1959.

tive.'[94] The continuing uncertainty and indecision as to whether the Hittite *Wilusa*—also found in the forms *Wilussa* and *Wilusija*—was to be identified with the Greek *Wilios* came to a definitive resolution in 1996. In that year the Tübingen expert Frank Starke succeeded in proving convincingly that the pile of ruins on the Dardanelles, whose once-proud predecessor Homer calls by turns 'Troy' and 'Ilios', really was the remains of that centre of power in north-western Asia Minor, known in the imperial correspondence of the Hittites by the names *Wilus(s)a* or *Wilusija*.

There was nothing at all sensational about Starke's presentation of his case. It relied on the same old, methodically tried and tested procedures which we have just seen in Garstang's reconstruction. However, Starke's procedure had two crucial advantages or assets to distinguish it from the earlier works: first, he was able to rely on newly discovered documents which allowed much greater precision, and, second, his work was distinguished by a caution and consistency unequalled by any of the preceding work in the field.

On account of the range of premisses and necessary length of the line of argument, it is unfortunately not possible to retrace the whole of Starke's case here. But mention needs to be made at least of the priceless consolidation brought to the reconstruction of the geography of the Hittite empire by a bronze tablet found in Ḫattusa-Boğazköy in 1986 and published in 1988 by Heinrich Otten,[95] which Starke was able to make use of. The tablet contained a treaty concluded between the Hittite Great King Tudḫalija IV (*c.*1240–1215 BC) and his cousin Kurunta of Tarḫuntassa. As Starke emphasized, with understandable delight, the text of the treaty presents 'a very detailed definition of the borders of Tarḫuntassa, explaining not only the geographical relations in southern and south-western Asia Minor, but also providing a firmer foundation by which to determine the position and environs of the countries in the *west* and *north-west* of Asia Minor'.[96]

When Starke first stated his arguments in two 'trial runs' in 1996—lectures at the universities of Tübingen and Basel—his professional audience realized at once that a breakthrough had been achieved. Before the eyes of his rapt audience, the map of the Hittite empire was gradually filled in step by step until only one area and one name were missing from it. This area was in the north-west of

Asia Minor, later known as Mysia—so no longer the whole area between the Dardanelles and the Sangarios, as Garstang had thought—and the name was *Wilusa*.

During the examination of all the details then available, this exemplary line of argument was crowned by bringing into play a letter written by the Hittite vassal king Manatabarḫunta of Sēḫa (which Garstang had correctly placed in the Kaïkos valley) soon after 1300 BC to the then Great King Muwattalli II. This letter had first come to assume importance in the geographical question in 1983–4.[97] The letter was about the aggressive military activities of a certain Pijamaradu, who operated out of Millawa(n)da (Miletos). Pijamaradu had interfered in the internal affairs of Wilusa. In response the king of Sēḫa, the sender of the letter, had come to the aid of Wilusa and at the same time requested reinforcements from Ḫattusa. But even before the Hittite force reached Wilusa, Pijamaradu had also attacked the island of Lazba and carried off craftsmen from there to Millawa(n)da. (The further course of events will be of interest to us in another connection.) The island named in the letter as Lazba, which according to the text lay within sight of both Sēḫa and Wilusa, can be none other than Lesbos,[98] the island which even today is as plainly visible off the north-west coast of Asia Minor as it was in the second millennium BC. This was sufficient to dispel any remaining doubt: the place now known in Turkish as *Ḫisarlık* was known in Hittite in the second millennium BC as *Wilusa* or *Wilusija* and in Greek as *Wilios*.[99]

In addition, an archaeological discovery made in Troy in the 1997 and 1998 digs, after Starke had established the geographical locations, must have given determined sceptics pause for thought.[100] On the western side of the lower town (squares t–u 14–15), directly in front of the presumed lower town wall, a deep cave cut into the hill was found, with one broad main arm 13 metres long and three narrow channels branching off it, one of them over 100 metres long (Fig. 18). This was originally a small subterranean reservoir, the overflow from which was carried through a high-set conduit to the outside, where it was stored in tanks. When it was uncovered, about 30 litres an hour still flowed into the inner storage from the left-hand tributary. Through all the channels together, 500 to 1,400 litres a day still drip or flow even today. According to a stone-dating

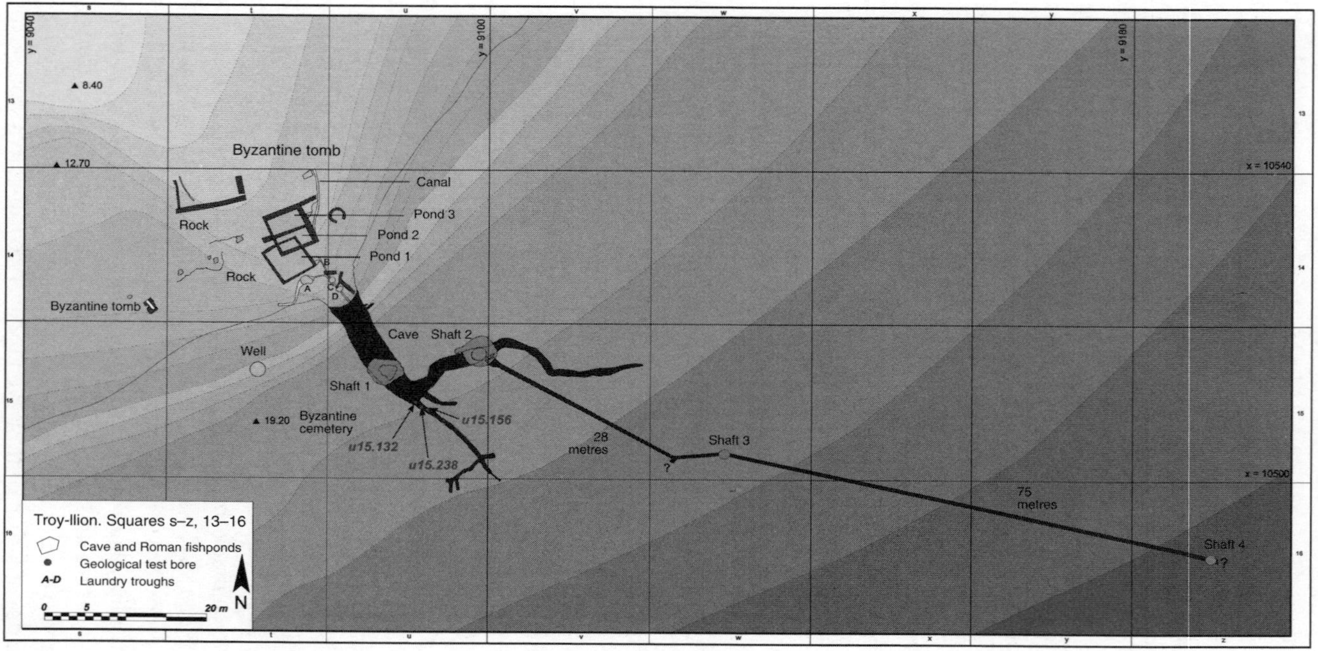

FIG. 18. The water supply system uncovered in Wilusa/Troy in 1997.

process carried out in 1999–2000 by the radiometry research team at Heidelberg Academy of Sciences (A. Mangini and N. Frank), this installation was built as early as the beginning of the third millennium BC as a 'water-mine'. What is of most significance for us about this discovery is not so much the installation itself—special though it is—but the fact that in the so-called 'Alakšandu Treaty' between the Great King of the Hittites and Alakšandu of Wilusa, in Paragraph 20 (see p. 110), where the swearing of oaths is recorded, as is customary in such treaties, among the 'gods of Wilusa' invoked is a 'subterranean watercourse of the land of Wilusa'. In treaties of this kind it was natural to invoke, in addition to great gods of supra-regional importance, local gods who were particularly dear to the signatories and whose vengeance—we may suppose—would smite the other party, in the case of breach of treaty, with particular fury. (From a later time we may compare formulae such as 'by my mother's head'.) It would be strange indeed if the 'subterranean watercourse of the land of Wilusa' recorded in this document were *not* identical with the ancient water-supply system discovered by Korfmann's excavation in the hill of Hisarlık.

Particularly attentive readers may have noticed the fact that the linguistic correspondence between the Hittite form *Wilusa* and the Greek *Wilios* is inexact after the initial three sounds: *Wil-*. Here it is essential to bear in mind that when *names* are borrowed by one speech community from another—including speech communities of the same language family, in this case Indo-European, to which both Hittite and Greek belong—a law applies which does not and cannot accord with the otherwise applicable sound laws. The normal word-stock, after all, is passed on from the proto- or 'parent' language to its individual descendants in conformity with the 'sound laws', by which we can usually predict the phonetic form of a given word in a given member-language of the family (Indian *pitar*, for example, must appear as Latin *pater* and German *Vater*).

Names, on the other hand, especially toponyms in times of population shift, are *discovered* by the new speech community and usually adapted by ear to its language. An attempt is made first to lend the foreign-sounding name a typical, familiar-sounding form, and, second, wherever possible to provide a meaningful semantic connection in the receiving language. The adoption of the Italian toponym *Milano* (from Latin *Medio-(p)lanum*—mid-plain) in German in the form *Mailand*, or of *Livorno* in English as *Leghorn*, may serve as prime examples. They cannot be explained by any phonetic laws. Starke pointed out in 1997 that the adoption of Hittite *Wilus(s)a* by Greek in the form *Wilios* 'can no more be explained by sound laws than, for example, the adoption of the toponyms *Milano* or *Ljubljana* in the German forms *Mailand* and *Laibach*: likewise the Greeks took from the name *Wilussa* what they thought they heard (and what they wanted to hear!), and brought the whole word into line with their own familiar patterns'.[101] Similarly in 1959 Garstang and Gurney, and many others, had pleaded for the primacy of facts over linguistic considerations, using the example of *Millawa(n)da—Miletos*:

> the form of the word Miletus does not suggest that a 'w' had been lost from the second syllable. But the development of place-names is not always governed by exactly the same rules as those established for a particular language, and in this instance there are strong factual reasons which lead us to prefer the equation with Miletus.[102]

Just how correct this position was emerged forty years later: in 1999 Wolf-Dietrich Niemeier, the co-excavator of Miletos, using the new discoveries in both archaeology and Hittite studies, was able to state categorically: 'Of all the proposed locations for Millawanda, Miletos is the only remaining possibility.'[103] In the case of *Wilusa* = *Wilios*, there is one further deductive step that should be taken: there is no doubt that the name of the hill derived from its earliest settlers, from a time approximately 3,000 years BC, and so was originally neither Hittite nor Greek (both peoples moved into the area much later), and most likely bore little phonetic resemblance to either *Wilus(s)a* or *Wilios*. In their respective new territories the Hittites and Greeks adopted the ancient place-names, which were foreign to them, and possibly borrowed them independently of each other, each in the form they thought they heard and the form that most closely matched the phonetic structure of their own language. In cases like this, insistence on phonetically 'pure' equations can do nothing to further the progress of science.

In the light of this, the matter of the so-called 'Wilusiad' also needed to be reconsidered. In 1984, at a symposium devoted to Troy and the Trojan War at Bryn Mawr College in the USA, the American Hittite scholar Calvert Watkins, in a paper on the language of the Trojans, put forward the theory that the four-word beginning of a Luwian cult hymn, quoted in the description of a Hittite ritual and evidently dating back to the sixteenth century BC, should be translated, 'When they came from steep Wilusa . . . ': 'This line could well be the beginning of a Luwian epic lay, a "Wilusiad".' When this theory was made public in 1986, it was treated by all the media as a sensation, although it was rejected by most colleagues in the profession.[104] While Starke proposed only the correction 'from the sea' instead of 'steep' ('when they came forth from the sea, from Wilusa'),[105] Neumann pointed out that the Luwian word *wilusa* seemed to contain the Hittite root *wellu-* 'meadow, pasture', so the translation should run: 'when they came forth from . . . the pastureland', or 'when they came down from the pasturelands', and was to be understood as simply the opening line of a shepherd's song, sung after the autumn return from the high grazing grounds.[106] Leaving aside the linguistic objections raised by some other specialists, this interpretation holds little attraction in the context of a cult hymn. A compromise suggested by Neumann himself seems more probable:[107] the name of the hill could have been taken by the Hittites or Luwians to be related, owing to a phonetic similarity, to the familiar *wellu-*, so that a toponym which was not transparent to them in their own language was reinterpreted as having the meaning 'meadow', or something similar. Place-names with the component 'meadow' are widespread in Indo-European languages.

In 1997 Starke presented to the public in more developed written form the arguments he had tested in his lectures.[108] But while *Studia Troica* No. 7, containing his article, was just appearing in Germany, another Hittite scholar, working independently of Starke, made a discovery in Turkey that confirmed Starke's result from a quite different perspective. Among the best-known evidence of 'Luwoglyphic' or 'hieroglyphic Luwian' script is, as we have briefly mentioned (see p. 56), a rock monument near Izmir, the 'Karabel Monument'. The monument is situated in the Karabel Pass over the Boz dağlari range (later the Greek *Tmolos*), which rises to a height of over 2,000 metres directly south of the Hermos Valley. The monument consists or consisted (as we shall very soon see) of ruler figures incised in two free-standing rock slabs, with the figures encircled by inscriptions in hieroglyphic Luwian. The total of four complexes were designated 'Karabel A, B, C1 and C2'. Karabel A was discovered in 1839 by Renouard. Until 1977 all four complexes could be seen and were visited and photographed by many researchers, and efforts were made to read or work out their general meaning; in 1982 the slabs known as Karabel B and C disappeared, having fallen victim to road-building.

Up to 1997 no satisfactory interpretation of this four-part monument had been arrived at, in spite of some partial success. In 1997 Starke wrote in the article we have mentioned: 'Although there is still a lack of clarity in the reading of the kings' names in the inscriptions, they are most likely local rulers.'[109]

While specialists were reading these lines, events had already overtaken them. In January of the same year, 1997, the British Hittite scholar J. D. Hawkins travelled to the Karabel Pass, driven by one of those hunches which have lain at the root of so many scientific discoveries. Some years earlier, with his colleague Anna Morpurgo Davies, Hawkins had made a new attempt to arrive at a satisfactory reading of the Tarkondemos Seal, published by Mordtmann back in 1872.[110] The occasion for the new attempt was provided by the impressions of two seals found in Ḫattusa in 1967 and published in 1975.[111] The seals in question showed great similarities in form and legend with the Tarkondemos Seal. Hawkins and Morpurgo Davies had compared the seals and their impressions and come to the conclusion that the name of the king depicted as an archer on the Tarkondemos Seal, previously interpreted in a completely different way (Mordtmann: *Tarkudimmi*; Güterbock: *Tarkasna-tiwa*; Nowicki: *Tarkasna-muwa*), should be read as *Tarkasnawa, King of Mirā*, and that this text was identical with that on the newly-discovered Ḫattusa seal. A king whose seal was also used in the capital of the Hittite empire, perhaps in a sort of consulate, can hardly have been a figure of no consequence. *Tarkasnawa, King of Mirā*, had therefore to be taken to be a historical figure of high standing.

Aware of this discovery, Hawkins later chanced to study outstanding new photographs of Karabel A. All of a sudden it struck him that the first line of the three-line inscription on Karabel A must be identical with that on the three seals. To check this on the site, on 11 and 12 September 1997 he visited the Karabel monument, and, when he had established the best possible sunlight conditions, he was able to read the first lines as *Tarkasnawa, King of Mirā*. In addition to this, he also succeeded in reading the two following lines: (2) 'son of X-li, king of the land of Mirā', (3) 'grandson of [...], king of the land of Mirā'.[112] Thus three generations of kings of Mirā in the period from the end of the fourteenth century to the end of the thirteenth were identified (even if the names of the father and grandfather of Tarkasnawa remain unknown)[113]—kings who had immortalized themselves in striking fashion on a rock-face in the immediate vicinity of the present-day port of Izmir, 'beside an important thoroughfare'.[114] (It was Hawkins's well-founded supposition that Karabel B and Karabel C had originally shown 'photographs' of the father and grandfather, to supplement the central inscription.) From this discovery, Hawkins drew the following conclusions (see the map on p. xix):[115]

Mira has been recognized as the most prominent Arzawa kingdom [...] The reading of the Karabel inscription confirms at a stroke the location of Mira in its vicinity and disproves all other proposed locations.

Mira itself is known to have had a common inland frontier with Ḫatti on the western edge of the Anatolian plateau in the neighbourhood of Afyon.

Karabel, being placed on the route northwards from the territory of Ephesos in the Cayster valley to the Hermos valley, shows by its reading that Mira extended this far west, in effect to the coast.

The probability is that this western extension of Mira represents the rump of the Arzawan state with its capital at Apasa, which is thereby doubtless confirmed in its identification with Ephesos.[116] [...]

Thus the size and importance of Mira is clearly revealed. Its neighbours too may be more precisely located by reference to its established location. [...]

In particular the Seḫa River land,[117] known to have shared a frontier with Mira, is confirmed in its identification with the Hermos valley [...][118] The attested interest of the state in the land of Lazpa (= Lesbos) may be understood by the recognition that its sway included the Caicos valley too,[119] and its connections with the Arzawa land Wilusa, which lay beyond but was reached through its territory, push the latter kingdom back into its home in the Troad, in the past so hotly contested.[120]

The fact that in a given issue two experts evaluating different documents at the same time have independently arrived at the same result has always counted in science as a strong indication that the result in question is probably the right one. In the matter of the site of Wilusa, given the mass of steadily accumulated archaeological evidence, which we have presented here, we may regard the fact that Starke and Hawkins are in agreement as the last link in the chain.

On 13–14 December 1998 an international colloquium on Troy was held at the University of Würzburg, drawing together scholars from various disciplines, including philologists, ancient historians, and eminent Hittite scholars (Hawkins, Neumann, Nowicki), in addition to archaeologists. Starke's theory that Wilusa and Wilios were one and the same was accepted.[121] From this time on there has been no doubt that, at least with regard to the *name* of the setting for Homer's story, he was not relying on his imagination. This meant that the fundamental prerequisite for at least taking Homer into account as a source had at last been met—a prerequisite that had seemed unrealizable as recently as 1992, when Donald F. Easton stated: 'Archaeology cannot give proof of the Trojan War if we are not sure that this site [that is, Hisarlık] was Troy. So far nothing has proved this.' Now it is proven. Where Homer might have found the name will emerge later, and with this, above all, the fact that he did not borrow it from any contemporaries who might have settled there and still remembered it from some oral tradition. For the moment it is sufficient to state one fact: at the very core of the tale Homer's *Iliad* has shed the mantle of fiction commonly attributed to it. Ilios or Wilios is not the product of the Greek imagination, but a real historical site. This site is located at the very place in which Homer shows it. And it was a place of sufficient importance to play a role in the politics of the leading powers of the second millennium BC.

It would be methodologically false, however, to jump to the conclusion that because the site is historically proven the stories set in it by Homer must also be historically proven. This error, repeatedly committed in the past and still committed today, was clearly pointed out over thirty years ago by Franz Hampl in a paper which was subsequently to become famous, 'The *Iliad* is not a History Book.'[122] Using various examples he pointed out that 'by this means we might demonstrate that absolutely any legend was historical reality', and cited a sentence from the 'historical layman' Hellmuth von Moltke as a warning: 'A story may be historically untrue and geographically fully precise.'[123] It is helpful to cite one of Hampl's examples in full, so as to make absolutely clear the distinction between 'reality of place' and 'reality of plot':

In some Austrian legends ... underground passages, sometimes linking two castles, have a role to play. And indeed, such passages have been found in the places where the legend has indicated. The conclusion that many have drawn from this—that the entire stories therefore really happened—is of course methodologically and objectively false. It should rather be assumed that the sinister passages aroused or stimulated the human story-telling imagination, and that pre-existing tales underwent suitable elaboration and found a new setting in the localities in question.[124]

Whether we should really assume precisely what Hampl suggests as an alternative explanation may remain an open question, but it is correct to say that the veracity of the site is no guarantee of the veracity of the events set in that site. On the other hand, the possibility that events placed in a particular location actually occurred in that location is not diminished by proof of the veracity of the site. Before *(W)Ilios* and *Wilusa* were shown to be the same, those who enquired about the degree of reality in the events recounted in the *Iliad* really did suffer from the disadvantage of not having the firm ground of the demonstrated historical reality of the setting under foot. Now they can proceed from a fixed point: the place which provides the setting for the *Iliad* is real. The old problem of 'Troy and Homer' has received a firm basis. It is now possible to embark upon an attempt to discover the nature of the relationship between the historical Ilios/Troy and Homer's Ilios/Troy.

We now need to state the first important result attained so far: since 1996, for the first time in the history of the study of Troy, it has been possible to give Homer's *Iliad* the status of a source text.

This result develops a powerful momentum. It compels us to take the next logical step and verify whether other names of places, regions, or inhabitants named by Homer, like Ilios, as the scene of the action or as actors are also matched in non-Greek documents of the second millennium BC. Should this be even partially the case, it would be proof that not only the narrowly defined setting of Homer's *Iliad* was historical reality, but also its broader geographical and ethnographic framework. This would be a great step forward. Since the narrowly defined setting for the *Iliad*—Ilios/Troy—still existed, if only as a ruined city, in Homer's time, it could well have served theoretically, in the spirit of Hampl's explanation, as a catalyst for the story Homer has to tell. But, as we shall see, the broader geographical and ethnographic framework for the *Iliad* did *not* exist by Homer's day. If, then, this framework was ever a historical reality, Homer, when he conceived the Trojan story as a narrative fabric that existed only in his imagination for the ruined city of Ilios/Troy, must have also invented for it a geographical and ethnographical framework which in his time was nowhere to be found but which had in fact once existed in precisely the form he proposes. Such a coincidence of the fruit of imagination and historical reality would be astonishing in the highest degree and require some explaining. We shall therefore proceed to an examination of the names.

The name of Troy, so heavily laden with meaning, is naturally the first candidate for such scrutiny.

Troy = Taruwisa/Tru(w)isa?

Side by side with the name *Ilios*, Homer employs another name for the setting of his story: *Troiē* (the long ē of the ending, in Homer's Ionian dialect, was matched in later dialects, which became more widespread, by a long ā, whence the form *Troia*). This name occurs over fifty times in the *Iliad*. From it Homer derives the name of the inhabitants: *Trōes* and feminine *Trōades* (used many hundreds of times), while never using *Iliadai* or *Iliades*.[125] Once one of the two names, *Ilios*, has been proven to be historical, it would fly in the face of logic to assume that Homer or his predecessors in the business of heroic poetry (to which we shall give more attention later) had simply invented the second name, when they already had a name for Ilios, in order to form a name for the inhabitants from the invented name. Why two names should be used at all is, of course, a question worth asking: we shall broach it later. However, when all possibilities are carefully considered, no reason for the invention of a second name can be found, so we are left with the conclusion that this name too was handed down by tradition, which means that it too had a historical existence. Are there any clues outside Homer, as in the case of *Ilios*?

In the so-called Annals of the Hittite Great King Tudḫalija I (*c*.1420–1400 BC), Tudḫalija reports on his martial enterprises. Much space is devoted to his report on a 'campaign against the Arzawa-lands'. We have already come across Arzawa or the Arzawa-lands several times, first in the Arzawa letters, which figured in the decipherment of cuneiform Hittite (see pp. 57–8). Earlier theories concerning the geographical location of Arzawa, which unanimously pointed to western Asia Minor (like the map in the Bavarian school textbook of 1953, referred to above), were confirmed conclusively by Frank Starke in 1997, when he demonstrated that Arzawa included the interior of western Asia Minor from the Maeander valley to the Tmolos mountains, just short of the Hermos valley, and had a royal seat, at times even its capital, in Abasa (Ephesos). With his successful reading of the Karabel inscriptions, the British specialist J. D. Hawkins arrived at the same conclusion, independently of Starke: the equation of *Apasa* with *Ephesos* is 'virtually confirmed by the new evidence of Karabel'.[126] The most recent Turkish excavations by the Selçuk Museum at the citadel of Ephesos, which among other things have already revealed a late Bronze Age fortress wall of the same technique as the Troy VI city wall, confirm this.[127] It is more than likely that Arzawa had developed a high level of culture even before the Hittite imperial expansion. Arzawa, as the Hittite documents show, was basically hostile to the Hittites, and especially in the fifteenth and fourteenth centuries BC the two powers frequently came into military conflict. Only at the end of the fourteenth century did the Hittite Great King Mursili II (*c*.1318–1290 BC), after a decisive battle in the area of the headwaters of the Maeander, succeed in terminating Arzawa's autonomy and dividing it up—the core area becoming the 'land of Mirā'—and installing Hittite vassal kings in the newly formed petty kingdoms.

A hundred years before the defeat of Arzawa, Tudḫalija I had waged his campaign against Arzawa and a number of other lands and smaller regions in the neighbourhood of Arzawa. After he had compiled his report on the subject, listing all these regions individually and declaring them conquered, including Sēḫa and Ḫaballa, which, as we already know, bordered directly on Arzawa from the north, there comes an unexpected change:

(13) [As soon as] I had turned back [to Ḫattusa], the following lands declared (14) war on me.

The names of some twenty 'lands' follow. Among those that are still legible are 'the land of Karkisa', 'the land of Kispuwa', 'the land of Dura', 'the land of Kuruppija', and some others. At the very end of the list are two names of particular interest to us:

(19)... the land of Wilusija, the land of Taruisa.

At this point the list ends, and Tudḫalija goes on:

(20) [These lands] had joined together with their warriors.

(21) [They] their [...] and put their army in the field against me.

(22) [But I,] Tudḫalija, led my army by night, (23) [so that] I was able to surround the camp of the enemy forces (24) and the gods delivered it to me: the sun-goddess Arinna, and the weather god of the heavens (25) [*names of five more gods*] (26) I neutralized the camp of the enemy forces. Furthermore (27–8) I advanced into those lands from which any army had ever entered the field.

(29–30) [And the gods] ran before [me], and the gods delivered to me these lands which I have named (30) as those which had declared war. (31) I set these all lands together in motion: inhabitants, large and small livestock and movable property of the lands (32) I drove forth to Ḫattusa.

(33) As soon as I had destroyed the land of Āssuwa, I returned to Ḫattusa (34) and brought in my retinue 10,000 soldiers and 600 chariot teams (35) with drivers to Ḫattusa (36) (and) settled (them) in Ḫattusa. Pijamakurunta, Kukkulli, (37) Mala(?)-zidi, the brother-in-law of Pijamakurunta, I also brought (38) [to Ḫattusa]. And their sons and their grandsons, who (39) were [...] ... (*illegible*), I also brought to Ḫattusa [*what follows deals with the conduct of the 'internees' Pijamakurunta and Kukkulli; then the scene shifts to other lands*].

As line 33 shows, the Great King brings together all the foregoing twenty-odd 'lands' (we have still to see what is meant by this term) under the heading 'the land of Āssuwa'. Where was Āssuwa? It cannot be identical with Arzawa together with Sēḫa and Ḫaballa, which Tudḫalija conquered first. And if the king 'turned back' after this victory (13), which can only mean that he started for home with his army and its plunder—'10,000 soldiers and 600 chariot teams', which represent a substantial baggage train—we must assume that he did not head south, south-east, or south-west, as this would have meant long detours and made for corresponding logistical difficulties. We can take it that he headed north-east, in the direction of Ḫattusa. While he was moving in this direction, the 'land of Āssuwa', with the twenty-odd constituent regions that we know of, declared war on him. This whole area had not therefore been involved in the war until now, and still possessed powerful forces. It clearly wished to avenge the defeat of Arzawa and its allies, for political and military motives of its own. So where can Āssuwa and its constituent 'lands' have been situated? Garstang and Gurney, relying on other considerations, had already concluded:

> In his preceding campaign, Tudhaliyas had defeated Arzawa together with its allies [so some of these allies who had been defeated were to be found *south* of Arzawa]. Thus the confederacy of Assuwa can only lie to the north of the Arzawa countries—as indeed is indicated by the suggestion of a reference to Troy and Ilios...[128] [A choice is then offered of equations for Āssuwa, with the later 'Asia', 'in the vicinity of Sardis', or with 'Assos' in the Troad.]

The use of Troy and Ilios as support for situating Āssuwa in the north implies that Garstang and Gurney equated the 'land of Wilusa', the penultimate name in Tudḫalija's list of regions, with Ilios and the 'land of Taruisa', the last name, with Troy. In the case of Ilios, their view has been fully confirmed, as we have seen. In the case of Troy, however, this question has not been completely resolved among Hittite scholars even today.

The equation of Taruisa and Troy was first proposed in 1924 by Emil Forrer,[129] whom we have already encountered as a co-decipherer of hieroglyphic Luwian (see p. 61). In the same year it was accepted by Paul Kretschmer in a supplement to his essay on 'Alakšanduš' (see p. 75). In 1932 Ferdinand Sommer sided with them in his epoch-making work *Die Aḫḫijavā-Urkunden*.[130] In 1952 Gurney, in his standard work *The Hittites*, referred to both equations (Wilusa = Ilios; Taru(w)isa = Troy), and, after voicing certain misgivings, concluded, 'Phonetically none of these equations is altogether impossible.' In 1959, working with Garstang, Gurney proceeded further. In *The Geography of the Hittite Empire*, they explained:

> The possibility that the last name in this list [i.e. Taruisa] might be identified with Greek *Troia*, i.e. the city of Troy, was observed in 1924 by Emil Forrer, and after much controversy philologists have agreed that the equation is possible by way of a hypothetical form *Taruiya.... The juxtaposition of the two names [Wilusiya and Taruisa] in this list strongly suggests that these attractive correlations are correct...[131]

After this, things remained quiet on the 'Taruwisa/Tru(w)isa' front for some time. In 1986 the doyen of oriental studies, Hans Gustav Güterbock, took up the matter again at the Bryn Mawr symposium 'Troy and the Trojan War'. Surveying the history of the problem under the title 'Troy in Hittite Texts', he first thought the equation theoretically plausible.[132] However, he then stated two reservations, within the framework of a new consideration of the Tudḫalija Annals. The first of these referred to the composition and geographical arrangement of the 'Āssuwa lands'. It was founded on a misinterpretation, accepted at the time, of Tudḫalija's list, and has now been superseded. The second referred to the fact that Tudḫalija termed both Wilusa and Taruwisa/Tru(w)isa 'countries', whereas Homer applied the name Troy to a region but Ilios only to the city.[133] If this were to be admitted as a valid argument (we shall return to this question later), and if it were correct with regard to Homer, one would have to point out that it was the Hittites' universal practice to name 'lands' after their capital cities, beginning with their own. Even when their sphere of influence extended as far as the Levant and the Aegean, after their numerous conquests, they continued to call these lands after their capitals: *Ḫattusas utnē*, literally 'Ḫattusa's land'. The same applied, for example, to the land of *Assura* (with its capital Assura), the land of *Karkamissa* (capital Karkamissa), the land of *Alalḫa* (capital Alalḫa), the land of *Ḫalpa* (capital Ḫalpa (Aleppo)), the land of *Ugaritta* (capital Ugaritta), and so on. In all these cases, the same word may denote both the city and the land. Where ambiguity may arise, the distinction is made by adding the words 'land' or 'city', just as modern German distinguishes 'Land Brandenburg' and 'Stadt [city] Brandenburg'.

The Greeks, on the other hand, in the second millennium BC (but also later), tended not to name regions or their inhabitants after the capital cities. If they had, Homer would have used *Mukēnaioi* (after Agamemnon's capital Mycenae), *Lakedaimonioi* (after Menelaos's capital Lakedaimon), *Orchomenioi* (after the capital Orchomenos), etc. In naming lands, regions, and their inhabitants, the Hittites and the Greeks clearly differed in their preferences. The difference in ways of applying names to lands cannot therefore serve as an argument against the equation of Taruwisa/Tru(w)isa and Troy.

Attempting a clear statement of the situation once again, we may say this: in a document listing place-names in the central administration of the dominant power in Asia Minor in about 1400 BC, two names appear next to each other—very likely indicating adjacent location. Even in their written form these names show a clearly recognizable phonetic similarity with two names which in Homer's *Iliad* also appear in clear relation to each other and may even be synonymous. Both pairs of place-names refer to the same geographical region. The natural conclusion may be that these place-names denote the selfsame places.

It would remain only to ask why Homer uses the two names interchangeably, while in Tudḫalija's list they appear separately, apparently designating two 'lands'. For this various explanations are possible. One might be that the Hittite text from about 1400 BC may illustrate an earlier situation, when the two places were still autonomous, under the leadership of Wilusa, whereas they later continued to exist under their former names but formed a single political entity, for which 'Taruwisa/Tru(w)isa', in the perception of outsiders, supplied the overarching regional name. The Greek text would then reflect the later state of affairs, in the Greek view, which persists to this day in the term 'Trōás' (from 'Trō(i)ás gē'—land of Troy). The Hittite term 'land' freely admits this interpretation. It is not identical with 'country' in the sense of 'state' or 'nation', but denotes political units which may be large or small (having a sense rather like 'district'). The cuneiform KUR placed before it merely indicates that a political and geographical unit is about to be named. Nothing is implied about the size, extent, population, or importance of that unit.

It is now clear that the word 'land' in Tudḫalija's list can be meant only in this sense. If we were to take it to mean a broader geographical unit, we should not know where to put those twenty or more entities, all termed 'lands', to the north of Arzawa/Sēḫa/Ḫaballa, since this region is occupied by the (large) land of Māsa (see map). In these circumstances the most likely theory is that Tudḫalija's list of 'lands' registered every settled area, no matter how small, in order to magnify the scale of the triumph.[134] This may well be why, besides 'Wilusija', it has scarcely been possible to identify even one 'land' from this list. The areas of settlement in question were evidently small enough to vanish without trace in the mantle of history. All except for one: Taruwisa/Tru(w)isa. It lay very close to 'Wilusija', and may even have formed part of it, but since it constituted an identifiable entity, with its own name, it was a welcome inclusion in the king's list, like the other 'lands'.

However, if Taruwisa/Tru(w)isa was a real historical locality situated close to the capital Wilusa, which in view of Tudḫalija's list is not in doubt, something very strange must have happened if this name had no relation to the Greek *Troia*.

Accordingly Frank Starke argued in 1997 that in the Hittite texts a land of Āssuwa can be identified as a political entity only in the latter half of the fifteenth century BC. The twenty-odd constituent lands named in Tudḫalija's list may 'be situated only in an area north of Arzawa, Ḫaballa and Sēḫa, since the same text names all three lands in connection with the Arzawa campaign'. For the lands of Wilusija and Taruwisa/Tru(w)isa, the last to appear in the list, what emerges is 'a position in the far north-west of Asia Minor. There in the Troad, or at least in the areas bordering it, Āssuwa has until now generally been located' (as in the map from the 1953 Bavarian school atlas). The name *Āssuwa* should be linked, said Starke, with Assos, as it was later called by the Greeks, on the southern coast of the Troad, rather than with the name Asia, which emerges relatively late and at first was restricted to Lydia and Ionia, situated further south. The land of Taruwisa or Tru(w)isa, whose name is listed with that of Wilusa, 'may very well have been situated in the neighbourhood of the land of Wilusa/Wilusija'. The relation to Greek 'Troia' is self-evident, he said, even though it 'could hardly be explained by the laws of phonetics'.[135] In this way the equation was acknowledged geographically, while linguistically set aside as unexplained.

This means that in the case of the name *Troy* used by Homer we are faced with essentially the same situation as in the case of the name *Ilios*: Troy also matches a similar-sounding real name recorded in a historical Hittite text of the second millennium BC. As in the case of *Ilios*, the locality which bears this name was situated, with all the probability we can now muster, in precisely the same narrowly defined area which provides the setting for the *Iliad*. However, using the methods of the sound laws now familiar to us, in this case too we cannot demonstrate the similarity of the Hittite and Greek names.[136]

As in the case of *Ilios*, the explanation for the impossibility of a purely Indo-European phonetic equation of the two toponyms may lie in the fact that the underlying form was prehistoric and seemed to the newcomers, both Hittite/Luwian and Greek, unconnected with anything in their languages, and therefore opaque. Both could have come into contact with the locality, each quite independently of the other, at different times. (The assumption—so far tacit—that the Greeks must have borrowed the name from the Hittites, forming *Trōiā* from *Taruwisa/Tru(w)isa*, is neither logical nor historically defensible.) When they first encountered it, both could have adopted in their own language what they thought they heard, in the case of *Wilusa-Wilios* and that of *Taruwisa/Tru(w)isa-Troy* alike.[137] After the first encounter, the actual geographical situation in the region could have altered in some way that we cannot (as yet) reconstruct, so that the two originally separate localities formed a single, presumably larger unit, whatever shape this may have assumed.

For Homer, however, and pre-Homeric Troy-related poetry, this internal shift, which in itself made only one name necessary, would be of no account. Greek Troy poetry could only welcome the availability of two names for the same geographical entity, since both names, with their differing metrical forms, made it much easier to work this fabled city into hexameters, as has recently been demonstrated.[138] It is after all a principle of Greek hexameter poetry (which we shall explore in more detail later) that where variant names exist for the same object and make hexameters easier to compose, they will be gratefully exploited. There was therefore no reason to drop one of the two names. In fact, there was every reason to use both of them concurrently—without making any real distinction.[139] If we still speak of Ilios *and* Troy today, it is thanks to the inner regularity of Greek hexameter verse, which has preserved both forms. Taruwisa/Tru(w)isa might otherwise have sunk into oblivion, like most other place-names in Tudḫalija's list.

Those not inclined to adopt an explanation of this kind face the question of whether the phonetic similarity is to be explained by mere teasing chance, thereby preventing the equation of the localities, purely because this similarity does not conform to the sound laws that the European discipline of comparative linguistics has deduced on the basis of certain linguistic phenomena (not from toponyms!). The other possibility, much favoured by renowned Hittitologists in this case and others like it, is to give in to the weight of *pragmatic* evidence and accept that in such cases our traditional linguistic methods may not (yet) have developed to match the facts.

It appears that here we face one of those instances that occur in science, when a path must be taken, however methodologically dubious it may be by existing criteria, in order to achieve a result which then by its evidence, if obtained, offers the chance subsequently to widen the path.

Conclusions: Troy and the Empire of the Hittites

Our initial question has been answered: in the Bronze Age Hisarlık was known to the Hittites as *Wilusa* and the Greeks as *Wilios*. Moreover, in the 'land of Wilusa', at the end of the fifteenth century BC, the Hittites knew an area called *Taruwisa* or *Tru(w)isa*, which can scarcely be distinguished from the Greek *Troia*. The city that Homer's *Iliad* tells of is therefore certainly a historical reality, and in the Bronze Age it lay in precisely that area of north-west Asia Minor where Homer places it.

Over and above this main result, other results have presented themselves:

1. The city of Wilusa, after which the Hittites named the whole land (which was commensurate with our 'Troad', at least, but probably larger), was no mere 'nest of pirates' on a mountain-top with a maximum area of 20,000 square metres, but an extensive walled settlement of over 200,000 square metres with between 7,000 and 10,000 inhabitants—a sizeable city by the standards of the day.

2. The city was laid out on the pattern of Anatolian settlements: a walled citadel with a densely built-up lower town, also walled and protected by an encircling ditch. During the second half of the second millennium BC the lower town expanded so far that a second ditch was deemed necessary. The population was therefore constantly increasing.

3. The town was at once a royal residence and trading centre. It was governed by the rulers of the citadel. Its prosperity, shown in increasing population and continuous expansion, rested on its importance as a trading centre. Its importance was a consequence of its exceptionally favourable economic and strategic position at

precisely that point in Asia Minor which afforded the closest control over trading movements between two seas, the Aegean and the Black Sea, but also enabled it to provide welcome support and protection for those movements.

4. This supporting and protective function determined the 'international' character of the city. Though Anatolian in its geographical situation and town-planning (perhaps also in its religious orientation), it did not isolate itself in 'Anatolian' fashion, but assumed the role of economic hub and organizational centre for the closer and further regions not only in Asia, but also for the European shores facing it, and naturally exploiting the economic structures focused there, to the advantage of all participants. The town thus served as a commercial harbour, storage facility, processing point for raw materials (metals, textiles, clay), market (among other commodities, it seems, especially for horses, which then provided the coveted latest form of locomotive power in peace and war), and entrepôt for the entire population of the hinterland in the Three Seas Region, consisting of the Aegean, the Sea of Marmora, and the Black Sea, that is, for the Troad and its Anatolian hinterland to the east and south, the off-shore islands (above all Imbros, Tenedos, and Lesbos), for the Asian and European coasts of the Dardanelles, Thrace and the Balkan area in the west and probably at least part of the southern Black Sea coast in the north-east. Manfred Korfmann has also suggested that the town served as an outpost for the coastal and island shipping lanes of the north-east Aegean, and thus as a kind of 'Hanseatic' centre. These functions and the associated opportunities for profit provided the source of its enduring wealth (the treasure hoard), which was clearly fabulous, especially during the Bronze Age.

5. It is plain that a city which radiated supra-regional importance and influence over such a wide area must have attracted the interest of political powers which combined great military potential with relative territorial proximity and expansionist tendencies. A power on this scale emerged on the further horizon during the second millennium in the form of the Hittite empire. The hieroglyphic Luwian seal found in the citadel of Troy, in a building close to the fortress wall, in 1995 can therefore hardly be a case of a displaced or accidental find. With the documents available today from the

imperial Hittite correspondence, it is much more probable that it points to a political connection, clearly a very old one, between the government of the Hittite empire in Ḫattusa and the rulers of the Wilusa citadel.

THE ALAKSANDU TREATY

In our reappraisal of the material so far, we have left open the question of the nature of this connection. At this point it is useful to return to it. Our starting point is again the treaty concluded between the Hittite Great King Muwattalli II (*c*.1290–1272 BC) and Alaksandu of Wilusa. To show that this treaty is not an isolated example to be handled with special caution, possibly even to be doubted as an authentic historical document, we set out below extracts from another treaty, of similar nature, which the father of Muwattalli II, Mursili II (*c*.1318–1290), had concluded some time previously with Manabatarḫunta, king of the Sēḫa River Land (which bordered on Wilusa, as we have shown):[1]

§ 1 (I. 1–3) Thus says My Majesty, Mursili, Great King, King [of the land of Ḫattusa, Hero]: Your father left you, Manabatarḫunta, [. . .], and you were (still) a child. [And . . . (personal name)] and Uratarḫunta, your brothers, attempted to kill [you] several times. They would have killed you, [but you] escaped. And they drove you out of [Sēḫa], so that you [went] over to the Karkisans, and they [took away] your land and the house of your father from you, so that they could take them for themselves. [I, My Majesty, had however recommended you, Manabatarḫunta], to the Karkisans and [repeatedly] sent gifts to the Karkisans. My brother (Arnuwanda II) also had repeatedly interceded [with them] on your behalf, so that the Karkisans protected you upon our word.

§ 2 (I. 14–18) When however, Uratarḫunta proceeded [to transgress] the oath, the oath gods seized him. And the Sēḫans (i.e. the Royal Clan of Sēḫa) expelled him, while the Sēḫans received you back upon [our] word and protected you upon [our] word.

§ 3 (I. 19–33) Then when my brother [Arnuwanda became a god (i.e. died)] I, My Majesty, [seated myself] on the throne [of my father] and then I, My Majesty, [backed] you from this time on. I [caused] the Sēḫans [to swear an oath] to you, [and] because of my [word they kept loyalty] with you. (*Four lines too fragmentary for translation.*) Then [when Uḫazidi, the Arzawan (= the king reigning in Arzawa)], waged war [against My Majesty, you, Manabatarḫunta, committ]ed serious [disloyalty] against My Majesty. You backed [Uḫḫazidi, my enemy], while [fighting against] My Majesty and not backing [me].

§ 4 (I. 34–62) [When] I [went on campaign] against Uḫḫazidi and against the [Arzawans], because Uḫḫazidi (as usurper in Arzawa) [had transgressed the oath] in regard to me, the oath gods [however] seized him, so that I, My Majesty could destroy [him]. And since you too [had taken the side of Uḫḫazidi], I [wanted] to destroy you as well. [But you did not] fall [at my feet], but [sent old] men [and old women] to me, [so that they] as your envoys [fell] at my feet, and you wrote [to me] as follows:

'My lord, preserve my (political) life! [May you, my lord, not] destroy [me], but take me as a (political) client and [keep loyalty] with me! Any dwellers of the land of Mirā, of the land of Ḫattusa, or of the land of Arzawa who have come over [to me] shall I [(re)turn/turn (over)] all of them from here[1] (*text offers*: from there) to you at any given time. So I, My Majesty, took an interest in you, acceded [to you] on account of that and accepted you on friendly terms. And as I, My Majesty, have taken an interest in you, [and] accepted [you] on friendly terms, seize each one of those [dwellers] of the land of Arzawa who have come over to you, and each one—whosoever has [fled] from me—of those of the land of Mirā and the land of Ḫattusa, who have come over to you, if someone of those is a person under oath, (seize) each dweller and hand him over to me! Leave not a single man behind, and let not anyone go out from your land nor let him cross into another land, but seize the(se) dwellers all in their totality and turn them over to me! And if you comply with all these terms, I shall accept you as a (political) client. So be a friend to me! [And] in the future you shall have this treaty! Observe it! It shall be placed under oath for you:

§ 5 (I. 63–6) Behold, I hereby give to you the land of Sēḫa and the land of Abbawija, and it shall be your land! Keep loyalty with it! Moreover you shall not desire an inhabitant of Ḫattusa or a border district of Ḫattusa! If you do desire in wicked fashion an inhabitant of Ḫattusa and a border district of Ḫattusa, then you will transgress the oath!

The train of thought is clear: (1) the addressee, the legitimate heir to the throne, who had apparently lost one parent and was at risk of assassination, was a nonentity, (2) but the Great King rescued him by his recommendation, (3) restored his rights, and (4) gave him constant support. (5) But the beneficiary defected from his benefactor. (6) The Great King magnanimously forgave the penitent and (7) gave him back his country (and another country with it). (8) Now the addressee must administer this country well on the Great King's behalf and (9) never be guilty of even the slightest hostile act against the Hittite empire.

Manabatarḫunta of Sēḫa is therefore a vassal king of the King of Ḫattusa—a petty king by the grace of the Great King.

Against the background of the form of this treaty, the political dimension in the background and significance of the treaty between Mursili's son Muwattalli II and Alaksandu of Wilusa will stand out more clearly and emerge in greater depth. In view of the importance of this text for the whole field of Trojan studies, it is set out here in full in an English translation by Frank Starke.[2] The level of detail may be wearisome for some readers, while at the same time giving cause for amazement. It is worth bearing in mind here that modern international treaties greatly surpass this one, which is over three thousand years old, in length and detail, that is, in the theoretical anticipation of even the remotest eventualities. However, the genre of the international treaty has remained the same. Then as now considerable specialized knowledge was needed to understand it fully.

§ 1 (B I. 1–2) Thus says My Majesty, Muwattalli, Great King, [King] of the land of Ḫattusa, Beloved of the Storm-god of Lightning, son of Mursili (II), Great King, Hero:

§ 2 (C I. 3–13) Formerly at one time the *labarna* (honorary title of the Hittite Great King), my ancestor, had made all of the land of Arzawa [and] all of the land of Wilussa (political) clients. Later the land of Arzawa waged war because of this; but since the event was long ago, I do not know from which king of the land of Ḫattusa the land of Wilusa defected. But (even) if the land of Wilussa defected from the land of Ḫattusa, they (= the Royal Clan of Wilussa) remained on terms of friendship with the kings of the land of Ḫattusa from afar and regularly sent envoys to them. (B I. 9–14) When Tudḫalija (I) [. . .], he came against the land of Arzawa [and . . .]. He did not enter the land of Wilusa, certainly, [since it was] on special terms of friendship [with him and] regularly sent envoys [to him]. And then [. . .], and Tudḫalija [. . ., . . .] the forefathers in the land [of . . .].

§ 3 (B I. 15–20) But the king of the land of Wilusa, [was] on terms of friendship with him, [and] he regularly sent [envoys to him]; and he did not enter (the land) against him. [When] the land of Arzawa [waged war once more], then my grandfather Suppiluliuma (I) [conquered the land of

Arzawa]. But Kukkunni, the king of the land of Wilusa [was on terms of friendship] with him, so that he did not come against him, [but] regularly sent envoys to [my grandfather Suppiluliuma].

§ 4 (A. I. 20′–34′) Then [the land of Arzawa waged war] once more [against the land of Ḫattusa]. The king of the land of Arzawa [...(*3 fragmentary lines*)...] my father (Mursili II) [...] the land of Wilusa [...] the king of the land of Wilusa [... came] to the aid [of...] he attacked and [conquered all of] the land of Arzawa. [He gave the land of Mirā] and the land of Kuwalija to Masḫuiluwa, [he gave] the land of Sēḫa and the land of Abbawija to Manabatarḫunta, [he gave] the land of Ḫaballa [to Tarkasnalli, and] the land of Ḫaballa [...].

§ 5 (A I. 35′–42′) *Highly fragmentary. Describes the circumstances in which Alaksandu succeeded Kukkunni in Wilusa* ('according to the word of your father').

§ 6 (A I. 43′–54′) When my father [became a god], I seated [myself on the throne] of my father. But you, Alaksandu, kept loyalty with me [concerning lordship]. Then when [...] waged war against me [and] entered..., you] called on me for help. [So] I, My Majesty, came to your aid, Alaksandu, and destroyed the land of Māsa. [... too] I destroyed [and...] and I [...] them in the Kupta (mountains). I [...] the dwellers [...]. I destroyed those lands [which had waged war] against you, Alaksandu. [...] and [I brought] them back to Ḫattusa. (55′–61′) *Highly fragmentary. A new paragraph appears to begin here, not observed in the enumeration of J. Friedrich:*

§ 6a...(A I. 62′–64′) no one in the land of Wilusa concerning kingship [...]. But since the people grumble?, [... When], Alaksandu, your day of death arrives, [...]. (65′–79′) Whichever son of yours you appoint for kingship—[whether he be] by your wife or by your concubine—and even if he is [...], so that the land says no and pronounces as follows: 'He [has to] be a prince of the seed (i.e. of dynastic progeny)!', I, My Majesty, will say no. Accordingly my son and my grandson, grandson and great grandson will keep loyalty [with that one alone]. You, Alaksandu, graciously keep loyalty with My Majesty. Accordingly keep loyalty with my son and my grandson, with my grandson and great grandson. And just as I, My Majesty, have benevolently kept loyalty with you, Alaksandu, because of the word of your father, and have come to your aid, and have killed the enemy on your behalf, accordingly in the future my sons and my grandsons will equally keep loyalty with your son, grandson and great grandson. If some enemy arises for you, then I, my Majesty, will not abandon you, just as I have not now abandoned you, and I will kill the enemy on your behalf. If your brother or someone of your family withdraws political support from you, Alaksandu,—

§ 7 . . . (B II. 5–14) or accordingly someone withdraws political support from your son (and) your grandsons—and they seek the kingship of the land of Wilusa, I, My Majesty will absolutely not discard you, Alaksandu, that is, I will not accept that one. As he is your enemy, in exactly the same way he is My Majesty's enemy, and only you, Alaksandu, will I, My Majesty, recognize. I will certainly [not recognize] him and additionally I will destroy his land. So you, Alaksandu, keep loyalty with My Majesty, and accordingly your sons, grandsons [and great grandsons] shall keep loyalty concerning lordship with [the sons], the grandsons and the great grandsons of My Majesty. They shall not plot [evil against them], nor shall they [de]fect [from them]! (A II. 8–14) As I, My Majesty, have now made the treaty tablet for Alaksandu, you Alaksandu, [(your) grandsons] and great grandsons, act thus with regard to the treaty tablet, and your [sons], grandsons and great grandsons shall accordingly keep loyalty with the sons only of My Majesty concerning lordship! Do not plot evil against them, nor defect from them!

§ 8 (A II. 15–33) *References—still visible—to the fact that His Majesty has made Alaksandu king in the land of Wilusa. In other respects fragmentary.*

§ 9 (A II. 34–57) *Highly fragmentary.*

§ 10 (A II. 58–74) [Furthermore: If in the vicinity of the land of Ḫattusa there arises some evil] case of withdrawal of political support, [(if) some land in the outer region (i.e. a federal state of the empire)] shows hostility [against My Majesty, but everything is well with My Majesty, then] await [instructions of] My Majesty, [as I, My Majesty, shall write to you. If in the inner region (i.e. in the interior lands of the core state of the empire) someone—either a Great One (i.e. a member of the imperial government) or a unit of the infantry or] chariotry, [or any person at all—carries out] against My Majesty a withdrawal of political support, I shall [so far as I, My Majesty, am able, seize that] person or [that unit of the infantry or chariotry. But if I write to you], Alaksandu: 'Let [infantry and chariotry] move forward [and let them come to my aid!'], come [to my aid] immediately and [move] them [up] to me [immediately! And if I write to you], Alaksandu, alone: 'Drive here alone!', then drive here alone! But if I, [My Majesty, do not] write [to you concerning this case of withdrawal of political support], but you [hear] (of it) in advance, [do not] ignore [it]! But if it, [nonetheless,] is not the right thing for you, place one Great One at the head of the [infantry and] chariotry, so that he sends them [to My Majesty's aid immediately]. But do not first take a bird oracle!

§ 11 (A II. 75–81) And if you hear in advance about an evil case of withdrawal of political support, either some man of the land of Sēḫa or [some] man of the land of Arzawa (i.e. a man from the Arzawan states, in particular from neighbouring Sēḫa) [carries out the withdrawal of political support], and if—knowing of this case in advance but not writing to My Majesty—you nonetheless show in some way lenience towards these *kuriwanes* (an elusive term probably derived from Luwian) who are now also your *kuriwanes*, saying as follows: 'Let that evil take place!', <do not do that>, but write in advance as soon as you hear about the case, without hesitation to My Majesty!

§ 12 (A II. 82–5) As soon as you hear of such a case, do not behave indifferently on behalf of the case! And do not change your mind and do not align yourself with such a man! As he is My Majesty's enemy, he shall likewise be your enemy!

§ 13 (A II. 86–III. 2) But if you hear of such a case and in addition behave indifferently on behalf of the case and make common cause with that man, behold, Alaksandu, you will then commit disloyalty before the oath gods, and the oath gods shall pursue you ceaselessly!

§ 14 (A III. 3–15) The stipulations concerning your army and your chariotry shall be established as follows: If I, My Majesty, go on campaign in the vicinity of those lands, either in the vicinity of Karkisa, the vicinity of Lukkā, or in the vicinity of Warsijalla, you too shall go on campaign at my side together with infantry and chariotry. Or if I send some lord (i.e. a member of the Hittite Royal Clan) in the vicinity of this land (i.e. of the core state) to go on campaign, you shall at any given time go on campaign at his side also. (*In exemplar C a paragraph break follows here.*) In the vicinity of Ḫattusa (i.e. of the empire) these campaigns concern you: If someone of the kings who are the equals of My Majesty—the King of the land of Mizra (Egypt), the King of the land of Sanḫara (Babylonia), the King of the land of Mittanna (Mittani);[3] or the man of the land of Assura (Assyria)[4]—commences battle there (*Exemplar C offers*: If someone . . . arises outside (the empire)), or someone within (the empire, i.e. domestically) carries out a withdrawal of political support against My Majesty, and therefore I, My Majesty, write to you for infantry and chariotry, then move up <infantry> and chariotry to my aid immediately!

§ 15 (A III. 16–25) Furthermore: Since there are also some treacherous people, if rumours circulate, so that someone whispers constantly in your presence: 'His Majesty is undertaking such and such to present you in bad light; he will take the land away from you, or will act in some way to your detriment', you shall nonetheless write about this rumour to My Majesty! And if the rumour persists, as soon as I, My Majesty, shall reply to you in writing, do not act hastily, create no confusion, and undertake nothing detrimental against My Majesty! As you have stood on the side of My Majesty, so (continue to) stand only on the side of My Majesty!

§ 16 (A III. 26–30) If someone says anything dangerous concerning My Majesty in your, Alaksandu's, presence, but you conceal it from My Majesty, and act hastily and undertake something detrimental against My Majesty, behold, you, Alaksandu, will then commit disloyalty before the oath gods, and the oath gods shall pursue you ceaselessly!

§ 17 (A III. 31–44) Furthermore: Among you who are the four kings in the lands of Arzawa—(among) you, Alaksandu, Manabatarḫunta[!] (of Sēḫa), Kubantakurunta (of Mirā), and Uraḫattusa (of Ḫaballa)—Kubantakurunta in the male line is a descendant of the King of the land of Arzawa, but in the female line he is a descendant of the King of the Land of Ḫattusa; for to my father Mursili, the Great King, the King of the land of Ḫattusa he was a nephew, and he is a cousin to My Majesty. But those who are his (political) clients and Arzawans (i.e. the members of the Arzawan Royal Clan) are treacherous. So if someone seeks to put Kubantakurunta in danger, you, Alaksandu, must be help and support and offensive force for Kubantakurunta, and keep loyalty with him; but he (too) must keep loyalty with you! If some (political) client withdraws political support from Kubantakurunta and joins you, arrest him and give him back to Kubantakurunta! So the one shall be the help and support and offensive force for the other, and the one shall keep loyalty with the other! (*Expected paragraph break omitted here.*)

(A III. 44–60) Furthermore: If some enemy mobilizes and moves against the borders of the lands which I have given to you, whose borders are, moreover, the borders of the land of Ḫattusa (i.e. borders of the empire), in order to attack, but you hear (of this) and do not write in advance to the lord (who is administrator) in the land and provide no assistance and are lenient in the face of the danger, or (if) the enemy attacks and holds his own, but you do not provide assistance in advance and do not fight the enemy, or (if) the enemy marches across your land and you do not fight him, but say as follows: 'Attack without fear and carry it out; I wish to know nothing of it!', then this too shall be placed under oath, and the oath gods shall pursue you ceaselessly! Or (if) you request infantry and chariotry from My Majesty <in order to> attack some enemy, and My Majesty gives you infantry and chariotry, but you betray them to the enemy at the first opportunity, then [this too] shall be placed under oath, and the oath gods shall pursue you, Alaksandu, ceaselessly!

§ 18 (A III. 61–72) Regarding fugitives, I have placed under oath as follows: If [a fugitive] comes from your land to the land of Ḫattusa as a fugitive, he will [not be given back to you]. It is not law to give a fugitive back from the land of Ḫattusa. But if some craftsman flees, [in order to enter the land of Ḫattusa], and does not do his job (in Wilusa), [he shall be seized and] handed over to you. [If] some [fugitive?] from <the land> of an enemy is captured, [fleeing from the land of Ḫattusa], that means that he crosses your land, and you seize him but do not send him on (to me), [but] give [him] back to the enemy, then that shall be placed under oath!

§ 19 (A III. 73–83) Furthermore: This tablet which I have made for you, Alaksandu, shall be read out before you three times yearly, so that you, Alaksandu, are familiar with it. But this wording is by no means based on reciprocity; it is issued from the land of Ḫattusa! So [you], Alaksandu, do not undertake anything to the detriment of My Majesty! And Ḫattusa will do nothing detrimental to you. Now, behold, in this [matter] I, [My Majesty], *labarna*, Great King, Beloved of the Storm-god of Lightning, have summoned [the Thousand Gods] (to the assembly of the 'Community'—i.e. the constitutional body of the Hittite Royal Clan, representing 'all the land of Ḫattusa' = the Hittite Empire—at which the treaty is issued and probably also handed over), in order to make them witnesses, and they shall listen [and be witnesses]:

§ 20 (A IV. 1–30) *List of the divine witnesses, enumerating the gods of the Hittite state pantheon; in the closing passage*: (A IV. 26–30) . . . all [the gods] of the land of Wilusa, the Storm-god of the Army, [names of one or two gods]. Āppaliuna (cuneiform writing: ^{D}]*A-ap-pa-li-u-na -aš*), the male deities, the female deities, [the mountains], the rivers, [the springs], the (divine) Underground Watercourse (cuneiform writing: ^{D}KASKAL.KUR) of the land of Wilusa. I, [My Majesty, Great King], Beloved of the Storm-god of Lightning, have summoned them in [that] matter.

§ 21 (A IV. 31–46) If you, Alaksandu, transgress these words of the tablet which stand on this tablet, then these Thousand Gods shall destroy you, together with your person, your wife, your sons, your lands, your towns, your vineyard, your threshing floor, your field, your cattle, your sheep, and your possessions, and erase your seed (progeny) from the dark earth! But if you observe these words, then these Thousand Gods whom I, My Majesty, *labarna*, Muwattalli, Great King, have summoned to assembly—the gods of Ḫattusa and the gods of Wilusa, and the Storm-god of Lightning of the person of My Majesty—shall graciously protect you, together with your wife, your sons, your grandsons, your towns, your threshing floor, your vineyard, your field, your cattle, your sheep, and your possessions! So enjoy welcome authority in My Majesty's sphere of responsibility and grow old in My Majesty's sphere of responsibility!

The structural similarity between the two treaties is striking. The preamble (more personal in the case of Sēḫa, political in that of Wilusa) is followed by a reminder of accession to the throne being due to the Great King, and of benefits bestowed, above all assistance in the war against Wilusa (§ 6), then the injunction to administer loyally the land held in trust, and finally a warning against defection, rebellion, or hostility against the overlord. In the case of Wilusa, detailed instructions follow concerning (1) the vassal king's duty to inform the Great King of any rumours of defection or rebellion in the neighbouring lands (Sēḫa and Arzawa are named), (2) his duty to supply supporting troops to the Great King himself and his commanders in case of war between Ḫattusa and any other vassal state in the immediate vicinity, and against any foreign power equal in status to Ḫattusa, (3) his obligation to provide support to the kings of neighbouring vassal states, (4) his obligation to inform the Great King or his district commanders without delay of any hostile troop movements directed against Wilusa itself and Ḫatti, (5) his obligation to prevent any hostile transit through Wilusa, (6) his obligation to extradite escaped prisoners to Ḫattusa.

The enumeration of the vassal king's duties and obligations to the Great King, in principle comparable to a modern treaty of similar content, concludes with the invocation of the gods, that is, with an indication of the sanctions to be expected should the treaty be breached, and on the other hand, of the rewards of abiding by it.[5]

Like Manabatarḫunta of Sēḫa, from the moment the treaty is signed, Alaksandu of Wilusa becomes a vassal of the Great King of Ḫattusa. Here it should be noted, however, that his treaty obligations—according to the text, at least—lie exclusively in the field of foreign policy. In domestic and economic policy his autonomy is unrestricted (by, for example, the payment of tribute, or the supply of permanent military contingents, and so forth). As long as he meets the obligations stipulated, he is relatively independent.

For the history of Wilusa in the second millennium BC, this state of affairs is of crucial importance: the archaeological excavation of the city has revealed steady economic expansion during the second millennium, until the Trojan high-culture phase in the latter half of the millennium. This continuous growth could have been possible only with external and internal political stability, combined with unrestricted opportunities for economic reinvestment. The Alaksandu treaty shows that the citadel rulers of Wilusa had every opportunity for this. It shows plainly, moreover, that throughout the history of the city they consistently availed themselves of these opportunities. We have no cause to question the fundamental accuracy of the historical sketch preceding the text of the treaty. This means that Garstang and Gurney were fully correct in 1959 when they took as the basis for the relations between Wilusa and the Hittite empire the 'unwavering loyalty of Wilusa to the kings of Ḫatti' for 'at least four hundred years'.[6] The treaty is specific in setting forth the following fixed points in the bilateral relationship:

(1) the subjugation of Wilusa by Ḫattusa in the time of the *labarna* (before 1600 BC);[7]
(2) no (effective) secession of Wilusa from Ḫattusa between this date and the reign of Tudḫalija I (*c.*1420–1400), when war was waged against Arzawa;
(3) no alliance between Wilusa and Arzawa, which was hostile to the Hittites, in the time of Suppiluliuma I (*c.*1355–1320);
(4) no Wilusan involvement in the war between Arzawa (under Uḫḫazidi) and Mursili II (*c.*1318–1290);
(5) conclusion of a vassal treaty between Alaksandu of Wilusa and Muwattalli II (*c.*1290–1272).

This brings us to a text identified in 1982 as an appendix to the so-called Millawa(n)da letter;[8] the Millawa(n)da letter was sent by Great King Tudḫalija IV (*c.*1240–1215) to a recipient not yet positively identified (the King of Mirā,[9] possibly Tarkasnawa of Mirā,[10] or, as has recently been suggested, the son of Atpa of Millawanda, the Aḫḫijawa representative deposed by the Hittites in the second half of the thirteenth century).[11] In this letter the Great King is at pains to restore the rights of Alaksandu's probable successor, Walmu, who had been overthrown in Wilusa and then seems to have fled into exile, to the recipient:

(36″) . . . (*highly fragmentary; part omitted*) he fled [. . .], (37″) and [they adopted] another man. [. . .] I (the majesty) have not recognized him. (38″) However, Kulanazidi has held ready the documents which were [prepared] for Walmu (by me/by somebody else). (39″) He will deliver (?) them (to you), my son. Look at them! (... *End of 39–40 omitted*), (41″) Therefore, my son, send me Walmu (who is in exile with you), so that I can restore him in the land of Wilusa (42″) to the throne. Just as he was previously king of the land of Wilusa, so shall he be again! (43″) Just as he was previously our vassal (and) soldier, so shall he again be our (44″) vassal (and) soldier![12]

To date this is the last known mention of Wilusa in the imperial Hittite correspondence.[13] It shows that Wilusa's apparently untroubled vassal status endured until the very last days of the great Hittite empire. The rulers of the Wilusa citadel were therefore well able to remain continuously on good terms with the dominant power in Asia Minor for almost half a millennium, and protect themselves in this way. A favourable geopolitical situation, combined with astute diplomacy and adherence to a policy of a kind of neutrality amidst the turbulence of the time, arising especially and repeatedly from nearby Arzawa, ensured for the city its relative autonomy, the results of which Manfred Korfmann's excavations are unearthing year by year in greater abundance.

Such a centuries-long policy of voluntary recognition and the resulting economic prosperity was naturally only possible because the citadel rulers permitted and consistently accepted the incorporation of the city and all of its hinterland in the network of multilateral dependencies by which the Hittite empire had subjugated all of Asia Minor since the fifteenth century BC. The individual paragraphs of the Alaksandu treaty proceed from a form of diplomatic co-operation which is taken for granted between Wilusa and Ḫattusa, presupposing on Wilusa's side a constant watch over political movements throughout north-western and western Asia Minor, and beyond. Complying with these obligations necessarily meant the integration of Wilusa in the political, military, economic, and other general communication practices of the Hittite empire, or, in short, Wilusa's self-categorization within the Hittite cultural space.

This must also have had effects in the area of language. We have indicated elsewhere that the hieroglyphic Luwian seal found in Troy in 1995 offers no proof that Luwian was the *colloquial* language of Wilusa, but that this find, with the documents of the imperial Hittite correspondence, points to Hittite or Luwian as the accepted *language of diplomacy* in Wilusa, as elsewhere. In 1997 Frank Starke arrived at the same conclusion:

> At the same time it emerges that the Wilusan envoys spoke Luwian, which—as I fully recognise—is no sure proof that Luwian was spoken in Wilusa. (It is possible that Luwian merely provided a shared linguistic basis for communication between the envoys and the Hittites.)[14]

This, however, leaves out of account the possibility that it is not a matter of oral communication alone (which, as Starke himself concedes, could also have proceeded through interpreters—as is known to have been in part the case for Hittite–Egyptian relations) but also, and primarily, of written communication. The detailed terms of the Alaksandu treaty concerning Wilusa's obligation to provide information so clearly presuppose constant written communication ('Write at once!', 'Send a report!', 'This tablet shall be read out to you three times every year!') that a regular postal service, used without any reflection, must have provided the basis for it.[15] From this it follows that a 'scriptorium and state chancellery' were established in Wilusa, which just as in the other Hittite vassal states (for example Karkamis and Ugarit) handled all diplomatic traffic—not only in Hittite/Luwian, to be sure, but certainly partly in it, since for a time it was the principal language of diplomacy in Asia Minor.[16]

In saying 'not only in Hittite/Luwian', we are taking account of the fact that Wilusa, being the major trading centre that we understand it was, during the two millennia of its existence, must naturally have come into contact with many Mediterranean languages and scripts. It would therefore be no surprise if Schliemann's finds had included remnants of Linear A, the pre-Greek Cretan script from the beginning of the second millennium BC—remnants which in Schliemann's day could hardly have attracted attention.[17] In view of the centuries-long relations between Wilusa and the Bronze Age Greeks ('the Mycenaeans'), whose presence in Wilusa is shown mainly by Mycenaean pottery, it would not be in the least surprising if one day remnants of Linear B, the writing of the Mycenaeans in the second half of the second millennium, came to light, and even Egyptian hieroglyphs would not come as a shock. The fact that so far nothing like this has been found in Wilusa/Troy can be easily explained: later construction in the hill area as early as the Hellenistic period and the later Roman age was linked with such thoroughgoing levelling of the remains of structures from Troy VI and VII that any ruins of the 'state chancellery', which must be regarded as firmly established at least for these periods, were scattered to the four winds. The Schliemann excavation must have meant the death blow. In these circumstances, the discovery of the seal in 1995 borders on the miraculous. We cannot rule out the possibility, however, that epigraphic evidence, in whatever script, may sooner or later surface in the ruins of buildings (particularly public buildings) in the lower town, which have so far been explored only at isolated points. And the many tons of Schliemann's rubble, tipped down from the hill during his excavations, could still hold some surprises.[18] The deployment of a 'special inscription-search squad' would probably pay dividends.

The 'core communication', however, which was essential to the existence of Wilusa in the second millennium BC, logically took place in Hittite/Luwian. The merest glance at the 'Pijamaradu affair', to which we shall return, or at the negotiations concerning the restoration of Alaksandu's successor Walmu, shows such close connections between Ḫattusa itself and the dynasties of its various western vassal states that the use of a variety of languages and the consequent need for permanent professional translation services may be ruled out, at least in diplomatic traffic. If we also take account of the realization, which came only in 1997, that the king of Mirā proclaimed his authority in Luwian at the Karabel Pass, 200 kilometres to the south of Wilusa, it will not seem rash to attribute to the dynasties of the western vassal states not only the use of Hittite/Luwian by salaried scribes, but also local competence—which conferred security—in that language. Starke's hypothesis that the Wilusan envoys, who were then regularly recruited by custom from the clan of the king,[19] spoke Luwian in other parts of the empire as well as in the capital, gains greatly in probability in the light of these considerations.

Starke's case for Luwian as the *main language* of Wilusa is less persuasive. He constructs the following line of argument:

1. In the Alaksandu treaty (§ 17), Wilusa is placed with Mirā, Ḫaballa, and Sēḫa under the heading of 'Arzawa lands'. Since this has no historical or political basis (Wilusa had already

distanced itself from Arzawa during its vassal-state phase, as we have seen), 'the juxtaposition is surely based primarily on language'.[20]

2. In Tablet I of the old Hittite law code the text of which dates from the seventeenth century BC, in § 19 the region to the west of the Halys is referred to as 'the land of Luvia'. In a copy from the fourteenth century, this is replaced by 'the land of Arzawa'.

3. The textual and onomastic material shows the whole area between Melitene in the south-east as far as the land of Sēḫa in the west of Asia Minor (the Kaïkos Valley, on the Wilusan border) as Luwian-speaking.

4. The probable consequence of this is 'that, like the rest of western Asia Minor, the extreme north-west, that is, the area of the land of Wilusa, is Luwian-speaking, and in fact the American Indo-Europeanist C. Watkins stated as early as 1986, primarily on the basis of personal names in the *Iliad*, that Luwian was spoken in Wilusa/Troy'.

As proof of Watkins's thesis, Starke then adduces 'surely the most striking equation of personal names, that of *Príamos* [the King of Troy in the *Iliad*] and the Luwian compound *Priiamuua*', which means 'exceptionally courageous', and is therefore 'certainly admirably suited to the world created by Homer'.[21] He concludes with another reference to the (probable) Luwian speech of the Wilusan envoys, 'which, against the general historical and linguistic background, here forms such an important piece of evidence, that in order to rebut it one would, in my view, need evidence of non-Luwian texts or inscriptions from Troy. As has been shown by the lucky find in Troy in summer 1995 of a biconvex bronze seal with hieroglyphic Luwian script from the late twelfth century, the likelihood of such evidence emerging does not seem very great, and the certainty is growing that Wilusa/Troy belonged to the greater Luwian-speaking community.'[22]

However much instinct may prompt us to accept Starke's argument, the step from 'Luwian as *official language*', which is practically beyond question, to 'Luwian as the *language in daily use*' still seems a dubious one. In the end all the arguments adduced point to Luwian being spoken, or of a command of it in addition to another language, among the citadel rulers. The correspondences in personal names make this plain. If we take seriously Homer's genealogy of the Trojans' ruling family in the *Iliad* (20. 215–40) at least linguistically (not historically)—and there is no reason why we should not—we find ourselves with a series of names, most of which have always been recognized as non-Greek. In Hans von Kamptz's standard work of 1958, *Homerische Personennamen* (Personal Names in Homer), which has still not been replaced, of the sixteen names *Dardanos*, Erichthonios, *Tros*, *Ilos*, *Assarakos*, Ganymedes, Laomedon, *Tithonos*, *Priamos*, Lampos, Klytios, Hiketaon, *Kapys*, *Anchises*, Hektor and *Aineias*, no fewer than nine (shown in italics) are either of 'pre-Greek Asia Minor' or 'Illyrian' origin ('Illyrian being a once favoured umbrella term for 'foreign and obscure').[23] A close examination of all the personal names of the extended royal Trojan clan in the *Iliad*, given that our knowledge of the Anatolian languages has greatly expanded since 1958, would show a much higher proportion originating in Asia Minor.

Here we should include the names of three Wilusan rulers known to us from the Hittite documents we have cited: *Kukunni*, *Walmu*, and *Alaksandu*. According to Starke, all three are Luwian. *Alaksandu*, however, is an exception. We have already pointed out that soon after Hittite had been deciphered this name was compared with the Greek name Aléxandros (see p. 76). Today most specialists agree that the name cannot be Hittite/Luwian in origin, but is a 'Luwianized' or 'Hittitized' form of a name from another language. It may easily be supposed that that 'other language' was Greek,[24] since in other cases Greek personal names were also 'Luwianized' or 'Hittitized', such as *Tawa-galawa* (= Greek *Etewoklewēs*, with loss of the initial vowel). (See n. 67.)

However, the fact that in the patently non-Greek Trojan dynasty a man with a Greek name should suddenly appear demands an explanation. The decisive proof seems to stem from the Alaksandu treaty itself. In § 6a it is stated,

> Whichever son of yours you appoint for kingship—[whether he be] by your wife *or by your concubine*—and even if he is [. . .], *so that the land says no* and pronounces as follows: 'He [has to] be a prince *of the seed* (i.e. of dynastic progeny)!', I, My Majesty, will say no.

From this it is clear that (1) the sons of concubines could succeed to the throne (cf. secundogeniture; see p. 65) and (2) non-biological offspring, that is, adopted sons (sons not 'of the seed'), could be contenders for the succession. Alaksandu himself, according to § 5, came to power 'according to his father's word', so probably not quite in accordance with the regular rules of succession. The very detailed rules set out in § 6a therefore seem to have filled a current need. Given the international character of the city, it is also possible that Alaksandu was the son of one of Kukunni's Greek concubines, or that Kukunni adopted an exceptional man of Greek extraction (as Garstang and Gurney suggested in 1959).[25]

The fact that this was a special case, however, if it happened at all, is suggested by the circumstance that the only treaty between a Hittite Great King and a Wilusan ruler to come down to us (so far) was concluded with none other than Alaksandu, who was clearly in need of help for internal political reasons as well. The ruling dynasty in Wilusa can be seen to be fundamentally Anatolian, possibly in some degree even Luwian (the unquestionably Greek names in the genealogy shown in the *Iliad* may be metrically determined 'fillers', as is the practice in compiling lists in Greek sung poetry; we shall take up the phenomenon of 'filling' later). That Luwian naming systems should be used in the dynasty of a vassal state under Hittite tutelage is of course natural. However, this is not yet sufficient to prove that Luwian was the spoken language of Wilusa. Nevertheless, at the Würzburg colloquium Günter Neumann specified a number of place-names and personal names from the Troad, including *Tros*, *Troilos*, *Daskyleion*, *Pedasos*, and the river *Satnioeis*, which indicate 'that here in the Ida Mountains a language which may have belonged to the Hittite–Luwian family was spoken'.[26] It seems, therefore, that Starke's thesis may be correct, but before the matter can be decided, further material must be collected and evaluated.

What is already clear, however, is that in the second millennium BC Wilusa was politically and culturally firmly anchored in the Hittite–Luwian sphere of influence.

This gives rise to one last question: the hieroglyphic Luwian seal discovered in Troy in 1995, which we may confidently treat as an artefact from the Wilusan 'state chancellery', was deposited, or disposed of, in the latter half of the twelfth century BC, according to D. F. Easton, the British archaeologist who discovered it, on the basis of a minute analysis of the context of the find.[27] By this time the Hittite empire had already disintegrated (*c.*1175 BC). Naturally, the date of manufacture was considerably earlier. Still, the date of deposit in relation to the collapse of Hittite supremacy was very late. The idea that the seal was kept for seventy or eighty years as a piece of antique decoration in the citadel only to be thrown away one day is less probable than that it continued in use as a seal in Wilusa even after the collapse of the central administration in Ḫattusa.

This opens up a new perspective for the status of Wilusa after the collapse of the overlordship in Ḫattusa: it had long been known that, as Starke put it in 1997, 'At the beginning of the twelfth century, in the east and south the secundogenitures of Karkamis and Tarḫuntassa came into their inheritance as great kingdoms', and moreover that, 'in the west the most important Arzawan vassal state, Mirā, seems to have attained the status of great kingdom by the time of Suppiluliuma II [*c.*1200 BC]'.[28] Further textual studies led Starke to increased certainty in this matter: 'Mirā therefore attained the status of great kingdom towards the end of the thirteenth century, a status which sovereign Arzawa already possessed in practice at the beginning of the fourteenth century.'[29] It is known that these petty kingdoms (which now styled themselves great kingdoms) assured political and cultural continuity in Asia Minor, in part at least, as far as the eighth or seventh century BC. As has been shown, Wilusa had traditional relations with Sēḫa and Mirā, in particular. This is apparent especially in § 17 of the Alaksandu treaty and the passage from the Millawanda letter, quoted above. The seal may be an indication that Wilusa too, after the destruction of Troy VIIa (*c.*1200), sought at first to uphold its Hittite–Luwian cultural tradition in the late flowering of Troy VIIb (after 1200).[30]

The Opposing Side: 'Achaians' and 'Danaans'— Two More Names Rehabilitated

Whether or not we assume that Taruwisa/Tru(w)isa can be equated with Troy, the name of the *besieged city* in the *Iliad* is historical, since it has been proven that Wilusa and Wilios are one and the same. But we must then proceed to note that the names of the besiegers in the *Iliad* are no invention either. The besiegers came from the region known broadly to us as 'Greece'. (We shall return to the matter of the geographical variations of the territory of 'classical' Greece.)

What does Homer call these people? It will surprise nobody to learn that they are never called 'Greeks'. 'Greeks' (Griechen, Grecques, Greci, etc.) is a modern term, which derives from the Latin. When the people of Italy first encountered those of the Balkan peninsula, they came upon a tribe which called itself 'Graikoí', which the newcomers adopted as 'Graeci'. The same principle explains why the Germans are known to the French as 'Allemands': the first Germanic tribe they encountered was the Alemani. However, the besiegers collectively are also never called 'Héllēnes' by Homer, that is, by the name this race has used for almost three thousand years, corresponding to 'Hellás', the name of the country. Instead, in the *Iliad*, the besiegers have three different names: *Achaioí*, *Danaoí*, and *Argeíoi*. All three are mutually interchangeable and do not denote separate tribes but rather all the aggressors collectively.

This trio has always been a cause of puzzlement in Homeric studies. Why is there no all-encompassing term? And if a choice of three exists, for whatever reason, why precisely these three? In the area of settlement of the people we term 'Greek', there had been a great number of different tribes and clans ever since they moved into their new homeland in about 2000 BC. Why should these three names have been selected? Furthermore, as far as we can tell, by Homer's day at least two of them, 'Achaioí' and 'Danaoí', as general terms for the Greeks, did not exist at all. In fact, there had apparently been no general term for centuries. It is highly likely that none had ever existed, except in bardic poetry. In reality, by Homer's time the only terms were 'Ionian', 'Aeolian', and 'Dorian' for the large groups. The name 'Achaian', centuries later, giving Latin *Achaei*—Achaea had been a Roman province since 146 BC—came from the region of Thessaly known as 'Achaia' (possibly for the second time in Greek history).

Here too the key to an understanding can only be found in the historical reality. Just as in the case of the twin names Wilios and Troy there was no conceivable motive for inventing a name, so here in the case of the trinity Achaioí/Danaoí/Argeioi no rational motive can be offered to explain why at a particular moment a particular poet should have invented three names for the attacking army. What would his audience have made of it? Given the abundance of real and available possibilities, would they not have found such inventions strange? But if the trinity comes not from invention but from hallowed tradition, what was the origin of the tradition?

'ACHAI(W)IA' AND 'ACHIJAWA'

It is easiest to answer this question in the case of the first name, 'Achaioí'. In the Hittite documents, 'Aḫḫijawā' (now usually written 'Achijawa') occurred at an early date as the name of a country. Not only does this name bear an obvious phonetic resemblance to the 'Achaioí' found in the *Iliad* (and to the adjectival form 'Achaiís', which appears five times)—as with 'Ilios', it is to be expected that the 'w' will be lost in the Homeric form, so originally 'Achaiwoí', 'Achaiwís'. But this word also, considered geographically and politically, seems to point to the people we know as 'Greeks'. So were the Homeric 'Achai(w)oí' the same as the inhabitants of Hittite 'Aḫḫijawā'? This question was posed by Emil Forrer as early as

1924.[1] After that the problem was turned this way and that for some time. In 1932 the state of research into the question of this equation was exhaustively reviewed by Ferdinand Sommer.[2] His book, in which he disputed the equation, marked the beginning of a prolonged scholarly controversy.[3] Fortunately there is no need to rehearse it here, as it may now be regarded as concluded. Today the equation is queried by hardly anybody;[4] Hittite scholars[5] and archaeologists[6] see it as certain, Mycenaean specialists are in agreement with them,[7] and Hellenists are coming round to this view.[8] Thus Hawkins was able to say in 1998: 'The scholarly tide in favour of recognizing in Ahhiyawa reference to some Mycenaean centre of power has been running very strongly since the early 1980s though some notable figures continue to swim bravely against it.'[9] The significance of this recognition, however, now extends far beyond the mere fact of the equation of the two names, since the latter also provides information of documentary status on the relations between the Hittites and the Egyptians on the one hand and on the other the Greeks in the second millennium BC—information which is, of course, completely independent of Homer's *Iliad*. And again we see not only agreement, but reciprocal enlightenment.

This can be truly striking only when seen in the original Hittite texts. The clearest example is that letter sent by the Hittite vassal king Manabatarḫunta of Sēḫa some time after 1300 BC to the Hittite Great King Muwattalli II—a letter whose value we have been able to appreciate only since 1984, and which has already been of use in the matter of equating 'Ilios' with 'Wilusa' (see p. 83). This text, it will be remembered, tells of a certain Pijamaradu, who attacked Wilusa and then Lazba, and carried off craftsmen from Lazba to Millawa(n)da (Miletos). The sender, the king of Sēḫa, reports to the Hittite Great King that Pijamaradu has handed over the craftsmen to his son-in-law in Millawa(n)da, one Atpā, *the representative of the king of Aḫḫijawā*. The latter at first refused to return them to their rightful owner, then, following the intercession of the king of Mirā (we should bear in mind that the land of Mirā lay between the land of Seḫā and Millawanda, so was well suited to the role of intermediary), he handed back only those who belonged to the Great King himself, while refusing to return those who belonged to the sender.

To Pijamaradu, who appears here for the first time in the Hittite correspondence—as a bitter foe of the kings of Mirā and Seḫā—we, from our scientific standpoint, have every reason to be grateful, unlike the Hittite rulers of the day. His tireless efforts are the reason why we are finding out substantially more detail about Aḫḫijawā. Since 'for decades to come in the reign of Ḫattusili III [*c.*1265–1240 BC], he repeatedly stirred up unrest on the entire western coast of Asia Minor, from Lukkā to Wilusa',[10] he appears in several more documents from the imperial Hittite correspondence.

One of these is the so-called Tawagalawa letter, named after the prominent individual who figures in it.[11] This letter—alas, in large part destroyed—is addressed by Ḫattusili III to *the king of Aḫḫijawā* (whose name, regrettably, does not appear in that part of the text which has reached us). The Hittite Great King consistently addresses the king of Aḫḫijawā formally, using the style 'my brother'. The significance of this is that the king of Aḫḫijawā is shown here as being placed on the same level as the king of Egypt and the Hittite king himself.[12] For the Hittite crown, therefore, at least at the time the letter was written, Aḫḫijawā was a political and military force to be reckoned with. But there is more. In this long letter Ḫattusili III describes at length the hostile activities of Pijamaradu, directed against him and his vassal kings, and complains that Pijamaradu is being protected by Atpā in Millawa(n)da and escapes by ship whenever Ḫattusili tries to seize him. Finally he comes to the main point of his letter:

> Further, look here! [it is reported], that he is saying: 'I wish to *cross* over from here into the land of Māsa or the land of Karkija, but leave the prisoners, my wife, my children, and my household here!'
>
> According to this rumour, while he leaves his wife, his children, and his household in the land of my brother, your land is granting him protection! But he is causing constant trouble in *my* land! And every time I stand in his way he returns to *your* land! Are you, my brother, well disposed towards his behaviour?
>
> [If not] then, my brother, at least write to him as follows:
>
> 'Arise and go forth into the land of Ḫatti. Your master has set aside his quarrel with you! Otherwise come *into the land of Aḫḫijawā*, and wherever I choose to settle you, [there must you remain!] Arise [with your prisoners,] your wives and your children [and] settle in another place! As long as you live in enmity with the King of Ḫatti, exercise your hostilities from [some]

> other land! From *my* land shall you exercise *no* hostilities! If your heart lies in the land of Māsa or the land of Karkija, go there! The King of Ḫatti has persuaded me, in that matter of *Wilusa* (?), over which we quarrelled, and he and I have become friends. [. . .] a war would not be good for us.' [My italics, JL.]

Unfortunately it is not quite clear from the text whether the 'matter over which we quarrelled' was really a dispute over Wilusa, because the middle part of the name is missing.[13] But there has certainly been a dispute between the Hittite kings and the king of Aḫḫijawā, and a little further on we read: 'Now my brother has [written] to me [as follows]: [. . .] 'You have acted with hostility against me!' [*But at that time, my brother,*] I was young; if I [then] wrote [*something hurtful*] [it was] not [*intentional*] . . . '. For us what is most important in this document is that it offers an insight into an exchange of letters which had evidently gone on for some time between the kings of Ḫattusa and Aḫḫijawā, with the periods of cool relations and rapprochement that are usual in diplomacy ('You complain about our previous unfriendly attitude. You are right. I beg your forgiveness . . . '). We also see that good relations with Aḫḫijawā matter a great deal to the Hittite king. Lastly, it is plain that Aḫḫijawā lies outside the Hittite sphere of influence, for what we have before us is in today's terms nothing other than an extradition request to a sovereign state, with a further request that the wanted man be interned there. For a long time it was not quite clear where this foreign sovereign state was situated. Expressions like 'by ship' and 'crossing' suggested that Aḫḫijawā could not be in Asia Minor, but only 'overseas', most likely to the west of Asia Minor—as the wanted man had fled from Millawanda (Miletos) and could apparently travel quickly between Millawanda and his place of refuge—but this was not quite certain. Where exactly that country might be, if it was really 'overseas', remained open to speculation.

In 1997 for the first time two specialists—again independently of each other and on the basis of different material—came to the same conclusion as to whether Aḫḫijawā lay in Asia Minor, and concluded that it could *not* have been in Asia Minor. First Frank Starke showed, in a new analysis of the Pijamaradu case,[14] that this man was of royal blood.[15] (He was probably the grandson of Uḫḫazidi, the king of Arzawa who was driven out by Mursili II before 1300 BC and went into exile in Aḫḫijawā.) Starke also showed that Pijamaradu had no country of his own in Asia Minor and was therefore obliged to 'conduct all his operations from Aḫḫijawan territory', since, owing to a geopolitical configuration which may have come about not long before, there was no place available in Asia Minor. By his study of sources Starke also made clear that Pijamaradu, who wished to regain his grandfather's lost kingdom, was able to be an effective trouble-maker only because, as the Tawagalawa letter shows very clearly, he had the support of Aḫḫijawā and because he had an operational base in Millawa(n)da (Miletos), which at this time functioned as a 'bridgehead on the mainland of Asia Minor for the king of Aḫḫijawā'.

Also in 1997, on the basis of his successful reading of the Karabel A inscription (see pp. 88–9), J. D. Hawkins concluded that, first, the equation of Millawanda with Miletos was 'virtually certain', and, second, that

> the web of interlocking locations arising from this cannot but bear on the vexed question of the land of Ahhiyawa. Now it may be argued more strongly than ever both that there remains no place for this country on the Anatolian mainland, and that Ahhiyawa lying 'across the sea' impinges mainly on the Anatolian west coast, above all at Millawanda-Miletos.

From this Hawkins concluded, 'This therefore remits the problem of the character and extent of the land of Aḫḫijawā under its sometime Great King to the field of Aegean island or perhaps mainland Greek archaeology.'[16]

For Hittite studies the consequences of this are clear: Aḫḫijawā has finally been removed from the sphere of Anatolian studies. It is a Greek region outside Asia Minor, with bridgeheads—Miletos principal among them—on the coast of Asia Minor.

In 1995, in a rigorously systematic archaeological and historical process of elimination similar to Starke's work on Troy, Wolf-Dietrich Niemeier, independently of Starke and Hawkins, reached the conclusion that all previous proposals concerning the whereabouts of Aḫḫijawā could be ruled out except for the one which placed it on the Greek mainland, extending to the Aegean islands and certain points on the south-west coast of Asia Minor.[17] This has now received definite confirmation.

This means that Aḫḫijawā is now the rightful property of Hellenists.

For their part, Hellenists, who now at last have full clarity and a free hand, had long supposed that 'Achaioí' must have been 'the name that at least some of the early Greeks of the Bronze Age applied to themselves',[18] and that 'Achaiwia' must have meant an eastern belt of mainland Greece as well as part of the eastern island region as far as Rhodes.

In 1996, following numerous far-reaching preparatory works within the framework of a comprehensive survey of international relations in the second millennium BC,[19] the ancient historian Gustav Adolf Lehmann first asserted that 'the question of a theoretical historical, geographical, and political connection between *Aḫḫijavā* and the ethnonym *Achai(w)oi/*Achawyos*, much used by Homer for the besieging Greek army at Troy (like the toponym *Achai[w]ia*), [is] now answered mainly in the affirmative'.[20] After pointing out that this might be the same country that is mentioned in a war report from the Pharaoh Merneptah (*c*.1209–1208 BC) under the name of *Aqajwasa*, as a 'powerful enemy "country of the sea"', Lehmann thereupon placed the kingdom of *Achaiwia* primarily in central Greece (southern Thessaly and Lokris) and in the southern and south-eastern Aegean: on Rhodes, in the Dodecanese, and Cyprus and Crete (as shown in the map in the Bavarian school atlas of 1953—with the name *Reich der Ahhijava*).

Even today the last word has yet to be said on the affiliation of some of the regions named here, but the basic geographical outline will certainly be confirmed—primarily by further excavations, but also by new documents or documents which have newly become decipherable. Cause for optimism is provided, for example, by the fact that, while the location of the seat of the 'king of Aḫḫijawā' has not yet been positively identified,[21] some Linear B tablets recently found in Thebes indicate that Thebes, shown on this tablet as a large kingdom which included the island of Euboia and had a harbour in Aulis, could have been a hub, perhaps even *the* hub, of the empire.[22] This would at a stroke explain many obscure details in various areas, including the key position occupied by Boiotia in the so-called catalogue of ships in the *Iliad*—a 287-line comprehensive enumeration of the Achaian fleet assembled in the alliance against

Troy (see p. 219). (Thebes had long been the capital of Boiotia; the catalogue of ships also included the name of *Boiōtía* in ancient times.) It would also explain the fact, which has always been cause for wonder, that the Achaian alliance sailed on its punitive campaign against Troy from Aulis (opposite Euboia).

The reconstruction of the history of this kingdom provides further cause for optimism. We already know, on the one hand, that relations between Ḫattusa and Aḫḫijawā had been established long before the Pijamaradu affair,[23] and, on the other, that Ḫattusili III's diplomatic offer of reconciliation, which we could follow so closely in the Tawagalawa letter, did not achieve its objective. Some twenty years after this letter, in about 1220 BC, Ḫattusili's son Tudḫalija IV (*c.*1240–1215) concluded a treaty with one of his vassal kings, who happened to be his brother-in-law, King Šaušgamuwa of Amurru (northern Lebanon). This treaty obliged Amurru to impose a trade embargo on Assyria, which would at the same time terminate any Aḫḫijawan trade with Assyria. Aḫḫijawā had developed close trading relations with Assyria, and the trading routes ran across Amurru. However, by this time Ḫatti was at war with Assyria, and Tudḫalija IV was consistently implementing a tight trade blockade on Assyria:

> No merchant of yours [i.e. of the King of Amurru] may go into the land of Assyria, and you may admit no merchant of his [i.e. of the King of Assyria] into your land, and he may not travel across your land! [. . .] [Let] no ship [of the land of Aḫ]ḫijawā [go] to him [i.e. to the King of Assyria]!

The degree to which relations between Ḫatti and Aḫḫijawā had cooled may also be seen in the fact that in this treaty the phrase 'king of Aḫḫijawā', at first evidently included automatically in the 'Great King formulae' (of Ḫatti, Egypt, Babylon, Assyria, and Aḫḫijawā), was later crossed out on orders 'from above'.[24] We may recall Ḫattusili's sentence in the Tawagalawa letter: 'A war would not be good for us!' Even to us, although our insight comes only from fragments of the historical reality of the period, it becomes plain how far relations had deteriorated by the end of the thirteenth century BC between Ḫatti—and this means the entire sphere of Hittite power and influence in Asia Minor—and Aḫḫijawā. First there was the encroachment into the Ḫatti empire from Miletos, shown when Pijamaradu's activities were 'condoned'. This was followed by the irritation caused to Ḫatti by the growth in trade with its great-power rival and military adversary Assyria across the Hittite vassal region of Amurru. It has been supposed correctly that the real motive for these incursions into Hittite territory lay in a marked increase in power and Aḫḫijawā's rising expansionist tendencies in the latter half of the thirteenth century BC: 'As a constant adversary of Ḫatti,... Aḫḫijawā may have attained the summit of its power in about 1200 BC and later... (that is, only in the late Mycenaean post-palatial period).'[25] This may provide us with the most natural explanation of the prominence in the *Iliad* of the name 'Achaioí' for the attacking force, as will become even clearer.

Against this detailed background, it is at any rate certain that Homer's appellation for the besiegers, 'Achaioí', is historical. The regions which research can now confidently demonstrate to be attributed to the land of Aḫḫijawā/Achai(w)ia play a significant role in the *Iliad*: Achilles, the hero of the story, comes from southern Thessaly (Achaia Phthiotis), and, in the description of his home region, the ethnic groups are called, from smallest to largest, 'Myrmidons', 'Hellenes'—because they inhabit the land of 'Hellás' (2. 684)—and 'Achaioí'.[26] From Lokris comes Aias the Lesser, from Crete Idomeneus and Mēriones (whose name has venerable connections: see p. 262), from Rhodes comes Tlepolemos, and so on. Opportunities arise here to form historical connections, which will be followed up.

'DANAOÍ' AND 'DANAJA'

The background to the second name applied to the attacking forces, 'Danaoí', cannot so far be illuminated in the same detail as 'Achaioí'. (The name survives to this day in the German expression 'jemandem ein Danaergeschenk machen'—'to send somebody a Greek gift', cf. English 'beware of Greeks bearing gifts'). Sources other than Homer are explicit enough, however, for us to consider this name historical too.

While in the case of *Achaioí* the Hittite epigraphic records provide the essential material, for *Danaoí* the Egyptian epigraphic records fill this role. This will come as no surprise to anybody who is familiar with the ancient tradition of Greek legends about Danaos, Danaë, and the Danaids. At their core lies the connection between the Greek land of Argos (later the Argolid) in the Peloponnese and Egypt. Danaos and Aegyptos, who were twins, were supposedly either born in Argos, as the sons of Io, the daughter of the river god Inachoa—in this version Danaos banished his brother Aegyptos to the land on the Nile, to which he gave his name (!)—or they were Egyptians, sons of Belos (Baal) and a daughter of the river god Nil (Neilos). In the latter case the brothers quarrelled over the right to rule, and Danaos fled with his fifty daughters (the Danaids) to Argos, where he apparently received his kingship. (According to the myth, his great-great-granddaughter Danaë was sought by Zeus, who in Argos transformed himself into a shower of golden rain.)

Only twenty years ago no classical scholar would have ventured to suppose that this legend might be the reflex of an ancient historical connection between Argos and Egypt. Thus, for example, in the widely distributed *Lexikon der Alten Welt* (1965), under 'Danaer', there is no mention of any relation to the eponymous mythical Danaos, and Homer's Danaans are described as 'a group of the Achaians . . . a tribe or, collectively, the warrior nobility'. In the equally widely distributed dictionary of the ancient world known as *Der Kleine Pauly* (1979), we read under 'Danaoi' that 'this is apparently the name of a lost Peloponnesian (originally Thessalian?) Greek tribe'. Almost twenty years later the state of knowledge had not advanced: in *The Oxford Classical Dictionary* (1996), under 'Danaus and the Danaids' (there is no entry for Danaans), we find an entry saying that 'Danaus' is 'the eponym of the Danaans (*Δαναοί*), a word of unknown origin used commonly to mean the Greeks'. Only in *Der Neue Pauly* (Volume 3, 1997), under the headword 'Danaer', does the user find a pointer (suggested by this writer) to the information set forth below, which has been available for over thirty years.

Dictionary 'information' of the kind shown above is irritating, not only because it reflects a period in the study of antiquity in which the mythic tradition as a whole, and not only that of the Greeks, was habitually confused with fairy-tales, but also, and above all, because it makes clear the long-standing self-isolation of the profession. To the cost of the discipline, this made it harder to look over the fence at the research landscape in ancient history (including oriental studies, Egyptology, and Anatolian studies), and it hampered the continuous updating of the knowledge base. The present interlinking of all accessible knowledge of the history of the ancient world is now yielding other, pragmatic results, which lend new impetus to research.

As far back as 1966, the Egyptologist Elmas Edel published a monumental Egyptian inscription of crucial importance to us,[27] found in the funerary temple of the Pharaoh Amenophis III (*c.*1390–1352 BC), the so-called necropolis of Egyptian Thebes, on the base of a statue. The inscription belongs to a series of five such inscriptions which list the important regions and towns of the parts of the world then known to the Egyptians and of political significance to them. It could be thought of as a kind of political *descriptio orbis*. The inscription which concerns us here, (E_N), enumerates the politically important regions and towns in northern Egypt. First, in the right half of the front of the plinth, the names of the lands of *Kafta* (*kftw*)[28] and *Danaja/Tanaja* (*tnjw*) are placed side by side 'as "kingdoms" of equal standing' (that is, under geopolitical headings showing equal status).[29] The first of these, *Kafta*, corresponds to the biblical *Kaphthor*, which in the Old Testament denotes the homeland of the 'Kherethites and Pelethites' (2 Samuel 15: 18), and the Ugaritic *Kaptara*, for example. Objectively, and given the phonetic similarity, this can only mean Crete, since under this heading only Cretan locations are listed. The second name, Danaja, is, as Gustav Adolf Lehmann (following some others)[30] asserted in 1985, 'the Egyptian reflex of the apparently native [that is, Greek] form "Tanaja". *Danaja, as opposed to "Kafta"-Crete, must be identified with the ethnonym *Danaoí* as a general term at least for the Peloponnese, including the island of Kythera'.[31]

Possible doubts as to the accuracy of these equations are banished as soon as one reads the thirteen surviving place-names of the original fifteen given on the left side of the front face of the plinth and the left of the side face, arranged under the headings *Kafta* and *Danaja*. Under *Kafta* these are: (1) *amniša*, the port of Amnisos, on Knossos, (2) *bajašta*, or Phaistos, (3) *kutunaja*, or Kydonia, (4) *kunuša*, or Knossos, and (5) *r/likata*, or Lyktos. Under Danaja appear (1) *mukanu/mukana*, or Mukania, in its later form *Mykēnē*, (2) *deqajis*, or *Thegwais*, later *Thebais* (the present region of Thebes), (3) *misane*, or Messana, later *Messēnē* (as it remains today), (4) *nuplija*, or Nauplion (as today), (5) *kutira*, the island of Kythera (as it is still known), which lies just off the Peloponnese, (6) *waleja/weleja*, Waleja, which later, with the familiar loss of 'w', became *Elis* (as it still is); one more name in this list, which the stonemason had tried to efface and replace with *amniša* (the first name in the first list), but which remains easily legible, is (7) *amukla*, or Amyklai, the old capital of Lakonia, or Sparta. In these equations it should be noted that the Greek vowel represented in transcription by 'y' was pronounced 'u' in the Greek of the period.

The structure of both lists is still less than fully understood; in 1996 a new study was foreshadowed. For the moment, at least the principle of the structure is clear: each list begins with a capital—Amnisos (Knossos) in the first, Mycenae in the second.[32] Then follow the most important regions and/or towns of the country in question—whether these were merely geographically or also politically dependent, that is, ruled from the capital, is not yet certain. (In the case of Thebes, which follows immediately after Mycenae, clarification would be particularly valuable; the newly discovered Linear B tablets in Thebes show that in the late Bronze Age Thebes was a great kingdom which included Euboia: see pp. 240f.). It is clear, however, that in List 2 (Danaja), following the list of capitals or central regions—that is, of what was probably Amyklai, and certainly Mycenae, Thebes, and Messenia—Nauplion, Kythera, and Elis describe a semicircle round the Peloponnese.

For Egypt between 1400 and 1350 BC, the Greek peninsula later known to its inhabitants as 'the Peloponnese' (island of Pelops), evidently with Boiotia and its capital Thebes across the Bay of Corinth, was the 'land of Danaja'. Knowledge of this land reached Egypt, as Peter W. Haider has plausibly demonstrated,[33] through Egyptian emissaries and/or traders. Haider also (following Helck)[34] pointed out the remains of a door-post revetment of blue-green faïence, found in Mycenae, displaying on both sides the throne name and birth-name of Amenophis III. In Haider's view, this is an imported 'Egyptian room', of unknown purpose, in the citadel of Mycenae in the fourteenth century BC. Haider's own suggestions of its purpose—Egyptian 'consulate', Egyptian medical practice, bed-chamber of an Egyptian—compete with the well-argued case made by other Egyptologists, that the fragments of six to nine faïence plaques found scattered in Mycenae could be dedications in a temple. Faïence objects bearing the name of Amenophis III or his queen Teje have been found at a total of six sites in the Aegean, including four which figure in the list of towns: Knossos, Phaistos, Kydonia, and Mycenae.[35]

The name 'Danaja' and the relations between the dynasties of Danaja and Egypt are much older, however, reaching back at least to the fifteenth century BC. Lehmann (again following others) has repeatedly pointed to an Egyptian document which in this context is as valuable as evidence as it is apparently unknown among classical scholars:

> The considerable importance and range of operation of the *Danajan kingdom in the fifteenth century BC is evidenced by the (casual) entry in the annals of Tuthmosis III (42nd year of reign, *c.* 1437 BC; 16th Syrian campaign: [IV 733. 3–4]), according to which the prince of *Danaja sent the pharaoh on the Levantine coast an expensive drinking set in gratitude ('a silver flagon in Kafta-work [that is, in Cretan-Minoan style!], with four copper beakers with silver handles, weighing altogether 56 dbn 3 kite [more than 5 kg.]'!).[36]

Haider had drawn attention to this entry in 1988, and deduced from it, in conjunction with the list of names, 'This means that there is no longer any need to doubt that the Egyptians were aware of the existence of much of the Peloponnese from at least 1450 BC.'[37] In 1991 Lehmann went one step further and concluded from this entry, surely correctly, that with this 'expensive gift . . . the prince of Danaja, in whom we may now see the ruler of the early Greek palace-fortress of Mykenai, was obviously attending deliberately to diplomatic relations with the victorious Pharaonic power which then controlled the whole of the Levantine coast (and northern Syria as far as the Euphrates)'.[38] This is in accord with an earlier observation made by Lehmann:[39] in Amenophis III's list of place-names the Cretan names have a non-Greek phonetic form, whereas the names from Danaja are in the familiar Greek form. These two observations taken together point to the conclusion that, first, relations between Egypt and Crete must be older, and at least firmer than those between Egypt and Danaja; and, second, that relations between Egypt and Danaja were deepening at the time when the people of Danaja, that is, the Myceneans, occupied Knossos in Crete (*c.*1450 BC).

The indications adduced and many others—not set forth here—allow us to accept as certain, as Lehmann emphasized in 1991,[40] first, that in the Peloponnese at least in the fifteenth and fourteenth centuries BC an extensive Danajan empire existed, with Mycenae as its capital. The princes of Mycenae appear, in this period at least, to have assumed a leading political position in the world of the then Greek palace centres. Secondly, it is certain that the Homeric Danaoí, like the rest of the Greek tradition of Danaos/Danaids/Danaë, had their origin in this Danajan empire, the centre of which was the plain of Argos (later the Argolid).

CONCLUSIONS

For the triad of names *Achaioí/Danaoí/Argeioi* in Homer, the following explanation now suggests itself:

1. The name *Argeioi* belongs in what is universally the most frequently encountered class of toponym, the topographically descriptive type. The word *argos* originally meant 'flat land, plain'; *Argos* as a name for a region or town therefore occurs so often in Greek that affixes are needed to distinguish similar names (compare German toponyms containing the components 'stein' and 'burg', found in up to twenty names in Germany alone). The central area of the Peloponnese which bore the name of Argos grew to be the 'plain' of greatest political significance in the southern Balkan peninsula in the first half of the second millennium BC. In view of the importance of this centre, the name of the inhabitants of this particular Argos was generalized before any others to denote the Greek-speaking people.

For Greek bardic poetry, which—as we shall see in more detail—was already practised in essentially the same form in the centres of Greek culture as it was several centuries later in Homer's day, this meant that the name *Argeioi* was adopted as the first of the three names to provide a substitute collective term for the Greek-speaking peoples.

2. As the Egyptian sources tell us, in 1500 BC a tribe or noble family called *Danaoí*, with its family seat in the same Argos (and with a fortress in Mycenae), rose to political dominance in the Peloponnese. *Danaoí* then became a new collective term, sharing equal status with the older *Argeioi*. Bardic poetry adopted it as a second term.

3. From the Hittite documentation it may be concluded that in the thirteenth century BC a Greek tribe named the *Achaioí*, who dominated the eastern belt of mainland Greece and the islands of the eastern Aegean, rose to the status of an internationally recognized power. It was logical that in bardic poetry the name of this group should join the previous two as a third collective term for the Greek-speaking people.

According to this hypothesis, the three names owe their penetration into Greek bardic poetry to a series of actual historical and political processes. However, their coexistence within this poetry—a phenomenon which can hardly be explained by logic alone, since any member of an ethnic group logically requires only one name for that group—then appears to be a natural consequence of their differing metric structure. This is a matter which we have not yet treated, as questions relevant to it have not yet arisen. We shall not need to delve deeply into the metrical principles of Greek bardic poetry, that is, into the technical matters of its prosody, until another point in our argument. But in order to make intelligible to non-specialists the hypothesis presented here, which relies on the versification of this poetry, we must anticipate matters somewhat and mention at least the relevant essential facts.

Greek bardic poetry takes the verse form of the hexameter, or six-foot line, exclusively. The hexameter, which was imitated first by the Romans and then in all related poetic cultures, consists of six units (measures, or feet), each of one long syllable and two short syllables; only in the last measure may one long syllable and either another long syllable or a short syllable occur, represented by the symbol 'x'. The pattern is therefore:

1 2 3 4 5 6
— ◡ ◡ — ◡ ◡ — ◡ ◡ — ◡ ◡ — ◡ ◡ — x

In each of the five 'normal' measures preceding the last, the two short syllables may be replaced by one long syllable (thus— — instead of—◡◡), producing the possible variant:

1 2 3 4 5 6
— — — — — — — — — — — x

The two variants may be mingled, producing a form such as this, for example:

1 2 3 4 5 6
— — — ◡ ◡ — — — ◡ ◡ — ◡ ◡ — x

An important rule of the Greek hexameter, which needs to be known in order to understand what follows, stipulates further that in building a line, for reasons of euphony, a word ending in a vowel should never be followed by a word beginning with a vowel. A so-called hiatus, that is, the non-closure of the articulatory organs between two words, is avoided.

Armed with this foreknowledge, we may now return to the three names used by Homer for the besiegers: their metrical structure differs: (1) Argeioi: — — —; (2) Danaoi: ◡ ◡ —; (3) Achaioi: ◡ — —. They also differ in their initial sounds. The words Argeioi and Achaioi begin with a vowel, Danaoi with a consonant. These differences mean that their parallel existence is exceptionally convenient for hexameter verse. They provide the poet with alternative possibilities that can only be welcome: in his verse, in almost any position in a line, he could always, at the shortest notice, apply the general appellation he needed for the besiegers in a poem dealing with the two parties (Greeks and Trojans), without having to reflect on this at length, and could select the name best suited metrically to the desired position in a line. All three names were thus retained as synonymous metrical variants. All denoted the same thing: the Greeks. The same principle operated here as in the case of the twin names (W)Ilios/Troiē.

So much for the hypothesis. (The purely metrical component is already of venerable age: it was explored by a Bonn scholar,

Heinrich Düntzer, in 1864.)[41] It is clear that the currently available material derived from sources extrinsic to Homer is still scant, and has gaps in it. The details of the hypothesis therefore still have to be filled in and consolidated. It is unlikely, however, that it completely misrepresents the actual processes. We may, then, sum up as follows: Homer's names for the besiegers, as for the besieged, do not spring from the poet's imagination, but reflect the real historical situation.

The Result: Homer's Backdrop is Historical

If one takes an overall view of the recent advances in research in various areas, which we have discussed from various angles, we can discern a dovetailing tendency in this research: from the east (Anatolia), west (Greece), and south (Egypt) the pieces move together and we can perceive a broader picture of the distribution of power in the second half of the second millennium BC in the Mediterranean area, in which three great centres of power and influence interact and counteract one another as they seek to maintain the balance. The power centres are the kingdom of the Hittites, the empire of the pharaohs in Egypt, and the kingdom of the Achaians in part of mainland Greece and the Aegean islands.

This picture disintegrates shortly after 1200 BC with the collapse of the Hittite empire. Homer lived in the second half of the eighth century BC, that is to say, about 450 years after the era when that picture was a reality. Nevertheless his *Iliad* contains elements which, as we have seen, can only derive from the time of that picture: not only have both names of the locale, Ilios and Troy, shown themselves to be historical in the period between about 1500 and 1200 BC, but so have the names of the besieging forces in Homer's story. It is the latter that is decisive, since the names of the locale, Ilios and Troy, so called by the Greeks between 1500 and 1200 BC, could have survived in the everyday speech of the local population for long afterwards, even after the site had been abandoned, in about 950 BC, according to Korfmann. Speaking purely theoretically, it is possible that a Greek bard could have learned these names even in the eighth century simply by visiting the site, always assuming that the site was still so called after being uninhabited for a considerable time (which is possible with place-names).

The position is different with the collective terms for the besiegers, *Achaioí* and *Danaoí*: given all that we know, these names could not have been in active use as general designations for Greek-speaking people in the eighth century BC. The Greeks no longer called themselves by these names; nor did anybody else call them this. In the eighth century there was simply no general term used by them or of them. These names must therefore have been somehow passed down from the time when they were in use to the time when Homer applied them as collective terms in his *Iliad*. It is precisely the question of 'somehow' that concerns us. How could a Greek bard of the eighth century BC have come into possession of knowledge of an era which by his lifetime lay some 450 years in the past? This question will comprise the second part of our search for solutions. For the moment we shall simply assert that Homer did possess this knowledge in the eighth century.

We may now state our second main result: for the first time in the history of Trojan studies, on the basis of recent research outside the Greek area, Homer's *Iliad* has achieved the status of source material. What are the consequences of this?

1. The excavations at Hisarlık can no longer be suspected of representing the pursuit of a phantom conceived in the imagination of a poet. The hill and its environs represented a power of supra-regional significance, at least in the second half of the second millennium BC. For as long as our civilization retains any interest in the knowledge of its origins, the study of the history of Troy is no less justified than that of, say, Mycenae, Tiryns, Pylos, Knossos, Luxor, Alexandria, and other centres of ancient culture. Owing to the exposed position of the city, on the dividing line between two continents (Europe and Asia) and two seas (the Mediterranean and Black Seas), the investigation of its erstwhile role acquires even greater importance.

2. The former exclusivity of the coupling of 'Troy' and 'Homer' has come to an end. The study of Troy is now no longer dependent on Homer. The eastward-pointing signals which have long existed, towards Anatolia under Hittite rule and before it, may now be taken up with renewed vigour. Disciplines such as Anatolian and Hittite studies will now assume a stake in the formerly exclusive claim of classical historians to the city. Troy will thus resume its original

historical role as a meeting point of peoples, at least in historical scholarship—as a point where different research disciplines intersect.

3. Nevertheless, now that its status as a source to be taken seriously is assured, Homer's *Iliad* with its almost 16,000 lines may become a welcome provider of supplementary information. This is because the Hittite, Egyptian, and perhaps other texts evaluated so far, yet to be evaluated, and yet to be found, are documents of central political administrations, concerned with large-scale structures in space and time. That is, they are concerned with dimensions which are much larger than the individual geographical unit, country, or town and exceed the viewpoint of a single *Iliad*, and can deal with this unit only from a bird's-eye view and only occasionally, when the need arises. Homer's *Iliad*, to be sure, can only illuminate the city it deals with from an infinitely smaller viewpoint, but may on the other hand, owing to the wealth of detail in it, transmit information which documents of state can never achieve. The *Iliad* should now at least be read with an eye to the changed premisses—with renewed impetus, but with a change of methodological approach.

One consideration must be seen as decisive for this change of approach: however much we may rejoice at having a new source for the history of Troy, we must never lose our sense of proportion. If adduced for information, Homer's *Iliad* can never be more than a marginal secondary source on the *political* status of Troy in the Mediterranean balance of power in the second millennium BC, since Troy, in all its two-thousand-year history, was surely subjected to more than one attack, by more than one adversary. For proof of this one needs only to consider the fortifications, which are increasingly strongly built from one settlement level to the next. But we also have written evidence, even documentary evidence. The Alaksandu treaty alone (§ 6) provides a historical record of several military conflicts, including a war with Wilusa's great eastern neighbour Māsa (later Phrygia), in which the Hittite Great King himself came to the aid of Wilusa. Events such as these, recorded in the sequence of construction levels as '*frequent* wars over Troy',[1] may have been extremely important for the participants at the time, but in the broader perspective of a general history of Troy each of these events could appear only as one event among many, and a report on that single event, whoever might have provided it, would be only one source among many. An Achaian war against Troy, if it really occurred, would be no exception here and any reflection of it in Greek literature would in this respect have only the status of a secondary source.

But not all secondary sources are the same. If the memory of a Greek assault on Troy really was preserved through the centuries and in the end flowed into the *Iliad*, this particular secondary source would have special status among all imaginable secondary sources for preserving the memory not of just one of many Trojan wars, but of the Trojan War which sealed the fate of the city. In view of the absence of any other comparable picture, the preservation of such a historical memory would represent an extraordinary piece of good fortune. It is now up to us to make the most of this good fortune: if it should be shown that the *Iliad* has preserved historical information from the second millennium BC, in addition to the essential facts of the locale and the central characters, that is, on the basic geographical and ethnographic framework, then Homer's *Iliad*—its secondary status notwithstanding—would be of no small importance for the reconstruction of at least one brief transitional phase in the history of Troy.

PART II

Homer

The Basic Facts

In the first part of this book, Homer was our constant companion. He was often spoken of as if readers already knew everything they needed to know about him and his poem. The present writer has been conscious that this cannot be the case for all those who are interested in Troy. However, anticipatory leaps in the story could not be avoided, since in the first part attention was directed primarily towards Troy, while Homer's role was that of a backdrop and point of reference. This meant that every time he entered the picture it was necessary to hope that for the moment the limited information in the Introduction about Homer and the *Iliad* would suffice. But in order to understand the problems now presented, after familiarization with the present state of research into Troy, the information about Homer in the Introduction is not sufficient.

The case of Homer is different from the case of Troy. Many people outside the fraternity of ancient historians and outside the circle of 'friends of the classics' already have some knowledge of Troy. In recent years there has been something of a boom in Trojan studies: innumerable press reports and television and radio programmes have dealt with it, many popular histories and novels have come onto the market, and in 1998 Troy was even able to provide the subject of a cover story in *Der Spiegel*. The American *National Geographic* was not slow to follow: in its German edition of December 1999 it published a lavishly illustrated and well researched article on Troy and Schliemann, occupying more than thirty pages. On 17 February 2000 Germany was brought to the highest pitch so far of 'Troy fever': on that day even the newspaper *Das Bild* offered its readers a large-scale reconstruction of Troy with a report on the results of the latest excavations. For the contemporary newspaper-reader, it was and is quite impossible to avoid Troy.

Homer, on the other hand, receives less publicity. To many people today his name has little meaning.[1] However, the fascination exerted by Troy would lack depth without the inclusion of Homer in the picture. It is surely no accident that after lectures on the subject of Troy, in which Homer is given a role, this single question looms large: 'What has Troy actually got to do with Homer?' The question demands an answer.

Troy has a great deal to do with Homer. How much can only emerge clearly when Homer, the second partner in the duo 'Troy and Homer', is 'reconstructed' before the eyes of the reader with the same care as the first. Of course this reconstruction of a parallel structure entitled 'Homer' means that the reader must be prepared for another major effort. The reward, however, once the end is reached, will be a state that might be described as 'illumination', replacing a state of disorderly gloom. One can promise no more, as the aims of science are limited to this.

To the Greeks, Homer is their first and greatest poet. Why the first? This can be seen by a glance at Greek history.

After the Greeks moved into their present home in the southern Balkan peninsula and adjacent islands from the north—their previous homeland remains unknown—in about 2000 BC, in the space of one thousand years they experienced an unprecedented cultural upsurge, followed by a disastrous decline.

The upsurge: in the second millennium BC the immigrants developed a homogeneous form of society with a high economic and cultural level over the greater part of their area of settlement. We term this the 'centralized palace culture'. In various areas particularly favoured by their geographical and economic conditions, the ruling stratum, the nobility, built large fortress complexes, which served as centres of government and administration. In modern times we might call these 'regional capitals'. The centres were autonomous, but connected one to another by family relations within the nobility. They communicated with one another by land and water, without permitting a hegemony to emerge. They traded not only among themselves, but also with the whole of the wider Mediterranean world, above all with Crete, which had its own culture, and with Egypt and the east. As modern excavations have shown, their prosperity and power increased steadily over a long period, leading to several successive stages of expansion and development, and naturally also of growth in the military power of the palaces. From the middle of that millennium and for an extended period one of these centres appears to have outstripped all the others: Mycenae in the Peloponnese, whose remains do not fail to impress any tourist in Greece. Compared with Mycenae, centres like Pylos, Ephyra (now Corinth), Sparta, Thebes, Orchomenos, and even Athens, which shot to prominence so rapidly, fall some way behind, at least for a certain period of time. Modern Hellenistic studies have learned their lesson from this: since Heinrich Schliemann's first excavations in Mycenae in 1874 and the years that followed, this first period of high culture in Greece has been known as 'Mycenaean' culture. It is important to understand that 'Mycenaean' does not include anything non-Greek, pre-Greek, or extrinsic to Greece. It means nothing other than the Greek culture of the second millennium BC, more particularly in its latter half.

In this second half of the second millennium, the centres began to expand. The most striking example of this outward growth, which was directed especially towards the southern and eastern Mediterranean, is the conquest of the main palace of Crete, Knōssós, in the fifteenth century BC. Such an enterprise was possible only with a powerful fleet, as the kingdom of Crete, which we call 'Minoan' after Minos, its legendary founder, held command of the seas in the Mediterranean at this period. It has not yet been explained in detail how this Greek move against Crete was effected, in particular, whether it was a single act by only one of the Greek palaces, or whether it was a common enterprise by several palaces, possibly under Mycenaean command. The only thing known for sure is that the breaking of Cretan dominance in the Mediterranean and the assumption of the Cretan inheritance meant for the Mycenaean Greeks the beginning of a new stage in their wealth, power, and prestige in the Mediterranean. The king of Mycenae could now deal as an equal with the king of Egypt, and later, as we have seen, the king of Achaia/Achijawa shared the same status as the Assyrian and Hittite kings. The overall increase in power also had important consequences for Mycenaean culture. Cretan, Egyptian, and eastern cultural influences, which of course had been present before, now became substantially stronger. As modern excavations have shown, this manifests itself in Mycenaean architecture, painting, and plastic arts, and in technology, as well as in everyday life, into which an insight is afforded by many remains.

Here writing plays an important part. To the best of our knowledge, before the conquest of Knossos the Mycenaean Greeks had no writing system of their own; their culture lacked literacy. They acquired this cultural asset by conquest: they adopted from the Cretans, who did not speak Greek, the syllabic script in use there, the so-called Linear A, which to this day remains undeciphered, and used it to write their own language, Greek. We call the Mycenaean form of this script, which was only deciphered in 1952, and to which we shall return, Linear B. During excavations in Greece, thousands of roughly shaped clay tablets have come to light showing writing in Linear B. But the expectations once attached to the reading of these, which is now possible, have not been met. The tablets have turned out to hold essentially what we would record in a card index: long lists of items and individuals, inventories, import and export catalogues, land registers, and the like. They bear witness to a singular pleasure in administrative efficiency. They help us towards a fuller understanding of the economic and social system of this first Greek high culture. But that is unfortunately all. 'Unfortunately' because lovers of literature had hoped for something literary, poetry perhaps, religious texts, prose . . . What emerged was none of this. There are plenty of reasons why this should be so, including the extremely complex writing system with approximately ninety different characters, the number and graphic complexity of which certainly rendered the rapid recording of linguistically sophisticated material difficult (see Fig. 19, p. 158). This of course is a separate matter, which we will not discuss here. What is of central importance to us is only this: in all probability, in this earliest period of Greek high culture, no written Greek literature which might have been transmitted at least in fragments down the centuries ever existed.

This does not, however, mean that there was no verbal artistry. Given the high level of development of all the other arts, it would be strange if there had been none. Until about twenty years ago, the existence of poetry in Mycenae and other centres could only be supposed. Since then, however, it has been proven. We now know that it was the art of oral literature. It did not depend on writing because its mode of being for centuries, from time immemorial, lay in an oral tradition. It was practised by artists who called themselves 'singers' (*aoidoí*, aoides). How these singers operated in practice, what their products looked like, what subjects they dealt with, and where they performed—all this will be explored later. At this point it is sufficient to stress that, according to the most recent research, their form of verbal artistry was the precursor of that which emerged centuries later in the form of Homer.

To many readers this assertion—and the very idea of verbal art-forms lasting for centuries—may seem dubious. Yet such art-forms of very long duration are not uncommon. German rhymed verse with 'pure' rhyme, for example, has existed for over 800 years, since the twelfth century, when Heinrich von Veldeke first created it. The Greek poetic genre of the epic in hexameter, that is, the oral improvisation of stories in poetic lines each consisting of six dactyls (— ⏑ ⏑), was every bit as long-lived, as we shall see. The significance of this is plain: Homer did not invent the genre. It is far more likely that he adopted it. He was a link in a chain which began centuries earlier and reached down to his time. For many reasons, this had long been supposed, but the proof of it was lacking, and the sceptics were therefore in the majority. Lately, however, compelling arguments have come to hand, which oblige the sceptics to reconsider. This material is so new that it is not yet generally disseminated even among specialists in Hellenistic studies. It will therefore be presented in detail.

First, however, we must return to Greek history. The protracted rise of Mycenaean culture came to an abrupt end. In the decades before and especially after 1200 BC there came an invasion of alien peoples from the north. The reason for this lay in the attractiveness of the wealthy region which had taken shape in southern Europe and the eastern Mediterranean (Asia Minor, the Levant, and Egypt). The composition of the attacking hordes and the exact progress of the invasion remain unclear. It may have had to do with a migratory irruption, a phenomenon well known from history. Intensive work to clarify this is now under way in detailed research projects on a world-wide scale and a long series of interdisciplinary conferences.

What is already clear may be summarized in one sentence: the invasion took place in waves and in several separate streams, both by land and sea, and in Greece and Asia Minor, including the Hittite empire, it led to the fall of the highly developed cultures, either directly by storming and destroying their centres, or indirectly by causing trading blockades, the collapse of administration, internal unrest, rebellion, and other structural breakdowns. The complete collapse of the Mediterranean cultures was prevented only by successful Egyptian defensive measures. In the borderlands between the Levant and Egypt the assault came to a halt.

For Greece and its highly developed culture, however, the consequences were devastating. The destruction of the palaces meant that the main organizational nerve centres were shut down. Since the machinery of administration and management was based on writing, that is, on written records of population numbers, livestock, and material possessions, the distribution of property, leadership hierarchies, taxation and liability, and so forth, the burning of the palaces and with them the archives was tantamount to the destruction of the entire system. (The fires had the unplanned side-effect of baking the clay tablets and thus preserving them in their original state, making reconstruction possible.) Many from the ruling stratum, or that part of it which survived the defensive battles, fled to remote regions and the islands, especially Cyprus. The ordinary people who stayed behind, left to their own devices, were compelled to take selective measures to ensure their own welfare—measures which helped to establish brand new structures. All in all a social and cultural regression set in, which led to a return to primitive conditions in many regions, especially of the mainland—in places even to a nomadic mode of life. These conditions favoured penetration by immigrant outsiders, but also by closely related but culturally backward people from the north, especially into the Peloponnese, which, as a once flourishing area for the whole of the Mycenaean culture, was particularly hard hit and, being reduced to rubble, could offer least resistance. As part of this penetration, the Greek tribe whom we know by the name of 'Dorians' entered the Peloponnese. This tribe had had no part in the cultural upsurge of their relatives, the Ionians and to some extent the Aeolians, whose territory lay further south.

This led to internal shifts in the areas of Greek settlement, this time, however, with positive results: these movements brought about an evasive eastward migration by the Aeolians and Ionians to the eastern Aegean islands such as Lesbos, Khios, and Samos, and—one jump further—to the western seaboard of Asia Minor. This movement, known as the Aeolian and Ionian migration, began in the north, probably at an early date, around 1100 or 1050 BC, and continued southward until about 950 BC. In the course of this movement, the details of which are now the subject of an intensive study, on the eastern Aegean coast there arose an eastern Greek colonial area, which, after the Dorians had joined the process in the far south, stretched from Lesbos and the adjacent Troad in the north to Rhodes and the mainland areas facing it in the south. The newcomers naturally brought with them their way of life and cultural traditions, and practised these—as colonists do—with particular zeal. This includes the poetic genre of which we spoke earlier, aoidean poetry. For our context, the essential fact to note is that the genre in which the story of (W)Ilios, the Achaians, and the Danaans is told did not originate in the Greek area of settlement in Asia Minor but on the Greek mainland, and that it was transported by the settlers, as part of their cultural heritage, to the new Greek settlements in western Asia Minor. We shall return later to the details of this process.

The reconfiguring of the Greek situation after the shock of the collapse clearly took some time, both in the homeland and the colonial areas to the east. (Cyprus is a special case, which we cannot go into here.) In any event, our present state of knowledge indicates a clear and general, not merely sporadic revival of Greek activity in the Mediterranean area from about 800 BC. The time between the catastrophic collapse and the emergence of a new, pan-Hellenic momentum therefore occupies some 350 to 400 years. The historical processes within the Greek-speaking areas during this period lay shrouded in deep darkness for so long that it was usual to speak of 'the Dark Age' of Greece. This term is at least a hundred years old.[2] Since then, however, research has provided so many indications that even in parts of mainland Greece life went on at a fairly high cultural level that an article title like 'The Dark Age Illuminated' now seems an understatement.[3]

In relation to the new colonies in the east, however, the term 'Dark Age', with its associations of poverty and insignificance, seems utterly misleading. As early as 1989 it was possible to state: 'The towns which the colonists established or re-established (Ephesos, Miletos, Klazomenai, Erythrai, Myus, Priene etc., with the settlements on the islands of Samos and Khios) soon became the richest in Greece.'[4] The results of excavations conducted since then have confirmed this. If we bear in mind the breadth and fertility of the alluvial lowlands of what is now the Turkish Aegean seaboard, there is nothing surprising about this. The revival of Greece from the eighth century BC, which we call the Greek eighth-century renaissance, had its beginnings in this eastern colonial region. It was marked by a general social leap forward based on a coming together of technical and structural innovations of all kinds. These included the adoption of an alphabet from the Phoenicians in about 800 BC and its expansion to a 26-character system, the establishment of regular long-distance trading by sea-routes from the Levant to the island of Ischia off Naples, and ultimately a large-scale colonizing movement which turned the Mediterranean virtually into a Greek lake. The pioneering focus of this expansion was Miletos. Here in about 600 BC the growth momentum of the Asia Minor region intensified into a flowering of economic and spiritual life which made Miletos the primary unofficial capital of the new Greece for almost a hundred years. This development, which we cannot trace here in any detail, must constantly be borne in mind as the background to our questions concerning tradition, culture, and poetry.

The reason is that all the information at our disposal points to this Ionian colonial region of Asia Minor as Homer's native land and the centre of his influence.[5] Of the numerous Greek towns which purported to be the birthplace of Homer and were later fixed in mnemonic jingles featuring the canonical figure of seven, at least three are in this region: Smyrna (now Izmir), Khios, and Kolophon. The site of Homer's death is also supposed to be situated here: the little Ionian island of Ios, south of Naxos. It is certainly beyond doubt that the Greeks of the historically known era could have had no documentary knowledge of the author of the *Iliad* or the *Odyssey*, because in his lifetime no culture of record-keeping existed, but the persistent tradition that he came from the area around Smyrna, along with the Ionian dialect used in his works, points to the conclusion, given the pioneering economic and cultural role that we must attribute to this same region, that any other suggested geographical origin for Homeric poetry is less likely.

The relative degree of certainty which we can thus claim for the poet's geographical home applies also to his time. Homeric poetry is, as will be more precisely shown at a later point, the product of a time of crisis in both its basic subject matter and its poetic technique. The social problems and conflicts reflected in it are those of the eighth-century renaissance. Its poetic technique points to the same period. It is of a kind which is rare in Greek literature: on the one hand it remains firmly within the oral tradition which marks the poetic forms of the Mycenaean era, and therefore shows that aoidean poetry is still alive, while on the other it already displays features of linguistic, intellectual, and structural compression such as can only have appeared with the deployment of writing. This itself points to a time of rapid change. The author of this poem must have lived on a critical fault-line in the development of European literature: he grew up with the old techniques of oral poetry, and grew into the new techniques of literacy. In his work he attempted to unite the two. A situation such as this can have existed only in a relatively short period, which coincided with the period of creativity of a particularly gifted individual—in round figures about fifty years. This critical juncture, unique in the entire literature of Europe, a point of radical change in the medium, must have occurred during the eighth century BC, no earlier, and no later. We know this because writing began to spread in Greece in about 800 BC, and the first evidence, in the form of inscriptions on vessels, dates from about 775 BC.[6] The literary products of earlier times show no evidence of having been written down, and all known literary products from a later date, beginning with the mainland Greek poet Hesiod, who dates from about 700 BC, show no clear sign of being orally transmitted—that is, of being genuinely oral rather than imitative of oral. The author of the *Iliad*—and very likely of the *Odyssey*—really was, as the Greeks themselves have believed throughout their history, with the possible exception of efforts of limited scope, the very first Greek poet to write his poetry down.[7]

Both the works attributed by the Greeks to this author, the *Iliad* and the *Odyssey*, are long epic poems with different subject matter and contents. The *Iliad* comprises nearly 16,000 hexameter lines, the *Odyssey* over 12,000. Later periods have divided both works into twenty-four 'books' each, corresponding to the number of letters in the Greek alphabet. The books vary in length: in the *Iliad* the number of lines varies between about 450 and 900. Both poems are coherent entities, that is, a single narrative thread runs through each. The *Iliad* tells the story of a human conflict and its consequences against the backdrop of a great joint military venture, a resolution to which is rendered impossible by this personal conflict. The *Odyssey* recounts the return of a hero, Odysseus, from this military venture to his homeland, Ithaca, which he left twenty years earlier, to his wife, his son, and his elderly father, and to his ancestral domain. The external point of departure of the narrative in both works is Troy. In the *Iliad* it is the setting for all the action; in the *Odyssey* it is the point at which the journey home begins, and the point which is left further and further behind, both outwardly and in the soul of the returning hero.

It is solely by virtue of this function as a point of departure in Homer's epics that Troy has enjoyed any life at all in Europe, and lives on to this day. As we saw in Part I, the Troy of history ceased to exist in about 950 BC at the latest. All that remained was ruins, quarries, and wasteland. In the Mediterranean area there were hundreds of such sites. Usually they were quickly forgotten. Many have been rediscovered in modern times and excavated in the interests of science. But on most of them we have no further information—in some cases, we do not even know if they ever existed. The same fate awaited Troy. The only thing that protected it was Homer. Homer's actual theme, however, was not Troy, but in both cases something else. There is a tension here, which calls for resolution. To this point we shall need to return.

As we said at the outset, the Greeks have looked upon Homer as not only their first, but their greatest poet. The history of the reception of both works justifies this. The extent, duration, and intensity of this reception have no parallel. Greeks, Romans, and the European modern age have all fed on Homer, learnt from him, used him to develop their own poetry and poetic studies, imitated him, sought to outdo him and to shake him off—and admired him. Poetry which lacks substantial quality can have no such reception. Homer studies in the modern age have endeavoured to explain this quality. Not, however, on account of Troy. The city has almost always formed only the mythical or historical backdrop. Of much more interest to scholars has been the poetry itself, as a work of art, and throughout the long period in which the two texts have been studied the high esteem in which they were held in antiquity has been confirmed in a multitude of new ways. Homer was indeed not only the first poet of Greece, but also the greatest.

Homer's *Iliad* and the Tale of Troy

THE TALE OF TROY—A PRODUCT OF HOMER'S IMAGINATION?

For all the emphasis placed by researchers on the artistic dimension of the *Iliad* and its pre-eminence for the cultural history of Europe and especially for the development of European literature, Homer studies in the modern era have been unable to simply disregard the question of the subject matter of the poem. Material which inspired a poet to produce a work of such unique artistic quality cannot be regarded as insignificant. Where did it come from? It has seemed implausible to most that the poet should have completely invented it. The framework of references is too extended, the number of characters too great, and the network of interlocking family and personal relations too complex for any single individual to have invented it and, moreover, endowed it with a meaning which was clearly not present at all in the basic structure of the raw material. These considerations were, as will be shown, fully justified. But where did the raw material come from? If Homer was not alone, how many poets were involved in creating it—before Homer's time, as a steadily evolving system? And beyond this, could it really have been simply the product of human imagination? Could it not contain something of reality, of a remembered past, of history?

SCHLIEMANN DISCOVERS THE SETTING: TROY AND MYCENAE

Into this picture of uncertainty in 1871 came Heinrich Schliemann. Troy, Mycenae, and Tiryns—mere names until this point, and places in a poem—appeared out of the ground. At the very least they plainly had a place in Greek history, were not invented, but had survived in human memory down to Homer's time. So how had this happened? And how great was the proportion of history in the stories about them, when the stories had been handed down over three or four centuries?

A period of discerning conjecture began, involving archaeologists, philologists, ancient historians, and specialists in religion, linguistics, mythology, and folklore. The discussion was fuelled by more and more discoveries. Having scented success, the archaeologists followed in Schliemann's footsteps in mainland Greece, Crete, and the Aegean islands, and uncovered more and more settlements and citadels which were definitely established and inhabited in the second millennium BC. These had later fallen into decline and were either never reoccupied or re-established as settlements only much later. The ancient Greece which had been known until then, the Greece that began with Homer, proceeded to the high classical period and on to world conquest under Alexander the Great—this Greece suddenly acquired a prehistory. This was no longer a beginning—it was a revival, and all the indications were that this revival was a second phase of *Greek* history. It was preceded—centuries even before Homer—by an extended era of prosperity, power, culture, and international renown: the Mycenaean era. The bearers of that flourishing culture really did appear to have been Greeks—just like those Greeks whose history generations of children had grown up with. In spite of differences in structure and social organization, religion, culture, and general way of life, these Greeks had much in common with their descendants of the known historical period.

How much they had in common, however, was disputed. On this matter the scholarly world was divided: one school emphasized the threads connecting the eras, the so-called continuity, the other school emphasized what separated them, the discontinuity. The adherents of discontinuity often doubted—logically speaking, with good reason—that the bearers of Mycenaean culture were really Greeks at all. Eighty years after Schliemann's archaeological discovery, this doubt was dismissed by a discovery in a different field.

NEW DISCOVERIES

Linear B deciphered

Since 1900 the British archaeologist Sir Arthur Evans had been excavating the palace of Knōssós in Crete, which dated from the second millennium BC—the palace of the legendary king of Minos, with its hundreds of halls, bedchambers, rooms, corridors, staircases, landings, and galleries, which had so baffled foreign visitors that they had adopted the term used by the inhabitants, *Labyrinthos* ('double axe building'), as a general term for a structure which induces fear and from which no exit can be found. The term has survived to this day. In this palace, Evans had found many clay tablets marked with rows of unknown characters—clearly a form of writing. Naturally the excavators and after them the linguists of the whole world had embarked upon an attempt to decipher the text. But all efforts were in vain. Only one thing could be established for certain: on these tablets, which were inscribed with linear characters arranged in rows, there were two different kinds of script: an apparently older one, which Evans called 'Linear A', and one apparently newer, to which he gave the name 'Linear B'. The newer variety first appeared in the fifteenth century BC. At first this was as far as it was possible to go.

Unexpected help came in 1939. In that year the American archaeologist Carl W. Blegen, who had continued the Schliemann–Dörpfeld excavations in Troy between 1930 and 1938, discovered the palace of Pylos, on the west coast of the Peloponnese, the palace which plays an important part in both the *Iliad* and the *Odyssey* as the domain of the wise old King Nestor. The ruins could be dated to the thirteenth or twelfth century BC. This meant that for the first time another site of Homer's epic poetry had emerged from the second millennium BC! But of much greater importance was the fact that Blegen's very first probe had struck a large archive of clay tablets. Some 600 tablets were found in the first dig. The writing on these tablets was unmistakably the same as the Linear B known from Knossos.

In this way not only was a connection in culture and writing established between Crete (Knossos) and Greece (Pylos in the Peloponnese)—a connection which had apparently existed from the fifteenth century BC to the thirteenth or twelfth—but the material basis for a possible decipherment of Linear B was also vastly expanded. However, due to the outbreak of World War II, the material could not be published. Before being consigned to the Bank of Athens (where it fortunately survived the war), it was photographed, but only in 1951 were the photographs published, by Blegen's colleague Emmett L. Bennett, Jr., an American specialist at the University of Wisconsin-Madison (*The Pylos Tablets*). Efforts to decipher the script proceeded on a world-wide scale. We have already spoken in this book of the trials and triumphs of the decipherers of scripts. In the case of both Linear A and B, the problems and disappointments were just as great as with other scripts. However, with Bennett's publishing of the Pylos tablets these efforts received a new and decisive impetus.

Among those who had already been working for years to decipher the scripts was the British architect Michael Ventris, who as a 14-year-old schoolboy in London had been fascinated by a lecture given by Arthur Evans in 1936 about the Knossos excavation and, in particular, the inscribed and not yet deciphered tablets found there. During the war he had served as a Royal Air Force navigator and handled decoding assignments. After the war he returned to the study of the Knossos tablets and informed collaborators throughout the world by means of photographic copies of his 'Work Notes' on his progress. From 1951 the Pylos tablets were available in addition to the Knossos tablets. This stepped up the pace of work. Ventris's Work Note No. 20, dated 1 June 1952, contained a hypothesis which would revolutionize our knowledge of antiquity. Three weeks later, on 24 June 1952, this was announced to the wider world. On that day Ventris gave a talk on the BBC Third Programme about his deciphering work and developed his thesis, that the language written in this script was—Greek! Until only a short time before, the scholarly community, including Ventris himself, had expected a very different result (Etruscan, for example). Now at a stroke this view had been superseded. The decisive point in Ventris's talk was this: 'During the last few weeks, I have come to the conclusion that the Knossos and Pylos tablets must, after all, be written in Greek—a difficult and archaic Greek, seeing that it is 500

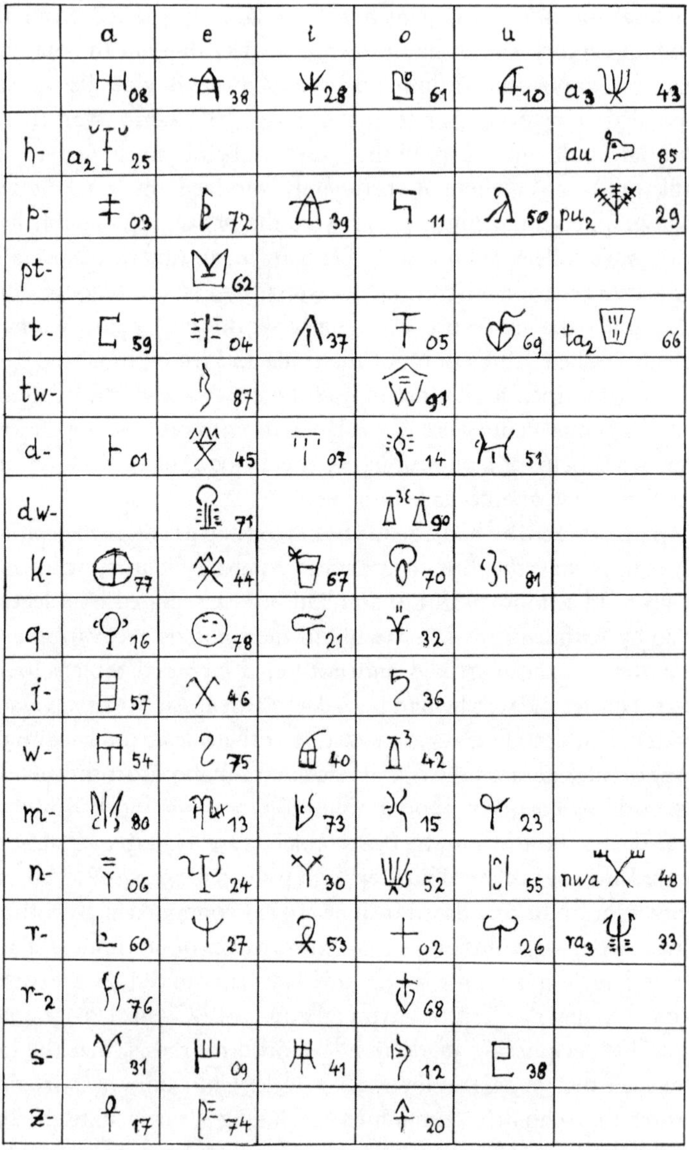
a e i o u
08 38 28 61 10 a3 43
h- a2 25 au 85
p- 03 72 39 11 50 pu2 29
pt- 62
t- 59 04 37 05 69 ta2 66
tw- 87 91
d- 01 45 07 14 51
dw- 71 90
k- 77 44 67 70 81
q- 16 78 21 32
j- 57 46 36
w- 54 75 40 42
m- 80 13 73 15 23
n- 06 24 30 52 55 nwa 48
r- 60 27 53 02 26 ra3 33
r-2 76 68
s- 31 09 41 12 38
z- 17 74 20

FIG. 19. The symbols of Linear B.

years older than Homer and written in rather abbreviated form, but Greek nevertheless.'[1] Among many others listening to the radio that evening was the Cambridge linguist John Chadwick, who had also worked to decipher this script. Sceptical at first, Chadwick tested Ventris's hypothesis over the next few days. His conviction grew and turned to enthusiasm. On 9 July he sent Ventris his congratulations. This was the beginning of a long period of collaboration between Ventris and Chadwick, culminating in 1956 in the publication of the standard work, *Documents in Mycenaean Greek*.[2] Since that time the accuracy of the decipherment has been beyond doubt.

The Mycenaeans were Greeks

The importance of this discovery can hardly be overstated. It lies in the fact that from now on there could no longer be any doubt that the bearers of the Mycenaean culture were ethnically identical with those of the revived Greek culture of the eighth century BC. Before Linear B was deciphered, this equation could only be inferred: (1) archaeology had established that a new race of people had migrated into the southern Balkan peninsula in about 2000 BC; (2) it was known that in the same region Greek had been spoken since the eighth century BC; (3) it had therefore been concluded that the immigrants of 2000 BC must have been Greek. As may readily be seen, this was no more than a hypothesis. Now the hypothesis was replaced by precise knowledge. In Chadwick's words:

> One fact stands out at once as of major consequence: the Mycenaeans were Greeks. Schliemann, when he excavated the first grave circle at Mycenae, had no doubt that he had unearthed a Greek dynasty, and in his famous telegram to the king of Greece claimed to have looked upon the face of one of the king's ancestors. But more academic judges were not so certain, and at one time theories of foreign domination were invoked to account for the precocious brilliance of the Mycenaeans at such a remove from the historical Greeks. The proof that the language of their accounts was Greek might be thought to have settled all controversy on that score.[3]

Indeed, this old controversy was now settled.

The tale of Troy is older than Homer

One particular consequence of the decipherment of Linear B, which necessarily follows from the first consequence, is of even greater importance for our topic. As Ventris's own words show, his very first impression was that this script reflected 'a difficult and archaic Greek'. He realized from the start that the closest linguistic relation of this 'difficult and archaic Greek' was the language of Homer. This suggested that a special relationship existed between the 'archaic' form and Homer's Greek.

In his radio broadcast Ventris had cited four Greek words which he believed he had deciphered. One of them was the word *chryso-worgós*, a well-known Greek word consisting of the elements *chrysós* (gold), which we still have today in 'chrysanthemum' (golden blossom), for example, and *worgós* (worker). (Greek *worgós* and English *work* are cognates, that is, forms of a word which Greek and the ancestor of English both possessed when they still constituted a single ethnic entity and had not yet been geographically and subsequently linguistically divided; this situation is only 4,000 to 4,500 years in the past.) A *chryso-worgós* is therefore a 'gold-worker', or goldsmith. However, the second element, *worgós*, is not found in this form in any known Greek text since Homer. Only the form *ergós* is found. In the later Greek as we know it, our 'gold-worker' is either *chryso-ergós*, or, since the final 'o' of the first element assimilates with the initial 'e' of the second element, giving -o + e-> ou, *chrysourgós*. Compounds of this type may be seen in modern German *Chirurg* and French *chirurgien* (surgeon), which consist of Greek *cheir* (hand; pronounced *chir*) and *ergós* (worker). A surgeon is thus literally a 'hand-worker'. The most obvious feature of the difference between the word in Linear B and the word as we know it in its later Greek form is the loss of the digamma 'w'. In the old Linear B form the 'w' is still written, which means that at that time it was still pronounced; in the later form it has been lost, meaning that by this time it was no longer pronounced. In itself this phenomenon is perhaps not particularly surprising. Languages change, and the Greek reflected in the Linear B is separated from the Greek of the time of Homer by several hundred years. Essentially the Greek word for 'goldsmith' remained phonetically unchanged over the centuries: *chrysoworgós*~*chrysourgós*, except that in the course of time the 'w' came to be increasingly feebly articulated, and, after passing through a transitional stage resembling English 'w', finally disappeared completely. This is the situation we find in the language of Homer: it is true that the specialized word *chryso-ergós* is not found in Homer, but instead we have *demio-ergós* ('demiurge, maker of the people/the world'), formed in exactly the same way, in whose second element the 'w' also no longer appears. But the loss of 'w' may be seen not only in the examples cited. The true situation is that in the language of Homer the sound 'w' no longer exists at all.

Here the matter would rest if there were not an additional and extremely important aspect to this phenomenon: as shown briefly in Part I, Homer's verse is written in hexameter lines. The basis of this versification lies in the difference between long and short syllables (not, as in some other languages, between stressed and unstressed syllables). A syllable is long if it contains a diphthong or a vowel which is inherently long. However, a syllable may also count as long if it contains an inherently short vowel followed by at least two consonants, because two consonants require more time to be enunciated than one and therefore lengthen the short syllable.

The hexameter (Greek *hex*, Latin *sex*, German *sechs*, English *six* + Greek *métron*, English *meter* = 'measure') comprises the six-times-repeated dactylic foot [— ⏑ ⏑], which may be replaced by a spondee [— —]. This means that a hexameter can be formed only by a series of six feet in the form 'one long syllable followed by two short syllables' [— ⏑ ⏑], or of feet in which the two short syllables are replaced by a single long syllable [— —]. It is therefore never possible to use a measure consisting for example of one long syllable, one short syllable, and one long syllable [— ⏑ —], or of three short syllables [⏑ ⏑ ⏑]. However, there are numerous hexameters in Homer's text which exhibit precisely these impossible measures. This example (in which for clarity's sake the more complex hexameter formation rules are left out of account) is from Book 22. 25 of the *Iliad* (King Priam looks down from the wall as Achilles attacks his son Hektor):

The aged Priam was the first of all whose eyes saw him.

In the original hexameter, here transcribed into Latin script, the line sounds like this:

Ton d'ho ge—ron Pri-a—mos pro-to si-de—noph-thal—moi-si
1 2 3 4 5 6
— ◡ ◡ — ◡ ◡ — — ◡ ◡ ◡ — — — x

It can at once be seen that the fourth measure violates the rule: it begins with a short syllable instead of a long one. Has the poet made a mistake? Any Homer scholar would recoil from this explanation, as Homer does not usually make mistakes. So what can have happened here? The answer was found in 1713 by the brilliant British scholar Richard Bentley.[4] By collecting and studying a great number of instances of the same type as our example, Bentley established that in all these cases the apparent error could be accounted for by the loss of an original 'w'. This will be clear even to those readers who are unfamiliar with the discipline of comparative Indo-European linguistics. They need only to be told that the Greek root *id-* is the same as the Latin root *vid-* in, for example, *videre* ('to see', whence the Italian *vedere*, French *voir*). Like these forms, the Greek *ide* must originally have had an initial 'w', so the word was at first not *ide* (saw, noticed) but *wide*. If we now assume this linguistic situation for our verse sample, the apparent error evaporates, because if the fourth foot was originally pronounced not as *to si-de* but *tos wi-de*, the syllable *to* was not short, as it appears to be in Homer's text, but long, because the naturally short 'o' is followed by two consonants: *-sw-*. The fourth foot, therefore, was originally not:

4
◡ ◡ ◡

but:

4
— ◡ ◡,

and thus was correct.

This is all somewhat complex, and the devil really is in the detail, but elaborately structured arguments can stand up only when constructed stone by stone. Here we must appeal to the reader's taste for problem-solving, since the problem of the sound 'w' is of paramount importance for the transmission of the tale of Troy through the Greek bardic tradition. This will be apparent when we have sunk new shafts from other angles into the mine of mystery.

Homer's prosody: late variants of an early ancestor

The results to date may be summarized as follows: a Greek bard of the eighth century BC like Homer, who did not pronounce the sound 'w' and therefore did not write it, composed his lines *as if he did* pronounce and write it. In primers of Homer's Greek, this phenomenon is usually described by the formula 'the effects of "w" are still felt', or words to this effect. What does this mean in practice?

It means, first of all, that the poet of our *Iliad* cannot have been the inventor of the genre in which he writes. If he had been, the 'w', which he did not normally use at all, would have played absolutely no role.

This is to say that the poet inherited the genre from his predecessors, who practised the genre at a time when the 'w' was still pronounced. Whether he took it directly from these w-speakers or from predecessors who themselves no longer pronounced the sound but had themselves taken the verse form from w-speakers remains unknown. In Greece a variety of dialects existed side by side for centuries, the three most important being Aeolian, Ionian, and Dorian. Of these, Aeolian, used for example by the poetess Sappho, still displays 'w' in the historical period. The (eastern) Ionian dialect, on the other hand, used by Homer, has no 'w'. It is possible that eastern Ionian bards had long been in the habit of dropping the 'w' when using the shared poetic genre, adopted from the 'w'-speaking Aeolians, but nevertheless composed their lines as if the 'w' were still present, because otherwise they would have been unable to preserve the hexameter metre. Whatever the case, Homer neither pronounced nor wrote the 'w', but was familiar with it as an integral part of the poetic language he had adopted, retained it from long habit as part of his ingrained sense of language, and plainly let it operate unconsciously, as it always had, in the composition of his lines.

Whatever the particular circumstances may have been, it is vitally important to realize that the *normal* form of that poetic diction found in Homer's *Iliad* and *Odyssey* is not the form we actually see in these epics. The normal form is not that of Homer, but a form developed and practised before Homer, of which Homer's form represents only a late variant, which may be termed deficient in view of the verifiable loss of essential elements of the normal form.[5]

In this variant Homer preserves a state of the Greek language which is older than the eighth-century Greek of (eastern) Ionia and which therefore, in the linguistic context of the eighth century, belonged to the past. This state, however, conforms in one significant respect to the state of the Greek preserved for us in Linear B, that is, the Greek of the fifteenth to thirteenth or twelfth centuries BC. It therefore occupies a position in time between Linear B and the Ionian colloquial of the eighth century. It is thus—as far as we can tell at this point—at least the second oldest stage of the Greek language that is still accessible to us, after Linear B. Ventris was therefore close to the mark when he proposed that a special relationship existed between the 'archaic' Greek which he had identified and Homer's Greek. Homer's prosody is closer to the spoken Greek of the period between the fifteenth and twelfth centuries than any other form of the language.

Unfortunately, we do not know exactly when the sound 'w' fell into disuse in the spoken Ionian dialect of Homer and his audience. As a result, we do not know the minimum period for which the poetic form that Homer followed (containing the 'w') had been in use before his time. But even if we did, it would still tell us only the end-point of the 'w-diction' form in Ionian, not its beginning. This may theoretically lie at any point in the whole period in which the spoken language possessed the 'w'.

Since we now know, thanks to Ventris's decipherment, that the digamma 'w' was written in Linear B and therefore pronounced at that time, and since this takes us back to the Greek of the fifteenth century BC, we can see that it is entirely possible, in purely linguistic terms, that the poetic diction favoured by Homer was in use among the Greeks as early as the time of Linear B.

Interim result: No linguistic or ethnic interruption between Mycenae and Homer

We shall see further on that the inference formulated above is actually correct. But for the moment we shall assert only that:

1. the decipherment of Linear B has demonstrated the continuity of the Greek language from the second millennium to the eighth century BC;

2. the decipherment of Linear B has raised the possibility that the poetic form used by Homer in the eighth century BC could have been in use at the time of Linear B, that is, in the period between the fifteenth and twelfth centuries BC;

3. since the introduction of Linear B to Crete with the conquest of Knossos in the fifteenth century BC was not the birth of the Greek language, but merely a 'technical innovation' which came about by chance, the poetic form that we see in Homer may be considerably older than the introduction of Linear B, that is, it may date from before the fifteenth century BC;

4. the decipherment of the Mycenaean script which we call Linear B deals a death blow to the thesis of discontinuity: a straight line runs from the Greeks of the second millennium BC to the Greeks of the eighth century. In view of our topic, we have been able to deal here with only one single element of this line: linguistic continuity. However, study of the contents of the tablets in the decades since they were deciphered has shown that the line comprises considerably more elements, more closely resembling a broad belt than a single strand. It includes the transmission of cultural features such as crafts, trade, transport, and communications, name-giving, food and eating habits, but also religion: the Linear B tablets bear the names of the gods Zeus, Hera, Athene, Artemis, Poseidon, Hermes, and Dionysos. These gods are therefore older than the tablets, and remained the same down to Homer's time.[6] Most recently the Cologne ancient historian Karl-Joachim Hölkeskamp has convincingly shown, in a refreshingly diversified survey, how strong and tight, for all the variation in the detail, are the ties between the Mycenaean era and the Greek renaissance of the eighth century.[7] From his comprehensive exposition of the facts, we can cite only one sentence here: '...the collapse of the palace system

and its consequences were far-reaching, but they did not amount to an abrupt or definitive break, because this break had no general effect on the underlying structures.'[8] Of course much had changed in Greece between the fifteenth century BC and the eighth, not only individual features of society but also more general demographic, economic, social, political, and other components of the superstructure, as is the case in the history of any people over a period of centuries. But the human society which was the bearer of these changes through the centuries, in the same area of habitation, was and remained the same.

The essential fact of the history of the Greek people from the second millennium to the time of Homer in the eighth century BC is therefore continuity.[9] This salient result of our study so far is one that must be emphasized.

IS THERE A HISTORICAL BASIS FOR THE TALE OF TROY? CONTROVERSIES AND POSSIBILITIES

The debate which has gone on since Schliemann's excavations about the 'historical basis' of Homer's tale of Troy was summarized in 1968 by the eminent Hellenist and Homer scholar Albin Lesky—aware of the decipherment of Linear B—in the form of a seven-column article in the largest and most serious dictionary so far produced in the field of ancient history. This article is distinguished by a masterful command of the relevant literature and great objectivity. It does not, however, reach a conclusion.[10] The views presented by Lesky ranged from complete rejection of any possibility of a historical nucleus—'absolutely no real event should be sought behind the story of a coordinated Greek campaign against Troy'[11]—to decisive exclusion of the possibility that a war did *not* take place between the Achaians and the Trojans: 'It can no longer be doubted, when one surveys the state of our knowledge today, that there really was an actual historical Trojan war in which a coalition of Achaeans, or Mycenaeans, under a king whose overlordship was recognised, fought against the people of Troy and their allies.' This last statement was five years old at the time of Lesky's survey and came from none other than the third excavator of Troy after Schliemann and Dörpfeld, the world-renowned American archaeologist Carl W. Blegen.[12]

After also setting out the opinions between these extremes, and the weightiest available arguments, Lesky concluded his article by saying, 'Mycenae and Troy are historical entities of great importance; that a conflict between them forms the historical background to the *Iliad* remains *one of the existing possibilities*, of course, *if no new sources come to light*—but no more than that.'[13]

THE NEW SITUATION SINCE 1996

Since that time more than thirty years have passed. There is little point in reporting here the continuing debate that went on until the early 1980s, that is, of pursuing Lesky's argument, since there were no really new arguments in it, and could be none, as the starting point had not changed. New sources had not come to light, or had not yet reached the great majority of the participants. Today the situation is different: since the 1980s new sources *have* come to light. The turning point came, as we have seen, in 1996. In order to stake out clearly the foundations for the conclusions which can now be drawn, at this point we shall provide a brief summary of the current state of affairs:

Since 1996 not only research on Troy but research on Homer too, in so far as these deal with the material base of the *Iliad*, have faced a new situation: before 1996 it was not established beyond doubt that Troy/Ilios, the setting for Homer's epic, could be equated with the ruins on the hill above the Dardanelles known as Hisarlık. In all conscience one could not call on Homer's *Iliad* to contribute anything to the reconstruction of the history of the historical city at Hisarlık. Nor, on the other hand, could the Hisarlık ruins seriously serve as proof that Homer's *Iliad* was grounded in history. Since 1996, however, there has been no doubt that the setting for the *Iliad* and the excavated ruins at Hisarlık must be equated, as shown in Part I: Homer's (W)Ilios is Wilusa, the city associated with the empire of the Hittites. Furthermore, it has become clear that the Greek besiegers of Wilios, called by Homer *Achaioí* and *Danaoí*, have equivalent names in the Hittite and Egyptian state documents of the late Bronze Age. Recognition of these facts could not fail to have further consequences.

The most important consequence of the new situation is easily seen: for Wilusa/Tru(w)isa we now have two sets of information at our disposal. On the one hand we have that mountain of research data accumulated by the combined efforts of numerous modern branches of science and still being added to today—archaeology with its sub-disciplines, history and cultural studies, linguistics and lately Hittite and Anatolian studies especially; and on the other the manageable body of evidence, definitively concluded some 2,700 years ago, offered by the Greek epic, the *Iliad*, which may now be exploited—for the first time in good scientific conscience.

Stones, documents, and the poem, the Iliad

At first glance it may appear that the increased body of material made available by the opening up of the *Iliad* as a second source should be cause for rejoicing. Need we not merely consider the two sets of sources side by side and use the one to fill any gaps in the other? Can Homer not leap into the breach as witness when the stones are mute and the Hittite documents sketch no more than broad outlines? As witness to bring to life the near-mute city? And conversely: cannot a walk through that city, which with every passing year is arising anew and ever more clearly before our eyes, inject palpable visual content into Homer's poem, which speaks only in broad terms of Troy, and thus make it more comprehensible?

That would be ideal, but matters are not so simple. The reason is that the two sets of data do not belong in the same plane: their periods, their perspective, and their authenticity separate them, so that they cannot directly intersect.

- Period: the stones date from between 3000 and at the latest 950 BC, and the Hittite documents belong to a period between about 1600 and 1100 BC, so are roughly contemporaneous with the heyday of Wilusa (Troy VI/VIIa). Homer's *Iliad*, on the other hand, arose between 750 and 700 BC, when even the last settlements of Troy had lain in ruins for at least two hundred years. The two sets of data are thus separated by a yawning temporal gulf. The first set is contemporary; the second is not.

- Perspective: the Hittite documents show us a view from the inland centre of the great and friendly protective power of Ḫattusa outward to the small vassal state of Wilusa, well known for centuries, on the fringes of the empire. Homer's *Iliad*, on the other hand, shows us Wilusa through the eyes of external enemies, who, moreover, seem to know nothing at all about the overarching system of the Hittite empire, of which Wilios/Wilusa is no more than a small part. The only entity which occupies all their thoughts, because they want to destroy it, is Wilios, the fortress dominating the passage to the Black Sea.
- Authenticity: lastly, the stones and the documents reflect nothing but reality. Put another way, the stones and the documents do not lie. Even if the Hittite documents may occasionally distort reality for the usual reasons of power politics, stones and documents essentially have no reason to lie, that is, to make Wilusa appear as something other than what it really was at the time. Homer's *Iliad*, on the other hand, is no document of state, but a poem. Poetry always purports to be something other and something more than a mere reflection of reality, but over and above this, the *Iliad* is a poem from the viewpoint of the victor, and the victor's viewpoint sits uneasily with objectivity.

If all these things are taken together the first conclusion must be that the two sets of sources represent different types of information. If the two types are assessed purely as types with regard to their supposed relative historical truth content, one would have to conclude in advance that the stones of Wilusa and the relevant contemporary documents from Ḫattusa, where Wilusa had been known for centuries, come closer to historical truth than the *Iliad*, a foreign poem of late date. To exploit the *Iliad* uncritically to complement and animate the stones and documents—as flesh to lend shape to the bare bones—therefore seems out of the question. It is necessary to state this, because this procedure is not unknown in the history of the problem. The eminent British Hellenist Denys Page, one of the few Homer scholars to refer to Hittite documents, was so filled with euphoria that in 1959 he declared not only the Trojan War to be historical, but also Homer's leading figures, such as Agamemnon and Achilles.[14]

While to this day nobody can actually prove conclusively that it is inappropriate to take a poem so literally, our general experience with poetry tells us that the burden of proof lies with those who would favour a literal reading. But so far the historicity of Agamemnon and Achilles cannot be proven from the stones, the non-Greek documents, or the *Iliad*. Only clues can be obtained, and these concern only the larger context of the tale of Troy and not details such as individual personal names or topography. This means that, even with our most recent knowledge, it is not advisable to try to wander, *Iliad* in hand, through a Troy which has been reconstructed in virtual fashion on the basis of recent excavations, equating a gateway here or a bastion there with some 'counterparts' in the text, or referring to Homer to conclude that this is how Troy appeared in its heyday in about 1200 BC, that here stood Agamemnon's headquarters tent, or that there Helen pointed out to Priam the heroes of the Achaian army from the wall of Troy. After all, Homer had never seen Troy in its undamaged and 'fully-functioning' state. He might, however, if he had ever visited the site, have seen the ruins, those ruins which in the eighth century BC may still have been visible as a 'topographical feature' or 'the ruins of walls' (see p. 33). What state they were in we cannot say, but certainly not in the cleanly exposed state of archaeological preparation which greets the visitor today. Homer may have wandered among these ruins, just as the modern archaeologist may do, but with one difference: as he walked he had the whole of the orally-transmitted tale of Troy in his head, not the *Iliad*, which he had yet to create, in his hand. Naturally he would have compared the picture he held in his mind with the reality of the ruins and formed impressions of the formerly living city. These are the impressions which we now read in the *Iliad*. That these would display certain similarities with the virtual images of our data-nourished computers is in the nature of things, since the ruins—the raw data—are the same, whatever their state of preservation at these different periods. However, the similarity of the images should never let us forget that they are only images and nothing more.

If this was really the case—and we do not know if it was—Homer was the first visitor with creative imagination known to have visited the ruins, and for this reason his testimony would have some value.[15] But he could not possibly have been a contemporary witness to Troy VI/VIIa.

What can the Iliad *tell us about Troy?*

At first all this sounds disheartening. What matters most, however, is the word 'uncritically', with which the discussion of the potential evidentiary value of the *Iliad* opened. After all, the *Iliad* cannot be totally unsuitable as a provider of information, since Homer knows things, as we have seen, such as the Bronze Age names of the besiegers, which he could not possibly have known if he had been privy to no historical information. This means that he does have evidentiary value. The only question is the nature of this. This brings us back to the heart of the problem, to the question which has been asked since the very moment when Schliemann first uncovered the Hisarlık ruins. At that time, however, the question and all its answers could be no more than an intellectual game, since whoever asked it assumed that Hisarlık was to be equated with Troy, and often wished to adduce the proof of this simply as a by-product, by comparing the text with the finds. All answers therefore remained in the realm of speculation. Consequently, while one had to admire the ingenuity of those who tried to find answers, nobody needed to take these hypotheses seriously, since nobody had any way of really knowing whether the *Iliad* dealt with *Schliemann's* Troy at all. Now we know that it does. The question of the level of the information value which the *Iliad* has for Troy and the historical events surrounding it can therefore now be placed on a firm foundation.

However, before trying to give any answer, we must first refine the question to encompass only what is strictly relevant. To formulate the question in an unfocused way would be to release a flood of answers which would have nothing to do with it, since Homer uses Troy only as a setting, as we shall later see in more detail. In this setting he places a wide range of varied events, including the most ordinary, such as sunrise and sunset, eating, drinking, love, giving and taking advice, arguments, conflicts, and so forth. But none of this will be at all helpful in the attempt to establish Homer's connection with Troy as the setting for his story. The question must be refined and fields of interest separated. For example, Homer has much to tell us about the gods and how they behave among themselves, how they remonstrate with one another and form alliances, how they watch over humans, guide them, encourage them, deceive them... All this is full of poetic charm and highly informative on the history of Greek religion. But with regard to Troy its information value is nil. Homer also provides very detailed and vivid descriptions of warfare, in the battles between besiegers and besieged. Where this deals only with different ways of throwing spears and different sword-thrusts, and not with definite localities in the Troad, this too is not instructive for us, since all of it could take place elsewhere, if the setting were different, in identical fashion. The *Iliad*, then, covers many fields which have little to do with our question: can Homer tell us anything about Troy? First of all, we need to ask: in which areas of Homer's narrative are we most likely to find information of the kind we seek? And this means asking at the same time, in which areas are we *least* likely to find it? We first need, therefore, to examine the *Iliad* from the point of view of historical significance, that is, with the aim of distinguishing the historically relevant and irrelevant areas. As soon as the historically relevant areas have been identified the information in this category will again have to be distinguished and weighed against the criterion 'invented or historically proven'.

If we wished to proceed systematically to the task of separating historically relevant and irrelevant areas, we would have to comb carefully through the entire 15,693 lines of the *Iliad*, and by a process of elimination exclude all material that had no historical bearing on Troy—the following passages, for example:

(1) everyday occurrences and household activities;
(2) scenes showing the gods (if irrelevant to the tale of Troy);
(3) battle descriptions of all kinds;
(4) accounts of sporting contests (almost the whole of Book 23);
(5) descriptions of objects, such as Achilles' shield in Book 18;

(6) dialogue scenes (again, if irrelevant to the tale of Troy);
(7) allegories.

The list could be continued. In analysing each one of these areas, we would need to take care not to excise references to Troy which occur here and there, in various ways and with varying frequency, even in these passages. It will already be clear that this would be a task of such a scale that, within our framework, we could not manage it in any systematic fashion. We elect to follow an abridged procedure, which will most likely appear to be an accelerated attempt to do the reverse: from the top, as it were, rather than the bottom, to isolate the Troy plot within the *Iliad*.

At this point many readers will ask: are the *Iliad* and the Troy plot not identical? Isn't the *Iliad* the Troy plot? It is not, as will be shown. The *Iliad* is something else. Recognition of this is the precondition for any answer to the question of the information value of the poem concerning Troy, since only when we understand what the *Iliad* actually sets out to tell us—and what it does not—will we be in a position not to demand too much of it. To put this another way: only when we grasp what information value the poem *can* possess will we be able to ask to good purpose what information value it actually *has*.

Two pictures of Troy: the Hittites and Homer

In order to put the Troy plot from the *Iliad*, behind which stands the poet's generalized image of Troy, in proper focus from the start, it is advisable to set it against the image of Troy provided by archaeology and Anatolian studies. Exaggerated expectations, of a kind often placed by archaeologists on the *Iliad*'s tale of Troy, may quickly be reduced to a more modest scale once this background is visualized.

The picture of Troy in archaeology and the Hittite documents

This picture is characterized by its long-term view, in which Troy is seen over a period of two thousand years. The detail retreats into the background, leaving only the broad outlines visible. The Troy which emerges is consequently a city of pragmatic rationality: a city with an extensive hinterland and a broad sphere of influence in north-western Asia Minor and neighbouring regions of Europe, the capital of a region which plays a significant role in the history of Asia Minor and the Mediterranean basin. We see this Troy before us as a living centre of trade, prospering for centuries at the meeting point of two seas and two continents, as a political entity in Asia Minor's network of states in the second millennium BC, as a treaty partner of the Hittite empire (the Alaksandu treaty) and member-state of the Arzawa lands, a group of countries of western Asia Minor. We see it embroiled in the power struggles of its neighbours (the Pijamaradu affair) and as a setting for intra-dynastic confrontations: Kukunni, Alaksandu, and Walmu. These are perspectives which reach far beyond the realm of archaeology. They do much to strip the city of its old aura of mystery. From this viewpoint, Troy can return to its hereditary place in the current of 'normal' world history.

The viewpoint of Homer is entirely different.

Homer's picture of Troy and the Troy plot

In Homer's *Iliad*, Troy is presented to us over a short period. We see the city in a time of crisis. It is a Troy filled with drama and tension, but also with ordinary life. We are shown a city fighting for its life. It is under siege by a foreign army and being starved into submission. For nine years it has been cut off from its more distant hinterland by the Achaian fleet, and as for the nearer hinterland, the besieging army beneath the walls is doing all it can to turn it into scorched earth. We get to know not only the Achaian leaders, but also the ruling stratum now in power in Troy itself, and we gain an insight into the conflict which has divided this stratum and which remains suppressed only because of the shared danger: a son of King Priam, the handsome Paris/Alexander, while travelling on business of state to Achaia/Greece, has abused the international right to hospitality by abducting the beautiful Helen, the wife of his host, the king of Lakedaimon/Sparta, along with considerable assets. The retaliatory force of the united Achaians, sent against Troy with 1,186 ships, demands the return of the kidnapped queen and stolen assets, in addition to the payment of reparations. The threat to the city, should these demands not be met, is spelled out ruthlessly, relentlessly, in a state of pent-up rage, by the supreme commander of this force, Agamemnon, King of Mycenae (6. 55–60). When his brother Menelaos, the rightful husband of Helen, wishes only to capture an opponent in battle, instead of killing him, he bursts out:

> 'Dear brother, O Menelaos, are you concerned so tenderly
> with these people? Did you in your house get the best of treatment
> from the Trojans? No, let not one of them go free of sudden
> death and our hands; not the young man child that the mother carries
> still in her body, not even he, but let all of Ilion's
> people perish, utterly blotted out and unmourned for.'

In the face of such threats the Trojans are naturally compelled to stand together, but there is ferment beneath the surface. All hinges on a matter of loyalty: how long can the city stand behind the abductor? The demand of the besiegers is still being refused, but the refusal comes through clenched teeth. Solidarity with Prince Paris and the royal house is gradually coming under intolerable strain. From the Trojan ruling stratum come more and more attempts to reverse the decision and accede to the demand of the besiegers. Here is the earnest suggestion of Antenor, for example, a member of the king's council, in the assembly recounted in Book 7 (lines 348–53), before the palace of Priam to the assembled Trojans and allied troops from the nearer and further hinterland:

> 'Trojans and Dardanians and companions in arms: hear me
> while I speak forth what the heart within my breast urges.
> Come then: let us give back Helen of Argos and all her possessions
> to the sons of Atreus to take away, seeing now we fight with
> our true pledges made into lies; and I see no good thing's
> accomplishment for us in the end, unless we do this.'

Of course Paris contradicts Antenor at once and declares him of unsound mind, but he knows all too well that the mood is against him. He therefore proposes a compromise: 'Helen? I'm not giving her up! But the captured property? All right! And I'll throw in one or two things of my own!' His father Priam receives this with relief. The very next morning he will send a messenger to the Achaians with this peace offer! The messenger arrives in the Achaian camp.

We expect transmission of the message to take place in the way this is usually shown in the *Iliad*, that is, the messenger repeats verbatim the words entrusted to him. But in this case Homer has the messenger do something different, and most unusual: the messenger does not simply convey the message. He also gives an unmistakable insight into the mood within the city (7. 385–93). Here the messenger's asides are shown in italics.

> Sons of Atreus, and you other great men of all the Achaians,
> Priam and the rest of the haughty Trojans have bidden me
> give you, if this message be found to your pleasure and liking,
> the word of Alexandros, for whose sake this strife has arisen.
> All those possessions that Alexandros carried in his hollow
> ships to Troy, *and I wish that he had perished before then*,
> he is willing to give all back, and to add to these from his own goods.
> But the very wedded wife of glorious Menelaos
> he says that he will not give, *though the Trojans would have him do it.*

So Paris is isolated in Troy. As the siege drags on, he finds himself driven so deeply into isolation that he needs to hire agents to sway public opinion in his favour. In Book 11, Agamemnon kills a number of Trojans, including both sons of Antimachos (11. 123–5)

> who beyond all others
> had taken the gold of Alexandros, glorious gifts, so that
> he had opposed the return of Helen to fair-haired Menelaos.

The citadel rulers are thus forced to wage a struggle to survive, a struggle they do not inwardly wish to be part of. And the solidarity in their ranks is put to even sterner tests by the behaviour of the one who originally brought this war upon them. Hektor, the brother of Paris, appointed by King Priam to supreme command of the defending army, returns to the citadel from the thick of the battle at a time of dire need, to organize a procession of supplication by the women of Troy to the temple of the goddess of the city. Passing the house of Paris and Helen, he calls in. What are the couple doing while battle rages outside the city, a battle begun for his sake? Paris is sitting in the bedchamber calmly polishing his weapons. Helen is giving domestic instructions to the servants, as usual. On seeing this, Hektor seethes with fury (6. 326–31):

'Strange man! . . .
The people are dying around the city and around the steep wall
as they fight hard; and it is for you that this war with its clamour
has flared up about our city. You yourself would fight with another
whom you saw anywhere hanging back from the hateful encounter.
Up then, to keep our town from burning at once in the hot fire.'

All these confrontations within the besieged city belie the hackneyed image of Troy so often reproduced in modern retellings of the *Iliad*, showing the city as the innocent victim of brutal external aggression, and make us aware in many different ways of the divisions within the threatened city, while also making us see the indescribable suffering and privations of the defenders and attackers on the field of battle. We experience their ordeals with them in every detail, fearing for their safety, and these ordeals have an immediacy about them which factual historical sources can never achieve. We are dealing not with laconic records of events, but with a poetic imagination, reifying the past with sensitivity and vision, trying to show not what actually happened, but what could have happened.

Up to this point all of this fully corresponds to what we generally expect of poetry. Aristotle used the criterion of factuality to define poetry, and to define factuality made clear and deliberate use of the example of 'history writing': 'history writing', he explained, reports what was, while poetry pictures to itself ('imagines') what might have been.[16] Thus far we may view Homer's picture of Troy, in the light of Aristotle's distinction, as belonging firmly in the realm of 'what might have been'. It would be difficult to imagine domestic Trojan scenes or dialogue of the kind cited above in an authentic battlefield dispatch kept in the Trojan state archives. These things have always belonged in the realm of fiction. We shall therefore fully embrace the view that the picture before us is the product of imagination. A bard is seated on a rock amid the ruins on the hillside, imagining what might once have happened here.

Now, however, an 'alien' tone enters the picture at many points: the poet's narrative does not remain in this realm of imaginative visualization and psychological empathy. Rather, it acquires a 'historical' underpinning. This means that the apparent openness and geographical transferability of the story comes to an abrupt end. We are no longer witnessing the course of some archetypical 'city siege', such as might take place anywhere at any time, of which Troy could be an example, as a name to be inserted in the structural framework under the heading 'siege story'. Instead we are suddenly made witness to a fuller treatment of a unique historical event. 'This is a quite exceptional siege,' we are reminded, 'of which humanity will go on talking for generations to come. Everything is predetermined. Troy will go up in flames, but these flames will still be visible centuries later on the horizon of world history!' The 'historical' underpinning, upon which Homer animates his characters, becomes particularly clear at one key point in the poem: Hektor takes his leave of his wife Andromache and young son Astyánax at the bastion of the Skaian gate of the fortress wall (6. 447–63):

> For I know this thing well in my heart, and my mind knows it:
> there will come a day when sacred Ilion shall perish,
> and Priam, and the people of Priam of the strong ash spear.
> But it is not so much the pain to come of the Trojans
> that troubles me, nor even of Priam the king nor Hekabe,
> not the thought of my brothers who in their number and valour
> shall drop in the dust under the hands of men who hate them,
> as troubles me the thought of you, when some bronze-armoured
> Achaian leads you off, taking away your day of liberty,
> in tears; and in Argos you must work at the loom of another,
> and carry water from the spring Messeis or Hypereia,
> all unwilling, but strong will be the necessity upon you;
> and some day seeing you shedding tears a man will say of you:
> 'This is the wife of Hektor, who was ever the bravest fighter
> of the Trojans, breaker of horses, in the days when they fought
> about Ilion.'

Here the 'little world' of private life and the 'wider world' of the course of history merge into one. When the chief defender of the city has this intimate conversation with his wife, into his mouth is placed the knowledge given by posterity of the futility of all his efforts, and this knowledge includes particular localities like the springs of Messeis and Hypereia in the homeland of the conquerors—localities which the speaker himself, Hektor, has of course never seen, and which therefore stem from the narrator's knowledge.

What poet who intends only to reflect human experience applies such specific colours? It is clear that whoever wrote these lines was consciously striving not, as it may at first appear, to recount the unchanging human reactions to the fall of any city. He wanted to give an expressive account of one particular and significant defeat, a defeat that 'made history', which, he suggests, all would know and speak of in his own time as well as later—a great, historic event, one might say, which would remain in human memory: '... the days when they fought about Ilion'. This is the event into which he wished to breathe life.

Is this part of Homer's picture of Troy also to be placed under the heading 'Invention, Fiction'? We shall return to this question anon. But first let us look at the end of the Troy narrative: after his nightmare vision, Hektor will not return from the battlefield. Achilles, the young prince of Achaia in Thessaly, will first send his friend Patroklos against him, then, when Patroklos fails and is killed, kill Hektor with his own hands. Hektor's father Priam, fearful and courageous at once, will go at night to the Achaian camp to pay a high ransom for the body of his favourite son. Achilles, filled with sympathy for the old king, who reminds him of his own ageing father, will let him take his mortal enemy. Hektor will be solemnly buried in Troy, and the struggle for Troy will go on to its predetermined conclusion.

This, in abridged form, is the Troy narrative as we have it in the *Iliad*.

This is a very different picture of Troy from the one provided by the archaeological finds and state treaties. It is extraordinarily rich in detail, and it seethes with life. At first sight it looks as if nothing of the kind could have emerged without the most intimate knowledge of the situation. How could this be? Was Homer actually present? If we can spontaneously ask this question (knowing full well that it makes no sense), we are exhibiting precisely the reaction Homer was consciously endeavouring to evoke. In the *Odyssey* (8. 487–93), he has Odysseus say to Demodokos, a bard like himself, after Demodokos' recital of a song of Troy:

> 'Demodokos, above all mortals beside I prize you.
> Surely the Muse, Zeus's daughter or else Apollo has taught you,
> for all too right following the tale you sing the Achaians'
> venture, all they did and had done to them, all the sufferings
> of these Achaians, as if you had been there yourself or heard it
> from one who was.'

Just as the bard Demodokos is praised by his listener Odysseus (who was present in the fiction of the *Odyssey* and therefore knows very well that Demodokos was not there), the bard Homer wishes to receive the praise of his listeners (and later, readers) for his *Iliad*—for filling out the bare facts by showing how they affect the participants, and doing this so realistically that the audience believes he must have been there himself, or at least have heard reliable reports from others who were.

His strategy succeeded: Homer's audience—even without the precise chronology we have today—has always known that of course Homer was not present. He himself stresses repeatedly in the *Iliad* that the story he is recounting took place in the distant past. None the less even Homer's very first listeners were fully persuaded that the kernel of the story he was telling was completely true. To them this kernel was the struggle for Troy. That this struggle had really taken place between their ancestors and the once powerful Trojans, that the 'Trojan War' was a historical reality, was never seriously doubted by Greek listeners and readers, or by the whole ancient world.

Even the most eminent of Greek historians, Thucydides of Athens, a clear-eyed and rational analyst in the enlightened fifth century BC, still takes Homer's *Iliad* so closely at its word as to use Homer's information on the Trojan War to argue his own case (Book 1, especially Chapters 9–11). How was this possible? After all, Thucydides knew that Homer was not an eyewitness: 'The best evidence for this can be found in Homer, who, though he was born much later than the time of the Trojan War...' (Book 1).[17] Just like almost all other Greeks before and after his time, Thucydides automatically drew the same conclusion as the poet of the *Odyssey* made Odysseus draw on hearing a bard tell the tale of Troy: that Homer had taken it 'from others', and was therefore a link in a chain of information which ran unbroken from the events themselves to his own time.

It should now be apparent that this conclusion was not prompted by the 'illustrative contribution' of Homer's Troy narrative, since nobody knew better than Thucydides that, for example, the direct speech and dialogue offered by Homer were a bonus supplied by the narrator. Thucydides made use of such elements himself. Rather, the conclusion was grounded in Homer's 'historicizing contribution'. This seemed to provide a reliable guarantee of the authenticity of at least the essential facts of the story—the parties to the conflict, the war, the conquest, the destruction. There seemed to be no room for doubt, especially in view of such apparently unmistakable signals of authenticity as the verifiable geographical information, of which the *Iliad* is full. Today, by contrast, many will at first be inclined to perceive a fallacy in this and view even the 'historicizing contribution' of Homer's tale of Troy as fiction. Everything that is no longer living, it will be argued, provokes in those who contemplate it or hear of it, not only a wish to visualize it in life, but also, if it appears to exceed certain limits of scale, the impulse to attribute historical importance to it. After all, experience tells us that everything of substantial size is conscious of its own weight and relies on it to predict its own after-life in the memory of posterity, while wistfully foreseeing its doom. In antiquity predictions of one's own immortality are almost a cliché, especially in poetry. A poet contemplating greatness—the ruins of massive walls, for example—will almost automatically be moved to place in the mouths of the formerly living bearers of that greatness the foreknowledge of their doom, and of the posthumous fame that will follow. And the more spectacular that doom appears in the light of the dimensions of the ruins, the stronger the poet's impulse to project into the minds of the imagined Trojans the familiar feeling of certainty at once of being doomed and never to be forgotten. An argument grounded in customary healthy scepticism will run roughly along these lines.

But it seems the matter does not end here. We have seen the scale of the Mycenaean world and what a catastrophe its downfall represented to the Greeks. This catastrophe left many sites of ruins in Greece, including some the size of Mycenae, Tiryns, Pylos, Orchomenos, Iolkos, and many more. However, so far as we know, their downfall never received a treatment comparable to that accorded the downfall of Troy. Why is it that no analogous reactions or projections were stimulated by these ruins, which to Greeks must have seemed scarcely less deserving of lamentation than those of the foreign city of the Trojan enemy? Must there not have been some additional element needed to make a ruined city 'lament-worthy'? And should this element not be sought in the real history? We are conscious of Albin Lesky's well-founded conclusion: 'Mycenae and Troy are historical entities of great importance; that a conflict between them forms the historical background to the *Iliad* remains one of the existing possibilities, of course, if no new sources come to light—but no more than that.'

A HISTORICAL BASIS FOR THE TALE OF TROY BECOMES MORE PROBABLE. CLUES FROM THE *ILIAD* ITSELF

In the light of the new material situation set forth in Part I, combined with the results of the decipherment of Linear B, it is now time to draw together the arguments—old and new—which from Homer's side speak in favour of this possibility.

One of the first arguments arises from the narrative emphasis of the *Iliad*: where is the main focus placed in the story? The distribution of emphasis is proof that—to state it as tentatively as possible—the tale of Troy must be considerably older than the one that is told in the *Iliad*. We shall explain this in more detail.

The tale of Troy is only a backdrop to the Iliad

In order to understand the *Iliad*, it is of fundamental importance to realize that it does not tell the story of the 'Trojan War'. Troy and the country around it, the Troad, and the struggle between the Greek besiegers and the Trojan defenders of the city form no more than the setting for the epic. What this poem in twenty-four books and a total of 15,693 hexameter lines actually relates is something else: in the ninth or tenth year of a great joint operation by an Achaian military alliance against Ilios, conflict erupts between two nobles who hold leading positions in the besieging Achaian army, Agamemnon of Argos/Mycenae, the supreme commander of the attacking force, and Achilles of Phthia in Thessaly, the commander of the Myrmidons, militarily the most effective allied contingent. After nine years of siege, at a time when the aim is felt to be within reach, this conflict threatens to thwart the entire Achaian operation. What is depicted is no mere squabble, but a dispute over principles. The dispute bears on the interpretation of social values not previously questioned: honour, position, and readiness to take up arms for the common good, and leadership. This dispute between two high-ranking and intelligent leading personalities becomes emotionally charged to the point where the younger of the two, Achilles, the prince, who commands the most important contingent in the allied army, is humiliated and feels his honour slighted. Achilles becomes deeply resentful and boycotts the whole venture. By the defamation of his person he believes that suprapersonal norms of behaviour are being set aside, and he wishes to see them reinstated. He believes that this is only possible if he by his boycott places the alliance in extreme jeopardy. Nothing less, he believes, will bring his detractor Agamemnon, the supreme commander of the alliance, to his senses. With the defeat of his alliance staring him in the face, Agamemnon will be forced to apologize, thinks Achilles. Thus, not only will he, Achilles, be rehabilitated, but—much more important for a character whom Homer delineates so expressively—norms of behaviour will be fully restored. This is Achilles' calculation.

The calculation proves correct and the desired effect is achieved. However, it is achieved only after both parties—the man who committed the outrage and the man who suffered it—and thus the whole alliance have had to sustain grievous external and internal losses, loss of reputation, losses in men, and loss of innocence. As all participants are forced to acknowledge at the conclusion of the conflict, these losses cannot be made good either by belated apologies in their own camp or by reprisals against the enemy. By this confrontation between its leading figures, the entire alliance is stripped of many illusions concerning their special qualities. The realization is sobering, and oppressive, and the alliance is thereby weakened. It will fight on, to be sure, but its old fighting spirit is gone.

That the first audience and earliest recipients perceived this to be the main emphasis and thus the meaning of the *Iliad*—a picture of a far-reaching conflict over ethical standards and its fateful consequences for a coalition—is demonstrated by other poems which arose later and brought Homer's tale to its end. These report that the alliance was no longer able to seize the citadel of Ilios/Troy by military means. The proud Achaian force—1,186 ships and over 100,000 troops, according to Book 2 of the *Iliad*—was able to triumph only thanks to a wooden horse, and then, after the frenzied and often brutal destruction of the hated city, the victors went their separate ways. No proud armada sailed into its home ports to cheers and rejoicing, with flags flying. Instead each unit sought to find its own way home. The heroes who survived were driven far off course by storms and scattered right across the Mediterranean, to reach home without fanfare many years later, like Odysseus, or, like Agamemnon, the renowned king of Mycenae and victor of Troy, who came home successfully, but only to be killed by his wife in the bathroom. An inglorious end.

This then is the story that Homer actually tells. As should by now be clear, it is not the story of the Trojan War. But what sort of story is it, and what does it really have to do with Troy?

Interpretative researches over the last fifteen years have made clear that the theme of the tale of Troy can be understood only from the viewpoint of the time of origin of the epic. The *Iliad* as we know it is a product of the second half of the eighth century BC. For the people of that time, the Trojan War, which provides the setting, belonged to ancient history. We know today that such a war, if it really took place, must have occurred some four hundred years earlier, not in the eighth century but in the twelfth century BC. Homer's audience did not know this. Having no precise means of measuring historical time and no chronologically ordered 'history', they took this war to be an event that really happened, but in a dim and distant past. This being so, to them in the eighth century, this war was of limited interest only, of historical interest, as we might say today. The time they now lived in had quite different concerns. What were these? In order to gain an understanding of the real bond between the poet and his audience, of the broad path of communication by which stimulus and response ran to and fro between the two parties, and see what was for poet and audience alike mere 'background' which fell away on both sides of that path as of lesser importance, though still necessary to ensure that the highway remained recognizable—in order to appreciate the context of delivery and reception in the case of the *Iliad*, we need to look in rather more detail at the historical situation in the eighth century BC.

The eighth century BC is a time of expansion in Greece after a prolonged period of stagnation. Following their immigration into the south of the Balkan peninsula, the Greeks had built up a flourishing culture, but had seen this culture utterly destroyed in about 1200 BC by an invasion of warlike peoples from the north. We have already discussed the disastrous consequences of this. Nevertheless, they had managed to maintain certain centres after the catastrophe, for example Athens, together with some regions in central Greece and on the island of Euboia, and new life could emerge from here. It is true that this took about 350 years from the time of the catastrophe to the great new upsurge, but by about 800 BC this stage had been reached. Now the Greeks were forming new external contacts, adopting numerous cultural achievements from neighbouring people and improving on them. These included the alphabet and long-distance seagoing trade, as we have seen. After this began the greatest colonizing movement in world history until the modern age: the Greeks founded a great number of new towns on all coasts of the Mediterranean—in Sicily and southern Italy, on the North African coast, in Asia Minor and the Black Sea—many of which exist to this day under their old names. An extended network of maritime traffic was established, with a lively exchange of goods and information. This brought with it a sudden broadening of the Greek geographical and spiritual horizon.

Of course, this did not happen by itself. Leadership was needed to give guidance, focus, and organization. This came from the new upper stratum whose origins lay partly in the old upper stratum which had ruled before the disaster. This new eighth-century upper stratum, the new aristocracy, was, on the one hand, the motor of the new upward trend, while on the other it felt itself threatened by the rapid development which it itself was driving. Until now it had had an undisputed monopoly on power. Now, however, seafaring, colonization, manufacturing, and commerce were bringing forward new classes, who also aspired to exert influence and threatened the monopoly of the nobility. The result was a feeling of uncertainty among the nobility. How should they react to the new developments? Should they relax their old value system, to which they had adhered unswervingly? Should they adapt? Should they take a rather more relaxed view of such values as honour, dignity, truthfulness, and reliability and adjust to the fickle new times, or should they cling to the old values? In the latter case, they all had to stick together, no one could resile, as the good of the community had to come before personal interests. There could therefore be no squabbling within the upper stratum. But if the argument was about precisely these basic values, did one not have to accept it, and even foster it, since long-term cohesion could only be guaranteed by socially binding norms? In certain situations, was not argument not merely permissible, but even absolutely imperative for reorientation?

It is questions of this sort—the burning issues of the eighth century—that the *Iliad* places on the agenda. Homer takes them up and makes them his theme.[18] At the time no other supra-regional medium existed to serve as a forum for discussion among the nobility. There was only this bardic poetry, which was the instrument by which the Greek upper stratum could again clarify its position and the requirements of the age—and this had been so for centuries, as we shall see in greater detail. Homer's Achilles epic, later known as the *Iliad*, represents an attempt to provide an answer to the new and still unresolved problem of an up-to-date self-definition of the nobility. The answer is put into the mouths of the leading personae—Achilles, Agamemnon, Nestor, Odysseus, Aias, Diomedes, and others—as they put forward and discuss various possible reactions. This takes place within the framework of a scenario which, by accentuating the conflict, makes it impossible to evade—as may have been common in reality—the debate on values, while making it possible to state the arguments in a clear and uncompromising manner which could never be achieved in the random configuration of real discussion.

As soon as we, as readers of the *Iliad*, adopt this point of view, and assume the natural receptive attitude of Homer's first and proper target audience, it becomes clear that everything that is of such outstanding importance for us, including the matter of Troy, was only of secondary interest to the first recipients, and to the poet, who was composing for this audience. Homer and his audience were not primarily interested in the Trojan War at all. They were interested in problems of their own time. Troy and the whole Trojan War were to the poet and his public nothing more than a backdrop.

But why precisely *this* backdrop? Why did the poet choose Troy, a city in Asia Minor, of which, by his time, nothing remained but ruins, and which he had never seen as a living city? The answer will emerge gradually, of itself.

The tale of Troy is familiar to the audience of the Iliad

First we need to clarify whether it is likely, according to the view still heard today, that the author of our *Iliad* himself chose Troy as the setting and invented the story that Troy was once besieged and captured by the Greeks.[19]

We begin with a phenomenon which all readers of the *Iliad* notice immediately and which is apt to irritate those who approach it without foreknowledge. The *Iliad* does not plunge the reader or listener wholly unprepared into the story—Horace (still eagerly quoted today)[20] was not quite right to say that Homer launches us at once *in medias res*. The opening of the *Iliad* is rather a *prooimion* (Latin *prooemium*, a proem or prelude, literally 'pre-song'), of seven lines:

> Sing, goddess, the anger of the Peleiad Achilleus
> and its devastation, which put pains thousandfold upon the Achaians,
> hurled in their multitudes to the house of Hades strong souls
> of heroes, but gave their bodies to be the delicate feasting
> of dogs, of all birds, and the will of Zeus was accomplished
> since that time when first there stood in division of conflict
> the Atreid, the lord of men and the brilliant Achilleus.

In the very first line, the reader who is completely unfamiliar with Homer will baulk at the word 'Peleiad'. What is a Peleiad? In spite of this, in the first line the reader will understand without difficulty that it denotes the same man as the personal name Achilles, that 'Peleiad' must therefore be something in the nature of a title, or at least some further qualifying term for Achilles, describing him in some more precise way. However, six lines further on this kind of conjecture will be less than satisfactory: who is 'the Atreid' here? This word, which looks very similar in form to the Peleiad of line 1, cannot be a personal name. But if it is some kind of title, as Peleiad in line 1 seemed to be, which individual does it refer to? Line 7 sounds as obscure as if it read,

> the grand duke, the lord of men and brilliant Achilles,

or with, for example, 'the army commander', or 'the president', or something of this nature instead of 'the grand duke'. The clearly individualized Achilles is thus being contrasted with an unidentifiable individual, denoted so far only by a generic term. Who is concealed behind the generic term?

This question confronts by no means only those with no knowledge of Greek, who will therefore be inclined simply to resign themselves to this, attributing the difficulty to their own insufficient preparation. The question arises just as much for those who do know Greek—in the past as much as the present. On hearing or reading the Greek word 'Atreid' they will recognize it at once as a 'patronymic' (analogous to the Russian Ivanovich and Ivanovna, indicating the son and daughter of Ivan), but are they any the wiser for this? After all, a Greek patronymic defines a person only as 'the child of X', without replacing a personal name, and a father may have many sons. We cannot, on hearing a patronymic, tell exactly which individual is meant. An Atreid is a descendant of Atreus. But there is more to the problem than this, because patronymics can indicate not only sons, but also grandsons, nephews, great-nephews and so on. So who is this 'Atreid, lord of men'? This is what readers or listeners, having heard the personal name of the other party, Achilles, free of encoding, would like to know. But they cannot discover until line 24 that it is Agamemnon! Before this, the same individual is called 'the Atreid' a further three times, and once—even more mysteriously—simply 'the king'. What can this mean?

Without attempting an explanation we shall proceed first to line 307 of Book 1. Before reaching this line, we have heard approximately 200 lines of argument between 'the Atreid, lord of men' and Achilles. This argument evidently takes place in the besieging army's assembly before Troy. The dispute is over for the moment, and we learn:

So these two after battling in words of contention
stood up, and broke the assembly beside the ships of the Achaians.
The Peleid went back to his balanced ships and his shelter
with the Menoitiad and his own companions.
But the Atreid drew a fast ship...

There is no longer any difficulty with 'the Peleid', as we heard 'the Peleiad' in the very first line, and it is clear that 'the Peleid' and 'the Peleiad' are the same as Achilles. We realize at once that 'Atreides' is merely another form of 'Atreid', and this 'Atreid', as we have seen, is identical with Agamemnon. But who is 'the Menoitiad'? In all the preceding 306 lines there has been no mention of any 'Menoitiad' (nor of any 'companions', who apparently belong to this 'Menoitiad'). Now we are suddenly faced with a 'Menoitiad', as if this were stunningly obvious. Apparently we are supposed to know at once who this 'Menoitiad' is, just as similar knowledge was expected in line 1 in the case of 'the Atreid'. What does this mean?

One might of course reply: this is a highly sophisticated narrative strategy, constantly presenting puzzles to which we eagerly await solutions or to which we find our own solutions. We might then have before us a fragmentary overture of the type known in literary studies as *in medias res*.[21] It is a technique we know from both novels and films. It is deliberately designed to surprise, even astound the reader. It offers the opportunity to enter, in the truest sense of the Latin expression, 'into the thick of things', making the listener/reader/spectator a direct participant in a completely unfamiliar situation in a completely unfamiliar series of events. If the narrative technique is executed with sufficient skill, it arouses curiosity and a desire to find out the whole context. Thus the primary objective of all narrative, tension, is often achieved to a greater degree than with the technique of sequential narrative which opens with scene-setting and a cast of characters. The puzzles posed at the beginning are resolved later, at suitable points in the progress of the plot, by the technique of 'delayed exposition' using flashbacks which often form multiple, fragmentary interconnections. Particularly in modern literature, this is a much favoured procedure, sometimes carried to excess. It requires of the narrator not only sophistication and total command of the overall picture, but also, if it is to be really successful and not unintentionally leave something open, the most alert intelligence.

In the case of the opening of the *Iliad*, however, this explanation must be ruled out, for several reasons. The most substantial of these is that it would make Homer introduce a narrative strategy which does not appear in Greek literature until the imperial period, that is, the first century AD. But if such a strategy had already been employed in the *Iliad*, given Homer's supreme importance as a model to the Greeks, he would certainly have had imitators. The strategy could not, therefore, have remained unknown to us.

This leaves only one possible explanation: the narrator takes for granted our foreknowledge of the individuals concealed behind the patronymics. When in line 307 we hear 'the Menoitiad', we should not be surprised but should realize, with the joy of recognition, that this can mean only one person: the son of Menoitios and friend of Achilles, Patroklos.

The progress of the narrative lines referring to this person shows that any other explanation must be ruled out: after the departure of Achilles, with 'the Menoitiad', from the assembly, we see him twenty-two lines further on (lines 329–30) in a different setting: in front of his tent. Agamemnon has sent two heralds to him to reclaim from him the object of the earlier dispute, the female captive Briseïs. Achilles receives these heralds, who might seem to be far from welcome, in unexpectedly friendly fashion. He says:

> Draw near. You are not to blame in my sight, but Agamemnon
> who sent the two of you here for the sake of the girl Briseis.
> Go then, illustrious Patroklos, and bring the girl forth
> and give her to these to be taken away.

In line 307 Achilles leaves the assembly with a 'Menoitiad'. In line 337 he calls a 'Patroklos' forth from his tent. Up to this point the listener or reader has not gathered from the story that these two individuals are one and the same. At four further points at which 'Patroklos' is mentioned we do not learn this (1. 345; 8. 476; 9. 190; 9. 195). Only in Book 9, lines 202–3, 4,873 lines after the first mention of the 'Menoitiad', do we find clarification, but again not in the form of information directed to the reader, rather as a self-evident variation of appellation. Again heralds come to Achilles, and again Achilles is seated in front of his tent. He invites the heralds, his equals this time in the profession of arms, to sit down and share food and drink with him. The poet then tells us:

> [Achilleus] at once called over to Patroklos who was not far from him:
> 'Son of Menoitios, set up a mixing bowl that is bigger,
> and mix us stronger drink...'

Only at this point can the listener with no foreknowledge conclude that 'the Menoitiad' and 'Patroklos' must be the same individual. That any such process of deduction is intended, however, must be ruled out as this process and its result have absolutely no function in the narrative. It is therefore plain that, at the very first mention of 'the Menoitiad' and 'Patroklos', the poet expects his audience to know that these are one and the same.

Other examples of this presentation of leading characters could be adduced. It differs markedly from the treatment of secondary characters. These are usually introduced in the familiar fashion: with their origins and home town named, their office indicated, and a background sketch and physical description etc. provided. For example, in Book 2 there is a small-scale mutiny in the Achaian army. A certain Thersites establishes himself as ringleader. Before making him deliver his fiery speech, the poet introduces him thus (2. 211–21):

> Now the rest had sat down and were orderly in their places,
> but one man, Thersites of the endless speech, still scolded,
> who knew within his mead many words, but disorderly;
> vain, and without decency, to quarrel with the princes
> with any word he thought might be amusing to the Argives.
> This was the ugliest man who came beneath Ilion. He was
> bandy-legged and went lame of one foot, with shoulders
> stooped and drawn together over his chest, and above this
> his skull went up to a point with the wool grown sparsely upon it.
> Beyond all others Achilleus hated him, and Odysseus.
> These two he was forever abusing...

It is clear that a person is being introduced who 'in all probability can be attributed to the inventive powers of Homer himself',[22] as indicated by his speaking name. ('Thersites' means literally 'impudent one'.) When compared with the procedure adopted in cases such as those of 'the Atreid' and 'the Menoitiad', the difference is striking. The inescapable conclusion is that the audience already knows the heroes of the story at the outset (or the narrator feels that these should be known). In view of its fundamental importance, this point should be stated once again, as emphatically as possible: the leading actors in the story are known to the audience in advance.

The focus of the Iliad*: not the tale of Troy but the tale of Achilles*

We now come to the next step: if the leading actors were known to the audience, it was not as isolated, free-floating figures, but as actors in a certain sphere of action, that is, within a certain narrative context. Hence the next question: from what narrative context or contexts did the audience know the actors?

The *Iliad* has one setting and four main actors: (1) Achilles, the young prince from Thessaly, (2) Agamemnon, the supreme commander of the besieging Achaian coalition, (3) Patroklos, Achilles' closest friend, and (4) Hektor, son of the king of the besieged city and leader of the defending forces. The setting is Ilios/Troy. Around these four characters and around Troy a rich array of other characters and interrelations is built up, on both sides of the front. This is a canvas with many figures in it. In the 'lower', human plane, it features heroic figures like Odysseus, Aias, Diomedes, Nestor, Helen, Paris, Priam, Hekabe, Andromache, Aineias, and many others, and in the 'higher' plane, numerous gods, from the supreme god Zeus down to the river gods, water nymphs, and godlike personifications such as 'fear', 'flight', 'sleep', 'dreams', and others—over 700 figures in all.[23] Even if we discount all those who are invented only to be killed in battle, well over 500 are left. This is an enormous cast.

However, the plot of the entire *Iliad* occupies no more than 51 days. One does not immediately realize this, supposing spontaneously that, given a length of almost 16,000 lines, the action must span a much longer period. But in fact there are only those 51 days, over which the vast narrative scope of the work is spread. This is best illustrated by a graph (Fig. 20).

Structure		Days	Nights	Lines	Segments	Content
Exposition (21 days) 647 lines		Day 1	-	41	**1.** 12b–52	Chryses - prologue
		Days 2–9	7 nights	1	**1.** 53	Plague in Achaian camp
		Day 10	-	423	**1.** 54–476	Quarrel Achilles-Agamemnon Embassy to Chryse
		Day 11	-	16	**1.** 477–492	Embassy returns Wrath of Achilles
		Days 12-20	8 nights	(1)	(**1.** 493)	Gods with the Ethiopians
		Day 21	+ night to day 22	166	**1.** 493–**2.** 47	Plea of Thetis Agamemnon's dream
Main narrative (6 days) 13,444 lines	First day of fighting	Day 22	-	3,653	**2.** 48–**7.** 380	Agamemnon tempts army (*Diapeira)* Catalogues (review of troops) Accord - duel Menelaos-Paris to decide outcome. View from wall (*Teikhoskopia*) Duel Menelaos-Paris Accord broken by Trojan Pandarus Aristeia (great deeds) of Diomedes Hektor in Troy (*Homilia*) Duel Hektor-Aias
		Day 23	-	52	**7.** 381–432	Truce Burials
		Day 24	-	50	**7.** 433–482	Achaians build walls
	Second day of fighting	Day 25	+ night to day 26	1,857	**8.** 1–**10.** 579 (3 books)	Achaians forced back Trojans camp on plain Mission to Achilles (*Litai*) [Dolonie]
	Third day of fighting	Day 26	+ night to day 27	5,669	**11.** 1–**18.** 617 (8 books)	Aristeia of Agamemnon Aristeia of Hektor Achaian leaders wounded Achilles sends Patroklos to Nestor Fight at the camp walls (*Teikhomakhia*) Trojans invade Achaian camp Fight by the ships Hera seduces Zeus (*Diós apátē)* Patrokleia Description of shield
	Fourth day of fighting	Day 27	+ night to day 28	2,163	**19.** 1–**23.** 110a (almost 5 books)	Quarrel settled (*Mēnidos apórrhēsis*) Fighting resumes Death of Hektor
Conclusion (24 days) 1,591 lines		Day 28	-	147	**23.** 110b–257a	Funeral of Patroklos
		Day 29	+ night to day 30	661	**23.** 257b – **24.** 21	Games in honour of Patroklos (*Athla*)
		Days 30–40	10 nights	9	**24.** 22–30	Hektor abused
		Day 41	+ night to day 42	664	**24.** 31–694	Priam goes to Achaian camp
		Day 42	-	87	**24.** 695–781	Hektor brought home
		Days 43–50	7 nights	3	**24.** 782–784	Truce; collection of wood
		Day 51	-	20	**24.** 785–804	Funeral of Hektor

FIG. 20. The chronological structure of the *Iliad*.

One notices immediately that battle scenes form the focus of the story. The battles occupy four days and almost twenty-two of the total of twenty-four books. Contrasted with this 'combat block' which goes into minute detail, the two books which precede and follow it, Books 1 and 24, each covering much longer periods, can only be described as the 'introduction' and 'conclusion'. The introduction, which includes Book 1 and the first part of Book 2, spans 21 days, and the conclusion, in the latter part of Book 23 and Book 24, spans 24, making a total of 45 days. These 45 days are dealt with in 2,238 lines, or one-seventh of the total. Between the introduction and the conclusion lie days 22 to 27, covered in 13,444 lines, or six-sevenths of the total. These lines form the core of the epic. But of these six days, detailed treatment is accorded to only four, the four days of battle (days 22, 25, 26, and 27). These four days occupy no less than 13,342 lines, in almost 22 of the 24 Books of the *Iliad*.

We have already discussed the poet's true intention and concluded that it did not consist in depicting the whole of the ten-year war over Troy. This conclusion is confirmed from another perspective in the graph: if this 16,000-line work has its narrative emphasis on only four days within a brief span of 51 days in the ninth or tenth year of the war, its true theme cannot possibly be the course of the Trojan War. The author must in fact wish to tell another story, a story of his own, and a relatively short one. As we have seen, this is his Agamemnon-Achilles-Patroklos-Hektor story, seen as the vehicle and 'debating forum' for the issues which were topical at the time the work came into being. We could go even further and say that it is his Achilles story, and on these grounds the whole huge work should be entitled not 'The Iliad', the 'Song of Ilios', but rather 'The Achilleid', the 'Song of Achilles'. We have shown elsewhere that this 'Song of Achilles' tells what is essentially a brief story, but one that is nevertheless compressed to the utmost relative to its central problem.[24]

But why does a short story need a cast of more than 700 characters, including many already assumed to be known to the audience? Can a story of this nature have been invented by the teller of the story alone?

The tale of Troy as a frame for the Iliad

If the 51 days constituted the whole of the story, we could perhaps, despite some reservations, give an affirmative answer. It does not seem unreasonable to suppose that one individual could compose a 51-day story. And it is theoretically possible that he might have introduced in some of his earlier stories the characters who are assumed to be already known—just as one does not introduce the characters anew in each episode of a serialized novel. We might perhaps be dealing with one episode of a series, and find the absence of the preceding episodes a cause of irritation. A contemporary audience, however, knowing the preceding episodes, would have been better informed. We shall see that in a certain sense this hypothesis comes close to the truth, but only in a restricted sense.

The reason for this is that the *Iliad* implies a narrative context which is incomparably larger than would be needed for the Achilles story alone. It can be asserted with full confidence that the broad narrative context in which the Achilles story is placed is so vast as to exceed by far the creative powers of any one individual. This needs to be shown in more detail.

The work itself makes clear near the beginning that the plot is not a chronologically closed entity, but a segment of a much longer continuum. Once again, it is not possible in our framework to enumerate fully and cite all the indications of this, which occur throughout the work. For present purposes it will amply suffice to outline the type of indication given. Three examples will be sufficient:

1. In Book 2, line 295, in a speech to an assembly of battle-weary and homesick Achaians, the narrator makes Odysseus say,

> And for us now
> this is the ninth of the circling years that we wait here,

and three lines further on (2. 299):

> No, but be patient, friends, and stay yet a little longer
> until we know whether Kalchas' prophecy is true or is not true.
> For I remember this thing well in my heart, and you all are
> witnesses, whom the spirits of death have not carried away from us;

> yesterday and before, at Aulis, when the ships of the Achaians
> were gathered bringing disaster to the Trojans and Priam...

[This is followed by the recollection of a certain omen seen in Aulis, and Kalchas' ensuing prophecy that the Achaians would conquer Troy in the tenth year.]

The narrator is therefore taking as given the knowledge that the siege on the plain before Troy has already gone on for nine years and that, before its landing on the coast of the Troad, the besieging Greek force had assembled as a naval expeditionary force in the Boiotian port of Aulis, in the straits of Euboia. This means that the narrator is forming a connection between this story and a preceding nine-year prelude, which he does not set forth in detail.

2. Shortly after this, the narrator gives a reason for the expedition of nine years ago, thereby once again extending his story into the past, this time over an undefined period. At the same assembly, he has Nestor deliver a speech in support of Odysseus, castigating the Greeks in the following terms (2. 354):

> Therefore let no man be urgent to take the way homeward
> until after he has lain in bed with the wife of a Trojan
> to avenge Helen's longing to escape and her lamentations.

Here the cause of the entire war is given: the abduction of Helen, the Greek queen of Sparta, by Paris, the prince of Troy. But this cause is not introduced by the narrator himself as a new element, with any of the flourish that such an important new motivation might deserve. Rather it is embedded in a speech by one of the characters, apparently as a component of a larger story, of which only a small part is told here, a component which the narrator assumes to be well known to his characters in the poem, as well as the audience outside it. He assumes this quite independently of his own Achilles story, so as to be able to utilize it as a building block in the way that he does here. However, this building block, the abduction of Helen by a Trojan, can have occupied a place in the chain of causes of the conflict only before the assembly of the Achaian fleet in Aulis, since this is the response to the abduction. So here the narrator has reached back to another segment—apparently of substantial length—in the period of the prelude, which he does not set forth, but which he uses in the expectation that he will be understood.

3. This still does not, however, take us back to the beginning of the assumed causal chain. In Book 24, lines 23 ff., the narrator reports how, in a kind of compulsive ritual, Achilles again repeatedly abuses the body of the Trojan prince Hektor, whom he has killed. The narrator then goes on:

> The blessed gods as they looked upon [Hektor's body] were filled with compassion
> and kept urging the clear-sighted Argeïphontes [Hermes] to steal the body.
> There this was pleasing to all the others, but never to Hera
> nor Poseidon, nor Athene, who kept still
> their hatred for sacred Ilion as in the beginning,
> and for Priam and his people, because of the delusion of Paris,
> who insulted the goddesses [Hera and Athene] when they came to him in his courtyard
> and favoured her who supplied the lust that led to disaster.

Here the narrator reaches back yet further into the objective time-sequence of the prelude, further than in the first two cases. Paris, who will later abduct Helen, is here shown as a very young man, who, according to the custom of the time, must tend his father's herds for a period in a kind of apprenticeship before his admission to manhood. The logic of the story requires that years must pass before he will return from the pastures to Troy as an adult, then as prince be entrusted with an official mission to Sparta, and there win Helen for himself and take her back to Troy. The same logic requires that the Greek reaction—the decision to mount a retaliatory campaign, the assembly of a coalition, the mustering of 29 naval contingents at Aulis (we learn the number in Book 2), and the crossing to Asia Minor—will also take some time more. The story into which our narrator embeds his 51-day plot therefore reaches back not just the nine years between Aulis and the ninth or tenth year of the siege, but many years before this.

In addition to this chronological dimension, however, there is something deeper hidden here: the cause of the Trojan War is not only named—hatred for the Trojan Paris and for Troy as a whole on the part of the humiliated goddesses Hera, the wife of Zeus, and Athene, his daughter. It is also given a psychological interpretation: Paris, who has spurned Hera and Athene in favour of Aphrodite, receives from his chosen goddess of love a very special gift, called *machlosýne*, which means 'aura of sexual attraction radiating onto others'. The barely comprehensible fact that Helen, the wife of a renowned king and mother of a little daughter, falls so completely under the spell of a foreigner from a distant land that she forgets everything to follow him to Troy is attributed to a god-given, demonic, almost magical power that nobody can withstand. Helen is exonerated. The Trojan War thus appears as something imposed by the gods.

These three forays into the past alone—and the *Iliad* has many more—and the casual manner in which they allude to clearly substantial components of an obviously extensive narrative context make it hard to believe that the narrator of our 51-day plot wished at the same time to create by his own efforts a larger framework for his modest story. In the first two cases, a sceptic might perhaps still hesitate—although here too the matter-of-fact way in which the chronological information ('the ninth year') is imparted in the first instance, and the geographical information ('Aulis') in the second, confirms the impression that the narrator is referring to an established temporal and spatial context which he knows the audience shares with him, and in which he wishes to embed his own story. The third of these forays removes any possible doubt: a narrator seeking to fabricate a larger frame-plot as background for his own smaller tale would not attempt profound psychological explanations for the fabricated interactions of fabricated characters in a fabricated background story. This would very soon involve him in a complex tangle of cause and effect. Furthermore, for the narrator's true purpose it would be an utterly pointless refinement.

The Iliad *elucidates and resonates clearly with the tale of Troy*

If we gather together in this way all the allusions reaching backwards, forwards, and laterally from the *Iliad*—the work contains over a hundred such references—and consider them together, the result is a dense network of assumptions, relationships, and motifs which lie outside the *Iliad* itself.[25] With the additional help of other texts produced in Greece after the *Iliad*, texts whose narrative course is known from the accounts of later writers, the so-called 'mythographers',[26] we can still today produce a highly reliable reconstruction of the total network. It displays no contradictions. It forms an immense, stable, and logically coherent narrative system, resonating with the most varied points in the *Iliad* and compatible with yet other components. Nobody who has ever followed the *Iliad* story, or who follows it today, could ever have any doubt that the *Iliad* as we have it now—as the tale of a 51-day period of crisis—is deliberately embedded in this narrative system. The narrator counts on his audience possessing the knowledge of this all-embracing network and being at least sufficiently familiar to appreciate its references correctly and make good use of the illuminating power of the background for the foreground story (and to some extent vice versa).

To us, unless we are Homer specialists, this broader context is naturally alien and largely new. We do not reside in it. The first audience of the *Iliad*, on the other hand, had long since been inducted by thematically similar stories heard from other bards, but also by prose tales, in rather the same way as our parents knew Grimm's fairy-tales or the Bible from earliest youth, so that, on hearing the name 'Little Red Riding Hood', or 'Moses', or 'Aaron' in some new version of a familiar story, they did not need to ask who these were or what role they played in the background story that was taken for granted. We, however, must first establish from the *Iliad*, that is, from the brief tale of a crisis embedded in that network, who the characters are and what position they occupy in the larger network of the overarching tale of Troy.

In this there is much for us to learn. The scope is such that here again the whole picture can be presented only in the form of a graph (Fig. 21).

This narrative web, of which no more than the main elements are shown here, contains such an extended and ramified wealth of events, characters, situations, and interconnections that the poet of our Achilles story, which we call the *Iliad*, could never have invented it by himself. It is more likely that he embedded his own 51-day story, as a relatively tiny excerpt, in this pre-existing and generally recognized overall context, and thus spared himself the need to construct a framework of his own. In this way the larger

Prologue on Olympus		**Story of the twenty years before the War**			
Zeus and Themis confer over the Trojan War	Zeus bgets **Helen** (with Nemesis/Leda)	**Wedding** of Zeus's grandson **Peleus** to Nereus's daughter **Thetis** on Mount Pelion (Thessaly); all the gods take part. (The union will produce **Achilles**)	**Judgement of Paris**: 'Aphrodite is the fairest!' His reward will be Helen.	Paris sails to Greece and **abducts** Helen from Sparta.	The **Achaians** muster to take revenge. First rendezvous of ships at Aulis and **first departure**; false landfall in Mysia (Teuthrania / Kaikos valley): too far south.
Zeus and Hera force the sea-goddess Thetis into a union with King Peleus		The goddess Eris sows discord among the three goddesses **Hera, Athene, Aphrodite**: 'Who is the fairest?'			**Telephos story**: Achilles wounds Telephos, king of the Mysians.
		The three goddesses go to handsome **Paris**, son of Priam and Hecabe, on Mount Ida near Troy: Paris to adjudicate.			Fleet leaves Teuthrania for Troy, but is scattered by storm. Second rendezvous at Aulis. Agamemnon's killing of the hart of Artemis leads to the sacrifice of **Iphigenia**, daughter of Agamemnon and Clytaemnestra.
					Arrival and healing of Telephos.
					Sparrow augury of Kalchas. **Second departure** from Aulis. Landing on Tenedos; landing on Lemnos. Philoktetes abandoned.

Ten Years of War before Troy			**Ten Years of the Return Home**		
9 Years	9th/10th Year			10th Year	
Landing in the Troad; death of Protesilaos. Achaian embassy to Troy under Odysseus and Menelaos fails.	51 days = our ***Iliad***: small episode: conflict of **Agamemnon** and **Achilles** and its consequences, above all death of **Hektor**.	Final events: the **Amazon Penthesilea** arrives and is defeated by Achilles. Thersites abuses Achilles and is killed by him. The Ethiopian king **Memnon** comes from Egypt and kills, among others, Nestor's son Antilochos.	**Return home** of all surviving Greek warriors.	40 days = our *Odyssey*: small episode of the *nostos* of **Odysseus** with his reunion with his wife **Penelope** and restoration of his estates.	**'*Telegonia*'**: the end of **Odysseus.**
Achilles kills Kyknos.		**Paris** and **Apollo** bring about death of Achilles.			
Great deeds of Achilles: he conquers 23 mainland and island towns around Troy (inc. Lyrnessos, Pedasos, and Hypoplakic Thebes) to isolate Troy; among the booty are Briseis and **Chryseis.**		**Aias** and **Odysseus** dispute armour of Achilles; latter is successful. Madness of Aias.			
(Chryseis serves as starting point for the *Iliad*.)		**Philoktetes** and **Neoptolemus**, son of Achilles, brought by **Odysseus.** The **wooden horse; fall of Troy:** 'Iliou Persis'. Priam killed.			

FIG. 21. The complete tale of Troy. The *Iliad* and the *Odyssey* may be seen to be small segments. The events shaded are mentioned in the *Iliad*; some of them also in the *Odyssey*.

story, of which knowledge is assumed, is to a degree segmented, and in the segment selected and magnified (as Aristotle stated in his study of the *Iliad*[27]) attention is deliberately focused on a few characters. The larger story of the Trojan War—with its cause, its course, and its consequences—thus becomes a framing structure, which needs only to be mentioned as background, and in the chosen segment a contemporary problem is explored.

This is a narrative technique which has since been applied a thousand times over in world literature—from the Greek tragedies in the fifth century BC, which are mostly fragmentary scenes from a larger canvas called 'myth' (predominantly the 'Troy myth'), through the Latin epics including Virgil's *Aeneid* which rework the myths, right down to the literature of today. (We have only to think of Christa Wolf's *Kassandra* and *Medea*.) Manfred Fuhrmann, the literary scholar from Constance, has termed this kind of writing *Mythenreprisenliteratur*, or 'myth-rewriting'.[28] Having in mind the beneficial effects of parasites, one might also call it 'parasitic literature'. The French scholar Gérard Genette has spoken of 'palimpsest literature', *palímpsēston* being in Greek a sheet of paper on which the original writing has been erased and overwritten. Genette has developed a highly elaborate theory of the 'palimpsest technique' in world literature.[29]

Of course this technique has also been applied to other overarching contextual systems, such as the Bible, and of course the technique has been refined in the course of centuries, in particular by the inclusion of a great number of earlier treatments of the same primary work (giving us what we now call 'intertextuality'). What remains common to all writing of this kind is that in each case it is embedded in a canonical narrative structure, the basis of which it does not change and cannot change, so that that structure remains recognizable and usable. Oedipus must never thrash his uncle and become engaged to his aunt, but must always kill his father and marry his mother. Within the pre-set parameters, however, much may be invented and much put to new uses. By this means the continued existence of the overall frame in which the parasitic story finds a host, and the existence of the genre of 'parasitic literature' may be assured possibly for thousands of years.

It is clearly this technique that the narrator of the *Iliad* employs and in which he takes as given the contextual frame for the insertion of his own theme. The story of Troy and the Greek struggle against the Trojans must therefore, by the time the *Iliad* was created, have existed as an entity with a considerable density of factual information. It would otherwise be impossible to account for the abundance of allusions to parts of this entity which are widely separated in time, to say nothing of the interpretative play with individual motifs of the story, as seen, for example, in the case of the judgement of Paris. This means, however, that the tale of Troy as a whole must already have been very old in Greece when the *Iliad* arose. How old—we shall explore later. In any case, it would have been heard so often, that is, performed by bards in ever varying oral versions for such a long time, that by the eighth century BC it constituted an elaborate narrative structure, a knowledge of which could be assumed in a large part of the audience, rather as a poet in Christian Europe could for centuries assume familiarity with the narrative structure of the Bible. What this meant for an eighth-century bard is clear: when he wanted to provoke debate about problems of his own time, there was no more effective method than to take this old story with its well-known characters—Agamemnon, Achilles, Priam, Paris, Helen, and others—and place the issues in the mouths of these characters. If he followed this procedure, there was no need to construct a new setting or create new characters. He could concentrate entirely on his own theme.

If we classify Homer and his Achilles story, to which some later writer gave the misleading title 'The Iliad',[30] in this tradition of 'myth-rewriting' or 'parasitic literature', this does not of course mean that Homer himself was the progenitor of this kind of literature. The broad scope of the story permits only the conclusion that long before Homer many bards had inserted their own chronologically determined individual stories in the narrative framework known as 'the tale of Troy', and thus contributed to its further internal consolidation. Bards who came later, like their confrères from an even later age, poets of the age of literacy in antiquity and the modern age, would have made use of the material inserted by their predecessors, of which they learned during their bardic apprenticeship and later from the performances of established bards. Intertextuality is not an invention of modern times, but has been an integral part of literature for as long as literature has existed, whether in oral or written form.

If we digress briefly and consider sung poetry in the living traditions of other peoples today, like those of the Serbs and Croats, for example, we see that all singers have a professional interest in learning as many versions as possible of the poems in their repertoire, as sung by their colleagues. Homer would have done the same.

It may therefore be assumed in advance that his story made use not only of the tale-of-Troy framework, but also of previous uses of that framework. Some scholars arrived at this realization by other routes several decades ago,[31] and attempts were made to reconstruct these uses from Homer's use. This has led to the growth of a whole new branch of research, known as 'neo-analysis' or 'motif study'.[32] Unfortunately, despite all the admirable ingenuity applied here, the reconstructions arrived at can never be more than hypotheses, because all earlier uses of the Troy-story framework are lost to us. They were transmitted orally, and since the Greeks had no form of writing until the eighth century BC each version faded away forever as soon as the bard reached the end. Only the adoption by the Greeks of the Phoenician writing system in about 800 BC brought with it the opportunity to write down a version which apparently struck contemporary listeners as particularly beautiful and successful, and thereby record it for posterity. This version was Homer's *Iliad*. For the European cultural area, Homer thus became the founder of this kind of literature, and the *Iliad* the prototype of a genre which has endured to this day.

CONCLUSIONS: HOMER'S *ILIAD* IS MERELY A SECONDARY SOURCE FOR THE TROJAN WAR

Summing up our argument to this point, we can state that:

In composing the Achilles story which we know as the *Iliad*, Homer cannot have invented either the form in which he wrote, or the material into which he embedded his story. To both he 'only' added new content. Both the form and the content were available to him.

The new content, the communication of which was Homer's real purpose, consisted of the Achilles story, with its statement of questions current at the time when the story originated.

The Achilles story is presented as a 51-day episode from the ninth or tenth year of the ten-year Trojan War and centres around one of the Achaian besiegers. In order to be able to explore this episode as a clearly illuminated foreground event, Homer was obliged to set out the familiar large-scale background event, the Trojan War, as a backdrop. For his purposes, however, as usual in this procedure, he had to set out only so much of this backdrop as was necessary and helpful for an understanding of his foreground story.[33] As a result, the *Iliad* shows the background, the larger-scale overall tale of Troy, only at relatively few brief points, each no more than a momentary glimpse, just as a modern story-teller, wishing to place a new episode in a biblical context, for example, will not retell the entire contents of the Bible.

This technique means that we cannot learn from the *Iliad* the whole of the tale of Troy or the whole story of the Trojan War in the form known to the original audience, but only glimpse isolated details which occasionally shine through. Homer's Achilles story, which we call the *Iliad*, can offer no more than a pale reflection of the complete tale of Troy, taken for granted by the poet, including the component dealing with the Trojan War.

Thus the sole written source which we have had to date for the history of the Trojan War, the Greek *Iliad*, turns out to be no more than a secondary source, offering only fragmentary information. We possess no primary source in Greek or any other language, no continuous presentation, that is, of the entire course of the war, such as Homer and most of his original audience must have held in their memory.[34]

Nevertheless, the *Iliad*'s very status as a secondary source lends it special value for the purpose of recovering the original form of the overall picture of the Trojan War. This is because the narrator of the *Iliad* not only cannot have had any interest at all in altering the structure of the frame, as he was concerned with something else, but also could not possibly have made serious changes to it because by doing so he would have distracted attention from his own inserted story and made it impossible to achieve his purpose. Those fragments of information from the larger story which he does convey may therefore be taken to be fundamentally authentic elements, until proved otherwise, of the original structural framework.

The Tale of Troy Independent of Homer's

It follows from these researches, on the one hand, that we will never be able fully to retrieve the original form of the whole tale from the *Iliad*, since it is no more than a pale secondary source. On the other hand, it also follows that we can at least reconstruct an outline of the tale from indications in our *Iliad*, supplemented by indications from our *Odyssey* and information from a collection of poems a hundred years younger and complementary to it, the so-called 'Epic Cycle'.[1] This outline reads then as follows.

THE OUTLINE OF THE TALE OF TROY

- A mighty king named *Priam* reigns in the wealthy city of *Ilios/Troy* at the southern entrance to the *Hellespont* (the Dardanelles) in Asia Minor.[2] One of his sons, named *Paris*, sails on a mission of friendship to the land of *Achaia* in the Peloponnese and reaches Sparta, where *Menelaos*, a son of *Atreus* (an Atreid), rules. Paris abuses the hospitality shown to him there by abducting *Helen*, the wife of Menelaos, to Troy. Menelaos asks for help from his brother *Agamemnon* of *Mycenae*. A delegation of Achaians, demanding in Troy the return of Helen, is turned away by the Trojans. Thereupon Menelaos and Agamemnon (the *Atreids*) resolve to compel the surrender of Helen by military means. Agamemnon asks all the more significant powers on the mainland and on the islands to supply contingents for a joint expedition to Troy. The appeal is widely heeded.

- The ships muster in the port of *Aulis* in Boiotia in the strait of the island of *Euboia* (the *Iliad* counts 29 contingents), each contingent under its commander or commanders. Agamemnon will assume overall command of the expedition. The fleet sails to the Hellespont by way of the islands of *Lemnos* and *Tenedos* (a distance of about 350 km.) and lands on the coast of the Troad. Once a first attempt to storm the city fails, as had initial negotiations, a siege begins, which, against all expectations, drags on from year to year because of the dogged resistance of the citizens and their allies among the neighbouring peoples of Asia Minor. It is marked by the besiegers' constant attempts to cut Troy off from its hinterland and support, taking, plundering, and destroying neighbouring cities, island settlements, and cultivated areas, and thus wear it down. The plan fails, not least because the gods are not at one over the fate of Troy. Only in the *tenth year of war*, when the pro-Trojan faction among the gods has finally given way, can the city be taken by a ruse: the *wooden horse* devised by Odysseus. King Priam and the male population are killed and the women and children carried off home as slaves.
- The return home (*nostos*) is not carried out in the same good order as the assault ten years earlier. There are contingents and single ships swept far off course. Many heroes reach home after many years of wandering and adventures (Odysseus!). Troy, however, is destroyed forever.

This is a sequence of events with a logic which appears basically realistic. Without damage to the coherence of the overall sequence, a few factors which are today perceived as irrational can easily be disregarded, for instance 'abduction' as the motive for war (which, however, hardly deserves the customary dutiful acid derision, particularly on the part of historians, given the liaisons which have triggered national crises and wars in modern history right up to the present). As can the acts of the gods or the wooden horse. To term this realistic, however, is only the first step. The state of knowledge attained today in Greek studies indicates that this sequence of events, both through the accuracy of its geographical detail, proved by re-examination today to be broadly correct,[3] and through the political configuration of powers reflected in it, is also thoroughly plausible *historically*.

One thing must be emphasized: the power relations, power distribution, and power capabilities mirrored in this sequence of events (above all the dominant position of Mycenae), according to Greek archaeology, appeared to be realized in Greece at a single point in time: not the eighth century, in which Homer recites this story, nor in the preceding three to four centuries, the so-called 'Dark Age', but only in the Greeks' first period of high culture, which we call Mycenaean, approximately in the third quarter of the second millennium BC (around 1500–1200/1150 BC).

Every one of the many attempts to place the tale of Troy in the Mycenaean age of the Greeks had naturally to remain a hypothesis as long as the only real information on this period in Greek history came from excavations and so could only be enunciated when imagination was employed to impose a system. Hence the decade-long discussion, often highly embittered, over the possibility or impossibility of a 'Trojan War' could at bottom be nothing more than a dispute over probabilities. As a rule, such discussions go in circles, take the case no further and tend to degenerate instead into training grounds for hurtful academic jibes. In this respect, the 'Trojan War' dispute has greatly damaged the scholarly world. In the light of the new set of facts, it could soon come to an end.

THE TALE OF TROY IN THE LIGHT OF SOURCES OUTSIDE HOMER

Constant attempts have naturally been made, following the rediscovery of Mycenaean Greece through the excavations of Heinrich Schliemann and succeeding generations of archaeologists, in the decades since 1874, to use evidence from written sources to bring to life the mute information wrung from the stones. The source material available was nevertheless weak: with few exceptions, place-names, geographical data, and internal and external political relations in the Mycenaean age of Greek history could only be taken from the Greek records themselves. These records began only when the 'Dark Age', which had no writing, ended and the Greeks adopted the Phoenician alphabet about 800 BC. That was about 400 years after the end of the period in question. And these 'alphabetically written' records consisted chiefly of Homer. There were also a small number of documents later than Homer, which in turn drew mainly on Homer and were able to add to him only here and there. These were various longer poems by the early Greek epic poet Hesiod (around 700 BC), then the aforementioned 'Epic Cycle', early Greek lyric poetry, and finally the writings of the so-called mythographers. These were the work of Greek writers who, since the sixth century BC, endeavoured to collect and collate in what they saw as the most sensible form possible the old myths, which could at that time still be gleaned from oral and written sources. In doing so, succeeding writers constantly relied, naturally, on what their predecessors had collected and assembled. Hence the material hardly increased, but was passed on as a block of information and essentially was merely rearranged and reinterpreted. Inasmuch as the information in these post-Homer writings extends beyond what we can gather from Homer, it can only come either from oral tradition in individual places in Greece or from later speculation.[4] There has been and is no known evidence in Greek, set down in alphabetical form, of the circumstances of the Mycenaean age, which either appeared before Homer or alongside him but was not at all influenced by him.

It is important to state these facts as emphatically as possible: our knowledge of the Greeks' Mycenaean age was for decades nourished, apart from the silent stones of the excavations, exclusively by *Greek* written sources, sources which, after a gap in which writing did not exist, began about 400 years *after* the time of the circumstances they treat.[5] Hence none of our written sources were contemporary with the Mycenaean age.

This situation has changed radically since 1952. Since that year three bodies of written sources contemporary with the Mycenaean age of ancient Greece have appeared—one Greek and two non-Greek. All three bodies have been discussed earlier—in the previous sections 'Achai(w)ija and Achijawa' (p. 121), 'Danaoí and Danaja' (p. 128), and 'Linear B Deciphered' (p. 156). This happened in separate places and in each case in another context. The situation as it appears today must hence be reformulated in summary for the new context.

1. The Greek-language corpus of sources, the Linear B corpus deciphered in 1952 by Michael Ventris and John Chadwick, consists of inscriptions made by Greeks in the form of speech in use at that time on clay tablets, seals, and vessels in the Mycenaean age, from the fifteenth to the thirteenth/twelfth century. The script used was a syllabary borrowed from Crete: Linear B. The objects so far discovered (others are constantly being found in excavations in Greece) derive from around ten sites in the area then settled by Greeks: the most significant are Knossos and Kydonia/Khaniá in Crete, Pylos, Mycenae, Tiryns, and Thebes on the mainland. The number of known inscriptions amounted in 1989 to 4,765. Among them place-names occur 189 times and names of peoples, tribes, occupational or social groups and similar groups 78 times.[6] Thus the texts give an insight into the following sectors of life at the time: the social structure and the administrative system, religion, agriculture (grains, spices, olives, figs, wine, bee-keeping, animal husbandry, animal products), crafts, commerce, and industry (construction, metals, household goods, fabrics, flax), weapons and war (arms, chariots, military organization).[7] Assembling and collating single pieces of information from this rich material enables reconstruction of a quite dependable picture of Greek geography, settlement history, economy, society, warfare, religion, and to some extent internal politics at the time in question, a picture *totally independent of Homer.*

2. Of the two non-Greek bodies of source material, the first is the *Egyptian,* the nucleus of which is an inscription discovered in 1965 on the plinth of a statue from the funerary temple of Amenophis III (*c.*1390–1352[8]). This inscription cites, for at least a part of the Mycenaean age of Greek history, an empire *Danaja* with a capital *Mukana,* which controlled, or in any case had contact with, besides *Messana* (= Messenia, up to the present) and, for a time at least, *Amyklai* (that is Lakonia, with the later capital Lakedaimon or Sparta), clearly also *Thebes* or the '*Thebais*' ('Land of the Thebans'). It seems certain that this is the empire, with its capital *Mykenai /Mycenae,* whose inhabitants appear in Homer's text as Danaans. Other references to various Mycenaean Greek place-names in the

Egyptian correspondence mentioned above supplement the plinth inscription.

3. The third body of source material, the *Hittite*, is the richest to date. Following the significant progress of recent years described above, the evaluation of the Hittite documents is now well under way—not only by Hittite scholars, but particularly also by archaeologists working in the formerly Greek cities of Asia Minor.[9] We have already, however, a picture of official (state) contacts between the Hittite empire and *Aḫḫijawā* (Achaia) which is rich in information. Provisional study of the correspondence currently reveals varied diplomatic activity by both sides to exert influence within the other's sphere of interest or to counter it in their own.

These three collections of written sources all refer to roughly the *same* period of Greek history, the time between about 1450 and 1150 BC.[10] So we have authentic and objective contemporary written documents of the Mycenaean age of Greek history, seen from within (Linear B) and without (Egyptian, Hittite).

None of the three reveals a Greek area of settlement which deviates in any geographically relevant way from that presented in our *Iliad*. All three bodies agree on a well-organized and economically prosperous culture for the area. The Hittite corpus adds that this culture was recognized politically as of equal standing by the two neighbouring great powers of the time, the Egyptians and the Hittites, right up to the thirteenth century BC.

The three sets of sources break off roughly simultaneously, reflecting the same catastrophe and the same cultural collapse indicated in material terms by the archaeology. In the course of the twelfth century, Greece vanishes from the light of Mediterranean history, to return into the light after about 350 years of darkness, from about 800 BC onwards, with changed structures re-emerging and then developing with great rapidity.

Comparing this documentary picture, totally independent of Homer, with the situation which forms the basis of the outline of the tale of Troy as it emerges from Homer's *Iliad*, one finds a clear correspondence. First, Homer's tale of Troy cannot be fully a product of imagination; second, it can reflect only the circumstances of the Mycenaean age of Greek history and no other.

Many researchers had come to this conclusion after the discovery of only the first of the three written bodies, Linear B. As an example, we refer here only to John Chadwick, who continued the analysis of the Mycenaean texts within the new science of *Mycenology* with particular success after the early death in an accident of Michael Ventris in 1956:

> Greece in the eighth century BC was a disorganised collection of petty states, still living at a comparatively low level of civilisation; houses were mainly of wood and mud-brick; precious materials were very scarce; the arts of painting and sculpture were primitive. Yet the Greece Homer describes is a network of well-organised kingdoms capable of joint military action; its kings live in luxurious stone-built palaces, adorned with gold, ivory and other precious materials. The scenes attributed to the shield made for Akhilleus by the god Hēphaistos argue a high degree of artistic competence. Nor does this situation square with what little we know of conditions in the ninth, tenth or eleventh centuries, the so-called Dark Age. In order to find a plausible setting for the Greece Homer describes we need to go back to the Mycenaean age, to the twelfth or more likely the thirteenth century at the latest.[11]

Once the two non-Greek sets of documents came to supplement the internal Greek written documentation, which in itself had made this conclusion inescapable, the last doubts were dispelled. The tale of Troy recounted in Homer's *Iliad* as a frame for the tale of Achilles is a reflection of the circumstances prevailing in Greece during the Mycenaean age.

When Was the Tale of Troy Conceived?

Once this point is reached, the same question presents itself to every observer: if the tale of Troy is a reflection of the Mycenaean age of Greece, an age which came to an end about 1200 BC or not very long after, how did it reach Homer, a Greek poet of the eighth century BC? Chadwick had put this question thus in direct connection with his conclusion: 'Is it possible that a poet of the eighth century could accurately describe events which happened five hundred years earlier?' And Chadwick went further in 1976:

'The answer to this question is perhaps yes.'[1] In what follows, we will try to make a 'certainly' out of Chadwick's 'perhaps', while significantly qualifying his 'accurately'. Hence we divide the question into two parts, which we put as follows:

First: When was the whole sequence of events at Troy which is retraced, along with its segment 'The Trojan War', *conceived*?

Second: How did those fragments, which represent our only means of reconstructing it, *find their way* into the epic of the *Iliad*?

The logical order of these two questions is clear: question number two can be put with the prospect of an outcome only when question number one is settled. Hence we devote the present chapter wholly to question number one.

It should be emphasized first that, with this question, the problem of the historicity of the sequence of events at Troy is left untouched. The point is how long the tale of Troy existed before Homer, not whether it is 'true'. Of course this is not a random question. The answer to it is crucial for the question of historicity, which we ultimately wish to address. Crucial, since the veracity of a story which relates to particular events, whether or not it has a historical core, is bound to decrease as the time lapse increases between its appearance and its underlying events. That applies, of course, only to oral transmission. In a culture based on writing, such time distances are relatively meaningless, since after centuries libraries and archives can produce simultaneity for the reader. In the case of Greece, however, as we have seen, it possessed during its Mycenaean age only an administrative script and no literature, then was without writing during the following so-called Dark Age. In oral cultures of this kind knowledge of past events is not totally lost as rapidly as many theorists in their generalizations have accepted, but it loses detail, depth of field, and structural correlations: it pales. Hence, the later the pattern of events in the tale of Troy, with its reflection of the Mycenaean context, was invented, the more experience indicates that the proportion of reliable Mycenaean reality in it is reduced.

This was, of course, always perceived, but two quite different conclusions were drawn. The result is that two quite distinct positions are represented in research on the question of the time at which the tale of Troy appeared (there are of course intermediate positions; for the sake of clarity, we restrict ourselves to the two extremes of the range):

1. The time of appearance of the story coincides approximately with the time of composition. It is less that the poet of the *Iliad* alone invented the story, than that it was a kind of common inspiration of Greek bards at the closing of the ninth and the opening of the eighth century BC. Since it was then that the cultural revival of Greece began, the ruling stratum had a strong interest in historical self-legitimation. This interest was served by the aoides, a guild of bards long closely linked with the ruling stratum, 'extrapolating' as it were to order the entire narrative fabric of the tale of Troy from remains in stone, ancient heirlooms from a dim past, fragmental recollections persisting in the collective memory, and contemporary political fantasies, all the while dreaming of greatness as they stood before the ruins of ancient cities.[2]

2. The time of appearance of the narrative is not long before or not long after[3] the collapse of the Mycenaean period of high culture. Accordingly the tale mirrors knowledge of the real Mycenaean situation on the part of its author or of its authors.

It must be made clear at this point what consequences each of these positions has in evaluating the historicity of the *core* of the tale of Troy:

- For those who uphold the first position, what appear in the *Iliad* to be 'fragments of information' from an originally very old, broader tale must constitute elements of a historicizing ('archaizing') new fiction. There would be then no 'fragments' of an original whole, only points on a projection curve. Consequently the adherents of this position can in no way recognize that the story of the war over Troy, which is part of the broader tale, has a basis in history.
- On the contrary, the adherents of the second position tend to ascribe to the story every conceivable historical substratum.

To decide between these two positions has been hitherto less a rational act than the spontaneous generalization of an impression. For the adherents of the first position, the decision often went along with the feeling that a scientific approach either implies a commitment to scepticism or is synonymous with scepticism. Feelings are certainly misplaced here. Science can afford to be led neither by scepticism nor by credulity, but only by facts and rigorous logic. To logic belongs the principle that rational conclusions can be based on even a limited number of facts. Were that not so, a large part of all scientific knowledge would not have come into being.

As regards the time of appearance of the tale of Troy, the decision between the two positions named depends on assessing how great the proportion of preserved reality is in that story.

'Assessing' is of course not the same as calculating. A subjective element is at work. This cannot be fully excised, since we, in order to calculate the proportion of reality in Homer, instead of assessing it, would have to know totally, that is absolutely, the reality of the Mycenaean age of Greece. Unfortunately, that will never be possible. In the future also, *how* individual researchers decide will depend on the standards they set personally for the amount of material that appears to them to be sufficient for a decision.

Recent research has adduced now a quantity of material and a level of knowledge which, in the view of this author, is quite sufficient to regard the second position as the more likely. Some of the facts which support this assessment have been set out above. In what follows, they will be repeated in compressed form and supplemented by other facts.

THE NAMES OF THE ATTACKERS AND THE CITY ATTACKED ARE MYCENAEAN

1. The global terms in the tale of Troy for the alliance ranged against Troy, 'Danaans' and 'Achaians', are indubitably historical. They were the names of the inhabitants of Greece in use internationally (Egypt, Ḫattusa) in the Mycenaean age of Greek history. It is improbable that they could have survived for long within the orally transmitted normal recollection of the period following the catastrophe when the unified Mycenaean structure disintegrated into its resulting parts and fragments, and no libraries or archives existed to support the memory. These terms are, however, no marginal elements, but load-bearing components of the framework of the tale of Troy. Had the story been 'extrapolated' in the ninth to eighth centuries, the attackers would have been given names current in Greece at that time, not names unfamiliar to the people of the ninth to eighth centuries; the terms 'Danaoí' and 'Achaoí' should not have been present in Homer's poems. Nevertheless they are not only present, but are even functioning elements of a metrical substitution system. The conclusion is obvious: not only they but the system they comprise derive from a time when this whole group of terms was living reality. This is the Mycenaean era.

2. The two terms used in the tale of Troy for the scene of the armed clash between attackers and defenders, *Wilios* and *Trōiē*, are likewise historical. They are variants in Greek speech of two place-names which appear in the Hittite documents as *Wilusa* (with variants) and (most likely) *Tru(w)isa*. These terms are also load-bearing components of the framework of the tale of Troy. The place *Wilusa* (leaving aside for the moment the still contentious matter of the name *Tru(w)isa*) was finally abandoned, according to the evidence of the Korfmann excavation, around 950 BC at the latest; that is, from that time on there was no permanent population there.[4] If the name of the place around 950 was *actually* the same as during the golden age of the settlement under the Hittites in 1200–1175, then it could only have been *Wilusa* or something similar, but not *Wilios*, as *Wilios* is the *Greek* form of the name. The successors to the advanced culture of the Hittite era settlement (Troy VI/VIIa) were, however, as we know, not Greeks, but new arrivals from the

Balkan area, speaking a non-Greek language—hence most unlikely to adopt a name used by Greek outsiders. Were we to proceed from local tradition, this name, different in form from *Wilios*, must have been handed down from about 950 onwards, passed on by shepherds and at best by more distant neighbours over two hundred years to reach Homer about 750 BC, with, of course, not without, the initial 'w'. Hence Homer in the eighth century must have heard a variant of the name *Wilusa* with an initial 'w'. There being, however, no 'w' in his Greek dialect, Ionian, he would first have dropped the initial sound, and second have changed the name—which was not Wilios, but something similar—to *Ilios*, but in doing so have left nothing in the poem to point to the former initial 'w'.

This is *not* the case: the name *Ilios* appears in the *Iliad*, in the various cases, a total of 106 times. In 48 of these places, i.e. about 45 per cent of instances, the line concerned is metrically correct only when we supply an initial 'w'. In a further 47 places, i.e. in about 45 per cent more instances, it cannot be determined whether the word was originally *Wilios* or *Ilios* (in 34 of these instances for the sole reason that the word stands at the beginning of a line; there the word could also have been originally *Wilios*). In only 11 places, i.e. about 10 per cent of instances, the initial 'w' cannot be reinserted without metrically destroying the line.[5] Hence the 'w' is firmly embedded in Homer's text.

It follows (in line with the conclusions which had to be drawn from the decryption of Linear B) that neither did Homer invent the name of the scene of his narrative himself, nor did he adopt it from the local tradition of the non-Greek inhabitants of the Troad in the eighth century. Rather, he could only have heard it from Greeks who used the 'w'.

Theoretically, these Greeks who possessed a 'w' could have been *Aeolian* Greeks. Aeolian Greeks, setting out from the island of Lesbos, however, came into close contact with the native inhabitants of the Troad at the earliest in the eighth century BC. Were we to take up the idea of local tradition, then the name *Wilusa*, or something similar, must have been retained among the non-Greek inhabitants of the Troad for some 150 years after the settlement was abandoned about 950. The Aeolian Greeks from Lesbos, who thrust into the area in the eighth century, must then have changed the name, on first hearing it, to the Greek form *Wilios*. And the tale of Troy, linked with the place-name? Either it must have been transmitted to the Greeks arriving from Lesbos, together with a non-Greek place-name, by the non-Greek inhabitants of the Troad, or it must have been invented and added by the Aeolians from Lesbos to the name they had adopted.

That would be so highly complicated an account of the appearance of the Greek name *Wilios/Ilios*, and a manner of emergence of the tale of Troy so verging on the miraculous, that both must be regarded as unrealistic. In view of the great age of the names for the *attackers* of the place, 'Achaoí' and 'Danaoí', and their firm anchor in Greek hexameter verse, we can let this whole complicated construction collapse without detriment. The most likely course is considerably more straightforward: like the terms for the attackers, 'Achaoí and Danaoí', the toponyms *Wilios* and *Trōiē* derive from the living reality of the Mycenaean age. They did not reach Homer through local tradition within the Troad. They entered Greek hexameter poetry in the Mycenaean age itself.

THE WORLD OF THE ATTACKERS IS MYCENAEAN

The tale of Troy in the *Iliad*, as has been shown by the reading of the Linear B tablets, describes political and economic circumstances which, taken together, were in fact reality once in known Greek history, though only during one era—the Mycenaean. Generalizations over the obvious resemblance in this regard have been frequently encountered. They do not need to be repeated here. What is needed is rather to sharpen the picture. If this were to be done comprehensively rather than in broad outline, it would, however, be bound to adduce and discuss so many facts that a separate book would be needed. Here we must demur. Instead, we shall extract a single fact which has long pointed to a Mycenaean origin of the tale of Troy, but the standing of which as research evidence has not yet been definitively confirmed. We have in mind the *places of origin* of the attackers recorded in the tale of Troy. Until the mid-1990s, research could not state definitively whether, among these places of origin named in our *Iliad*, there were places whose names and exact locations could only have been known in the Mycenaean age. Since 1994/5 this uncertainty has finally been ended through a new discovery which is currently still being worked on and is as yet scarcely known even in specialist circles. In order to assess the significance of this new discovery, we must, however, go somewhat further back. It concerns a special topic in *Iliad* research, the so-called catalogue of ships.

The 'catalogue of ships'

The facts

The *Iliad* contains an extensive enumeration of the ships in which the Achaians sailed to Troy and the places of origin of their crews. The poet embeds this list in his tale of Achilles before the Achaians advance to their first battle. The list embraces 267 lines of the second book of the *Iliad* (2. 494–759). Twenty-nine contingents of attackers are listed, each forming a geographical and political entity. Each of the 29 entries has the same structure: (1) name of the region and enumeration of the places furnishing men for the expedition to Troy; (2) names of the respective commanders; (3) the number of ships and the crew numbers for each. In all there are 1,186 ships and some 100,000 men.

Before putting our actual question, let us try to clarify a preliminary question: how is it that the poet of an epic narrative comes to present such a statistic in his poem? Are not statistics rather unpoetical? What kind of poetic lure is there in versifying long tallies of place-names and personal names? And from the point of view of the audience: was it not fearfully boring to listen to 267 hexameters consisting essentially of nothing but names? Seen from today, such questions are apposite, yet not from the point of view of listeners to an ancient epic. Lists of this kind had a long tradition in bardic poetry. This tradition rested on a real fact. Since writing had existed, from about 3200 BC, kings and generals of all cultures possessing writing favoured making known in figures the greatness of their victories in their campaign reports following the conclusion of great military enterprises, often chiselled into temple walls and cliff faces. How many warriors and chariots came from which places; how many countries and towns were finally conquered; how many captives taken; and so on. Such enumerations (catalogues) astonish simply through the mass of individual items, impress, and emanate power (an effect equally sought after today, as is shown by the familiar graphics and pictograms which flicker on our screens in the run-up to every military conflict). Enumerations of this kind are but a reflection of reality: whoever wishes to go to war must first weigh his chances, so be aware of his own strength and that of his opponent. That of his opponent he can, as a rule, estimate only roughly; his own he seeks to assess as completely as possible by parading, counting, and registering. So numbers, names, districts, and places of origin combine. This knowledge enables regiments, divisions, formations, and armies to be mustered, equipped with command structures, and trained for an operation. To calculate troop numbers is therefore an integral part of taking up arms, a constant in every war.

The epic as a literary genre recounts great deeds and therefore not only resembles the reports of kings and rulers, but might in point of fact be said to offer a transposition of these from monumental inscriptions into a detailed, imagined narrative for a wide public hungry for particulars and emotions. If the background of the Greek *Iliad*, which belongs in this epic tradition, is the history of a war, then a catalogue of troops belongs in it. The question could certainly be asked whether it had to be as long as in our *Iliad*, an epic being no official document from the army command, nor a report or record for the imperial annals.

Not only a public less familiar with the ancient epic, but certainly many experts also have not properly grasped the real significance of this catalogue of troops in our *Iliad*. As has been said, it takes up 267 hexameters and counts 29 contingents. As each of these 29 contingents comes from a different district of the land of the Achaians, we have something like a map of Achaia. That, certainly, is not intended, since, according to the introduction (2. 492), only those crews, with their captains, are named which sailed to Ilios, which means (a point often overlooked in research) that districts *not* sending crews to the expedition to Troy are not to be named. Hence it is not a complete description of the country that is attempted, but a record of contingents. If, however, in an area so small in geographical terms as Greece, 29 districts, some quite extensive, with islands included, are enumerated, there must be something of a 'map in words', not complete, but reasonably comprehensive. This results from not less than 178 geographical names being recorded, names which have been largely retained until today, so that in this list of troop contingents we can recognize Greece. Edzard Visser, the author of the latest comprehensive analysis of this *pièce de résistance* of Greek hexameter verse,[6] a subject of repeated study since ancient times, in 1997 described the area covered by these names thus: 'The area described covers the whole of Greece: north–south from the mouth of the Peneios [Thessaly, south of Olympus] to Crete; east–west from the island of Kos, lying just off the coast of Asia Minor, to the Ionian Sea with the isles of Ithaca and Zakynthos . . . '.[7] The 178 place names describing this area, in groups of from one to three names, take up 91 of the total of 267 lines. Hence it can be said that one third of the entire catalogue consists of place-names.

To make our argument clear, it will be useful to explain as clearly as possible what system underlies this enumeration of place names. We will attempt this by means of an analogy. Imagine hearing a text like this:

> The men then of Yorkshire, the shire of broad acres,
> The men of York city and Kingston-upon-Hull,
> They who were masters of Wakefield, Bradford, and beautiful
> Beverley,
> Who had settled in Pontefract, Ripon, and in Halifax too,
> Dwelt far off in Richmond and Scarborough and herring-fishing
> Whitby,
> Tilled the land at Skipton and Malton and Yarm where the river is
> crossed—
> The Earl of Northumberland led them, Earl Marshal of England,
> And there were forty ships followed him, all black-caulked with pitch.

There are 29 blocks of text taking this form. Because they begin with either the name of a region (exemplified here by 'Yorkshire') or the largest city of a district (in our model therefore the large cities of York and Hull), and because the respective town names and the settlements indicated have, since being named in the catalogue, in many cases remained the same ever since Homer (often up to the

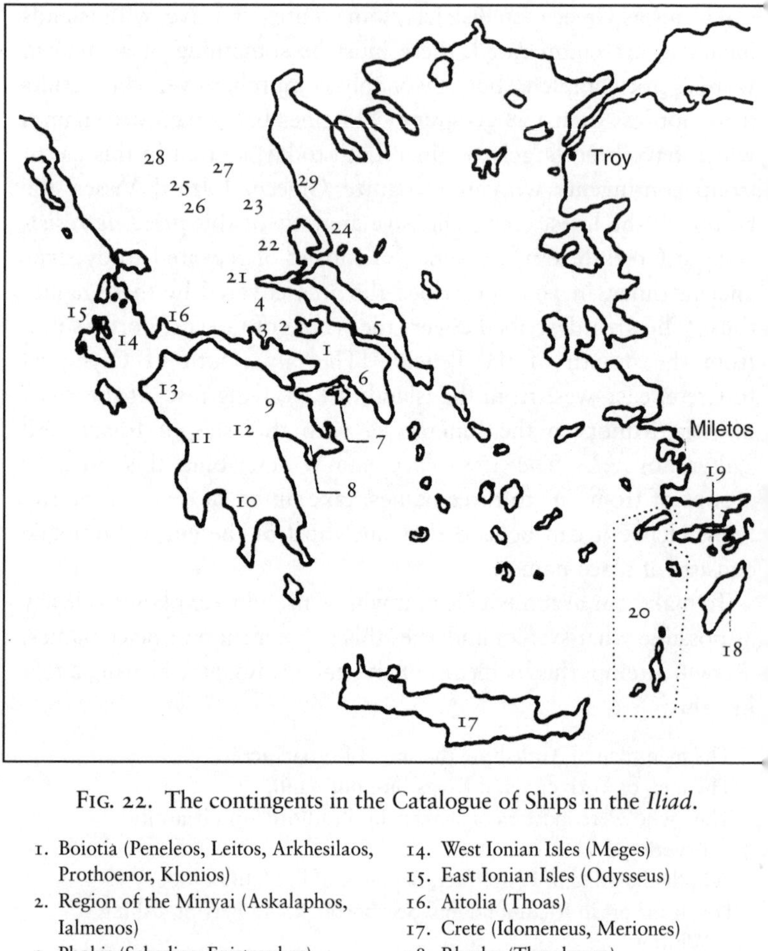

FIG. 22. The contingents in the Catalogue of Ships in the *Iliad*.

1. Boiotia (Peneleos, Leitos, Arkhesilaos, Prothoenor, Klonios)
2. Region of the Minyai (Askalaphos, Ialmenos)
3. Phokis (Schedios, Epistrophos)
4. Lokris (Aias the Lokrian)
5. Euboia (Elephenor)
6. Athens (Menestheus)
7. Salamis (Aias the Telamonian)
8. South Argolis (Diomedes, Sthenelos, Euryalos)
9. North Argolis/Achaia (Agamemnon)
10. Lakonia (Menelaos)
11. North-West Messenia (Nestor)
12. Arkadia (Agapenor)
13. Elis (Amphimachos, Thalpios, Diores, Polyxeinos)
14. West Ionian Isles (Meges)
15. East Ionian Isles (Odysseus)
16. Aitolia (Thoas)
17. Crete (Idomeneus, Meriones)
18. Rhodes (Tlepolemos)
19. Syme (Nireus)
20. South Sporades (Pheidippos, Antiphos)
21. Spercheios region (Achilles)
22. Phthiotis (Protesilaos, Podarkes)
23. Pelasgiotis (Eumelos)
24. Magnesia (Philoktetes/Medeon)
25. Hestiaotis (Podaleirios, Machaon)
26. Thessalotis or Tymphaia (Eurypylos)
27. Perrhaibia (Polypoites, Leonteus)
28. Pindos region (Guneus)
29. Peneios/Pelion region (Prothoos)

present day), we are able today to identify at least the district, territory, or region meant. It becomes more difficult with the names of the individual small settlements (villages). The Greek geographers who began scientific research some 150 years after Homer did not themselves know in the case of many of the names where the relevant settlements lay. Modern research knows much less.

That raises a series of questions. We first pick out just one, though the most important: how did the author of this catalogue encounter this huge mass of names? We cannot presume that he learnt it at school or took it from an encyclopaedia or atlas. There were none in the eighth century BC. So we face the situation that a Greek bard in the part of Greece located in Asia Minor wishes to tell the tale of a great military expedition of the past, mounted by his Greek forefathers against the fortified city of Troy in Asia Minor, and needs a list of the home towns and villages of the Greeks fighting against Troy at that time. Where can he get it? We have seen from our model that a single contingent entry in our *Iliad* not only contains a number of names of towns, but also some which are quite unfamiliar. Which of us, for all our current wealth of knowledge, could give a spontaneous description of Yorkshire as the author of the catalogue does with the regions of Greece? Most could name York and Hull, perhaps also Bradford and Scarborough. Who, however, apart from locals and neighbours of the district, would be able off the cuff to name Yorkshire towns like Beverley, Pontefract, or Ripon, Skipton or Malton? And this would apply, not only to ordinary mortals, but to politicians and businessmen right up to the top. The catalogue author does this, not in a single case only, but in twenty-nine at once. And the most recent researcher to study the catalogue intensively says this about the outcome: 'Nowhere in Homer can real errors . . . be established.'[8] So far as we can test his geographical data today, in the entire catalogue there is in fact not one instance of misplacement—to adhere to the analogy, of Stockton appearing in Yorkshire or Richmond in County Durham. So we have neither an imagined list (all the place-names which we can check are, as has been said, real), nor an arbitrary jumble, since the names apply to places which, as far as we can see, do belong in the region described.

We can now repeat our question: how did the author of the catalogue achieve this? Naturally, one is inclined first to give the obvious answer: he travelled through Greece, visiting all the places he names, noting down their names and then using that material to construct and name individual regions. Indeed, at least one of the many catalogue researchers in the long history of dealing with this problem once tentatively offered this answer. In 1969 Adalberto Giovannini, the Geneva ancient historian, presented this formula:

> Remarkably complete and precise, the geographical data in the catalogue raise the difficult problem of their origin and of the intention of their compiler. If the cataloguer is to be seen as a wandering bard with a passion for geography, the question answers itself: it is with the direct intention of enumerating the participants in the Trojan War that the names of the cities of Greece have been collected, a task which must have cost its author a great deal of time and above all considerable perseverance.[9]

The final words show the scepticism which the researcher brings to his own reasoning. Indeed, this reasoning is rejected in the very next sentence: 'But everything points to the cataloguer not having assembled his data himself, but having made use of a list compiled with a different intention, adapting this source to the requirements of his poem.' In 1960 another experienced researcher, Wolfgang Kullmann, a philologist specializing in Homer, drew the same conclusion from his investigation: 'First of all the view that the catalogue was, with certain changes, taken from a source is borne out.'[10] What were the considerations which must have led to the rejection of the 'obvious' answer? Giovannini pointed to them in the first reference, naming as factors enthusiasm for geography, time, and endurance. In order to ascribe to a bard the collection and arrangement of the 178 place-names in the catalogue, we would have to make a series of assumptions unrealistic in the light of the development of Greek culture. The first would be to assume that the 'wandering minstrel' in question was research minded. Research mindedness to the extent required emerges amongst the Greeks *after* the Mycenaean age, not until about 600 BC, at Miletos, under the pressure of a huge surge of information brought about by the colonizing movement of the eighth/seventh centuries BC.[11] We have to be clear precisely what a 'wandering minstrel' would have had to achieve. In order to search out all the places named in the catalogue, he would have had to walk or ride the length and breadth of Greece. Then, in addition to these travels on land, he would have had to undertake a series of sea voyages to the islands, to Ithaca, Leukas, Kephallenia, Zakynthos, and many others in the west, to Crete, Rhodes, Karpathos, Syme, and Kos in the south and east. He would have had to record the results each time and finally map all this material into a coherent general picture. Moreover, not only the factors of time and endurance noted by Giovannini, and funds too, would have been needed on a scale difficult to imagine in a lone 'wandering minstrel', but also the use of writing and an associated awareness of scientific method, which we encounter in the area of geography in Greece with the first *histores* (enquirers), Hekataios of Miletos and Herodotos of Halicarnassos in the sixth/fifth century BC.

Such an elaborate research project, impeccably executed and moreover correctly anticipating the findings of modern Greek studies, as is presupposed by the geographical record of Greece in the catalogue of ships is unthinkable in the whole area of Greek settlement in the eighth or seventh century BC. The loophole occasionally suggested, that the data could have been collected by *several* bards, does not stand up against this fact. It is quite unrealistic to suppose that one bard might have begun at one time, for others then to make the necessary additions and fill in the gaps. A joint project of this kind does not come about spontaneously. It requires planning. We have no indication of any central point on the mainland of Greece or in Ionian Asia Minor in the eighth/seventh centuries BC (or earlier in the 'Dark Age') which could, for whatever purpose, have commissioned, co-ordinated, and assessed such a gathering of data.[12]

Our question was this: who collected the geographical data brought together in the catalogue of ships? Sober reflection excludes the obvious answer, that the data were collected by a bard (or a number of bards), together with the view sometimes put forward that the poet of our *Iliad* was responsible. Another consideration suggests that the bard who composed our *Iliad* and whom we call

Homer, had he been *able* to collect the data in the catalogue of ships, would in any case not have collected it for our *Iliad* (but for a history on a much larger scale).

The cataloguing is based on ships: 'The men of region A were led by X. Ninety ships followed him.' 'The men of region B were led by Y. Forty ships followed him.' And so on. Such an account of ships can make sense only in a history intending to tell of a maritime expedition by a combined fleet (note that ships are not needed for a war on land) and hence having first to establish the fleet. The tale of Troy *is* the history of a maritime expedition. So it is more than possible that the assembly of a fleet was from the beginning an integral part of it. In all logic, then, this account of the assembly of the fleet will be placed in the narrative at the point where the Achaians muster for the maritime expedition against Troy, not where we now find it in our *Iliad*, that is before the Achaian troops advance to give battle in the ninth/tenth year of the siege.[13] That indicates that the catalogue of ships cannot have been compiled for the tale of Achilles.

This is confirmed by many details which, for reasons of space and clarity, cannot be fully gone into here. We must restrict ourselves to one point: the catalogue lists as captains of particular contingents commanders whom it expressly 'deletes' as characters in our *Iliad* immediately after naming them. Two examples of this:

Example 1: Book 2, lines 716–23:

> They who lived about Thaumakia and Methone,
> they who held Meliboia and rugged Olizon,
> of their seven ships the leader was Philoktetes
> skilled in the bow's work...
> Yet he himself lay apart in the island, suffering strong pains,
> in Lemnos the sacrosanct, where the sons of the Achaians had left him...

The story of Philoktetes is subsequently briefly recalled: at a halt during the crossing by the Achaian fleet, Philoktetes was bitten by a poisonous snake, sustaining a festering wound in the foot, the intolerable stench of which induced his comrades to set him down on the island of Lemnos.

Example 2: Book 2, lines 695–9:

They who held Phylake and Pyrasos of the flowers,
The precinct of Demeter, and Iton, mother of the sheep flocks,
Antron by the sea-shore, and Pteleos deep in the meadows,
Of these in turn Protesilaos was the leader
While he lived; but now the black earth had closed him under.

Protesilaos, we are briefly told, was the first to leap ashore as the fleet landed on the coast of the Troad, and was killed by a Trojan.

In respect of these passages, Geoffrey Kirk in his 1985 commentary to the *Iliad* was right to put this question: 'what is the point of creating something that has to be immediately corrected in the case of Protesilaos and... Philoktetes?'[14] Kirk himself pointed to the solution: the poet of our *Iliad*, the tale of Achilles, had found these two heroes in the tale of Troy (whoever its author had been). They had been participants in the maritime expedition it told of *before* the fleet sailed from Greece, and hence were included in the assembly catalogue. At the point at which the poet of our *Iliad* placed the catalogue in *his* story, nine years after the departure from Greece, the general tale of Troy, having run on for those nine years in the meantime, had ensured that these two heroes were either not present before Troy (Philoktetes) or already dead (Protesilaos). Hence our *Iliad* poet, having found them in the assembly catalogue of the tale of Troy, could not have them active in his compact 51-day tale in the *ninth/tenth* year of the siege. Yet to leave them out was clearly also impossible. Why? One reason only suggests itself: since they were known both to the poet himself and to all his audience from the original fleet assembly catalogue, once having been included in the tale as 'great heroes', their names were naturally expected to be found. So what was to be done? The poet finds his best solution is indeed to include the two, only to eliminate them promptly.

The significance of this device, one which is unavoidable from the standpoint of our poet as narrator, is clear: the poet of our tale of Achilles was aware of a catalogue of ships as part of the tale of Troy (naturally, it need not have been the same, word for word or in extent, as his, which we now read). However, since we have seen that, in his tale of Achilles, he uses the tale of Troy only as a frame, not telling it chronologically and sequentially, but spotlighting it at certain points, and since in the tale of Achilles he intends to deal in detail only with something taken from the ninth/tenth year of the siege, not from the time before the departure of the fleet from Greece, he has to move the catalogue of ships away from its original position in the narrative (Aulis in Boiotia, the assembly point of the fleet), if indeed he wishes to specify the strength of the attackers. In the restricted frame of his 51-day story, set in the ninth/tenth year of the siege, only a position directly before the onset of combat is open as a new location: the advance of the contingents on the battlefield before Troy. For a catalogue of *ships*, this position is illogical, but could nevertheless appear acceptable to the audience.[15]

A catalogue of ships as we now read it in our *Iliad* cannot then have been compiled originally as a basis for the context it now serves in our tale of Achilles, but only as a basis for the wider context of the 'Trojan War'. Since, however, the poet of our tale of Achilles can make very good use of this catalogue, the main figures in the tale of Troy (and so in the 'Trojan War') being also the main figures of his *small-compass* story, he adopts *en gros* the existing catalogue, adapting it wherever necessary to the *new*, restricted context through explanations within individual entries.

Hence we return to our initial question: by whom was the geographical data of the catalogue of ships collected and how was it achieved? If it was not a bard, nor Homer either, then who was it?

Probabilities hitherto

Hitherto we have merely demonstrated once again that the tale of Troy, of which the catalogue of ships is a part, was known to the poet of our *Iliad*. Another question still remains open: *how long* at that time had the tale of Troy been known, i.e. when was it conceived? It has become clear from the earlier chapters, before the catalogue of ships was introduced, that it cannot have been conceived in the eighth/seventh centuries, since the author of our *Iliad*, working in the eighth century, embeds his tale of Achilles in it. The previous chapter has also shown:

- First, the tale of Troy, as the narrative of a maritime expedition, must logically *always* have contained a catalogue of ships.

- Second, this catalogue of ships, in however modified a version, is still comprehensible in our *Iliad*.

Hence we now possess a key: through the catalogue of ships we can now, with prospect of success, try to determine the time when the tale of Troy as a whole came into existence. In the present chapter, we first recapitulate the findings of previous research on this topic.

All further considerations must start from the fact that thus far not one of the 178 geographical names in the catalogue of ships has been proved to be fictitious. Moreover, the overwhelming majority are known to us from sources outside Homer, in by no means all cases traceable back to Homer.[16] The second most important point is that the area covered by these names, as has been shown, encompasses almost the entire area of Greece, though its political divisions in some instances do not correspond to those of the known periods of Greek history.

Hence the question is this; which is the earliest age of Greek history to coincide with this area of settlement? Until not long ago, research had always two answers ready. One is that the area of settlement providing the catalogue of Achaian ships for the campaign against Troy is identical with that of the time of the poet of our *Iliad*, the eighth century BC, in which case the catalogue is a product of that eighth century. However we have seen that this solution is invalid. The alternative is that this area of settlement is identical with that of the Greeks of the Mycenaean age, in which case the geographical information contained in the catalogue derives from the Mycenaean age. The latest scholar to work in this problem area opted for the second possibility, for reasons not identical with ours: 'this area coincides reasonably well with the extent of Mycenaean culture in stages III A and B (i.e. the time between 1400 and 1200 BC).'[17] 'Reasonably' in this statement is made necessary by the fact that, from a purely theoretical point of view, it is no longer possible for us today to be one hundred per cent certain in deciding between these two alternatives, not knowing precisely the areas of settlement of the two epochs (we have no map of Greece from either). We can only balance the probabilities. In doing so, we believe, however, that, despite our lack of knowledge, we can today perceive this: the Greeks of historical times were unable to locate almost one quarter of the places named in the catalogue,[18] which can only mean that, by the eighth century, these places were no longer populated. Had they been so in that eighth century and hence been included by a poet of the eighth century in a catalogue he himself compiled, given the significance of the *Iliad* for Greek culture in the years which followed, either their names would never be surrendered, or, if those places were ever abandoned after being included in the catalogue, the sites where they had stood would never be forgotten.

If, however, places bearing these names did not exist in Greece in the eighth century, then, to sustain the premiss that the catalogue was compiled by a poet of the *eighth* century (or even later), the only option would be to prove that this poet devised all these place-names, for instance for metrical reasons, i.e. to fill out one or other incomplete hexameter. This proof cannot be furnished. Such a supposition would, however, be improbable, first because these place-names would all have to be unspecific, universal, and easy to devise, of such a kind as 'Meadowdale', 'Waterside', 'Hightown', which they are not, and second because the author of the catalogue moreover regularly applies *adjectives* to the place-names ('of the flowers', 'leaf-trembling', 'rugged', etc.) to fill gaps and end lines, a device he could have used equally in those instances, rather than taking the trouble to invent place-names.

The most likely solution of the problem is to assume that these place-names and places indeed no longer existed in the *eighth* century (or later), yet had once existed and been large enough to provide crews for a seaborne expedition. To do so, they would have had to be fairly significant or at least known in their time. In the nature of things, this time could not have been the 'Dark Age', but only that of Mycenae. Hence the place-names must have been retained in tradition because of the former significance of those places during the Mycenaean age.[19]

The information contained in the catalogue of ships of our *Iliad* can hence only refer basically to the Mycenaean age of Greece. Nevertheless, that is not yet to say that this information, as the kind of geographical inventory we have today in the list of 29 contingents, must have been *compiled* in the Mycenaean age of

Greece. While the content is basically Mycenaean, it could also have been compiled into the list of 29 contingents at a later time. After all, data can survive independent of lists.

However, it is improbable also that the data were *compiled* into a catalogue in a later age. This conclusion is based on Edzard Visser's examination of the catalogue in 1997, the most thorough hitherto, and his brief evaluation of that examination in his article of 1998.

In his analysis, Visser indicated three important points, significant for this question, which had, however, attracted little or no attention before:

The elaborate structure of the catalogue as a geographical list of names resembling an 'extract from a geographical register drawn up by an administrative authority' suggests that lists of names as a narrative form are very old.[20]

This narrative form, widely used in the *Iliad* outside the catalogue of ships, like catalogues of people in genealogies or descriptions of groups, catalogues of suitors, the dead, and other such lists, shows a striking resemblance to bureaucratic record-keeping in Greek palace cultures in the Mycenaean age as we encountered it in the Linear B tablets.[21]

The inclusion of a *geographical* catalogue, which by its very nature is static, in a heroic poem which is oral and *narrative* is best understood in the function the catalogue of ships indeed performs in our *Iliad*: as an order of march. Yet how does such a voluminous list of armed forces, clearly bringing the population of almost the whole of Greece together in a common purpose, come to be in our eighth-century *Iliad*? It is likely to have been difficult for the idea of such a large-scale common enterprise by the Greeks to emerge in the so-called 'Dark Age', given the prevailing fragmentation and weakness of the Greek world at the time:

> Between the collapse of the Mycenaean palaces and the Geometric period [the eighth century is meant], it is impossible to connect such an occurrence with an actual historical event.... If it were a joint expedition which gave rise to the literary form of the geographical catalogue, then at that time such a thing is... scarcely imaginable. This would suggest that large joint expeditions in which individual districts combined to carry out some kinds of raids were certainly known in Mycenaean times...[22]

What follows from this? The idea of great combined military assaults on a foreign power was alien to the Greeks of the 'Dark Age'. It was still alien in the eighth century, though there were then some overseas colonial expeditions, but no notion of invasion. On the other hand, such an idea must have been far from alien to a great power whose king is addressed as 'my brother' by the Great King of the Hittites and whose fleet dominated the south-east Mediterranean once the Cretan fleet's mastery was ended: Aḫḫijawā. A catalogue of ships as found in our *Iliad* must therefore originally have belonged in fact to a tale composed in Mycenaean times. As a *form* it could have belonged to every Mycenaean tale recounting combined maritime expeditions. There could have been more of these in Mycenaean times than we know of. The aggressive maritime expeditions to the island of Crete and from there to Miletos on the coast of Asia Minor, of which we do know, were only among the most significant, which is why they are known to us.

That Mycenaean tale, however, with which the catalogue of ships which has come down to us is firmly linked, on account of the characters enumerated in it, can in its unadapted, unmodified form only have belonged to the tale of Troy. The tale of Troy must therefore have been composed in Mycenaean times.

There is another circumstance congruent with this, long observed, but yet to find a reasonable explanation. The catalogue of ships in our *Iliad*, otherwise not lacking much in coverage or in detail, with its 29 contingents enumerated and 178 geographic names, extends the area of settlement of the 'Achaians' over the greater part of what is still today mainland Greece (less Macedonia and Thrace, with the off-shore islands like Thasos, Imbros, and Lemnos[23]), together with part of the island realm which is still Greek today—the western Greek islands, Crete, the Southern Sporades including Rhodes, Syme, Nisyros, Karpathos, Kasos, and Kos. Nevertheless, it omits the Cyclades and the entire west coast of Asia Minor between Troy and Halicarnassos with the off-shore islands (Lesbos, Chios, and Samos). Yet the whole of this latter area (leaving aside the Cyclades) was successively settled by Greeks at the latest from 1050 BC onwards.

When exactly Greek settlement in Asia Minor began remains unknown even to modern scholarship. Nor is it possible that the

Greeks themselves, having no long-term calendar, no writing, and no archives, therefore no documents either, before 800, could have known any more in the eighth century (despite all assertions to the contrary). What was certainly known by every Greek in the eighth century BC, more than two hundred years later, however, whether in Asia Minor or in the motherland, was the fact that this whole area, from Lesbos in the north to Rhodes in the south, together with the adjacent coastal strip of Asia Minor, was unquestionably part of Greece *at that time*. That means that, following the Greek settlement of western Asia Minor, every poet devising a catalogue of Greek naval forces preparing to sail against Troy would automatically have had ships from this, then densely populated, area join the Achaian array against Troy. Since the assembly point at Aulis in Boiotia would have made no strategic sense for these contingents (a *double* crossing of the Aegean), he would either have placed the point somewhere else, or had the Greek contingents from Asia Minor join the mainland Greeks at a rendezvous in the Aegean, preferably an island, to incorporate them then in his order of march of the Achaians on the Trojan plain. Had it been the work of a poet of the eighth century, the order of march in the second book of our *Iliad* would therefore, in one way or another, have contained contingents from the great port cities of Miletos, Ephesos, Smyrna, and others.[24]

Nevertheless, in our *Iliad*, and not only in the catalogue of ships but throughout the whole of the 15,693 lines, this area not only does not belong to Greece but, with a few exceptions which we cannot go into here, but which are easily explained,[25] simply does not exist. This 'blank space' in our *Iliad* has been conspicuous since the beginning of modern research on Homer. From the outset two contradictory explanations for this have repeatedly been put forward: (1) the poet of our *Iliad* (or his predecessors in arranging the material) deliberately 'archaized'; (2) the poet of our *Iliad* did not include these districts when rearranging the Troy story because nothing about them was passed down to him within the poetic tradition which he followed.

Let us consider for a moment the first explanation, since it still finds support even today and even with renewed vigour. According to it, Homer in the eighth century or his immediate predecessors in devising the tale of Troy would have been perfectly aware that many contemporary places had not yet come into existence at the time of the 'Trojan War'. These were: the Aeolian League cities on the west coast of Asia Minor—Cyme, Larisa, Neon Teichos, Tamnos, Killa, Notion, Aigiroessa, Pitane, Aigai, Myrina, Gryneion, and Smyrna; the Ionian League and island cities further south—Samos, Khios, Miletos, Myus, Priene, Ephesos, Kolophon, Klaros, Lebedos, Klazomenai, Erythrae, and Phocaea; and the Dorian cities still further south around Cnidos and Halicarnassos, including their smaller settlements.[26] Accordingly they would have taken pains to say not a word about any of these places or any of these regions, rivers, and mountains in extrapolating an Achaian–Trojan conflict from the ruins of Troy, still to be seen in their day.

Since Benedikt Niese in 1873,[27] those who take this position have worked with the concept of a certain 'suppression' of better judgement:

It is conspicuous that in recreating Asia Minor the poet has succeeded in suppressing the present and in creating a landscape populated by peoples such as the Lycians, Carians, Phrygians, Maeonians and Paphlagonians... There is no hint in the *Iliad* proper [meaning apart from the catalogue in Book 2] of the Ionian cities of Miletos, Smyrna and Ephesos, not to speak of the lesser foundations, that must have been well-known to the poet of the *Iliad*.[28]

Although Albin Lesky, the doyen of recent Homer research, had warned against forcing to extremes the principle of 'archaism' in interpreting Homer ('We admit to being mistrustful of accepting a planned archaism...'[29]), this course has been further pursued in recent years. It has even been suggested that the poet of the *Iliad* extrapolated from the ruins of Troy, still to be seen in the eighth century, and from 'complex archaeological discoveries', not only 'the mighty fortress of Troy VI' and 'a campaign once undertaken by Mycenaean Greeks', but even 'various layers of remains' and 'several hostile attempts on Troy',[30] in fact that very fortress of Troy which is *today* known as 'Troy VI' and those very various layers which *modern excavations* have uncovered. That would turn a traditional Greek bard of the eighth century BC into a modern archaeologist and historian of the type of Schliemann/Korfmann combined with Starke/Hawkins, though with the added gift of clairvoyance superimposed.

We do not propose to deal in detail with any of the more exaggerated notions in this vein, which might see the entire tale of Troy arise from the elements of 'extrapolation', 'speculation', 'retrojection', and 'information passed on by members of literate societies with whom the Greeks were in contact, such as the Phoenicians, the Babylonians—and possibly Anatolians'.[31] That would mean our having to imagine, in respect of those places which excavations have shown to have once been Mycenaean settlements (provided that their remains were still to be seen in the eighth century), that Homer (and/or other bards before him) sat before the ruins of Mycenae, Tiryns, Thebes, Orchomenos, and a hundred and more other sites in Greece, just as he did before the ruins of Troy, employing all possible methods of collecting information to make a projection of the erstwhile size, appearance, and suzerainty of each place, including its political and diplomatic relations with other places and much more. In view of what the early Greek bards and Homer are regarded as capable of and what is expected of them when the projection thesis becomes so complicated, one can only take Franz Hampl's cry, 'The *Iliad* is not a History Book!' and add, 'nor Homer a history professor'.

Finally, however, apart from these considerations of principle, the *intention* which might have made a 'projection' of the tale of Troy necessary must also be looked at. Its aim, when the basic lines of its plot were set (the destruction by armed force of a non-Greek city), can only have been to acclaim the Greeks' own forebears. Were then the authors of this tale, themselves from Ionian Asia Minor, to cut out of the common enterprise which they projected none other than the markedly tradition-minded eighth-century Greeks of Asia Minor, in whose lands it was that they composed their projected *Iliad*? Would that not run directly counter to their own objective?

Hence, when we test the first solution proposed to the question why Greek Asia Minor is ignored in the *Iliad*, the result is this: once its actual basis is called into question, the projection theory can presently only offer vague assumptions and conjectures. It can provide no rational explanation why the Greeks of Asia Minor are neglected, nor for the whole process of the emergence of the tale of

Troy in the ninth/eighth century BC as it sees it. It would indeed be methodologically correct, as a trial, to set it up and develop it as a possible explanatory model, though it has now reached a stage at which it becomes apparent that its implications lead *ad absurdum*. Before it can once more be taken seriously as one hypothetical explanation amongst others, it must disprove this surmise by proposing specific scenarios. In any case, in its current form it cannot answer the question why the *Iliad* passes over the area of settlement of the Anatolian Greeks. Let us then go on to test the second solution proposed.

As early as 1959, Denys L. Page, the British philologist and supporter of the second proposed solution, put a number of questions to the adherents of the projection theory which have substantially remained unanswered since:

> many places named in the catalogue could not be identified by the Greeks themselves in historical times... some of them were abandoned before the Dorian occupation [i.e. about 1000 BC and after] and never resettled. How could a poet of the post-Dorian era have selected such places for his list? How could he even have known that they existed, or what their names were? The importance of the great fortresses, such as Mycenae, might have been conjectured from visible remains: but how could the poet learn about *Dorion*, abandoned at the close of the Mycenaean era and never reoccupied? How could he come to select numerous other places for which the geographers in historical times sought high and low without ever finding a trace of them?—*Nisa*, which 'cannot be found anywhere in Boeotia';[32] *Calliaros, which is 'no longer inhabited'*;[33] *Bessa* and *Augeiae*, which 'do not exist';[34] *Mideia* and the vineyards of *Arne*, which 'must have been swallowed up by the lake';[35] *Eiones*, which has 'disappeared';[36] *Aepy*, a name unknown to posterity;[37] *Pteleos*, which was identified with an uninhabited copse;[38] the Arcadian places, *Rhipe, Stratie*, and *Enispe*, of which Strabo says, 'It is difficult to find these and you would be no better off if you did find them, because nobody lives there';[39] *Parrhasia*, which survived only as the name of a district;[40] *Elone*, which has 'changed its name' and 'is in ruins';[41] *Neritos* and *Aegilips, Ormenion* and *Orthe*, and at least a dozen more?[42]

The most recent research on the catalogue of ships in 1997, forty years after Page, based on all the special studies published since Page's book, cannot yet find anything else to say about these places: Dorion—'definitive clarification impossible';[43] Nisa—

'remains an unknown quantity... nothing really firm can be said about this name';[44] Kalliaros—'clearly no longer known to Greek geographers since the fourth century BC at the latest';[45] Bessa—'today still an obscure entity';[46] Augeiai—'almost entirely unknown';[47] Mideia—'a definitive and unambiguous identification of Mideia [...] "hopeless"';[48] Arne—'the name of Arne is still a riddle';[49] and so on.

Of course the adherents of the projection theory could still object to Page that, at the time of the poet of the *Iliad* in the eighth century BC, all these places still existed, were inhabited, and could be found. Only in the *following* centuries might they have been abandoned, with only the later Greek geographers unable to discover anything about them. Page, however, had already closed this escape route:

> It is vain to plead that the places might have fallen into oblivion at some time between the ninth and the third century: the supreme authority of 'Homer' was an absolute guarantee that places mentioned in the Catalogue which still preserved their names in (say) the eighth century would never again lose those names,—or at least the memory of them.[50]

What Page means is this (cf. p. 230 above): the catalogue of ships contains the names of places about which, for two to three centuries after Homer, Greek geographers, competent researchers, could no longer find out anything. 'How was that possible?' Page wonders. Had Homer in the eighth century simply taken these places from contemporary reality and incorporated them in his catalogue, they would thus have been immortalized! Even had they all been abandoned by their inhabitants in the period after Homer (an implausible hypothesis, given their number), descendants of these inhabitants or people from neighbouring districts must have said to the geographers enquiring later with Homer's text in their hand, 'Yes, this Arne in Homer was once *here*. Only the people who lived here have moved away. But look: there are the remains of the settlement!' Yet this did not happen in any of the cases. Page concludes that there can be only *one* explanation for such an extraordinary phenomenon: no Greek could tell anything about these places, since by Homer's time they were unknown. The question then arises: how did Homer come to know of these places, which in his time were known to no one else? Page muses: then it must be from some source. Yet this source must have stemmed from an *earlier* age when these places were still living. 'What age could that be?' asks Page, and so do we. After all that research has assembled and everything we have adduced, can any age other than the Mycenaean come into consideration? If there remains only the Mycenaean period, then the 'blank space' with which we are concerned here is explained, and in fact astonishingly simply: the Greeks living since about 1050 BC in Asia Minor do not appear in the catalogue of ships, since there were no Greeks in Asia Minor at the time when the original catalogue was composed, i.e. in the Mycenaean age.[51]

This was the point which could be reached by a rational evaluation of the research *before* 1994. Everything went to show:

- First, that the geographical data in the '*Iliad* catalogue of ships' derive in the final account from the Mycenaean age;
- Second, that the original catalogue in which the data were compiled as an inventory of ships must have been compiled in the Mycenaean age of Greek history;
- Third, that hence the entire tale of Troy, in which a catalogue of ships must always have been present because of its maritime nature, must have been conceived in the Mycenaean age of Greek history.

However probable this series of deductions might have been, it could not yet be proved to be correct. The turning point came in 1994.

New certainty: the Linear B discoveries of the 1990s from Thebes

Thebes in Boiotia has a history of unbroken settlement of about 4,500 years. In Mycenaean times it was one of the principal centres of the palace culture of the day. As we have seen (pp. 131ff. above), along with Knossos, Mycenae, Messenia, and other towns and districts in Greece, it was well known to the pharaohs in Egypt in the fourteenth century BC. It plays a prominent part in Greek myth. Amongst other things it is the setting for the birth of the god Dionysos, the world-famous story of Oedipus and Antigone, the campaign of the 'Seven against Thebes', the Amphitryon story with the birth of Herakles, the son of Zeus, and many other legends which have lived on ever since in literature and art (and in many other fields—for example the 'Oedipus complex' comes to mind).

The Greeks believed that the founder of Thebes was *Kadmos*, a brother of *Eurōpē*, who gave her name to Europe. The city of Kadmos was called *Kadmeia*, so the Thebans are called *Kadmeians* in Homer. Today the city centre of modern Thebes stands on the site of Kadmeia. The streets crossing this larger area bear the names of famous prehistoric figures: Oedipus Street, Antigone Street, Pindar Street (Pindar came from Thebes), Pelopidas Street (Pelopidas was a famous general of Thebes and Boiotia in the fourth century BC). No further explanations are needed for the difficulty of carrying out archaeological excavations today in the heart of the city. Nevertheless, in the last hundred years, numerous spot excavations have been carried out in conjunction with new construction projects and have brought to light extensive material, including numerous Linear B documents: the typical inscribed clay tablets, together with inscriptions on vessels, seals, and other written evidence, though in relatively modest numbers. This material had always indicated that Thebes must always, and especially in the Mycenaean age, have

FIG. 23. A new Linear B tablet from Thebes.

been one of the richest and most politically powerful centres in Greece.

On 2 November 1993 a large Linear B tablet with substantial written text was found in Thebes when the municipal water corporation was laying water pipes in Pelopidas Street. Vassilis Aravantinos, the then Director of the Museum and the Antiquities Office of Thebes, obtained an indefinite suspension of the work with the support of the Greek Ministry of Culture. Subsequent excavations undertaken by Greek archaeologists over 495 days brought to light between November 1993 and February 1995 the third largest find of Linear B tablets in Greece after Knossos (about 3,500) and Pylos (about 1,200): more than 250 tablets and fragments of tablets.

Aravantinos and two Mycenaean experts brought in by him, Louis Godard and Anna Sacconi, presented a first preliminary report on 11 March 1995 at a session of the Italian Academia Nazionale dei Lincei in Rome.[52] It was clear that the find not only gave new impetus to Mycenology and to history, but would profoundly influence, if not transform, our picture of the Mycenaean age. Subsequent publications dealing with various selected aspects of the find have only reinforced this impression.

Unfortunately, at the present time, publication of the tablets in full, several times announced, is still awaited.[53] However these points are already clear:

1. The tablets belong to a palace archive of Kadmeia, destroyed in a fire.

2. The time of the fire can be dated with certainty from the considerable number of objects found with the tablets: it happened in about 1200 BC.[54]

3. The texts do not differ in writing technique or content from previously known Linear B texts from Thebes itself or from the six other sites of Linear B finds (Knossos, Kydonia/Khania, Pylos, Mycenae, Tiryns, Midea); most of the content refers to economic and religious items (income, taxes, rations, offerings to local and foreign deities, etc.).

The texts have already, through partial and sporadic publication,[55] added substantially to knowledge in all possible fields, though the full extent will be seen only when we have complete publication of the texts and the whole world can join in reading and interpreting them. What is, however, decisive for *our* question is the *geographical* information provided by these new tablets, though even here the full extent of the material is still unknown. Attention was nevertheless drawn to what emerged from the preliminary publications: the tablets not only referred several times to a 'man from Lakedaimon', that is, from Sparta, confirming political and commercial ties between Thebes and Sparta around 1200 BC, but the naming of *Amarynthos* and *Karystos* in unambiguous contexts made it clear that around 1200 BC Thebes not only ruled Boiotia, but evidently the large island of Euboia too. The extensive network of relations which around 1200 BC linked Thebes with the greater Mediterranean area was evidenced by place-names like Knossos appearing beside names of Cypriot, Egyptian, and Anatolian towns (including Troy).[56]

Certainly this was at first all unconnected and preliminary information. There was as yet no systematic study. This was presented only in 1999 by Louis Godard and Anna Sacconi in a paper with the title 'La Géographie des états mycéniens'.[57] It set out for the first time our entire current knowledge of the geographical extent of the seven Mycenaean centres already substantially known to us from the Linear B texts, together with their relations with each other and with other places and regions. The most important methodological principles followed by the authors and which they set out in the introduction have to be quoted verbatim (in translation):

> The toponyms recorded in the book-keeping archives brought to light in the ruins of these various palaces sometimes correspond to place-names used in the first millennium BC or even still today to denote familiar localities or regions of Greece. In these specific cases, the Mycenaean settlement was probably located at the same site as that known in historical or in modern times, or at least in its vicinity. This probability becomes a quasi-certainty when we are dealing with modern settlements built upon strata going back to the Bronze Age or even beyond and with names corresponding to the ancient names. Knossos is an example. [... the world-wide practice of using the same name for places in different areas must be taken into account].
>
> More often these Mycenaean toponyms have no equivalent in alphabetical Greek. Then context must serve to try to determine whether a place

with a mysterious name belongs to one or another known geographical area. [...] Thus, the tablets of series Co from Knossos, [...] record herds of sheep, goats, pigs and cattle in which female animals predominate in six localities in Crete named as *a-pa-ta-wa, ku-do-ni-ja, si-ra-ro, wa-to, o-du-ru-we* and *ka-ta-ra-i*. These are probably animals selected for breeding and pastured on plains or in valleys which were well watered. Western Crete has these characteristics. Since two of these toponyms in series Co, *a-pa-ta-wa* and *ku-do-ni-ja*, denote cities in western Crete, it is logical to think that the four other localities in the series, *si-ra-ro, wa-to, o-du-ru-we*, and *ka-ta-ra-i*, should also be located in western Crete.

The authors use this method to go through the seven palace centres individually. Taken together, the results are of the greatest interest in reconstructing Mycenaean geography, yet for our purposes they can and must be left out of consideration, especially since the first six previously known archives have nothing more to offer for our question. We concentrate on Thebes alone, the new find of tablets there being about to change radically our picture of the Mycenaean age of Greek culture. Godart and Sacconi write:

We know nothing of the political situation in mainland Greece at this time (the fourteenth century BC), since the archives of the mainland palaces have not been preserved. Against that, we can say that, in the following period, the thirteenth century, the greatest kingdom in terms of territory was indubitably the kingdom of Thebes. The area under the sway of the palace of Kadmos was far more extensive than the territory held by the monarchs of Khania, Pylos, Mycenae, Tyrins and Midea. Does that mean that Thebes played a leading role on the Mycenaean stage at the end of Late Helladic IIIB? We would be prepared to believe so.[58]

It is not only Godart and Sacconi who would be prepared to believe so. Without knowing their work on the material, Sigrid Deger-Jalkotzy had already stated the same view. Moreover she had proposed Thebes as the long-sought seat of the ruler of Aḫḫijawā, a view which Wolf-Dietrich Niemeier also, after earlier support for Mycenae, now inclines to, for reasons hard to dismiss:

1. There is in the south-east Aegean no late Bronze Age centre which could have served as the seat of a ruler of a great power recognised as of equal standing by the Hittite great kings and at times by the great kings of Egypt, Babylonia and Assyria also...

2. The isles of the Dodecanese and the adjacent coastal strip do not provide sufficient resources in land and population to found an international great power.

3. The local ruler of the land of Millawanda is a vassal of the ruler of Ahhijawa. Millawanda is never described as a specific part of Ahhijawa. Of all the lands named in the conflicts in west Asia Minor, Ahhijawa has a special political role: it is only of Ahhijawa that we learn nothing in respect of its geography or political and social structure . . . Hence Ahhijawa was for the Hittites a remote and unknown[59] land.[60]

Should the Thebes hypothesis prove to be true, then *inter alia*, as we have indicated elsewhere (p. 127 above), the old problem of why it has to be that the catalogue of ships begins with Boiotia and the Theban region and why the fleet assembles at Aulis is at once explained: Thebes dominated Mycenaean Greece at the time,[61] and Aulis, for reasons of physical geography in the region, had always been the natural harbour of Thebes.[62]

These sentences appeared in the German edition of this book early in 2003. In this English translation a small but sensational new discovery may now be added (for a preliminary report see Linsmeier 2003). On 9 and 11 August 2003, at two press conferences in Troy for German and Turkish journalists, the Tübingen Anatolian specialist Professor Frank Starke was able to present the first cuneiform letter in Hittite to be sent not from east to west, from Ḫattusa to Aḫḫijawā, but from west to east. The sender of this letter (which has been known since 1928 but completely misunderstood) was a king of Aḫḫijawā, and the recipient the Great King of the Hittites. Palaeographic evidence dates the letter in the thirteenth century BC, and further evidence makes it likely that it was addressed to Ḫattusili II (*c.*1265–1240 BC), the writer of the so-called Tawagalawa letter (see p. 123). Linguistic features of the text confirm that the writer spoke Greek, rather than Hittite, as his mother tongue.

In the letter the Great King of Aḫḫijawā cites a previous letter from his correspondent, the Great King of the Hittites. This means that by the time this letter was written a regular exchange of correspondence was established between Ḫattusa and Aḫḫijawā.

The letter deals with the matter of the islands which originally belonged to Assuwa. The Hittite Great King had asserted in his message that these islands belonged to him. The king of Aḫḫijawā objects that an ancestor of his received the islands from the king of Assuwa. Since Assuwa was the predecessor-state of Wilusa until the end of the fifteenth century BC, this can only refer to islands in the northern Aegean. Lesbos is out of the question, as it formed part of the Hittite empire, as 'Lazba'. Tenedos is too insignificant to play any part. The islands further south, Khios, Samos, etc., may be dismissed as they do not lie 'off Assuwa'. This means that the 'islands' in question are most likely Lemnos, Imbros, and/or Samothrace. Here we see the earliest prehistory of a later and still current conflict between Greece and the leading Anatolian power of the day over the islands off the Anatolian coast.

All this is significant enough. Still more exciting, however, is the fact that in a question of rights the king of Aḫḫijawā argues from *history*, as is still common practice in diplomacy today: he explains that a forebear of his had given his daughter in marriage to the then king of Assuwa (which after the chronology of kings known to us must have been in the fifteenth century) and that consequently the islands had come into the possession of Aḫḫijawā. As luck would have it this forebear is named in the letter: his name is *Kadmos*.

Kadmos, however, is inseparably linked with Thebes; the Greeks have always held him to be the founder of Thebes, and the royal city of Thebes was and is still called *Kadmeia*.

There can be many other conclusions drawn from this discovery. We simply state that with this letter the conjectures put forward above regarding the role of Thebes within Aḫḫijawā in the thirteenth century become hard facts, and—still more importantly—the empire of Aḫḫijawā is demonstrated to have been an equal partner in the power structure of Anatolia and the Aegean in the late Bronze Age.

Amongst the many reasons to justify a conclusion that Thebes had special political significance in the thirteenth century BC, not least is the large and geographically dispersed number of toponyms occurring in the new tablets. Regarding the special question of the age of the catalogue of ships, which is of particular interest to us in this section, these toponyms, thirty in all, hold a peculiar surprise, the following three being amongst them:[63]

1. Eleōn
2. Peteōn
3. Hylē

All these three names appear, linked together, in one line in the catalogue of ships (2. 500):

> they who held Eleōn and Hylē and Peteōn.

This line belongs to the Boiotian entry, hence to Theban territory. The three places named represent classic instances of the phenomenon discussed above—the Greek geographers after Homer having nothing or as good as nothing to say about certain places named in the catalogue of ships, since they were unable to locate them. In 1997 Edzard Visser put together everything that can be discovered about these three places in Greek literature of the historical period.[64] His conclusions are:

Eleōn: 'In the context of his description of Boiotia, Strabo gives no firm details for Eleōn, but mentions an Eleōn on Parnassus, hence in Phocis, about which there was nothing else to say; that had been established by Demetrios of Scepsis.' And a footnote states: 'Strabo IX 5, 18. Strabo names as his source Crates of Mallos, but this Eleōn on Parnassus is now quite unknown. Not once does this Eleōn rate a lemma in the *RE* [the *Realencyclopädie*, the world's most extensive archaeological lexicon], which tries to achieve full coverage of antiquity.'

Hylē: 'Apart from these myths (which all occur only in the *Iliad*), somewhat problematical in a synthesis, we know nothing of a polis named Hylē. All attempts to locate this place are totally unconfirmed . . . any traces of a historical significance are no longer plausible.'

Peteōn: 'The mention of Peteōn in 2. 500 appears to be the source of all subsequent references . . . Identification with a particular place in Boiotia is therefore uncertain.' 'Peteōn remains a totally unknown entity.'[65]

These three cases, which could be significant enough in themselves, are followed by a fourth, supplying the keystone in the argument: the case of *Eutrēsis*. This place also appears in the catalogue of ships in the Boiotian contingent, hence in the Theban region. For this place, in contrast to the three previously mentioned, archaeological evidence produces something very substantial. Visser reports the outcome:

Archaeological excavations have brought to light in Eutrēsis significant remains covering a period from the middle Helladic age to SH III B [= 1300–1200 BC]. Eutrēsis was then destroyed (presumably in connection with the migrations of the sea peoples) and appears to have been abandoned for a long period. It was resettled from about 600.[66]

It is this name Eutrēsis which we now find on the Theban tablets.[67]

In order for the reader to see clearly the new state of knowledge, we reproduce a drawing of that Linear B tablet, on which two of the four names can be clearly read (Fig. 24. The tablet is numbered TH Ft 140 in the general register of the find).[68]

Anyone with a knowledge of Linear B can read clearly the place-name *te-qa-I* in the first line. It is in the locative, meaning 'in Thebes'. The largest number of grain units (38) comes from here, as does the second largest number of oil units (44). The second line contains clearly a form of a name *e-u-te-re-u*, which, given our geographical information about the region around Thebes, can only be read as the locative form of a place-name 'Eutreus'[69] or similar. It is evidently not by chance that this 'Eutreus' occupies second place after the capital, Thebes, in the table on the tablet. It delivers only a modest number of grain units (14), yet by far the largest number of oil units (87). Aravantinos, who carried out the excavation, writes in connection with this name:

The second name *e-u-te-re-u* brings to mind the very important prehistoric city which is referred to by the name Eutresis in historical times and which belonged to the area of Thespiai... If in actual fact the relation is valid between the Boiotian toponym *e-u-te-re-u* (Eutresis) with the certainly identified, extensive and fortified citadel and city of the Mycenaean period, it could be deduced that Mycenaean Eutresis or Eutreus occupied a second place in the hierarchy of the settlements of the state of Thebes.[70]

In the fifth line, the place-name *e-re-o-ni* can be understood only as the locative form of 'Eleōn'.[71]

As stated, the place-name *Eutrēsis* is listed in line 2. 502 in the catalogue of ships under the Theban contingent, the place-name *Eleōn* in line 2. 500.

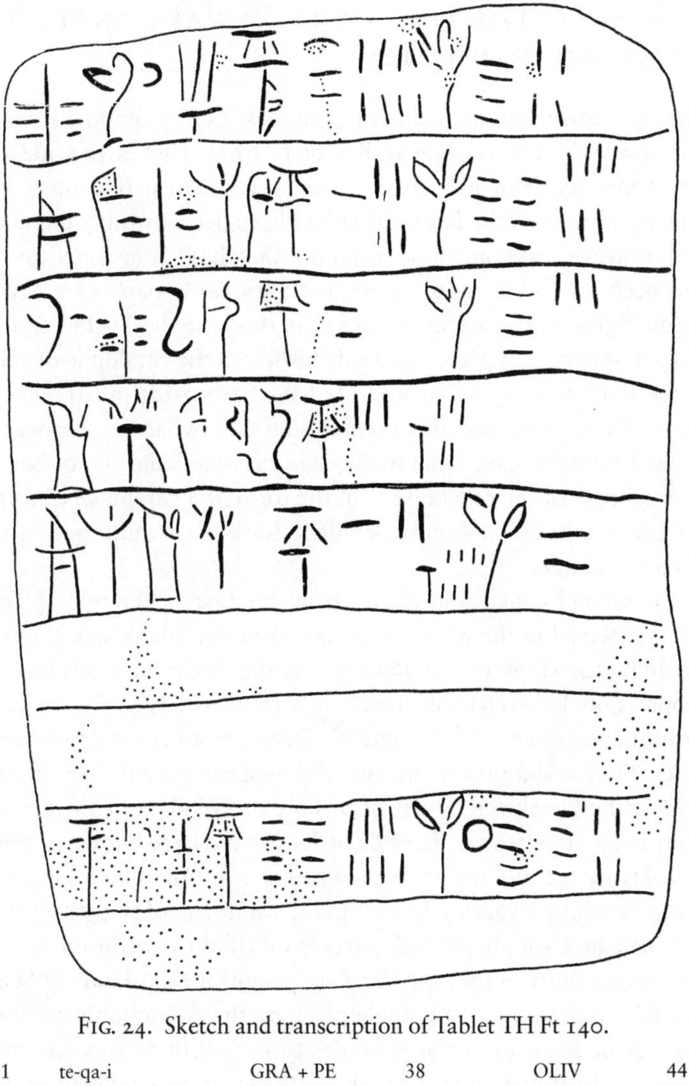

FIG. 24. Sketch and transcription of Tablet TH Ft 140.

.1	te-qa-i	GRA + PE	38	OLIV	44
.2	e-u-te-re-u	GRA	14	OLIV	87
.3	Ku-te-we-so	GRA	20	OLIV	43
.4	o-ke-u-ri-jo	GRA	3 T 5		
.5	e-re-o-ni	GRA	12 T 7	OLIV	20
.6	*vacat*				
.7	*vacat*				
.8	to-so-pa	GRA	88	OLIV	194

OUTCOME: THE TALE OF TROY WAS CONCEIVED IN MYCENAEAN TIMES

The first conclusion to be drawn from these facts is an obvious one: the newly discovered Linear B tablets from Thebes provide the proof that places which, in the post-Mycenaean period up to the time of the poet of the *Iliad*, either had been demonstrably uninhabited (Eutrēsis) or in any case could not then have been in existence, had been around 1200 BC quite unquestionably parts of a Mycenaean region under a central palace, in this case the Thebes region. The compilation of place-names, from which the catalogue of ships in the *Iliad* derives, can hence only have been made in Mycenaean times. Since, however, this compilation (for whatever purpose it might originally have been made) had become from the outset an integral part of the tale of Troy in the form of a catalogue of ships, the entire tale of Troy must definitely have been composed in the Mycenaean age.

The second conclusion ensues from the first: if the tale of Troy was conceived in the Mycenaean age, then the 'blank space' in the catalogue of ships in the *Iliad* is not the result of a strategy of suppression by archaizing bards in the 'Dark Age', but a quite natural consequence of the state of Greek settlement in Mycenaean times. Greece did not yet include the western coastal area of Asia Minor; the Greek settlement of this area took place at the earliest from 1100 BC onwards. The tale of Troy could have known nothing of it. Hence it could not have had Greeks from Anatolia taking part in the expedition against Troy. If in the catalogue of ships the list of regions which supplied Greek participants in the expedition against Troy stops short of the coast of Asia Minor at the islands of Syme and Kos and names not a single place on the Anatolian mainland, nor any of the isles of the Sporades to the north of Kos (see map above, p. 222), then it clearly reflects the state of settlement in that area of the Aegean in the thirteenth century BC.[72]

W.-D. Niemeier recently undertook a comprehensive reappraisal of the state of discoveries in the eastern Aegean. He explains that the probability of the presence of an ethnic group in a particular region can be proved when three categories of evidence coincide: (1) undecorated kitchen and household pottery; (2) cult objects; (3) burial practices. Mycenaean discoveries in all three categories have been made over a long period on Rhodes and Kos, in Miletos and Müsgebi (on the peninsula of Halicarnassos/Bodrum), and, furthest north, sporadically on Samos, yet

No undecorated Mycenaean kitchen and household pottery from the eastern Aegean islands to the *north of Samos* or from the late bronze age settlements on the Anatolian coast north of Miletos are yet known, with the exception of a few examples from Troy. There are no tholoi of the Mycenaean type there . . . Unlike in Miletos, where Mycenaean wares make up about 95% of the total range of ceramics in the fourteenth century BC finds, in the coastal settlements further north the ratio of Mycenaean to local ceramics is very small. Hence at Troy VI F–H Mycenaean ceramics represent about 1–2%, and in the bronze age settlements of Panaztepe, Ayasuluk in Ephesos /Selçuk and Klazomenai-Limantepe the ratio of Mycenaean ceramics is small. On the islands, SH III A–B ceramics in the settlements of Thermi [on Lesbos] and Antissa [also on Lesbos] are also in a very clear minority against the local red and grey wares.

From the sum of these findings Niemeier draws this conclusion:

Mycenaean Miletos was the Millawanda of the Hittite texts, a vassal of the empire of Aḫḫijawā, the centre of which is to be sought on the Greek mainland, probably at Mycenae or Thebes. The settlements lying further north . . . along the coast, on the other hand, were of a local nature and formed part of states with Luwian speaking populations. Of the places named here, Ephesos, as Apasa, was the capital of the Luwian empire of Arzawa, Klazomenai-Limantepe and Panaztepe were in the Seha river land and Troia in Wilusa.[73]

Here archaeology coincides with what the texts say: for the Hittites, according to their imperial correspondence, the area of the state of Aḫḫijawā extended neither across to Asia Minor nor further north into the Dodecanese from Kos. The correspondence shows that the closest contact between Hittite and Aḫḫijawā territories was in the area between Millawanda (= Miletos) and the South Sporades. The catalogue of ships presents the same picture from the opposite side.[74]

How Did the Tale of Troy Reach Homer?

Up to this point we have argued at great length to demonstrate conclusively that the tale of Troy could have been conceived in no other period of Greek history than the Mycenaean. Some readers may indeed find that the argument has been altogether too long. It must be clear, however, that Homer can contribute something to the 'Troy question' only if the information on Troy and the Trojan War which we obtain from his *Iliad* (and the *Odyssey*) is not his own fabrication (nor that of a company of bards), but derives from the actual era of Troy. Now that this has become so apparent that the burden of proof no longer rests on us, but on those who continue to doubt, we can put the question to which everything has increasingly pointed and which the reader has long been impatient to ask: if the tale of Troy was really conceived hundreds of years earlier than the eighth century, how can it have survived the cultural void of the so-called 'Dark Age', so that its fragments remain palpable in our *Iliad*?

Transmission over such a long period and with such continuity was long dismissed from consideration. Ethnological research was quoted which followed the narrative traditions of existing peoples who possessed no writing. This research was collated in 1985 by the Dutch ethnologist Jan Vansina in his book *Oral Tradition as History*.[1] His conclusion was that an oral tradition lasting more than some three generations is unknown in such societies; everything before is a 'floating gap'.[2] The book had a not inconsiderable influence on various disciplines in the study of antiquity dealing with 'transmission gaps' in the history of the peoples under investigation, including Roman and Greek history. There was, however, too rash a leap from the knowledge base to its application. Vansina's knowledge derived mostly from ethnological work among African tribes.[3] If it was applied to Roman and Greek history, an important distinction was overlooked. Unlike the history of inward-looking African tribes, Roman and Greek history was played out in a larger area which was not without writing when the migrating later Greeks and Romans arrived, but had possessed writing for more than a thousand years (cuneiform and hieroglyphics), confronting the immigrants with this written culture from the outset.

Naturally, peoples without writing who are newcomers in a zone possessing writing may have a fictional form of history in the sense described by Vansina. In the Romans' case this is to some degree even probable. In the Greeks' case, clearly, other rules apply. Relatively soon after penetrating the southern Balkan Peninsula, the Greeks had established close contact with societies in the Near East and Egypt which possessed writing. They began to write themselves at the latest in the fifteenth century, when they took control of Knossos on Crete, adopting the syllabic script which had been in use there for centuries, adapting it to their own language and employing the new product (= Linear B) throughout their area of settlement uninterruptedly through to the collapse of their first high culture about 1200. Certainly no proper historical records have come down to us from this first period of the use of writing by the Greeks. The Linear B documents, however, show that in this first period of Greek (Mycenaean) high culture there was a highly developed awareness of accuracy, precise description, and proper balancing of accounts.

Following the collapse of the system which operated on this basis and the concomitant eclipse of writing,[4] we encounter the same awareness again some four hundred years later after the second adoption of a script, in the first evidence of alphabetical writing by the Greeks. The 'gap' between the first and second phases of Greek writing is hardly comparable with what Vansina calls a 'floating gap'. It is more a period of suspension, the interruption of a continuum, which as such was never forgotten by the Greeks themselves. We can see this *inter alia* in the pool of stories which traversed the 'void' and which the Greeks and we after them call 'myths'.

The term myths now has a derogatory overtone, since one is quick to associate them with 'fantasy'. Originally there was nothing of this in the concept. The word quite simply designated 'what is told, recounted', hence the subjects of speech and narrative (today we would probably say 'items of information'). The *mythoi* which we know from written transmission by the Greeks from 800 BC onwards tell of events and actors which cannot be placed in the eighth century or later, but must be placed in times long past. In most cases too these were clearly and indisputably Mycenaean times. The stories of what happened to Oedipus and of the ensuing Theban wars, of the Argonauts and their voyage of discovery into the Black Sea, and even of maritime expeditions from Greece to Asia Minor can only derive from Mycenaean times. That means that the stories we know as 'myths' appeared in Mycenaean times and crossed the 'void'.

The next question is, of course: how? Naturally the first answer will be: by being repeated from generation to generation. Equally naturally there will be the usual misgivings regarding the reliability of this method of transmission. How can we judge what, in the final version of a myth as we know it, might correspond with the initial version of that myth four hundred years earlier? Must not a great deal have changed in the interval, since the changing moods of men at different stages in the course of history inevitably find expression in the point of view they adopt and so, without their being aware of it, change the interpretation of an old story? The end product consequently is *bound* to deviate from the initial version. These are highly plausible ways of thinking. If we knew of only this method of transmission of prose narrative among the Greeks, this is the point at which we would have to lay down our arms.

Fortunately we know of another method among the Greeks, one shared (as far as we know) by no other society: poetry in rigidly structured lines fundamentally unchanged throughout centuries—hexameters.

THE ORAL POETRY OF THE GREEKS

We have earlier briefly touched on the metre in which the *Iliad* and the *Odyssey* were composed (see p. 161): the hexameter. It is important to be clear that this metre never varies in the two epics. That means that the *Iliad* consists of exactly 15,693 *hexameters*. Not a single line departs from the rigid dimensions this metre imposes by consisting only of some five or of seven or eight stresses. Not a single line departs from the conventions which give the hexameter its internal structure, forming an aesthetically harmonious rhythmic unit.

That the *Iliad* and the *Odyssey* were composed in verse is not surprising. There was and there still is poetry of the type of these two epics, 'heroic poetry', and not only in Greece. Verse of this kind exists throughout the world, occurring in every possible language. These poetic traditions have been researched and compared and certain rules established which they all follow. One of these is the unity of the line. Sir Maurice Bowra, one of the foremost researchers of this type of poetry, observed in his standard work, *Heroic Poetry,* which appeared in 1952:

> Heroic poetry requires a metre, and it is remarkable that . . . it is nearly always composed not in stanzas but in single lines. The line is the unit of composition, and in any one poem only one kind of line is used. This is obviously true of the dactylic hexameter of the Homeric poems, in line with the four 'beats' of *Gilgamesh*, the accentual alliterative verse of Old German and Anglo-Saxon . . . the verse of the Russian *byliny* with its irregular number of syllables and fixed number of artificially imposed stresses, the ten- and sixteen-syllable trochaic lines of the Jugoslavs, the eight-syllable line of the Bulgarians, the *politikós stíchos* πολιτικὸς στίχος or fifteen-syllable line of the modern Greeks, the sixteen-syllable line, with internal rhymes, of the Achins, and the Ainu line with its two stresses, each marked by a tap of the reciter's stick. Each line exists in its own right as a metrical unit and is used throughout a poem.[5]

And added later: 'Heroic poetry seems always to be chanted, usually to some simple stringed instrument, like the Greek lyre, the Serbian *gusle*, the Russian *balalaika*, the Tatar *koboz*, or the Albanian *lahuta*.'[6] Metre and musicality are also integral to this type of verse. In this respect Homer conforms. Nevertheless there is one point at which he does not conform. That is the unprecedented consistency, we should say rigour, with which he maintains the metre. This rigour is so extreme that for the sake of the metre the normal spoken language is modified, at times even distorted. The later Greeks themselves noted this peculiarity of Homer's expression, for example in the following passage (*Iliad* 8. 555):

As when in the sky the stars about the moon's shining are seen in all their glory...

The Greek Homerian philologists described this expression as 'an impossibility' (*adynaton*). How can the stars be 'seen in all their glory' about the *moon's shining*? The expression 'in the sky the stars are seen in all their glory' can only be logically true when the moon is *not* 'shining'. There are, however, many such instances in Homer's text. At 21. 218 the river god of the Skamander says: 'For the *loveliness* of my waters is crammed with corpses'. In the *Odyssey* (6. 74) Nausikaa fetches dirty washing from the laundry to wash: 'and the girl brought the *bright* clothing out from the inner chamber'. Was Homer not aware of the contradiction in these instances? Was he nodding?

This cannot be implied of the great poet. So a plausible explanation of this phenomenon was finally found in a roundabout way. It went like this: 'this quality has been taken, not from the circumstance described, but from nature'. In the case of the moon's 'shining' the explanation ran: the contradiction is solved in Homer's diction. 'Shining' does not refer to the moon in that ephemeral context, but to the intrinsic nature of the moon, as also do the 'bright' clothing and the 'loveliness' of the waters. So it had been recognized that certain epithets in Homer's diction may indicate intrinsic qualities ('shining' is characteristic of the moon—otherwise we would not see it at all) and hence can be applied independent of context.

If these epithets are not suppressed even in those cases where striking logical contradictions arise from their retention, it shows that they are not intended to serve a *present* purpose, that their function is therefore only 'decorative' ('cosmetic', 'ornamental')—hence the technical term *epitheton ornans*—and that bards and audience alike perceived no contradiction between them and the immediate context. The reason is that these epithets, with their associated principal concept, i.e. 'shining' with 'moon', form a unit which evidently had so often been heard that no thought was given to the logic of its use in certain contexts. In present-day English a comparable effect might be produced with sentences like 'The good Lord has punished me', where the epithet 'good' is at variance with the general sense of the sentence. One who suffers punishment would not normally use the word 'good' of the castigator.

Yet this solution left unexplained how such an illogical way of speaking could have arisen. It was modern Homeric research which found the explanation. In the nineteenth century three German scholars arrived at the same idea: Gottfried Hermann, Johann Ernst Ellendt, and Heinrich Düntzer.[7] Considerations of space make it impossible to follow their reasoning individually, so we go straight to the outcome: the reason for the illogicality is the force of the metre. Why?

That is quickly seen. A poet has need of a quite particular technique to make his work easier, if he lacks the support of writing, and does not sit undisturbed at a desk, combining words to make lines, continually experimenting and improving, but must develop his tale on the spot, purely orally, in front of an audience hanging on his every word. This he must do in a particular metre, from which he may not deviate without disappointing his audience, or maybe having it jeer or boo him off. It is impossible for him to find new words within the metre for every single event he would like to introduce. That would be such an effort, so challenging, that he would be forced to concentrate on that alone and not come to attend to what *really* matters to himself and his audience: to tell a tale, a tale with internal consistency and coherence, with living characters who speak to each other naturally, and with suspense which grips and rivets the audience. In sum, he has to produce a work of spoken and narrative art, at the end of which an audience can applaud enthusiastically, and which thus gauges his standing as a bard. In order, however, to concentrate wholly on this 'higher' aim, he needs prepared phrases, coined earlier and long proven, phrases which are cast iron certainties to fit the metre and hence can be relied on. We call such phrases 'formulae'.

Those bards throughout the world who recite their stories to an attentive audience, not so much off by heart as composing as they go along, improvise in this way and regularly employ such formulae. We can now also understand why 'shining' *has to* be combined with the moon in our example. The phrase is a formula, one of the most frequently employed kind, a so-called line-closure formula. Why most frequently employed?

It is evident that an improvising bard has most freedom to compose within the metre when beginning a line. The closer he comes to the end of the line, the greater the danger that he will not finish precisely at the point prescribed, but might complete his thought too early. He might fall one or more beats short, or overshoot the end of the line, his last word being perhaps too long. The bards seek to avert this danger by concluding the main thought, if at all possible, in the middle or shortly after the middle of a line. They 'top up' the remaining part of the line up to the prescribed end with something suitable and decorative. The line-closure formulae serve this purpose. 'About the moon's shining' is a line-closure formula of this kind. In Homer's hexameter language it is *phaeíníēn ámphi selēnēn.* The rhythm is ⏑⏑— — — ⏑— x ||. That closes the hexameter. So when a bard wishes to recount an event involving the moon, he will, as a rule, try to employ this reliable fixed formula. Whether something in the old formula clashes with the immediate context is thus of secondary importance. The force of the metre is the stronger.

There may be readers sceptical of this explanation. We may perhaps be able to persuade them if we quote similar examples from other traditions of improvised verse. Bowra assembled many. A few of them: for example, we have in Russian heroic poetry 'damp mother earth', 'free open plain', 'silken bowstring', 'honeyed drinks', but also 'rebellious head', 'splendid honourable feast', then set expressions for names, such as 'young Volga Svyatoslavovich', 'Tugarin, the dragon's son', 'bold Alyosha Popovich', and, a step higher on the social scale, 'Vladimir, prince of royal Kiev', 'the terrible Tsar, Ivan Vasilevich', or 'Sadko the merchant, the rich stranger'. Place-names have fixed attributes, such as 'glorious city of Kiev', 'Novgorod the great', 'glorious rich city of Volhynia', etc. Already we seem to hear Homer. We come even closer to him in the formulae of Kara-Kirghiz heroic poetry, for example, 'Alaman Bet the tiger-like', 'Adshu Bai the sharp-tongued', 'bald-pated Kongir Bai', or even 'Er Joloi with a mouth like a drinking-horn'. The Kalmucks tell us of 'the white champion of lions' and 'Ulan-Khongor of the red bay'; the Yakuts of 'Suodal, the one-legged warrior' and 'Yukeiden, the beautiful white butterfly'.[8] The function of such combinations is the same everywhere: 'The formulae are important to oral improvised poetry because they make it easier for the audience to listen as well as for the poet to compose.'[9]

Now we understand not only why in Homer's poetry individual heroes constantly warrant the same epithet, Achilles in the *Iliad* always being 'swift-footed Achilles' (*pódas ōkys Achílleus*) or Odysseus 'long-suffering brilliant Odysseus' (*polýtlās dīos Odýsseus*), etc., but also that *repetitions* are intrinsic to verse of this kind. Repetition *must* be a distinguishing mark of this kind of verse if the same language formulae are employed in all the following and many other instances: for characters who appear repeatedly; for places which are repeatedly the scene of action; for events which in real life repeatedly follow the same course (a person washes, a person sits down to eat, someone makes a visit, a person says farewell, sets sail, sacrifices to the gods).

We suspect, however, another outcome of this poetic technique: formulae on this scale cannot have been the work of a single poet, nor of a number of poets in a short period of time. We must take into account that all these formulae are not something like 'small change', but are, in their own right, when taken out of their context, striking and moreover aesthetically highly satisfying articulations. We have only to think of the famous 'rosy-fingered dawn' which Homer uses to describe sunrise—a short poem in itself. Few can achieve this. It requires a combination of the greatest technical and poetic gifts. The abundance of formulae of this high quality in Homer suggests a long lead-time before a system such as we encounter in our *Iliad* and *Odyssey* can come into being. So this form of poetry must have a long history. It must have been practised long before Homer and passed on from generation to generation of poets. Homer is not its inventor, but its highest peak.

These are conclusions which were drawn seventy years ago in a study signifying a minor revolution in Homer research. This was the doctoral thesis of the American Milman Parry in 1928 entitled 'L'Épithète traditionnelle dans Homère'. Parry studied under the Parisian philologist Antoine Meillet. He had read virtually all the works on Homer's language which had appeared at that time, including those of the above-mentioned German scholars Ellendt and Düntzer. On this basis he was able, in a new approach which surpassed all previous work in its range of material and careful treatment, to set out a range of findings which are still valid today and which anyone who wishes to understand Homer must be aware of. These are the most important:

1. The Homeric 'stock epithet' (*epitheton*) is, in the overwhelming majority of cases, employed 'generically'. That means that it signals neither a particular attribute of a certain individual or object nor a characteristic feature, the social status, behaviour, etc. of the relevant person or object at a particular moment in the narrative. The characters in the narrative all belong to a heroic world and hence all warrant ennobling epithets ('divine, god-like, sublime, gleaming, strong, brave, wise, great-hearted, noble, blameless', etc.).[10] Objects have attached to them epithets commonly applicable to that object, but bringing out no individual quality and at the same time suggesting esteem; for example, the ship has twenty-three different epithets, but all thoroughly positive. When an epithet is applied, a logical connection with the immediate context is in no way sought, nor is it expected by the audience.

2. Certain epithets, having fused in the course of tradition with certain key concepts to which they were constantly applied, form fixed combinations with these concepts which themselves act as building blocks, *formulae*, available to be inserted as units in appropriate places in a line, particularly at the end of a line ('brilliant Odysseus', 'lady Hera'). If necessary, these units can be lengthened backwards along a line; fixed formulae are available for this too—thus our two examples can be lengthened to: '*long-suffering* brilliant Odysseus', '*ox-eyed* lady Hera'.

3. A formula can be defined as 'an expression regularly used where the same metric conditions exist to convey a certain essential idea' ('une expression qui est régulièrement employée, dans les mêmes conditions métriques, pour exprimer une certaine idée essentielle').[11]

4. The aim of the bard is rigorously to reduce to a single one the number of theoretically possible formula applications at a particular point in a line, so as to be freed at the outset from the anguish of choice as the improvisation flows on. The result in practice is that, for one and the same character or object (Agamemnon, Achilles; sword, ship), there are several formulae in the repertoire and in use, but, so far as is possible, to ease the burden on the memory, only

enough to make one formula available for a particular point in a line.

5. Since a technique of this kind and so rich a repertoire of formulae need generations to develop, this epic diction must have a tradition. The abundance and the generally conspicuous technical and aesthetic excellence of Homer's epithets leave only one conclusion: this pre-Homeric tradition goes back an extraordinary length of time and is in all probability hundreds of years old.

6. Analysis of the still living oral improvisation epic in Serbia and Croatia can show that such a technique of spontaneous recitation of epic ballads, employing a stock of formulae and associated rules to be learnt for combining them, is not only possible, but is the prerequisite for all oral poetry, where it does not consist of repeating something composed in advance.

This is the technique used in the composition of Homer's *Iliad* and *Odyssey.* They far surpass this technique in what is most important in all poetry—poetic quality. That the *Iliad* and the *Odyssey* were composed with the aid of writing, the stage of purely oral improvisation having been left behind, contributes greatly in this respect, yet the technical foundation on which these two great edifices were built was the technique of formulae. Hence the *Iliad* and the *Odyssey* are part of an old *tradition* of poetry.

THE ORAL POETRY OF THE GREEK BARDS IS MYCENAEAN

Parry had assumed that this poetic tradition of the Greeks must be very old. No one at that time, however, could say how old. A few decades later, following the deciphering in 1952 of the Greek script of the second millennium BC, Linear B, one could at last postulate that the Mycenaean Greeks must have had sung poetry. Geoffrey Kirk, for example, stated this in a fundamental article in 1960:

> [Yet in spite of the absence of assured Mycenaean formulas or usages] the possibility still remains that the Greek poetical tradition reached back to Mycenaean times. Taking this possibility together with the knowledge preserved in the Homeric poems of Mycenaean objects, geography,

mythology, and customs, and adding the argument that even if all these could be supplied in the early post-Mycenaean period it is unlikely that the idea of narrative poetry, and the hexameter itself, were invented then, we may feel inclined to accept Mycenaean narrative poetry of some kind as a probability.[12]

Eight years later Albin Lesky, in his major review of research in Pauly's *Realencyclopädie der classischen Altertumswissenschaft*, was considerably more definite:

There is every possibility that the epic bards were firmly installed in the Mycenaean cities. M. P. Nilsson and T. B. L. Webster... have reinforced this view. Welcome confirmation came from the fresco of bards at Pylos... the lyre player depicted may have been a human... or a god.[13]

In the meantime we have been fortunate enough to take another whole step forward. In the last twenty years or so, specialists in Greek and Indo-European linguistics have erected a logical structure, widely accepted among themselves, yet still little known among representatives of the general discipline of Greek philology. It states that this tradition of hexameter verse was in use amongst the Greeks at least in the sixteenth/fifteenth century BC, being thus the current form of poetic recitation some eight hundred years before Homer. What is the basis for this discovery?

This is where we reach the most difficult stage of our exposition. To follow the specialists' argument requires not only excellent knowledge of Greek and especially of Homer, but also solid training in and wide knowledge of Indo-European linguistics. Nevertheless we will try to make the outcome plausible. Let us try with an example from English poetry.

If one reads lines like these today:

For one thing, sirs, safely dare I say,
That lovers each other must obey,
If they will long keep company...

we cannot perceive a metre in the lines and are left with a feeling of dissatisfaction. Yet if we read the same lines in this form:

For o thyng, sir*e*s, saufly dar I seye
That freend*e*s euerich oother moot obeye
If they wol long*e* holden compaignye...

the uncertainty is swept away. The first version is present-day English, the second the lines as found in an early manuscript of *The Canterbury Tales*.[14] Going back from the language of today to the language of the Middle Ages has restored the proper metre.

The same phenomenon appears in numerous hexameters we read in the *Iliad*. As they stand in our text, which derives from the eighth century BC, they sound 'false', since they do not conform to the usual conventions of prosody. If though we make use of historical linguistics to change them to the form which they would have had in the *sixteenth* century BC, they sound right. This can only imply that these lines were composed hundreds of years *before* Homer. How many hundreds can also be determined by historical linguistics. Frequently a hexameter, in the form in which it has come down to us, sounds false because it contains a relatively *long* word form which destroys the rhythm. Try as we might, we cannot 'scan' the hexameter, i.e. speak it in correct rhythm. If, however, we make use of linguistics to return a word to the form which, according to indisputable linguistic laws, it must have had in the sixteenth/fifteenth century BC, a *short* form emerges and the hexameter becomes speakable and 'regular'.

We wish to produce at least one example of this point, since it has fundamental importance for the question.

Three times in Homer's text there appears a formulaic line describing an Achaian hero named *Mēr ionēs*, the charioteer of Idomeneús from Crete:

Mērionēs atalantos E-nyaliō^{i} andreiphontē^{i}

Meriones, like to Enyálios (= Ares, the god of war), the killer of men.

In *metrical* notation a regular hexameter has this form, as we saw on p. 161:

1 2 3 4 5 6
–UU –UU –UU –UU –UU –x

This line, however is different:

1 2 3 4 5 6
–UU –UU –UU –UU – – – –x

Mē-ri-o-nē sa-ta-lan-to sE-ny-a-li-ō^{i}*an-drei*-phon-tē^{i}

It can be seen that the fifth foot of this line contains the two syllables *an-drei* where the rules require two short syllables or one long syllable. If it is known that, in the hexameter, only those syllables can be short which do not end in a diphthong[15] and which are open (i.e. end in a vowel, not in a consonant), then it will be recognized that the sequence of syllables *an-drei* is unmetrical. The *an-* is not an open but a closed syllable (ending in a consonant) and the *-drei* ends in a diphthong. Hence both are long. Their position in the hexameter, however, requires, as has been said, two short syllables or one long syllable. The line, then, is metrically 'false' and does not scan in this form. Replace it by this line, linguistically reconstructed:

Mārionās ḫatalantos Enuwaliō^{i} anrq^{w}hontā^{i}

which appears in metrical notation thus:

1 2 3 4 5 6
–UU –UU –UU –UU –UU –x_

Mā-ri-o-nās ḫa-ta-lan-to-sE-nu-wa-li-ō^{i} a-nr-q^{w}hon-tā^{i}

and the hexameter is correct. The closed syllable *an-* becomes the open syllable *-a* and the closed syllable *-drei* becomes the open syllable -nr-(the /r/, a so-called syllabic /r/, counts as a vowel,[16] in fact a short vowel—cf. instances in modern languages like Czech, for example the city of *Brno*). This form of line, however, takes one back to (at the latest) the fifteenth century BC.[17] This linguistically irrefutable date finds corresponding historical support, since the name *Marionas* is indistinguishable from the Hurrian *maryannu* (superb charioteer), a term that was widespread throughout the Near East in the sixteenth/fifteenth century BC, the age of the Eurasian war chariot.[18] For his part, Homer's *Mērionēs* is also a charioteer, and moreover the possessor of the boar's-tooth helmet, a type notoriously Mycenaean.[19] He is the sixth in the succession of proud owners of this valuable helmet, as is recounted at length (*Iliad* 10. 260–71), which also indicates tradition and great age.

This line, which gives the appearance of antiquity in its structure as a four-word line,[20] was clearly also composed some eight hundred years before Homer. Naturally, we no longer know the context for which it was composed. Since the line speaks of a hero from

Crete, it could be supposed that there is a connection with the assault and final conquest of Crete by the Mycenaean Greeks.[21] This event would certainly have immediately become a subject of Greek bardic poetry.[22] Evidently the line was then carried further within that tradition and emerged in verse the subject of which was no longer Crete. The two great heroes Idomeneus and Meriones could well be used in other stories too, and so the line was handed on from bard to bard.

While this protracted process of transmission was going on, there were certainly changes creeping into the Greek in everyday use, which ran along its own rails parallel to the language of the poets. Among other changes, it lost the syllabic /r/, changing it to /ra/ or /ro/ or alternatively /ar/ or /or/.[23] The old word *anrq^{w}hontās*, 'killer of men', was affected. In this process it underwent various mutations and became *andreiphontēs*.[24] Since the bards, on the one hand, were unwilling to abandon the fine old four-word line, yet, on the other, could not or would not entirely ignore the changes which had occurred in the language of their day, they simply replaced the old form *anrq^{w}hontās* with the modern *andreiphontēs*, while retaining the line they had inherited. The metre was thus disrupted, but this they accepted.[25] The line then continued its life in hexameter poetry until it came to Homer.

This is just one example among many. In respect of hexameter style the linguistic proof is now so comprehensive and coherent[26] that there is nothing to suggest any other conclusion: certain Homeric lines as we read them in our editions of Homer were recited by Greek bards in the sixteenth/fifteenth century BC in a form which was virtually the same, only being rhythmically correct. They must therefore have been passed down in the traditional poetic diction of the Greek bards over the period from the sixteenth/fifteenth century to the eighth.

Many who are less well acquainted with the facts will find this hard to accept. We must, however, bear in mind that we are dealing with a form of poetry which had developed into a monopoly as the medium of public recitation and presentation at a time when writing did not exist. It was unaffected by the relatively short period when Linear B was in use, Linear B being useful for administrative purposes, but unsuitable for recording long texts. Hence hexameter poetry continued throughout Mycenaean times uninfluenced by the adoption of the Cretan script, and there is nothing surprising in its continuation *after* the collapse of the Mycenaean palace culture. An independently practised poetic technique, it was linked neither to administrative structures nor to writing. The collapse of the period of Mycenaean culture did not inevitably entail its own collapse. As long as there were bards who knew the old tradition and handed it on, and as long as there were people who would listen to them (we shall come to this shortly), there was no reason to abandon the practice, nor to change the technique and replace the good old formulae with something new.

If this medium of hexameter verse as we describe it was Mycenaean and survived the 'Dark Age', then tales which were conceived in Mycenaean times and were expressed in this medium in Mycenaean times *could* have been handed down right through the period between 1200 and 800 BC.

Naturally, in the process they were not retained in precisely the same version as they originally had. We have seen that the sung poetry of the Greeks was a *living* poetry. It was not verse composed and recited at one time by a bard in a certain form, to be then learnt off by heart and handed on by others. That would have been verse which set like cement. It would have led to petrification. In the end there would have been an antiquated repertoire of ready-made tales, comparable with the repertoires of modern singers of opera, oratorio, or lieder, who accumulate pieces learnt off by heart, in which they neither change anything nor add anything new or change their presentation.

In contrast, it is characteristic of Greek bardic poetry that it continued to work on the old tales from performance to performance, both unconsciously, through automatic adaptation to ever new circumstances, and deliberately, through placing new emphases, redrawing characters, finding new motives for actions, and many other things. For example, it is clear that a tenth-century bard would have Helen speak to Paris differently from a ninth- or eighth-century bard. Had he not done so, he would not have been able to hold his audience. Moreover he would presumably have failed to make the subject of his verse intelligible himself.

In the hands of successive generations, the old tales changed, not only in the way characters were drawn, their speech structured, and their actions motivated, but also in the way the general circumstances of life were represented. For example, it was natural for new realities to be constantly introduced into the old tales as one generation of bards succeeded another. Thus a quite automatic process came about. Social structures and economic developments contemporary with each successive generation of bards, and also objects such as weapons, household articles, or clothing, were bound to percolate into the old tales.

Research on Homer has long been quite clear about this unremitting *internal* change in the tales. It describes as an 'amalgam' the two products of sung poetry which have come down to us in written form from the eighth century, i.e. from Homer, with the titles of the *Iliad* and the *Odyssey.*[27] As early as 1968 Albin Lesky, in a long section of his article entitled 'Homer' under the heading 'Culture', defined the nature of this amalgam accurately and finally summed up his definition thus: 'elements from different ages operate in an internal combination which cannot be mechanically dismantled.'[28] This is incontestable. What is crucial, however, is that this amalgam appears as constant movement *within a rigid frame*. It is the content which goes on changing, not the frame. To visualize quite what happens, the best comparison would be with the ageing of a person. What changes is above all internal; change in the outward appearance is limited. On the whole a person remains the person he or she always has been. At the end of life his or her identity is the same, and from the outside he or she is still entirely recognizable.

The tales handed down through many generations of Greek bards are of the same nature. They change internally, while remaining always within their original frame. This original frame is determined by key data. These data include, of course, the settings for the action and the characters, together with certain basic configurations, family relationships, friendship/enmity, love/hate, and many other things of this kind (we are acquainted with the key data of the tale of Troy: p. 206 above). To change these would mean making a tale unrecognizable and destroying it as 'that particular tale'. That means, nevertheless, that the *frame* of a tale *can* certainly be preserved through centuries.

Names will be particularly important in this, since names, which form the framework of a tale, are not subject to linguistic change or, if they are, only to a severely limited degree. Hence they will be first to be preserved, in their own right as names, or more particularly as names tied into a rigid rhythmic system, especially in those positions in the line where they were always favoured on account of their rhythmic structure. That is crucial, however, since the tales depend on names. We know this from our own experience. A name uttered in a circle of people who have something in common rapidly recalls to mind the events and circumstances connected with that name. Piece by piece information from the members of the circle, be it a family celebration, a class reunion, or a sporting competition, will be put together, until often a detailed picture emerges, one which will have a fair amount of interpretation superimposed, but in which the basic data 'fit'.

The *Iliad* and the *Odyssey* are full of names: of persons, peoples, and places. Naturally, when certain names were pronounced, entire stories were called up by association. When 'Helen' was heard, thoughts turned immediately to 'Paris' and simultaneously to the love story between the two, to the 'rape of Helen' and the consequent campaign of the Achaians to take vengeance on Paris's native city. When 'Oedipus' was heard, thoughts turned immediately to the story of Oedipus murdering his father and marrying his mother. Nevertheless, however confident we can be that these associations were made, we cannot be so confident about their relation to reality. Whether there really was ever such a 'Helen' or 'Oedipus', or whether these are merely cover names for certain figures or types, we shall never know. The tales themselves exist, palpable as coherent narratives and constantly accessible, but a quondam real existence of individual characters cannot be proved.

Names of peoples and places are a different matter. The names of peoples like 'Achaoí' and 'Danaoí' were, as has been shown, taken from reality. The written documents of non-Greek peoples enabled us to infer that these names once denoted historical communities of people which, in the second millennium BC, were known to the whole Mediterranean area. After all that research has recently discovered regarding the age of Greek hexameter poetry, there can be no doubt that these names came into sung poetry, already flourishing in Greece at that time, in the course of the second millennium BC. Hence the tales connected with these names are entitled to be tested for the degree of reality they contain.

Basically the same applies to place-names. Names like Mycenae, Nauplion, Thebes, and many others, as has been shown, have been well verified in non-Greek documents of the second millennium as really existing and standing for centres of power. It must now be regarded as natural that they found their way at that time into contemporary Greek hexameter poetry. When precisely that happened, and in which narratives, must remain open for the present, since these centres existed for centuries and for centuries were also the home of bardic poetry. They would therefore have given rise to ever new tales. The tale of Troy would be only one of them.

The name of the city to which the tale of Troy is inextricably linked is a special case. Following established custom, we have referred in this book principally to 'Troy' and throughout to the 'tale of Troy '. We have nevertheless indicated that in Homer 'Troy' is only one of two names for the city. The second name, '(W)Ilios' (from which the *Iliad* takes its name), has a stronger claim to give its name to the tale, both because of the greater frequency with which it occurs in the *Iliad*[29] and especially because of its identification with the city and land of *Wilusa* verified in Hittite sources. We ought properly to refer to the 'Tale of (W)Ilios'.

What however has to be of most interest to us in this place-name 'Wilios' is whether any indication can be found *in Homer's text itself* of *when* the name appeared in Greek hexameter poetry. In this way Homer's text itself, in addition to the non-Homer and non-Greek documents, would provide an indication of when the tale of Troy/Wilios was conceived. Such indications do exist. After all that has been said, it will be hardly surprising if they point to a very great age for this name in bardic poetry.

(W)ILIOS IN GREEK BARDIC POETRY

In our *Iliad* we find, in the total of 106 occurrences of the name 'Ilios', an 'Ilios' formula which stands out because of its peculiar metrical structure. It is the formula (and here we must introduce for once the original Greek, if only in Latin transcription) *Iliō proparoithe(n)*. It means literally 'before Ilios'. (In Greek a preposition, here the word 'before', can follow the noun; we call it then a 'postposition'. The Greek word *proparoithe(n)* is such a postposition.) This formula appears three times (15. 66; 21. 104; 22. 6), always at the beginning of a line (on one of these occasions it is continued by *pylaōn te Skaiaōn*—'and before the Skaian gate'). The metrical structure is peculiar because, in the other 103 cases, the word 'Ilios' always follows the structure – ∪ ∪, beginning with a long /i/ followed by two short syllables. Note that the second /i/ is therefore short. In the formula which stands at the beginning of a line, however, if we pronounce *Ilio* in the usual way, the hexameter lacks scansion, it does not 'come out'. In order to make the hexameter scan, we should have to make the second /i/ long also.

Exceptions of this kind in the hexameter are not entirely unknown. The bards had particular difficulty with names, since names could not be changed, yet did not always fit the hexameter rhythm. In such cases the bards would here and there resort to compromise and would for once pronounce as long a syllable which in normal speech was short.

In our case this explanation is not plausible. In the first place, it concerned not just an infrequent word with which the bards had to deal as something of an exception. On the contrary, it contained the key setting of the whole epic, which had to be referred to hundreds of times. Consequently, how to insert the name into the metre in all possible positions in a line had long ago been worked through, no special rules being needed. In the second place, a compromise of that kind might perhaps have had to be resorted to once in an unusual and isolated context, but it would never have occurred to virtually any bard to construct an entire formula, a whole building brick to be used over and over again, on the basis of a compromise. Another explanation, were it to be found, would be preferable.

There is such an explanation. The form *Iliō* is a genitive form. However, in linguistic history, it is a recent genitive form. The genitive form of *Ilios* which we would normally expect to find in bardic language is *Ilioio*. That is the normal genitive form of words like *Ilios* found in Linear B texts, i.e. in the Greek written language of the second millennium. At that time, if the name *Ilios* had indeed been known in contemporary Greece, it should have had the genitive form *Ilioio*. Even in Homer, in the majority of instances, words like *Ilios* have that genitive form, since the general practice in the traditional bardic language, even *after* the collapse of the Mycenaean palace culture, was to form the genitive of words, including names, ending in *-os* automatically with the ending *-oio*, whether these names were current in Mycenaean times or not. In Homer, however, the name *Ilios* in fact does not take the ending *-oio* (so *Ilioio*). Does that mean that the name *Ilios* was *not* yet known and current in the Mycenaean age?

Here another observation comes to our aid. As we have said, Homer, alongside the genitive ending *-oio* which was current in the Mycenaean stage of the Greek language, makes use of an alternative genitive ending which is exactly as we know it from classical Greek: *-ō* (spelt */ou/* in classical Greek). This long */-ō/* can, however, have developed only from the old *-oio*, through the /i/ between the two /o/ being pronounced less and less distinctly until it finally became inaudible and only an *-oo* was pronounced. At the end of the process this *-oo* was shortened again, the two /o/ in *-oo* no longer pronounced as two separate /o/, but combined in a single /o/, which nevertheless was pronounced not short (it had after all developed from two /o/ sounds), but long: *-ō*.

We now know that this change from the old Mycenaean *-oio* to the more recent *-ō* had long been completed by Homer's time. In the spoken Greek of Homer's time no one any longer formed the genitive of words in *-os* as *-oio*; everyone said *-ō*. Only the bards continued to use the old genitive ending *-oio*, which derived from the Mycenaean stage of their art. They did so because it gave them a huge advantage in composing hexameters. The bisyllabic *-oio* was at its most useful especially at the end of line segments with the rhythmic structure — ∪ ∪ — ∪ ∪ — x (the monosyllabic *-ō* by contrast was less useful here).

If now we look at our Ilios formula *Iliō proparoithe(n)* once more, taking into account this development of the genitive ending, scales seem to fall from our eyes. The compromise theory of an improbable forced lengthening of the second /i/ can be immediately discarded, once we perceive that this formula was employed at a time when the old *-oio* had become *-oo*. As soon as we say *Ilioo proparoithe(n)*, the lengthening of the second /i/ is no longer required and the name *Ilios* retains its old structure – ∪ ∪ in the genitive as well: the first /i/ is long; the second /i/ is short.

– ∪ ∪ – ∪ ∪ – ∪
I – li – o – op – ro – pa – roi – the(n).

Thus we have restored a line form as it was evidently pronounced *before* Homer, but no longer by Homer's time. Hence the line cannot have been composed by Homer. It must have been formed by bards *before* Homer and then handed down through the ages until it reached bards in the age when the genitive in everyday Greek was no longer formed in *-oo*, but in *-ō*. If nevertheless at that time this line was to be retained, logically the traditional *Ilioo proparoithe(n)* would have to be changed to *Iliō proparoithe(n)*. If the hexameter was still to scan, there was no other course than to lengthen the second /i/ in *Iliō*. Thus the authentic pronunciation of the old name *Ilios* was distorted, but that was accepted for the sake of preserving the formula.[30]

The author of the latest grammar of Homer's language, the Basel scholar Rudolf Wachter, summed up the process in this way: 'the restitution of *-oo in formulae is very plausible for *prehomeric* poetry. 15. 66 is such a case . . .'.[31] (15. 66 denotes our Ilios formula).

The latest editor of the *Iliad*, the leading Greek scholar Martin L. West, concurring with this version of the development of the genitive ending, made direct use of the spelling *Ilioo proparoithe(n)* in two of the three relevant places in the text (21. 104 and 22. 6) and declared himself in favour of that spelling in a footnote to the third (15. 66).[32]

This knowledge naturally has consequences. It is true that the exact years cannot be fixed when the changes from *-oio* to *-oo* and then from *-oo* to *-ō* took place, since such processes within a speech community take time. Nevertheless Geoffrey Kirk in 1960 had good grounds for accepting that certainly *-oo* was still pronounced in the period before the Greek colonization of the east, i.e. before about 1050 BC.[33] As far as we can tell, no convincing counter-arguments have been advanced.[34] We cannot of course be absolutely sure of the time.

What we can be sure of is, as stated, that long before Homer's time the *-oo* ending was no longer used. That means that in any case the entire formula *Ilioo proparoithe(n)* was current in Greek bardic poetry long *before* Homer. Accordingly Martin L. West concluded in a *Companion* entry in 1997:

to mend the meter we have to restore *Ilioo*, a genitive form which is not attested but which must have existed as an intermediate step between the older *-oio* and the later *-ou* (= *-ō*), both of which are common in Homer. *Iliou proparoithe* may have been a formula established many generations before Homer.[35]

This implies more. It implies that Greek bards certainly long before Homer were recounting events which took place 'before Ilios' and 'before the Skaian gate'. What can these events have been? What can have happened 'before Ilios and the Skaian gate', before a town across the sea on the mainland of Asia Minor, that had significance enough for bards in Achaia/Greece to tell of it in hexameter verse in Greek? Certainly not some peculiarly Trojan local issue and even more certainly not something which did not involve their own rulers. It can only have been a matter arising from contacts between states. The basic subject matter of the Greek poetry invites the conclusion that these contacts were more warlike than peaceful.

In terms of time, Homer's text itself takes us even further back with the tale of Troy/Wilios, and the time of its existence in Greek poetry can be even more closely determined. Unfortunately it is too difficult to set out here the relevant series of conclusions in detail. Too many prerequisites would have to be met and special disciplines like Greek dialectology too deeply explored. Hence we wish to content ourselves with a few references.

One of the leading researchers in Greek dialectology, Richard Janko, after an extensive study, came to this conclusion in 1992:

Mycenaean speech and legend may have migrated directly from the Peloponnese to the Asian area of the *Aeolians*, especially if there is some truth in the assertions of the Penthilides[36] of Lesbos that they are descended from the line of Atreus[37] ... Achilleus is an *Aeolian* hero ... Phrases like *proti*

Ilion hirēn or *Hektoreēn alochon* show that *Aeolian* bards recited tales about a war at Troy.[38]

What does Janko mean when he repeats *Aeolians* and *Aeolian*? Aeolian was one of the principal dialects of Greek. The Greek dialect of the *Iliad* and the *Odyssey* is, however, as has been said many times, predominantly Ionian. Nevertheless this Ionian contains a large number of *Aeolian* dialect words and forms, often representing a very old stage of Greek. In many cases the Ionian bards would have been able to replace these words and forms with metrically equivalent words and forms from their own dialect. This they did not do. Hence it is a widely held belief among Greek dialectologists that Mycenaean bardic poetry survived the collapse of Mycenaean culture either entirely or at least particularly vigorously in the *Aeolian* dialect of Greek, possibly passing only after an interval into other dialects, like the Ionian, with those Aeolian forms being simply retained. Many dialectologists even infer, with good grounds, that fundamentally Aeolian was the *continuation* of the speech of the Mycenaean Greeks.[39]

If that is correct, Aeolian words and forms, within the traditional Ionian texts of the *Iliad* and the *Odyssey*, are to a degree warning signals for us: 'Attention! There can be a particularly old stratum of bardic poetry here!' The phrase Janko quotes, *proti Ilion hirēn*, 'away to sacred Ilios', bears all the signs of great age.[40] Hence it must be asked: 'When could this phrase have been coined?' Martin L. West replied in 1988: after the eastward migration of the Aeolians.[41]

The (northern Greek) Aeolians, according to all we know today, were the first Greeks to migrate to the coast of Asia Minor after the disaster on the mainland. The first destination of this migration was naturally the island of Lesbos, which lies off the coast of Asia Minor. It is on Lesbos that West would like to think this phrase was coined. Since the most recent comprehensive archaeological research of Nigel Spencer indicates that Lesbos did not begin to be settled before 1050 BC,[42] that means that the Ilios phrase was not coined until after 1050.

Nevertheless there is a weighty circumstance which argues against so late a date. In the *Iliad*, Lesbos belongs unambiguously and explicitly to the realm of Priam, so to Troy. In Book 24, lines 543–6, the narrator has Achilles say to Priam:

> 'And you, old sir, we are told you prospered once; for as much
> as Lesbos . . . confines to the north above it
> and Phrygia from the north confines, and enormous Hellespont,
> of these, old sir, you were lord once in your wealth and children.'

And Book 9 of the *Iliad* mentions several times (129; 271; 664) that Achilles had sacked Lesbos and carried off women from there to the Greek camp.

These statements cannot derive from a time when Lesbos was already part of Greece. Never (even in retrojection) would Greek bards have had a Greek hero in a Greek war against foreign enemies attack his own compatriots and carry off Greek women as slaves. Greek bards whose home was Lesbos could certainly not have made such statements in the matter-of-fact manner we find in our *Iliad*. This whole range of information about Lesbos must also derive from the time *before* the acquisition of Lesbos by the Aeolian Greeks,[43] that is, before 1050. Expressions like 'away to sacred Ilios' therefore were also contained in the bards' repertoire before this point.

Hence it can be confidently held that (W)Ilios was named in Greek bardic poetry on the mainland of Greece before 1050. With this established, it will readily be seen that, in the case of *Ilios*, the genitive form *-oio* was the original genitive of the name *Wilios*, which must then also have had a role in bardic poetry of the Mycenaean age.

So we have a point *before* which Greek bards told of (W)Ilios—a *terminus ante quem* in technical terms. Let us now look in the other direction and test the expressions containing *Ilios* and mentions of *Ilios* in the *Iliad* to see if one at least of them on linguistic grounds has to be dated *before* the Greek spoken by the Mycenaeans, i.e. before the Linear B period, like the *Meriones* line referred to above. Not one can be found. That means that the expressions containing *Ilios* must have been coined at the earliest after the Linear B period began, that is, after *c.*1450 BC (=*terminus post quem*), and at the latest before 1050 (=*terminus ante quem*).

If we put all this together, we see our conclusions regarding the age of the tale of Troy confirmed from this standpoint also. We have taken different paths to return to one and the same point: the tale of Troy is Mycenaean. The keystone, so to speak, of our argument is the recognition emerging from the *Iliad* itself, in fact from hexameter formulae in which the name *(W)Ilios* appears, that *(W)Ilios* was the subject of Greek hexameter poetry in any case some 300 years before Homer, very probably even earlier—in the Mycenaean age.

At this point we will resolve to ask no more questions and eschew speculation on exactly how the story could have emerged at that time—whether for example it can be assumed that the Mycenaeans shared with early Eurasian cultures the widespread practice of bards, the chroniclers of those days, accompanying some military expeditions in enemy territory side by side with the military leaders, as was later the custom in new forms, with Alexander the Great taking historiographers with him on his staff. Nor will we ask what the tale of Troy might have looked like in detail, what characters might have made up the original cast, etc. In these areas we must leave the detail to future researchers. We had from the outset a limited objective: to demonstrate that the tale of Troy as such, i.e. a tale of Wilios/Troy with certain basic structural contours, cannot be the product of later imaginings. We wish here to establish one fact alone: the lines of argument we have followed from various directions come together to form the following picture:

The tale of Troy was conceived in the Mycenaean age and handed down from that time to Homer through the medium of Greek hexameter poetry *in the form of a framework*.

THE BARDS' AUDIENCE

To complete the argument, we now need to answer the question whether, in the interval between Mycenae and Homer, there was in the Greek-speaking region any *sounding board* for Greek bardic poetry and thus for the tale of Troy. Had no one wished to hear the old tales, no doubt they would have vanished. Happily we can spare ourselves an extensive exposition of this point, since research in roughly the last fifteen years has clearly shown that Greece had not become a total cultural desert following the collapse of the Mycenaean palace culture. The great centres did lie in ruins, but lesser courts continued to exist in Greece. Excavations, for example, at Elateia in Phokis, but also at Lefkandi on Euboia have made it clear that life in these minor centres went on, indeed in luxury: lavish buildings went up; imports of luxury commodities, for instance from Egypt, went on; rulers were buried in great magnificence. It is, however, particularly important for the question we ask that the bard, with his phorminx, his lyre, appears as a constantly recurring motif on small art works in these minor centres. One of the most active researchers in this area of the 'Dark Age', Sigrid Deger-Jalkotzy (Salzburg), in 1991 on the basis of her own widespread excavations wrote:

The general nature of the SH IIIC period (i.e. the late twelfth/early eleventh century BC), briefly sketched here, but particularly the middle SH IIIC with its prosperity, its small domains and residences, with its apparently warlike ruling stratum looking back with nostalgia to the age of palaces, together with the work of epic bards at these courts, evidenced in vase paintings—all this suggests that the illiterate Mycenaean age without palaces, and particularly the courts of minor princes in the middle SH IIIC, played a significant role in the development of the early Greek epic.[44]

Knowledge acquired since, principally in the field of pottery research,[45] has confirmed this picture. The author attempted a summary in an article of 1994.[46] Subsequently the Cologne ancient historian Karl-Joachim Hölkeskamp, whom we have already quoted, in 2000 drew a comprehensive picture of the so-called 'post-palatial' period from about 1200 to 1050 BC. We take an extended passage from it:

A whole range of settlements and burial places from this period have in the meantime been excavated in Achaia, in northern Elis and other parts of the Peloponnese, in Phocis and East Locris in central Greece, in the area of the former palace of Iolkos in Thessaly, and also in Macedonia and on Crete.

Some of these settlements even experienced a second flowering round about 1100, turning many for the first time into 'centres', if still without a palace. There was such a centre in the vicinity of Perati in eastern Attica, where a burial place with at least 220 graves indicates the existence of a large settlement between the early twelfth century and about 1075. Many of the numerous burial gifts, some of them rich (vases of various forms, jewellery and seals, utensils of all kinds and weapons), also indicate through their origin that supraregional contacts were still maintained, not only with adjacent Argolis and with Euboia, but for example with Crete, Cyprus, Rhodes and Cos and as far as with Syria and Egypt. The far-reaching connections with the Levant were not abruptly and totally disrupted, even if the closely knit system of the age of palaces no longer existed.

In this phase of relative prosperity around 1100 a number of domains or 'principalities' became established, for example at Mycenae and Tiryns, in some places in Achaia, Arcadia and Laconia, on Euboia and Paros. There arose fortified villas, sometimes with living quarters of at least two storeys and surrounded by large settlements. There developed a style of life which, through nostalgic retrospection in the direction of the typical forms of expression of the palace culture, appears virtually 'courtly'. They include living quarters following the traditional megaron plan, a reinvigorated fresco art and the renewed use of Mycenaean graves. Particularly characteristic of the culture of this period of late flowering were the 'noble' ceramics, serving as an overt indication of the status of the owner; the richly decorated wine-mixing bowls, and the broad range of flagons and drinking vessels must have been intended for sophisticated hospitality and the kind of feast that was to reappear in Homer's epic.[47]

Recently the insights obtained in this area have been expanded by Gabriele Weiler in a special systematic study of 'The Forms and Architecture of Rule in the Dark Age Settlements', carried out in contact with Mrs Deger-Jalkotzy:

Following the collapse of the palace centres in the Greek motherland within one or two generations, far-reaching changes eventuated in the economy and in politics around the turn of the thirteenth/twelfth century. The final destruction of most Bronze Age villas resulted in the near collapse of the highly specialised economy and the production of luxury goods linked with the palaces. The political and administrative élite . . . appears to have gone under with them. Supraregional contacts were to a large extent interrupted by the general unrest of the invasion by the sea peoples; writing, linked with administration, was lost; cultural and material standards were progressively reduced. Even after the catastrophe the areas of the erstwhile Mycenaean koiné in the Greek motherland remained moulded and influenced by Mycenaean culture (SH III C). . . . Destroyed as they were, Mycenae and Tiryns reveal a still significant post-palace period of flowering in SH III C. Other cities, like Athens and Perati in Attica, Grotta on Naxos and Amyklai in Laconia continued to exist. Areas in Phocis seem to have been entirely spared. The SH III C period of about 150 years is still clearly under Mycenaean influence in architecture and ceramics, even though a general decline in material culture is noticeable. Lesser, local principalities take shape instead.[48]

The finding of more recent research is therefore clear: precisely because of its relatively restricted circumstances, the lesser nobility in the so-called Dark Age of Greek history held on as best they could to the old standard of living. The bards' old tales of fame and greatness provided support and constant encouragement. When the great migration of the Greeks began, across to the west coast of Asia Minor, from about 1100–1050 onwards, the settlers naturally took with them this art and its practitioners. Ever since the phenomenon of migration has existed, colonists have clung to their roots in the motherland with peculiar tenacity and affection. Hence Greek hexameter poetry continued uninterrupted. Seen in this way, Homer, the bard who grew up in the eastern Greek colonies of Ionia in Asia Minor, is for us not so much a beginning as the end, the zenith, of a centuries-long tradition. The tales within which he seeks to realize his new poetic aims were not his own discovery. They were known to him because countless others had performed them and then he in his turn had done so. The tale of Troy was one.

Did Homer, like perhaps many east Ionian bards before him, try to 'verify' the tale of Troy, one of many such in the bards' repertoire (as Manfred Korfmann has proposed in several recent articles[49])? Did Homer make the none-too-distant journey from Smyrna/Khios to the scene at Ilios/Troy and enrich the tale with one or another element of reality from his own times, culled from the remains of the walls, then still visible. We do not know, nor is it likely that we ever will. There is no doubt that it would have been possible.

Let us sum up what we can know. There was a medium through which the tale of Troy could be passed on: the Greek hexameter poetry of the bards. There was a social stratum which could and would offer a home to such a medium through the centuries. Now that this point has been reached, the decisive question can and must be put: can the tale of Troy, with its component part 'The Trojan War', be based on something historical?

The Tale of Troy and History

The Achaians had known of Troy since the middle of the second millennium at the latest. That can be deduced from the best indicator we have available to prove contacts among peoples and cultural zones: ceramics. Greek pottery of the Mycenaean age, i.e. 'Mycenaean' or 'Achaian' pottery, begins to spread increasingly on the west coast of Asia Minor from about 1500 (and is very soon imitated in large quantities by local producers). The latest research[1] names Troy among places with the strongest Mycenaean influence, together with Miletos, Iasos, Ephesos, and Klazomenai. This is not unexpected, given the importance of Troy for overland and especially overseas trade, particularly as a port, storehouse, and centre for trade with the Black Sea region.

The Mycenaean Greeks therefore were in contact with Troy at the latest from the middle of the second millennium. Until now, however, the nature of this contact could only be roughly outlined, as there have been no documents of state available to us, unlike the evidence of the Trojan–Hittite contact. In respect of letters, we know so far only some of those which passed from Ḫattusa to Aḫḫijawā, not those which passed in the other direction. (For the first exception, see above, p. 243.) This is probably a consequence of differing stages in the development of a culture of writing. While the Hittites very rapidly made use of the existing, relatively flexible cuneiform script, the Mycenaean Greeks came to writing late, in the fifteenth century at the earliest, and the syllabic system which they adopted from the Cretans following the conquest of Knossos and adapted to their own language was, as we have seen, cumbersome and not properly 'presentable' internationally. Hence correspondence had to be in the international diplomatic script of the time, cuneiform. Relevant passages of Hittite royal letters show that Mycenaean correspondence with at least the Hittites did indeed take place and was regarded as self-evident.

One of these passages, the famous letter written by the Hittite Great King Ḫattusili III (*c*.1265–1240 BC) to the 'king of Aḫḫijawā' about the middle of the thirteenth century BC, the so-called *Tawagalawa* letter, has already been quoted at length (see above, p. 123). In it Ḫattusili III complains to the king of Aḫḫijawā, very cautiously and seeking understanding, that the latter does not put a firm stop to the depredations of *Pijamaradu* throughout western Asia Minor from *Wilusa* and *Lazba* (= Lesbos) to *Millawanda* (= Miletos). We have seen that Pijamaradu was the grandson of a king of Arzawa, a country on the coast of Asia Minor with its capital at *Apasa* (= Ephesos), constantly in conflict with the Hittites, who had fled the Hittites to Aḫḫijawā. Among other places, he had attacked *Wilusa* (= Wilios/Troy) and *Lazba* (= Lesbos), taking slaves there to be carried off to *Millawanda* (= Miletos), Aḫḫijawā's bridgehead in Asia Minor. Ḫattusili would have liked to eliminate him, but could not lay hands on him, since he always escaped by ship to Aḫḫijawā at the critical moment.

Discussing the Pijamaradu affair, we have already emphasized that the Hittite Great King Ḫattusili in his letter of complaint always addresses the king of Aḫḫijawā formally as 'My Brother', thus according him the same rank as the king of Egypt and himself. We have, however, also emphasized that the whole letter is a diplomatic juggle of plea and threat. When, in that section of the letter in which the Hittite king virtually dictates to the king of Aḫḫijawā a draft of a letter to the troublemaker Pijamaradu of which he would approve, the last sentence says that the king of Aḫḫijawā should please write to Pijamaradu as follows, 'The king of Ḫatti has persuaded me, in that matter of *Wilusa* (?), over which we quarrelled, and he and I have become friends. [. . .] *a war would not be good for us*', the implied threat is obvious. Even if we cannot, unfortunately, say whether the dispute and the subsequent reconciliation between the kings of the two realms was in fact over Wilusa, since the reading *Wilusa* is not confirmed,[2] the text is nevertheless meaningful enough. It shows that the correspondence between the two and their territories clearly had gone on for some time. Further, it shows that there were peaks and troughs in relations between the two realms. Finally, it shows that the king of Aḫḫijawā is informed about the whole 'Pijamaradu case' and also about Pijamaradu's activities in the Wilusa area. This is confirmed by the continuation of the text: 'Now my brother has [written] to me [as follows]: [. . .] "You have acted with hostility against me!" [*But at that time, my brother*,] I was young; if I [then] wrote [*something hurtful*] [it was] not [*intentional*] . . . '. For his part, the king of Aḫḫijawā also wrote to the king of Ḫattusa. It can only have been in cuneiform (by way of the palace scriptoria then customary). There must therefore have been a regular post between Ḫattusa and Aḫḫijawā. This postal traffic must have lasted a considerable time. Otherwise the Hittite king could not have referred to an old exchange of letters with 'My Brother has now once [written] [the following]. The term '[*But at that time, my brother*,] I was young' reinforces the time span: the writer is *now* old, so letters must have been exchanged over decades. Thus contacts were close and clearly frequent.

Unfortunately, the relevant letters of the Mycenaean kings to Ḫattusa have not so far come to light either in the Hittite archives or as copies in the Mycenaean residences, with the exception of the letter mentioned on p. 243. Hence we have for the present relied substantially on indirect deductions in reconstructing relations between the two realms.

Of the many possibilities offered by this field (we could, for example, refer to Mycenaean commodities and weapons in Asia Minor, representations of Mycenaean warriors on objects from Asia Minor, etc.), we intend here to mention what is most obvious: place-names from Asia Minor on Mycenaean clay tablets in the Linear B script. A recently published study[3] compiles the following place-names or their derivations providing information relevant to our question:

1. *Trōs and Trōia* = 'Trojan' and 'Trojan woman': recorded three times, once at Knossos on Crete, twice at Pylos in the Peloponnese; there is now a further record from the great clay tablet discovery at Thebes.[4]

2. *Imrios* = 'man from (the island of) Imbrios': recorded once at Knossos.

3. *Lāmniai* = 'women from (the island of) Lemnos'; recorded several times at Pylos.

4. *Aswiai*; recorded several times at Knossos, Pylos, and Mycenae; evidently refers to women from the region called *Āssuwa* by the Hittites, which has been linked with the place *Assos* in the Troad.[5]

5. (possibly) *Kswiaia* = 'women from (the island of) Khios'; recorded several times at Pylos.

6. *Milātiai* = 'women from Miletos' and *Knidiai* = 'women from Cnidos'; recorded several times at Pylos and Knossos.

These then are references to foreigners in Aḫḫijawā; where the reference is to women, in the context of the time, clearly, work teams of women are meant—so foreign female workers.

The tablets from Pylos and Thebes have a confirmed archaeological dating of the period around 1200 BC; those from Knossos are older. All the tablets had been originally notes or daybooks, the contents of which, as has been discussed elsewhere, would have been transferred at the end of a year to yearbooks of (for those times) more durable material. The tablets which we have were preserved by chance, since in the relevant year the palace and with it the archive went up in flames and the clay was thus hardened. The names listed above, sadly, therefore, provide a snapshot of the situation during one single year. Hence it becomes impossible to deduce from the names any reliable historical sequence of events. Had we tablets from several years, then the differences and changes we would expect from year to year would probably make at least a rough reconstruction possible of the background of these work teams of women from the Anatolian region.

These names do, nevertheless, provide us with substantial evidence. They reveal a natural familiarity on the part of the Mycenaean Greeks with the coastal region of Anatolia, the offshore islands, and Troy. The frequent incidence specifically of *women* from these areas, entered as foreign workers, leads to further deductions: evidently there were Mycenaean raids on Anatolia and the offshore islands. That would add to and fill out in real terms the account in the letter of King Manabatarḫunta to the Hittite Great King Muwattalli II (after 1300): Pijamaradu has attacked *Lazba* (= Lesbos) and carried off craftsmen from there to *Millawanda* (= Miletos).

One thing is now clear: raids with the objective of procuring labour are confirmed in Hittite sources and indeed for the Hittites themselves. Evidently it was a common international practice of the time. In this respect the Mycenaean Greeks were no exception. One point, however, stands out: in the *Hittite* documents, of which we possess far more than of the Achaian Linear B documents, these raids are restricted to areas in Asia Minor. Women from *Aḫḫijawā*, for example from Pylos, Mycenae, or Thebes, have *not* yet emerged. What appears to be clearly defined is expansion, but in *one* direction only: from west to east, from Aḫḫijawā to Asia Minor, not the reverse.

That this expansion had, particularly in the thirteenth century, become a lasting situation could be seen from the treaty of the Hittite Great King Tudḫalija IV with his brother-in-law and vassal King Šaušgamuwa of Amurru, contracted around 1220 (see above, p. 127). In it the king of Amurru was not only expressly instructed to impose a strict trade blockade on Aḫḫijawā, but the Great King of Aḫḫijawā was deleted from the evidently very longstanding formula of great kings—'The great kings of Ḫatti, Egypt, Babylon, Assyria and Aḫḫijawā'. That no longer points to cooling and discord in relations, but to downright hostility—as had occurred before. The Tawagalawa letter made this clear (see above, p. 123).

The Result:
There Probably Was a War over Troy

In 1998 one of the leading Hittite scholars, Trevor Bryce, attempted to collate some of these facts, if far from all, in order to present a general picture in a separate chapter of his book, *The Kingdom of the Hittites*, which he entitled 'The Trojan war: myth or reality?'[1] He concludes that there can no longer be any doubt that the story of the Trojan War has a basis in history. Four of his five items of evidence will be quoted here (the fifth is not directly connected with the first four):

1. Mycenaean Greeks were closely involved in the political and military affairs of western Anatolia, particularly in the thirteenth century.

2. During this period the Hittite vassal state Wilusa was the subject of a number of attacks in which Mycenaeans may have been directly or indirectly involved. On one occasion, its territory was occupied by the enemy; on another occasion its king was dethroned.

3. Wilusa lay in north-western Anatolia in the region of the classical Troad.

4. In philological terms, Wilusa can be equated with the Greek (W)Ilios, or Ilion.[2]

Despite this evidence, for the present Bryce considers a series of Achaian attacks on Troy to be more likely than a single campaign. What was actually a series of attacks over time would then have merged in the course of time (Bryce reckons on a hundred years at least) into one great event in the bardic poetry of the Greeks, these thrusts by their ruling stratum across the sea to the longed-for 'Promised Land' being naturally a topic of consuming interest.

Bryce reiterates this view in his latest book, of 2002, a milestone in Hittite studies.[3]

This thesis finds support from many directions, yet, as the author himself is fully aware, it is purely speculative. It is indeed still difficult to move beyond speculation, even though research has greatly advanced since the time of Bryce, who completed his manuscript, according to the preface, in June 1996. Nevertheless there is an increasing likelihood that behind the tale of Troy there lies, not numerous pinpricks, but a single military strike by the Achaians. This is supported by a finding recently published by the German archaeologist Wolf-Dietrich Niemeier, the co-excavator of Miletos. An archaeological discovery shows clearly that the regime in Miletos changed in the second half of the thirteenth century. Achaian control of Miletos was replaced by Hittite. Niemeier states:

> In Millawanda (which may have included the area between the estuary of the Meander and the Bodrum peninsula... with Iasos, with its strong evidence of the influence of a Mycenaean presence), Ahhiyawa had a foothold on the south-west coast of Asia Minor, from which it intervened in the affairs of western Asia Minor and supported enemies and rebellious vassals of Hatti, but seldom initiated direct actions.... Unfortunately we do not know how it was that Ahhiyawa disappeared from the western Asia Minor scene, nor how it was that Millawanda came under Hittite control in the second half of the thirteenth century. Most probably Tudhaliya IV wished to eliminate this persistent hotbed of unrest on the western boundary of Hatti's sphere of influence.[4]

This is archaeological confirmation of a conjecture made by Denys Page in 1959 following his analysis of passages in Hittite letters: 'I suppose that this district [i.e. the district of Millawanda/Miletos] (like others in the neighbourhood) may have varied its allegiance from time to time.'[5] A totally new discovery provides further confirmation of the conflict over the district and of the apparently frequent changes of control in the region of Millawanda = Miletos. In the spring of 2000 the archaeologist Anneliese Peschlow discovered a Hittite inscription on the eastern slopes of the Latmos Mountains near Miletos in the region of the road from the inland to Miletos.[6] Until now only two such Hittite inscriptions on cliff faces had been known in western Asia Minor: Karabel and Akpinar, both not far from Izmir. These rock inscriptions, always with a likeness of the Hittite vassal king or one of his closest relatives in Hittite costume and with Hittite text, were in their time a signal to the whole world: 'Ḫatti rules here!' This new inscription derives from Kubantakurunta, the adopted son of Mashuiluwa of Mira, installed as vassal king of Mira by Mursili II about 1307/1306, and dates from between 1307 and about 1285.[7] It shows, if not that Miletos actually belonged then to the Hittite vassal state of Mira, none the less that Miletos was constantly under threat from Ḫatti, and implies a Hittite claim to Miletos. Such a claim seems only natural. Geopolitical circumstances must have made it appear only logical to the great powers of Asia Minor, as they succeeded one another through history, to lay claim to the *entire* area of western Asia Minor, at least as territory in which their hegemony was recognized, as far as the Aegean Sea, including the inlying offshore islands as a natural boundary. This claim has been among the constants of great power politics in Asia Minor from the Hittites of the second millennium, through the Persians of the first millennium, to the Turkish state of modern times. Against this background, the reconquest of Millawanda/Miletos by the Hittites in the second half of the thirteenth century BC, proved archaeologically by Niemeier and now supported[8] by a new reading of the famous Millawa(n)da letter from Hittite imperial correspondence, is anything but surprising.

The scenario runs thus in one direction, on which, even previously, everything seemed to converge: Aḫḫijawā in the second half of the second millennium was an expanding power in the Mediterranean area. In the fifteenth century it reached out to Crete and, once Minoan command of the sea in the Aegean was ended, took over the Cretan legacy in Asia Minor also, gaining a firm foothold at Miletos. From there it attempted to spread further. Mycenaean finds around Miletos and the Pijamaradu affair are unambiguous. The attempts of Aḫḫijawā to do mischief to the greater Hittite empire, which the Hittites saw as including the islands lying off the shore of Asia Minor, were finally ended by a counter-blow by those it had attacked. Aḫḫijawā lost its bridgehead in western Asia Minor, Miletos. Simply to accept this setback would have been difficult for the king of Aḫḫijawā. Aḫḫijawā's interest in the 'feeding trough' of Asia Minor had lasted for hundreds of years—and would be renewed after the collapse of its Hittite adversary around 1175. Greek colonization in the east, beginning around 1100, merely continued a long-standing trend, as we now see. To strike at Miletos, a place from which they had just been driven, would not have been particularly astute strategy. It could appear attractive, however, to try to gain a foothold at another place on the coast of Asia Minor, a place which had long been a target for the Aḫḫijawans because of its increasing wealth and political importance as a trading centre: Troy.

We cannot here enter further into a question much discussed in this context: how could a military expedition of the Mycenaean/Aḫḫijawan Greeks towards the end of the thirteenth century BC, if indeed it took place, be consistent in terms of time and of cause with the collapse of the Mycenaean central palace culture about 1200? We will content ourselves with pointing out that the history of the world is full of examples precisely of an expansionist undertaking at the zenith of the life of a state, through its defeat, combined with other factors, bringing about the steep decline and eventually the collapse of that state.

We deliberately take no position with regard to the old debate whether the two great cataclysms so far archaeologically recorded around 1200—an earthquake around 1250 (the end of Troy VI) and a great fire about 1180 or little later (the end of Troy VIIa)—have anything to do with an assault from outside, possibly aggression by the Aḫḫijawans. The traditional causal link between these catastrophes, recorded in the stones and the political movements of the time, perhaps only leads to a needless narrowing of the possibilities. Incursions and devastations do not become history merely on account of archaeological evidence. Such evidence is valuable only as corroboration.

We can then formulate our conclusion thus: at the point which research has now reached, it may be that we cannot yet say anything definite about the historicity of the 'Trojan War'.[9] However, the possibility that a historical event could underlie the tale of Troy/Wilios, with its great array of Greeks confronting a power which in every way constituted an obstacle on the coveted coast of western Asia Minor—that possibility has not diminished as a result of the combined research endeavours of various disciplines during the last twenty years or so. Quite the reverse: it has grown ever stronger.

The abundance of evidence pointing precisely in this direction is already almost overwhelming. And it grows with every month in which new shafts are driven into the mine of mystery by archaeologists, scholars in Anatolian, Hittite, and Greek studies, linguists, and many other representatives of divergent disciplines, all working with strict objectivity and all under the spell of the problem of Troy. So we can look forward today to the continuation of research with keen anticipation. The earlier uncertainty dissolves and the solution seems nearer than ever. It would not be surprising if, in the near future, the outcome states: Homer is to be taken seriously.

NOTES

PREFACE

1. A reference to the writer Erich von Däniken (1935–), famed for his writings on the ruins of antiquity and extraterrestrial visitors, *Chariots of the Gods*, *Gods from Outer Space*, *Gold of the Gods*, and others.
2. 'Troy in Recent Perspective', *Anatolian Studies*, 52 (2002), 75–109.

INTRODUCTION

1. The English versions of the *Iliad* and the *Odyssey* cited here are by Richmond Lattimore, adapted where necessary to suit the author's purpose (*The Iliad of Homer*, trans. R. Lattimore (Chicago, 1951); Homer: *The Odyssey of Homer*, trans. R. Lattimore (Chicago, 1961). The Hittite treaties are given in an English version made for this edition by Professor Frank Starke of Tübingen from the original Hittite. Translations from sources in other languages are here made from the original languages by RI and KW unless otherwise stated.
2. Since the first Hisarlık Conference (1988), in scholarly writing the various national variants of the name of the city (English *Troy*, German *Troja*, French *Troie*, Spanish *Troya*, etc.) have been regularly replaced by the authentic ancient Greek form *Troia*. In this version, following convention, the traditional English form 'Troy' is retained.
3. The form of the name used in Homer's *Iliad* and *Odyssey* is 'Ilios' (feminine), not 'Ilion' (neuter) as most commonly found in the modern literature. In *The Iliad*, this name occurs over a hundred times, but only once in the neuter form (Book 15. 71). The authenticity of this occurrence has been disputed since ancient times. The new Greek city (Troy VIII) established on the same site in *c.*300 BC was called 'Ilion' and retained the neuter form ('Ilium') under the Romans. In this book, 'Ilios' is therefore used for the prehistoric settlement (Troy I–VII), and 'Ilion' for the Greek city (Troy VIII and IX).
4. In the Turkish script, the word is written with only one 's' and an undotted 'i' (pronounced like the vowel 'schwa') in the final syllable. The Turkish word is an attributive, meaning 'furnished with a citadel'. The noun 'tepe' (hill) is understood.

5. For a detailed personal and archaeological biography of Schliemann, see e.g. Richter 1992 (very well documented, objective, though not always sufficiently critical), and Cobet 1997 (somewhat malicious).
6. Two and a half months before his death on 9 October 1890, he admitted in a postscript to a letter to Richard Schöne, the director of the Berlin Museum, that the 'Homeric' Troy was not Troy II but Troy VI. See Easton 1994: 174.

PART I. *Troy*

THE OLD SOURCES: A LACK OF AUTHENTICITY

1. 'Like some others, we have always assumed that the Trojans could read and write.' (Korfmann 1996: 26.)

THE FUNDAMENTAL PROBLEM: WAS HISARLIK REALLY ONCE TROIA/ILIOS?

1. Schliemann 1874: 161. 'Relying on information in the *Iliad*, in which I had the same faith as I had in the Gospels, I supposed that Hisarlık, the town which I had been digging over for years, was the Pergamos [citadel of Troy]... But Homer was no historian but an epic poet, and we have to allow for some exaggeration...'.
2. Hachmann 1964: 109 f. (my italics, JL).
3. In prehistoric times in the Mediterranean area, besides stone, metal, wax, etc., much writing was done on clay. The clay came in the form of rectangular or oval tablets. As soon as they had hardened, the tablets could be stacked (in a similar way to the pages of our books). 'Linear B' is the name given to the syllabic script in which thousands of clay tablets found especially in Knossos (Crete) and Pylos (Greece) since 1900 are inscribed. The script was recognized as Greek and deciphered only in 1952.
4. Easton 1992: 69.
5. Korfmann 1997*a*.
6. Cobet 1994: 12 with note 73 (my italics, JL); also Latacz 1988: 389: 'If new written sources—indeed, documentary sources—are not found (these could only be *oriental* texts or Greek Linear B texts from the second millennium BC)...' (my italics, JL).

STAGING POSTS IN A SEARCH: WHAT WAS HISARLIK CALLED IN THE BRONZE AGE?

1. More detail on Korfmann's scholarly career (which is of more than personal relevance to this research) may be found in Latacz 1988: 390 f.

2. Korfmann 1996: 29.
3. Schliemann 1884: 1 f., 5.
4. Schliemann 1891: 24.
5. A. Brückner in Dörpfeld 1894: 123; cf. Korfmann 1992*a*: 127.
6. Dörpfeld 1902: 25.
7. Blegen *et al.* 1953: 370 ff.
8. In 1991 Jerome Sperling, who had taken part in the Blegen excavations, commented as follows on the examination of the 1934 finds: 'The humbleness of the burials was puzzling, since it contrasted with the relative magnificence of the large houses in the citadel. Carl Blegen commented that evidently the cemetery was used by the humbler ranks of society. What had not been considered, however, was the possible relation of the cemetery to a lower town, of which virtually nothing was known in 1934.' (Sperling 1991: 155.)
9. Korfmann 1991: 17.
10. Korfmann 1991: 19.
11. Korfmann 1991: 26.
12. Korfmann 1992*a*: (the quotation) 144.
13. Becker, Fassbinder, and Jansen 1993: 122 (with Fig. 4).
14. Korfmann 1992*a*: 138.
15. Kolb 1984: 46.
16. Faced with the evidence of later research, Kolb himself subsequently conceded this: 'My earlier conclusion that Troy VI and VIIa were "wretched little settlements" was inaccurate with reference to Troy VI, even given the then state of knowledge, at least as far as it concerned the architecture.' (Kolb 2002: 33, note 4.)
17. Korfmann 1993: 27 f.
18. Jablonka 1994: 52.
19. Becker and Jansen 1994: 109.
20. Jablonka 1994: 66 with note 18.
21. Jablonka 1994: 66.
22. Jablonka 1994: 65 f.
23. 'However, it is very probable that the earth and rock from the ditch was used to build a wall or at least a rampart, since otherwise considerable effort would have been required to remove it.' (Jablonka 1994: 48.)
24. Korfmann 1996: 1.
25. Korfmann 1997: 62.
26. 'Outside the area of the tower no trace has been preserved of a palisade following the defensive ditch.' (Korfmann 1997: 62.)
27. Korfmann 1996: 42.
28. Korfmann and Becks 1999: 15 f.
29. Korfmann and Becks 1999: 7; Korfmann 2000*a*: 4.

30. Korfmann 1996: 46–8.
31. Jablonka 1996: 86.
32. Mannsperger 1995.
33. Korfmann 1996: 48.
34. Korfmann 1997: 38.
35. Korfmann 1998*b*: 118.
36. Korfmann 1993: 27 f.
37. It should, however, be pointed out that, for example, the Greek fortress of Tiryns also possessed a sizeable lower town, and recently the *Pylos Regional Archaeological Project* has also proven the existence of a lower town with an area of 200,000–300,000 sq. m. below Nestor's Palace at Pylos (Bennet 1995; reference supplied by W.-D. Niemeier). A lower town and defensive system of the Trojan type has not yet, however, been found there. Possible lower-town precincts for Mycenaean (and Cretan) palace-fortresses have so far hardly been observed. This will surely change with the new excavations at Troy. Should anything similar to the Trojan lower town emerge, one would immediately need to enquire where it originated: the Greeks did not bring it with them, so this too would appear to be a borrowing from the east (via Crete?).
38. Iakovides 1977: 161–221; Iakovides 1983, taken up by Korfmann 1995*a*: 181.
39. Naumann 1971: 125, 307.
40. Müller (1930: 74; reference supplied by W.-D. Niemeier) thought it probable that mud-brick structures were built over Mycenaean city walls.
41. Naumann 1971: 252 and figs. 324, 325.
42. Korfmann 1998*a*: 371.
43. Easton 1992: 67 and fig. 10.
44. Korfmann 1998*a*: 373.
45. Korfmann 1996: 34 and fig. 27; Korfmann 1998*a*: 373.
46. Korfmann 1998*a*: 373–7; Korfmann 1998*c*.
47. In Homer's *Iliad*, from Book 1 onwards (Book 1. 9), Apollo is Troy's main protective god. He helps build the defensive wall of Troy for Priam's father Laomedon (7. 452 f.), and with Priam's son Paris slays Troy's mortal enemy Achilles at the Skaian gate (22. 359 f.). As Smintheus, he is a local deity of the Troad (controlling Chryse, Killa, and the island of Tenedos) (1. 37 f.), and as such answers the prayers of his priest Chryses by bringing down upon the Achaians the plague which resolves the deadlock (1. 43–52). *Appaliunas*, on the other hand, is one of Troy's three main deities in the oath-swearing section of the Alaksandu treaty (see p. 110), and, significantly, found nowhere

else (so far). (B. H. L. van Gessel, *Onomasticon of the Hittite Pantheon*: I (Leiden etc., 1998), 37 (reference supplied by W.-D. Niemeier)). As *Apollon Agyieus*, the Greek Apollo was protector of the gates and streets, and linked with the stone cult (Fehrentz 1993). Wilamowitz saw Apollo as an import from Asia Minor (Wilamowitz 1903), and Nilsson followed him (Nilsson 1967: 559–64); Nilsson (1967: 562, note 5) also pointed out the gateway *stelai* before the fortress walls of Troy, introduced into the debate by Dörpfeld (1902: 132–5) and Blegen (1953: 96–8, 452). The etymology of 'Apollo' remains unclear even today (Burkert's attempt to derive it from Doric *apella* 'people's assembly' (Burkert 1975) has not been borne out.) West (1997*a*: 55) does not go into the west Anatolian connection.

48. Korfmann 1986: 1–16; Latacz 1988: 395–7.
49. Latacz 1988: 396.
50. It is still not fully clear whether (laden) merchant ships could be anchored in the same manner as (lighter) warships (on whose certainly traditional anchoring technique, which needed no port installations, see the *Iliad* 1. 430–9, with commentary in Latacz 2000 I. 2: 148, with further reading). The fact that in the Bay of Beşik no port installations have yet been found (breakwaters or piers), which is not the case in Limantepe, the present Urla, near Izmir, does not mean they were unsuitable as anchorages. On the Bronze Age harbour of Limantepe, see H. Erkanal in Cobet *et al.* (2003).
51. The first detailed description and analysis of some of the 'Treasure of Priam' was provided by Schliemann himself (Schliemann 1874: 289–97; in the 1990 reprint: 216–23; metal analysis by Damour and Lyon in the same edition 237 f.).
52. P. Jablonka in Korfmann 1998: 52.
53. See Starke 1995.
54. *The Art and Thought of Heraclitus*, an edition of the fragments with translation and commentary by Charles H. Kahn (Cambridge, 1979), Fragment VII, 31.
55. Korfmann 1995: 181 f.; Korfmann 1998*a*: 380–3.
56. The protracted scholarly dispute over whether there was maritime traffic between the Aegean and the Black Sea in the second millennium BC has recently been tending strongly towards an affirmative answer. See Korfmann 1995: 182, note 52, and the relevant discussions at the International Symposium 'Lebensraum Troia zwischen Erdgeschichte und Kultur', 2–5 April 2001 (Akademie der Wissenschaften Heidelberg).
57. This branch of research can best be seen today in the regular reports on the wreck of a sunken cargo vessel from the fourteenth century BC,

found off the Turkish town of Kaş (*Antiphellos*, in Lykia) in 1984 and the subject of systematic study since then. The reports have been appearing in *The American Journal of Archaeology* (from No. 90, 1986).

58. Easton 1996: 115, 118. Also Korfmann 1996: 60, note 54a.
59. *Studia Troica* 6, 1996: 111.
60. For a long time the purpose of the hole was not known. It was thought that the seal might have been worn round the neck as a pendant, or even an amulet. Only in the 1980s was this clarified by the discovery at Ras Shamra (Ugarit) of a biconvex seal with the reversing mechanism fully preserved. (See Gorny 1993: 167, note 29.) Of particular interest is Gorny's reference to a *bronze* biconvex seal with the reversing mechanism still in place, from Boğazköy, furnished by K. Bittel as early as 1969. (Bittel 1969: 8 f. and note 4.)
61. Gorny 1993: 167.
62. Korfmann 1996: 25 f.
63. The following explanation is based on the superb work of Ernst Doblhofer, to whom I am very grateful (Doblhofer 1993).
64. Rawlinson 1850: 8.
65. From the orginal Hebrew 'Hittīm'.
66. Mordtmann 1872: 625–8.
67. Starke 1998a: col. 522. (The Greek name Eteokles < *Etewo-klewēs, for example, appears as *Tawagalawa*, as shown in Güterbock 1990: 158.)
68. Neumann 1999: 16.
69. Neumann 1992: 25 (my italics, JL).
70. From Starke 2001: 37 and Starke 1998: cols. 191–2.
71. Starke 1999: Abschnitt B ('Die luwischen Dialekte').
72. 'Pictographic Luwian' (Bildluwisch) is recommended by Klengel (1989: 234) in place of the meaningless and misleading term 'hieroglyphic Hittite' (Hieroglyphen-Hethitisch). In this book, following convention, the standard term 'Hieroglyphic Luwian' is used.
73. Neumann 1992: 27 f.
74. Riemschneider 1954: 93 f.
75. Hawkins and Easton 1996: 111.
76. Gorny 1993: 187.
77. Korfmann 1996: 26.
78. Neve in Gorny 1993: 180, note 102.
79. Neumann 1999: 19. (Besides the Perati seal, five more seals and one seal impression are known. See N. Boysan, M. Marazzi, and H. Nowicki, *Sammlung hieroglyphischer Siegel. Bd. 1: Vorarbeiten* (Würzburg, 1983), 102 f. Reference supplied by G. Neumann.)

80. Korfmann 1996: 26.
81. Neumann 1999: 19.
82. Neumann 1992: 27 f.
83. See Heinhold-Krahmer 1977.
84. Starke 1997: 472, note 70.
85. Kretschmer 1924.
86. Gurney 1990: 46 f. (my italics, JL).
87. The English translation is by Frank Starke, from the original Hittite. (*Wilussa* with double 's' is a variant spelling in the Hittite.)
88. Starke 1997: 474, note 79.
89. Starke 1998: cols. 185–98 (Anitta ruled in the *eighteenth* century in *Nēsa*).
90. We shall refrain from adducing the misleading and stylistically singular statements of Fritz Schachermeyr 1986, although much of the detail would support the case presented here.
91. Garstang and Gurney 1959: p. vii.
92. Otten 1966: 155, Fig. 9.2.
93. Heinhold-Krahmer 1977: 351.
94. Heinhold-Krahmer 1977: 167.
95. Otten 1998.
96. Starke 1997: 448 (my italics, JL).
97. Houwink ten Cate 1983–4.
98. Houwink ten Cate 1983–4: 44; Starke 1997: 472, note 58 (the 'islands off the Anatolian mainland were for the most part claimed as Hittite territory in the thirteenth century').
99. The differing spellings and forms of the name may easily be explained by Hittite place-naming and writing practices, as Starke 1997: 468 f., note 4 shows at length. Limitations of space preclude repetition here of the specifics.
100. Korfmann 1998: 57–61; Korfmann 1999: 22–5; for more extensive treatment see Korfmann 2000; and most recently Korfmann in 'Rundbrief an die "Freunde von Troia"', 20 Aug. 2000: 5 f.
101. Starke 1997: 468 f., note 4.
102. Garstang and Gurney 1959: 80.
103. Niemeier 1999: 144.
104. Watkins 1986: 58 f.
105. Starke 1990: 603; cf. Starke 1997: 473, note 78.
106. Neumann 1993: 290.
107. Neumann 1999: 21, note 20.
108. Starke 1997.
109. Starke 1997: 470, note 41.
110. Hawkins and Morpurgo Davies 1998.

111. Güterbock, Bittel, *et al.* 1975: 51–3.
112. See Hawkins's 'Summary' (Addendum), distributed at the colloquium 'Homer, Troia und das dunkle Zeitalter', held on 13–14 December 1998 at the University of Würzburg. Also Hawkins 1998 (published 2000): 4–8.
113. Hawkins 1998 (published 2000): 18 now tentatively reads the name of the father as *Alantalli* and that of the grandfather as *Kupanta-D. KAL.*
114. Neumann 1992 (see above, p. 66).
115. Hawkins 1999: 10; for more detail see Hawkins 1998 (published 2000): 1–31.
116. The evidence for equating *Apasa* (also written as *Abasa*) with *Ephesos* is set forth in detail in Hawkins 1998 (published 2000): 22–4.
117. Non-specialists often object to toponyms like these, which sound as if they come from fairy-tales. However, this shows a timeless naming system, like those in English and German; cf. 'Rhineland', 'Saarland' (from the river Saar), 'Ruhrgebiet' (Ruhr region), or 'Merseyside'.
118. The Hittites were fond of fashioning rock sculptures of the Karabel type on their borders. (Even today the border crossings of neighbouring states are marked with their national emblems.) F. Starke correctly concluded in 1997 that the Karabel reliefs 'mark a political frontier' (Starke 1997: 451). The border marked here, as is now apparent, was that between Mirā (in the valley of the Maeander and Kaÿstros) and Sēḫa (in the Hermos valley).
119. Starke 1997: 451.
120. Hawkins 1999: 10. For more detail see Hawkins 1998 (published 2000): 23, 'Wilusa = Ilion [i.e. Ilios]. The evidence of the treaties and also of the Manapatarhunda letter suggests that Wilusa was more remote than the other Arzawa states and specifically reached through the Seha River land, with which it may have shared a frontier. With the Seha River land and Mira attached to either side of the Karabel pass, *Wilusa is inexorably pushed into the north-west*' (my italics, JL); also 29, 'and so *the land of Wilusa is going to return here to its Troad home*, so strenuously debated since its proposed identification with Ilion [i.e. Ilios]' (my italics, JL).
121. Since then it has become accepted by other specialists beyond the circle of participants in the Würzburg conference. Little more than five years have passed since the conference; the results were published only in early 2000 (*Würzburger Jahrbücher für die Altertumswissenschaft*, 23 (1999; published 2000), 5–41), and acceptance in the specialist literature can of course emerge only in gradual and piecemeal fashion. However, one powerful voice has already spoken: that

of Wolf-Dietrich Niemeier, the veteran scholar in this field and collaborator in the Miletos excavation (and director of the German Archaeological Institute in Athens since 2001), who stated in a well-documented survey of the recent discoveries (including those of Starke and Hawkins) published in 1999, 'Thus the Troad with Troy most probably was the country Wilusa, as has been suggested by a series of scholars' (Niemeier 1999: 143). As for opposing views, such as those which were heard in readers' letters in response to M. Siebler's report on the new discoveries (*Frankfurter Allgemeine Zeitung*, 16 Feb. 2000), these may be taken seriously only when their authors have fully grasped in every particular the course of the research conducted in the last ten years as described in this book. The number of those in agreement has continued to rise. These include Günter Neumann, the Würzburg Indo-Europeanist and specialist in ancient Anatolia (letter to the author, 21 Apr. 2001, p. 3: 'Your arguments have convinced me') and Gustav Adolf Lehmann, the Göttingen ancient historian and Bronze Age specialist, in *Die Welt*, 27 Oct. 2001: 'And the land of Wilusa [may] at least [be identified] with the area around the hill of Hisarlık, where Korfmann is digging.' Finally the leading Hellenist Martin West has endorsed not only the Wilusa = Wilios equation but all the Hittite–Achaian equations in the present book:

> Everyone today admits, on historical and geographical rather than on linguistic grounds, that Ahhiya/Ahhiyawa was a Mycenaean kingdom (wherever its borders are to be placed), that Wilusa/Wilusiya was in the Troad and inseparable from [Greek] Filios, that Lazpas is Lesbos, Apasas Ephesus, and Millawanda Miletus. Of the personal names, it is accepted that that of Alaksandus, ruler of Wilusa, is not Asiatic but a rendering of [Greek] Alèxandros, and that Tawagalawas or Tawakalawas, the name of an Ahhiyawan king's brother, is a rendering of [Greek] EteFokléFes (not the son of Oedipus, of course, but a homonym). (West 2001 [published 2003], 265).

The objections of the opponents in particular of Wilusa = Wilios were comprehensively refuted in a detailed rejoinder to the sceptics by David Hawkins in 2002 (published 2003), who points out that the sceptical position is outdated and concludes:

> The identity of Wilusa with Hisarlık-Troy is reaffirmed, as is its position and status as a regional capital, the seat of an Arzawa king. Our knowledge of the political geography of southern and western Anatolia has been transformed in the last 15 years, even if this advance has escaped the notice of those who continue to deny the possibility of constructing a plausible historical map for the Arzawa

lands. (Hawkins in Easton, Hawkins, Sherratt, and Sherratt 2002, 101).

The sixteen authors of the collection which appeared in autumn 2003, *Der neue Streit um Troia* (Ulf 2003), were apparently unaware of the total dismissal of most of their objections. The majority of the contributions in this volume were therefore out of date even before they were published. (This matter will be explored separately elsewhere.) On Wilusa-Hisarlık see also the special treatment in Latacz 2002*a*.

122. Hampl 1962: 40.
123. Hampl 1962: 62 with note 42. The sentence has been used by another historian as the motto for an essay on the 'question' of the 'localization' of Plato's *Atlantis*. The difference between a philosophical model, such as Plato's Atlantis, and a real historical site, such as Wilusa, once grasped, may be of particular value in clarifying the question of Troy.
124. Hampl 1962: 40.
125. From 'Ilios' there is only one derived adjectival form: *Ilēios*. It occurs only once in the *Iliad* (21. 558).
126. Hawkins 1998 (published 2000): 22.
127. Niemeier 1999: 142 (with details of Turkish publications of 1998); see also Hawkins 1998 (published 2000): 24 with note 148.
128. Garstang and Gurney 1959: 106.
129. Forrer 1924: 6.
130. Sommer 1932.
131. Garstang and Gurney 1959: 105 f.
132. Güterbock 1986: 35.
133. Güterbock 1986: 40 f.
134. A parallel is provided by the so-called 'Madduwatta Text'. Under the Hittite Great King Arnuwanda I, the Arzawan prince Madduwatta rebelled against Ḫatti, following a well-established pattern, and occupied a substantial group of 'lands' of the Hittites: Zumanti, Wallarimma, Iyalanti, [Zumarri,] Mutamutassa, Attarimma, Suruta, Hursanassa. All these 'lands' lay in the lower Maeander valley! (Hawkins 1998: 25). Other similar examples of the Hittite concept of 'lands' are easily found. Comparisons with the Greek notion of the *polis* (in its geographical sense) suggest themselves.
135. Starke 1997: 455 f. with notes 82–94.
136. Nevertheless G. Neumann (1999: 18) now counts the two related Homeric princely names 'Tros' and 'Troilos', from which the name of Troy is supposedly derived (17, note 4), among the 'points of

detail' which make it 'likely that to the north of Lydia too, in Mysia, and probably also in the Troad, the Lydian language, or a closely related Indo-European Anatolian tongue was dominant'. Since Neumann uses the term 'Anatolian' as a synonym for 'Hittite–Luwian' (15, note 2), this would give a Hittite–Luwian stem *trō* (or better *trōw*), side by side with a toponym 'Taruwisa/Truw(isa)', recorded in Luwian Hittite. There may yet be more work to be done here (cf. *Tlōs* and *t[a]lawa*).

137. A similar case is made, as I have recently learned, by the Oxford linguist Anna Morpurgo Davies, for the equation of Greek *Miletos* (and earlier *Milatos*, a Cretan city) with Hittite *Millawanda*: 'If the Minoans did indeed call the place with a name similar to Μίλατος (the evidence we have is later, i.e. Mycenaean and Greek, and we must allow for some phonological differences), the Hittites would have come across a name which they did not recognize and which they might well have tried to integrate into their language by adding the suffix *-wanda* which is common in place-names such as Wiyanawanda. Jic's *Retrograde Glossary* lists some 50 *-wanda* names. Hittite is rich in words which start with *mil-*; this could have led to the development of a form such as *Millawanda* which would have been based on an attempt to integrate the name *Milatos* into Hittite through a simple process of popular etymology.' (Letter from Anna Morpurgo Davies, cited in Hawkins 1998 (published 2000): 30, note 207.)

138. Visser 1997: 88–90.

139. See Latacz 2000 (Prolegomena): 50 f.

CONCLUSIONS: TROY AND THE EMPIRE OF THE HITTITES

1. The English translation is by Frank Starke.

2. From J. Friedrich, *Staatsverträge des Ḫatti-Reiches in hethitischer Sprache*, Part 2 (Leipzig, 1930), 50–83. The letters A, B, and C denote the three available copies. The translation in each case is based on the best-preserved copy. Roman numerals denote the columns of the cuneiform tablets and Arabic numerals denote the line numbers.

   [ ] = not preserved in the Hittite
   ( ) = explanatory insertion by the translator
   < > = not stated in the Hittite

3. In fact not 'equal'! Possibly an error. [Note by F. Starke]

4. 'Man' (sic! cf. foregoing series of kings). The equal status of Assyria has not so far been explicitly recognized. [Note by F. Starke]

5. The 'template' for the Hittite treaties, of which the Alaksandu treaty is a variant, is presented fully by Klengel (1989: 240 f.). Klengel further points out that 'after the death of the vassal . . . the treaty was renewed with his successor—in partially revised form'. The Alaksandu treaty may, he claims, represent such a revision.
6. Garstang and Gurney 1959: 101 f.
7. Garstang and Gurney 1959: 102; Starke 1997: 473 f., note 79.
8. Hoffner, Jr. 1982: 130–1.
9. Starke 1997: 454; Starke 2001: 43.
10. Hawkins 1998 (published 2000): 19.
11. Niemeier 2003*b*, referring to Gurney 1992: 220 f., note 58 and Bryce 1998: 340, and supporting this choice with the latest archaeological discoveries (see p. 284 above). Güterbock before him (1986: 38) had suggested that the recipient of the letter was the then ruler of Millawanda (Miletos) himself, rather than a vassal ruler in a region bordering Miletos.
12. From the German translation by F. Starke (Starke 1997: 473 note 74). Lines 36–40 of the German version were amplified following correspondence between Starke and the author. 'Our vassal' = a vassal of the Great King and the King of Mirā. Cf. the Alaksandu treaty § 17. [Note by F. Starke]
13. Heinhold-Krahmer (1977: 349) has enumerated the 20 references known up to 1977. Those which have come to light more recently are from no later than 1200 BC. The fragment of a letter KBo XVIII 18 = No. 215 Heinhold-Krahmer (with four references to Wilusa), in which Wilusa appears to be at the centre of a dispute between the two parties, was described by Heinhold-Krahmer (1977: 350) as undatable. Hagenbuchner (1989 Part II: 317) dates it at between *c.*1265 and 1200. Starke (2000, end of Section B) places it in the reign of the last Hittite great king Suppiluliuma II and 'later than *c.*1215'. Hagenbuchner regards the king of Aḫḫijawā as a possible recipient. Starke opts for the last known king of Mirā, Mashuitta. In view of these discrepancies, it would be prudent to await further clarification.
14. Starke 1997: 459.
15. Cf. Klengel 1979: 240 f. on state treaties in general: the arrangement 'brought with it a regular correspondence, appropriate to the diplomatic practice of the time, with enquiries and good wishes, and linked with the conveyance of precious gifts'.
16. Thus far the study of the Hittite correspondence has unfortunately been less than systematic (understandably, given the wealth of material, the relative youth of the science, and the relatively small number of specialists). This is illustrated by the following quotations from

Hagenbuchner: 'There is no complete published catalogue arranged by year and place of find' (1989: 3); 'In the letters recovered during Winckler's excavations [i.e. in Ḫattusa, before 1931: "almost 50% of all fragments discovered"], it is possible only in a few cases to state the site of the find [i.e. the precise location in the excavation area]' (1989: 4); 'Very frequently only the site itself is indicated, with no information on the exact context, which is sometimes lacking even in the preliminary reports' (1989: 5). In view of this lack of archaeological documentation, the writer's conclusion is fully logical: '*From the results of the excavations*, it seems that [Ḫattusa] had no special archive for its correspondence' (1989: 6, my italics, JL). In reality, however, such an archive must have existed, for without one the empire, which relied for its continued existence on diplomacy (the letters constantly refer to earlier letters), would have descended into chaos within a matter of months.

17. Neumann 1999: 19, note 12, referring to Godart 1994*a* and 1994*b*. The identification of the material as Linear A is, however, disputed by some specialists in the field: Olivier 1999: 432; J. Bennet and Th. Palaima (oral communication).
18. At the commemorative symposium 'The Aegean and the Orient in the Second Millennium', 18–20 April 1997 at the University of Cincinnati, the eminent American archaeologist and Troy expert Machteld J. Mellink strongly urged the participants to encourage the Korfmann excavation to sift Schliemann's rubble systematically. 'We don't say that the next campaign will produce a copy of the "Alaksandus Treaty", but . . . there is evidence of historical contact, correspondence as well as friendly relations with the Hittites. . . . And the profit of that operation will be a search for historical records, for whatever written documents, or copies of documents, were preserved in the central buildings (palaces, if you want) of Troy VI and VII A.'
19. See Hagenbuchner 1989: 17: 'For their international correspondence the rulers employed as envoys well educated and trained diplomats, who held high positions in the hierarchy of their country.'
20. Starke 1997: 456.
21. Starke 1997: 456–8.
22. Starke 1997: 459; Starke 1999, Section A (Luwian also in western Anatolia: Arzawa, Mirā, Sēḫa, and Wilusa, except in the south and south-east).
23. von Kamptz 1982: 380–8.
24. Starke 1999 (Section E: 'Kontakte'): from the Mycenaean **Aleksandros*, which is attested in the feminine form **Aleksandra* (a-re-ka-sa-da-ra MY 303 = V 659).

25. There are astonishing parallels here with the Greek story of King Priam's first-born son Aléxandros/Páris, who first appears as an adult in Troy (having been abandoned as a child by the king and queen because of evil omens) and who then naturally encounters resistance within the dynasty. We should be careful, however, not to be too quick to equate the historical *Alaksandu* with the *Alexandros* of the *Iliad*: *Aléxandros* is one of the commonest Greek names. It is significant, however, that the Alexandros of the *Iliad* bears another name, a non-Greek name, Paris (probably a shortened form; 'Illyrian' according to von Kamptz 1982: 340), in addition to his Greek name. It is out of the question that Homer, a poet of the eighth century BC, could have produced the idea of diglossia in Troy. This can only be explained by a tradition.
26. Neumann 1999: 18.
27. Hawkins and Easton 1996: 118. Some time later Easton declared himself in favour of 'early VIIb2' (see Korfmann 1996: 60, note 54a). This would mean *c.*1100 BC.
28. Starke 1998: col. 193.
29. Starke 2000 (Section B, end).
30. See Starke 1998B, col. 531. 'Even if nothing is so far known of the further fate of this great kingdom [i.e. Mirā], the bronze seal of a scribe (i.e. a representative of the state administration), found in Troy in 1995 and inscribed in hieroglyphic Luwian, makes clear that administrative continuity must be assumed even in the region of the Arzawan states.' For the moment, perhaps 'must' should be replaced by 'can'.

THE OPPOSING SIDE: 'ACHAIANS' AND 'DANAANS' —TWO MORE NAMES REHABILITATED

1. Forrer 1924; Forrer 1924*a*.
2. Sommer 1932.
3. The book by the English philologist Denys Page (Page 1959), which is important for the *overall* framing of our question, merits special mention. On the question of Aḫḫijawā, Page, who was firmly *in favour* of the equation, gave a correct judgement on many points of detail (ch. 1, 'Achaeans in Hittite Documents'). In general, however, he was often obliged to resort to suggestive rhetoric rather than precise argument, as the clear geographical basis now available to us was then lacking. (See the totally erroneous map of the Hittite empire, p. 14a, taken from Garstang 1943; the *Geography* by Garstang and Gurney (1959) was not yet available.)
4. On the matter of the *linguistic* equation of *Aḫḫijawā* and *Achai(w)ia*, Page (1959) followed the same line of reasoning represented in all these

Hittite–Greek equations: 'but I suggest that that problem has now become one of philological interest only and is no longer a matter of historical importance. The identification of Ahhijawā with an Achaean land is to be proved, if at all, by documentary and archaeological evidence, apart from all speculation about place names' (Page 1959: 17).

5. Starke 1997; Hawkins 1998; Bryce 1998: 659–63, 321–4, 342–4.
6. Mountjoy 1998; Niemeier 1999.
7. Parker 1999: especially 497: 'communis opinio'.
8. Bennet 1997: 519; Latacz 2000 (Commentary on the *Iliad* 1. 2, p. 16).
9. Hawkins 1998 (published 2000): 30. Hawkins goes on, 'I have to declare my opinion that the evidence offered in this article strongly supports the view that Ahhiyawa does represent the Mycenaean Greeks, whether on the Aegean islands or on the Greek mainland (see P. Mountjoy, this volume).' One of those resisting the tide is G. Steiner, 'Neue Überlegungen zur Ahhijawa-Frage', in *X Türk Tarih Kongresi. Kongreye sunulan bildriler*, II Cilt (Ankara, 1990), 523–30; A. Ünal, *Bulletin of the Middle Eastern Culture Centre in Japan*, 4 (Wiesbaden, 1991), 39–44. [Note by Hawkins]
10. Starke 1997: 453.
11. Tawagalawa (= Greek *Etewo-klewēs) was a brother of the king of Ahhijawā: Güterbock 1990: 158; Starke 1997: 472, note 61; Hawkins 1998: 26, 'Tawagalawa, the brother of the king of Ahhiyawa'.
12. Hagenbuchner 1989: I. 45 f., 'Kings of equal status usually address one another as ... "my brother"'.
13. Heinhold-Krahmer 1977: 175 f. Schachmeyr (1986: 207 f.) cites a private letter from Güterbock, according to which the reading 'Wilusa' is possible; to make it possible, however, Güterbock has to fill out a syllable. An argument concerning a point of such importance cannot seriously be constructed on this basis.
14. Starke 1997: 450–4.
15. Hawkins 1998: 17. 'It seems to have become accepted to refer to Piyamaradu as a "freebooter", but in fact there is no reason to doubt that he was another refractory Arzawan prince pursuing traditional goals.'
16. Hawkins 1998: 2.
17. Niemeier 1998.
18. Latacz 1st edn. 1985 = 3rd edn. 1997: 49.
19. The principal works are Lehmann 1985 and Lehmann 1991.
20. Lehmann 1996: 5.
21. Page 1959: 17 made the case for Rhodes; as Page himself realized (17 f.), the fact that in the third century BC a fortress in the town of Ialysos (at the northern end of the island) was known as 'Achaia pólis'

proves nothing. Rhodes alone could hardly have inspired such fear in the Hittite empire as the documents show.

22. Niemeier 1999: 144. For more detail on the matter of the location, see pp. 242–3.
23. Summary in Niemeier 1999.
24. For quotations and references see Lehmann 1991: 110 f., 114; Niemeier 1999: 153. For more detail see p. 282 of the present work. In private correspondence, F. Starke holds that the translation 'a merchant of *his*' is incorrect and reads this as 'of *yours*' (adopted above; the remaining modifications of Lehmann's translation also follow Starke). However, this in no way alters the fact that the King of Amurru is being placed under an obligation to prevent the transit of freight by sea from Aḫḫijawā to Assyria as well.
25. Lehmann 1991: 114.
26. Commentaries on this line which lead in other directions (see Visser 1997: 658 f. for a survey) must necessarily seem contrived. It is suggested that even the name of 'Achilleus' himself, for which no rational etymology has yet been found, may be traced through a possible connection with the name 'Achaia'. As early as 1958, von Kamptz (1982) broke the name 'Αχ-ιλ-εύς down into three components, comparing -ιλ-with the 'pre-Greek Anatolian suffix -il' in the Trojan name τρωιλος, and affixing these to the 'pre-Greek stem' 'Αχ-.
27. Edel 1966: 33–40.
28. The transcription of the Egyptian hieroglyphs is simplified here, following Lehmann.
29. Lehmann 1991: 107.
30. e.g. Haider 1988: 9.
31. Lehmann 1985: 10.
32. Why Amnisos should appear twice remains unclear.
33. Haider 1988: 13–15.
34. Helck 1979: 97 (with fig. on p. 96); amplified by Haider 1988: 139, 14, note 48.
35. See Cline 1987 and 1994: 39 f. (reference supplied by W.-D. Niemeier).
36. Lehmann 1996: 4, note 3; Haider (1988: 10) reads 'iron' instead of 'copper'. In this period iron was naturally extremely valuable.
37. Haider 1988: 15.
38. Lehmann 1991: 109.
39. Lehmann 1985: 10, note 10.
40. Lehmann 1991: 109 f.
41. Düntzer in Latacz 1979: 99 f.

THE RESULT: HOMER'S BACKDROP IS HISTORICAL

1. Korfmann 1991*a*: 92.

PART II. *Homer*

THE BASIC FACTS

1. In December 2000 the results of a poll entitled 'Who was Homer', conducted by German pupils studying Greek at a grammar school in Upper Franconia, were published on the Internet (*http://www.casiopeia.de/ausgabe45/Homer/homer.html*). Correct answers were given by 92% of grammar-school pupils, but of 154 citizens questioned only 30% gave a correct answer, and of these 50% gave an incomplete answer. Only 7 of the 154 could name the *Iliad* and the *Odyssey*.
2. The first attested use of the term seems to be in Tsountas and Manatt 1897: 363. In the past decade, however, it has become clear 'that the terms "Dark Age", "Dark Centuries" and "Greek middle ages" have more to do with the state of modern knowledge than with what they were intended to designate', Deger-Jalkotzy 1991: 128; see also Latacz 1997: 54—'dark to *us*'.
3. Blome 1991; Latacz 1994.
4. See Latacz 1997: 61 for more detail.
5. We shall not tackle the question of whether the poet of the *Iliad* (and perhaps the *Odyssey* too) was really called *Hómēros* (in the original Greek form), as there is no point. The *Iliad* and the *Odyssey* must have had authors. The Greeks themselves gave *Hómēros* as the name of the author. There is nothing to be gained by using any other name (or an anonymous X).
6. See Latacz 2001.
7. For more detail see Latacz 1991*a*. Ongoing attempts to locate the poet of the *Iliad* in a later age, even *after* Hesiod, proceed from points of detail in the body of the text which has come down to us, rather than from the broader context. Such attempts must necessarily remain superficial.

HOMER'S *ILIAD* AND THE TALE OF TROY

1. *The Listener*, 10 July 1952, cited in Chadwick 1959: 68.
2. Ventris and Chadwick 1956, 2nd edn., 1973.
3. Chadwick 1959: 101 f.
4. On Bentley's importance in Hellenistic studies, see the chapter 'Richard Bentley und die Klassische Philologie in England', Pfeiffer 1982 (p. 195 on Bentley's rediscovery of the digamma 'w').

5. To simplify the argument, we have considered only the loss of the 'w'. A systematic treatment of the phonological aspect alone would need to trace and explain the loss of other sounds, above all 'j', and the partial loss of 's' and 'h'. For more detail see Wachter 2000, §§ 15–27.
6. The full extent of the common ground shared by Greek culture of the Mycenaean age and that of the eighth century BC and later is still best judged on the basis of the comprehensive survey in Chadwick 1979.
7. Hölkeskamp 2000.
8. Hölkeskamp 2000: 43.
9. Historical judgements such as 'continuity' and 'discontinuity' depend on the choice of segment to be studied and the consequent magnification or reduction of the structures observed. Microscopic studies produce the judgement 'discontinuity'; macroscopic studies (as practised here)—'continuity'.
10. Lesky 1968: cols. 750–7. (The encyclopedia article appeared in offprint form in 1967.)
11. See Lesky's report (col. 750) on Carpenter's thesis (Carpenter 1956).
12. Blegen 1963: 20.
13. Lesky 1968: col. 755 (my italics, JL).
14. Page 1959, 253 f. ('The Achaeans did fight the Trojans, and Agamemnon was the name of Mycenae's king. Achilles is certainly not less historical.')
15. Manfred Korfmann 2001 follows roughly this line of thinking. It is quite possible that new insights will be achieved by this means and by developing carefully differentiating hypotheses. The primary task will be to attempt to reconstruct as faithfully as possible the appearance of the site as it was in the eighth century BC.
16. Aristotle, *Poetics*, translated with an introduction by Gerald F. Else (Ann Arbor, 1976), 32–3. The writing of history depends to a great extent on filling gaps, evaluating probabilities, and setting forth suppositions, and cannot therefore report 'how things really were', but this is a question of a different order.
17. Thucydides, *History of the Peloponnesian War*, translated with an introduction by Rex Warner (Harmondsworth, 1954), 14.
18. Note also the most recent extensive study, by Elke Stein-Hölkeskamp, of 'the world of Homer' and her correlation between reality and poetry: 'The very choice of the quarrel between Agamemnon and Achilleus as the starting point for the plot of the *Iliad* shows that selfish insistence on one's own personal interests is seen in the text as abnormal behaviour with dramatic consequences for the community as a whole'; 'Were these texts by poets of genius chosen for preservation in the medium of writing because they served the interests of all—the

aristoi and the *laoi*—in an age of far-reaching change?' (Stein-Hölkeskamp: 58).

19. In the study of the *Iliad* we frequently refer to 'our *Iliad*' because we need to bear in mind that we do not know the exact scope of the *original Iliad* as recited by Homer in the eighth century BC, only the scope of the work passed down to us, 'our' *Iliad*. This version became canonical only in the third century BC in the philological school of Alexandria. For the period between the eighth and third centuries, variations in its scope are likely. For example, the whole of Book 10—the description of a night patrol—most likely did not belong to the original *Iliad* but was introduced later.
20. In *Ars Poetica*, lines 147–9, Horace rebukes poets who tell interminable prefatory tales before turning to their actual subject, and upholds Homer as a shining example of one who launches straight away *in medias res*. Here Horace was nearer to the mark than he himself suspected, as will shortly be seen.
21. For more detail see Latacz 1997: 92–6.
22. von Kamptz 1982: 26.
23. Stoevesandt 2000: 173–207.
24. Latacz 1995.
25. See Kullmann 1960: 5–11.
26. For more detail see Latacz 1997*a*, cols. 1154 f. These additional texts (bracketed in Kullmann 1960: 5–11), combined with certain passages in the *Iliad*, yield about fifty further references.
27. Aristotle, *Poetics*, translated, with an introduction, by Gerald F. Else (Ann Arbor, 1976), ch. 23 (61–3).
28. Führmann 1984: 213.
29. Genette 1982.
30. See Latacz 1995: 87, note 82.
31. Pestalozzi 1945; Kakridis 1949; Kullmann 1960.
32. The best survey of this line of research is given in Kullmann 1992. The entire framing of the question is naturally based implicitly on the assumption of an enduring bardic tradition on the theme of Troy for a long period before our *Iliad*.
33. In their content—though not the technique—the so-called 'information prologues' of later Attic tragedy, for example, especially Euripides, are comparable. Here the elements of the framework essential as background for an understanding of the internal episodes are placed *before* the beginning of the episodes. In the *Iliad*, since the outer framework can be taken for granted, they are recalled during the exposition of the episodes.

34. Once the *Iliad* had become available in written form, this lack was felt by generations immediately following, who no longer shared their predecessors' familiarity with the tale of Troy, as such a profound hindrance that it was remedied by the later creation of an all-encompassing Trojan narrative in writing (the so-called epic cycle; see Latacz 1997: 80 and 114 ff.). This work, however, being preserved only in fragments, cannot provide us with a substitute (see Latacz 1997*a*).

THE TALE OF TROY INDEPENDENT OF HOMER'S

1. See previous note.
2. In this summary the key terms in the tale are in italics.
3. See Visser 1997.
4. See Cook 1975: 773. 'The local historians of the individual cities may here and there have preserved genuine memories of earlier times . . . But their works are almost totally lost.'
5. Accurately in terms of fact, though dubiously in terms of language, all these records have been collectively termed 'memory': Schachermeyr 1983.
6. Bartoněk 1991: 308 f.
7. Here we adopt the chapter and section structure of Chadwick 1979.
8. Lehmann 1991: 107 ff.
9. Alongside Manfred Korfmann (Troy) and Wolf-Dietrich Niemeier (Miletos), whose works in this area are more often referred to, P. A. Mountjoy deserves to be named as particularly active (most recently: 'The East Aegean–West Anatolian Interface in the Late Bronze Age: Mycenaeans and the Kingdom of Ahhiyawa', in *Anatolian Studies* 48/1998 (published 2000), 33–67).
10. The latter date marks the downfall of the last palace settlement in Mycenae, *Mycenaean IIIC*.
11. Chadwick 1979: 240.

WHEN WAS THE TALE OF TROY CONCEIVED?

1. Chadwick 1979.
2. Most recently strongly held by Kullman 1995, Kullman 1999, Kullman 1999*a* (esp. 200 f., 'extrapolated').
3. An appearance *after* the collapse is allowed for by those who hold this position, to take into account the possibility that the life span of the inventor or inventors might have *bridged* the collapse; even in this case the nucleus of the tale would have been formed beforehand.
4. This dating relies above all on the one place on the hill of Hisarlık where up till now a clear sequence of layers can be followed from Troy

VI/VII to Hellenistic times: square D9. On this see Koppenhöfer 1997 (esp. 314 and table 4, p. 346); M. Korfmann, lecture, Basel, 17 May 1999, manuscript pp. 10–15 (with extensive discussion).

5. These eleven references are enumerated for those interested: 5. 204; 6. 386; 6. 493; 7. 345; 13. 349; 17. 145; 18. 270; 21. 81; 21. 128; 21. 156; 24. 67. Occasional non-observance of the 'w' is understandable in non-'w'-speakers like Homer. That it occurs so infrequently can only be explained by the influence of a very old tradition.
6. Visser 1997.
7. Visser 1998: 30.
8. Visser 1997: 746.
9. Giovannini 1969: 51.
10. Kullmann 1960: 166.
11. Latacz 1998: 512–16.
12. Giovannini's own proposed solution, that the catalogue of ships in our *Iliad* could have been created by the priests of the oracular shrine at Delphi for propaganda purposes, stemming from lists of invitations to religious occasions at Delphi which required the Greeks to observe a religious peace, and inserted into the *Iliad* for the sake of panhellenic nationalism, fails to recognize the structural function of the catalogue within the tale of Troy, as will be shown, and is unacceptable for a number of other reasons. Since that idea is a function of Giovannini's basic assumption that the catalogue reflects the Greece of the *seventh* century, it can at once serve as the most compelling counter-argument so far. In view of the knowledge obtained since 1969 concerning the background of the catalogue, the renaissance enjoyed in recent work (e.g. Kullmann 1993; Kullmann 1999: esp. 111) by this position, which had been rejected by Kirk 1985 (238), does not amount to a step forward.
13. To invert the argument and assert that, since where the catalogue of ships is placed in our *Iliad* makes nonsense of the notion of 'ships', 'ship' must have become a unit for counting troop numbers (as does Beye 1961; cf. Visser 1998: 39) can only be understood as an act of desperation.
14. Kirk 1985: 231.
15. Particularly if the audience understood the retrospective device used by the author of the tale of Achilles to mirror in books 2 to 7 of his smaller-compass tale a large, coherent part of the greater tale of Troy; on this see Latacz 1997: 161–8.
16. See above all Hope Simpson and Lazenby 1970; Kirk 1985: 168–240; Visser 1998.
17. Visser 1998: 30.

18. Kirk 1985: 238.
19. Kirk 1985: 238. Kirk's evaluation of the situation here is, however, uncharacteristically muddled. I have attempted above to reproduce what he may have had in mind. That the reason for the preservation of the names of these places would have been precisely their participation in the 'Trojan War', for example, does not follow therefrom.
20. Visser 1998: 30, 41.
21. Visser 1998: 33 f., 40.
22. Visser 1998: 41 f.
23. Macedonia, Thrace, and the islands named were a non-Greek-speaking area and still foreign territory for Greeks in the eighth century BC and for a long time thereafter (see Neumann 1975 and 1975*a*), even if in some of those areas (Macedonia, Lemnos) the ruling dynasties at least for a time appear to have been of Greek origin.
24. It is remarkable that those researchers who tackle the problem of the absence from the *Iliad* of the Greek population of Asia Minor regularly note that reference to these cities is missing, not from the Achaian, but from the Trojan catalogue (Allen 1921: 172; Page 1959: 139; Giovannini 1969: 42; Kirk 1985: 263; Kullmann 1993: 144; also Kullmann 1999*a*: 195; etc.). Would the compiler of an extrapolated list of Trojan allies in the 'Trojan War' have originally made Greeks into defenders of Troy and then deleted them, recalling that there had not been Greeks in Asia Minor at that time? If the Anatolian Greeks, by dint of intentional extrapolation, had had to be deleted from somewhere in the *Iliad*, then it would of course have been from the Achaian catalogue. The logical error results from the widespread confusion of lists of allies with descriptions of territories.
25. See below, note 74.
26. The Greeks of the post-Homer period in fact always believed that their Anatolian colonies had been founded only after the Trojan War. Where did they learn this? They took it from the *Iliad*, from the point under discussion here. Since in the *Iliad* there were no Greeks in Asia Minor, yet the *Iliad* 'described the Trojan War', Greeks could have settled in Asia Minor only after the Trojan War.
27. B. Niese, 'Der Homerische Schiffskatalog als historische Quelle betrachtet', Dissertation (Kiel, 1873). Other earlier advocates of this position are listed in Giovannini 1969: 42, note 2.
28. Dickie 1995: 38 f.
29. Lesky 1968: col. 749.
30. Kullmann 1999*a*: 200 f.

31. 'This epic possesses a historical consciousness. This historical consciousness is constituted of three factors: (1) extrapolations of Greek singers on the basis of the visible walls of Mycenae, Tyrins (and originally perhaps Pylos) and Troy and other ruins from former times; (2) speculations by the Aeolian settlers in Asia Minor concerning the time of the decline of Troy that was then inhabited by foreign people; (3) memories of events that had occurred in the more recent past and were projected back into the time of the ruins, and information passed on by members of literate societies with whom the Greeks were in contact, such as the Phoenicians, the Babylonians—and possibly Anatolians (i.e. Lykians)': Kullmann 1999*a*.
32. Strabo 9. 2. 14.
33. Strabo 9. 4. 5.
34. Strabo 9. 4. 5.
35. Strabo 9. 2. 35.
36. Strabo 8. 6. 13.
37. Strabo 8. 3. 24.
38. Strabo 8. 3. 25.
39. Strabo 8. 8. 2.
40. Burr 1944: 70.
41. Strabo 9. 5. 19.
42. Page 1959: 121 f.
43. Visser 1997: 521.
44. Visser 1997: 279 f.
45. Visser 1997: 401.
46. Visser 1997: 401.
47. Visser 1997: 402.
48. Visser 1997: 279.
49. Visser 1997: 277.
50. Page 1959: 122.
51. On the 'Miletos case', which appears to contradict this conclusion, see above, p. 285.
52. Aravantinos, Godart, and Sacconi 1995; expanded English version by V. Aravantinos in *Floreant Studia Mycenaea I* (Vienna, 1999), 45–78.
53. It is available on subscription from the *Istituti Editoriali e Poligrafici Internazionali Pisa/Roma* press as V. L. Aravantinos, L. Godart, and A. Sacconi (eds.), *Thèbes. Fouilles de la Cadmée. I: Les Tablettes en Linéaire B de la 'Odos Pelopidou'. Édition et Commentaire*. The academic world awaits avidly the already announced volume III: V. L. Aravantinos, L. Godart, and A. Sacconi (eds.), *Corpus des textes en Linéaire B de Thèbes*.
54. Godart and Sacconi 1996: 101.

55. To the two publications already cited we add: Godart and Sacconi 1998a. Shorter specialist articles are not cited.
56. Aravantinos, Godart, and Sacconi 1995: 18.
57. At the time of writing this paper had not been published, but by courtesy of the authors was available to the writer in manuscript. It has been published in the meantime: Godart and Sacconi 1999 (published 2001).
58. Godart and Sacconi 1999: 545.
59. That is, unknown in respect of the details of its geographical, political, and social structure.
60. Niemeier 2001 (forthcoming), manuscript: p. 16, notes 132 and 133. I am grateful to Wolf-Dietrich Niemeier for making his manuscript available.
61. There is no reason to assume that the changes in dominance in *classical* times, *inter alia* between the Peloponnese and Thebes, would have had no precedent in Mycenaean times. The myth of the 'Seven against Thebes', i.e. Argos against Thebes, may have reflected this. Speculation which sees the myths as a figment of fantasy derived from the Orient (Burkert 1984: 99–106; cf. West 1997*a*: 455–7) here also soars too rapidly above historical reality.
62. The various attempts of the ancients to explain the choice of Aulis for the fleet rendezvous, dictated as they were by incapacity, are collected in Visser 1997: 247, note 2. On this question the state of knowledge up till now could indeed lead to no other conclusion than that formulated by the English commentator of the *Iliad* M. M. Willcock: 'there is no reason *inherent in the Iliad* why the Boiotian contingent should have the honour of being named first, nor why it should have more leaders and come from more named towns than any other contingent' (Willcock 1978–84: 68; my italics, JL). In fact there is no reason for it to be found in the *Iliad*, an Achilles poem of the eighth century BC. The reason must be found outside the *Iliad*. Visser's own attempted explanation did point in the right direction: 'A place like Aulis . . . for the Greek reader of the time was always identical with the mythical Aulis, the rendezvous of the Greek fleet before sailing for Troy . . . This rendezvous of the fleet was taken to be an event as "true" historically as, for example, the part played by Aulis in the . . . political conflicts of the fifth or fourth centuries. The heroic myth . . . represented evidence of a historical and geographical reality . . . '(21). As we now begin to see, it was absolutely right.
63. Godart and Sacconi 1999: 542.
64. On Eleōn: Visser 1997: 261–4; on Hylē: Visser 1997: 264 f.; on Peteōn: Visser 1997: 265 f.

65. Visser 1997: 315.
66. Visser 1997: 269.
67. Godart and Sacconi 1999: 540, 542; cf. following notes.
68. For those interested: each line of writing ends to the right with two totals consisting of horizontal strokes (= tens) and vertical strokes (= units). The grand total in the last line is made up of a circle (= one hundred) + 9 horizontal strokes (= nine tens) + 4 vertical strokes (= four units): 194. In the individual lines the first of each two totals begins with the 'standard lamp' sign, representing a stylized ear of grain and signifying 'grain' (Latin *gra[num]*); the second, with the stylized olive tree sign (Latin *oliv[a]*), signifies 'oil'. So the tablet is a calculation of quantities of grain and oil. Before each pair of totals come the places providing the relevant quantities at the time of registration and probably delivering them to the palace of Thebes.
69. On Mycenaean place-names ending in *-eus* see Aravantinos 1999: 56, note 43. On the locative form see R. A. Santiago, 'Mycenaean Locatives in *e-u*', in *Minos* 14 (1975), 120.
70. Aravantinos 1999: 55 f. The place-name variation *Eutreus* (Myc.) / *Eutrēsis* (Homer) is not yet explained.
71. Aravantinos 1999: 57. The Linear B script makes no distinction between /r/ and /l/ and for both sounds uses the same sign (which today we represent by /r/).
72. On Miletos see p. 284 above.
73. Niemeier 2001 (forthcoming), manuscript, pp. 15–17 (my italics, JL).
74. As the tale of Troy passed down through generations of bards in the period following the catastrophe, individual bards, particularly hailing from the west Anatolian coastal districts settled by Greeks in the meantime, introduced some west Anatolian geographical features into the tale (for example the river Kaÿstros, which flows into the Aegean near Ephesos: 2. 461). They also settled peoples of their own time in the area in Asia Minor left empty in the tale of Troy in the form in which it was handed down. This corresponds to the customary practice of bards in all they sang of (such as weapons, household implements, textiles, architectural forms, and also customs, speech patterns, etc.). It remains crucial, however, that in respect of geography the *basic framework* was handed down unchanged. Not one of the innumerable Greek towns and smaller settlements founded on the Anatolian west coast after 1100 appears in the entire *Iliad* (on the special case of Miletos see p. 284 above), not because these settlements were all deliberately left out (such an instance of total *damnatio memoriae* is unthinkable in view of the free, unconstrained practices of the

aoides), but because they were (naturally) not mentioned in the tale of Troy as it was handed down.

HOW DID THE TALE OF TROY REACH HOMER?

1. Vansina 1985.
2. Vansina 1985: 23.
3. 'The reader will no doubt also notice that there is a preponderance of African examples and of examples deriving from my own researches within that body itself': Vansina 1985, XIII. To conclude similar circumstances for all places and all times on the basis of this highly restricted view ('I hold that all human thought and memory operates in the same way everywhere and at all times': ibid.) is a rash generalization.
4. Nevertheless it is highly probable that it did continue to exist at least on Cyprus throughout the period of the 'Dark Ages' (= Linear C or 'Cypriot syllabary'): see Heubeck 1979: X. 70–3.
5. Bowra 1952: 36.
6. Bowra 1952: 38–9.
7. This complex of problems is studied extensively in Latacz 1979; shorter version: Latacz 2000 (Prolegomena, section 'Formelhaftigkeit und Mündlichkeit').
8. Bowra 1952: 223–5.
9. Bowra 1952: 226.
10. Parry (1928: 112) 1971: 89–91 (table).
11. Parry 1928: 16.
12. Kirk 1960: 201.
13. Lesky 1968: col. 694.
14. G. Chaucer, *The Canterbury Tales*, edited from the Hengwrt Manuscript by N. F. Blake (London: Edward Arnold, 1980), 346. (Italics added.)
15. To simplify the argument we leave out of consideration the phenomenon of so-called hiatus shortening.
16. See Meier-Brügger 2000: 88 § L300.
17. We present here the original data for those with a knowledge of Greek. Meriones, the charioteer of the Cretan leader Idomeneus, appears 57 times in the *Iliad*. In three of these places (2. 651; 7. 166; 8. 264) he appears in the whole-line formula Μηριόνης ατάλαντος Ἐνυαλίω ανδρειφόντῃ. In this form the line does not scan. Yet if we insert a reconstruction of the original form *Mārionās* ḫatalantos Enuwaliō^i *anrq*^{w}*hontā*^{i}, the line scans correctly. This form of the line must, however, be older than the Greek speech form passed down in Linear B (*c.*1450–1200), since it contains a short syllabic /r/ in *anrq*^{w}*hontā*^{i}

which no longer exists in Linear B, becoming *-or* or *-ro* (Meier-Brügger 1992: II. 117, L 401.2: 'The vocalization of these consonants had already come about in Mycenaean Greek'; Horrocks 1997: 202 f.; further evidence available at the time listed with literature in Latacz 1998*a*). The highly complicated hypotheses and speculations of Berg 1978 and Tichy 1981: 56–63 (examined by Meier-Brügger 1992: I. 93, E 404.5), that the hexameter had perhaps developed from combinations of lyric metres like glyconic + aristophanean, in my view take no account of the reality of the bards' practice of recitation with improvisation, with its impulse towards forms with relatively simple rhythms.

18. West 1997: 234; West 1997*a*: 612 (original findings by Schachermeyr, 1968).
19. Borchhardt 1977: E 62 and E 73.
20. On the peculiar effect of the four-word line (*versus tetracolos*) see Latacz 2000: Commentary on the *Iliad* 1. 75.
21. 'the poetry of the high Mycenaean age has already featured some of the heroes familiar to us from Homer, with their characteristic epithets and weaponry. It told of warfare involving Minoans: the Mycenaean conquest of Crete?' 'We seem to have here [in Idomeneus and Meriones] a pair of genuine Minoans from the heyday of Knossos': West 1988: 159.
22. 'Evidence from other traditions tends to show that the commemoration of historical events in epic generally begins soon after they have happened': West 1988: 161; cf. the examples in Latacz 1997: 106 f.
23. See Meier-Brügger 2000: 92 § L306, 2.
24. See R. Wachter in: Latacz 2000 (Prolegomena): 70 § 15.
25. 'bards did not hesitate to modernize their material in line with developments in the spoken language (whenever this could be done without collateral damage) . . . ': Horrocks 1997: 208.
26. The purely historico-linguistic evidence listed in Latacz 1998*a*: col. 12/15 is now supplemented by Stefan Hiller's recent observations. Going beyond the single word, he posits that 'fixed speech units' ('fixer Sprachbestandteile') found their way simultaneously into the Linear B language and the hexameter language of the bards of Mycenaean times (Hiller 1999, the quotation: 298).
27. Lesky 1968: cols. 717, 719.
28. Lesky 1968: cols. 740–50; the quotation: 749.
29. 'Ilios' is mentioned in *The Iliad* 106 times, 'Troy' 49 times. On the two names and their metrically governed interchangeability in Homer see Visser 1997: 83–94 ('Das Beispiel Troia').
30. 'Limited damage (entailing further adjustment) was, however, clearly tolerable, and apparently sometimes preferable to the simple retention of archaic forms': Horrocks 1997: 208.

31. Wachter 2000: 80, note 24.
32. West 2000 (see the relevant passages). Whether nevertheless the form of text reproduced is that which *Homer* at these points spoke and wrote is uncertain. We do not know whether Greek bards of the eighth century like Homer, alongside the old genitive ending *-oio*, recognized, spoke, and wrote the transitional ending *-oo* as well, the ending *ō* being merely an adaptation made later in the process of handing down. If Homer himself had spoken and written *-ō*, then the insertion in the text of *-oo* would reproduce, not *Homer's Iliad*, but a '*Wiliás antehomerica*'.
33. Kirk 1960: 197.
34. The most recent German-language description of Greek linguistics by M. Meier-Brügger provides only a description of this process of change (Meier-Brügger 1992, II: 79 f., F 313.3: *-osjo*> *-ojjo* > *-ojo* > *-oo* > *-ō* [written *-ou*]; see also Chantraine 1986–8, I: 194, § 80), but no indication of its *absolute chronology.*
35. West 1997: 230.
36. 'Penthilides' was the name of one of the most prominent noble clans on the island of Lesbos about 600 BC.
37. Atreus was, as we have seen above, the father of Agamemnon and Menelaos.
38. Janko 1992: 19. There is a summary of the linguistic facts which demonstrate this also in Latacz 1997*b*: 30–2.
39. Overview in Horrocks 1997. We cannot here take a position in the controversy between the adherents of the 'Aeolian stage' and the 'diffusionists'.
40. West 1988: 163; Latacz 1997*b*: 31.
41. West 1988: 163.
42. Spencer 1995: 276.
43. Cf. Spencer 1995: 275, note 29: 'It is perhaps also worthy of note that even in the *Iliad* Lesbos is grouped very much with Anatolia, since Achilles speaks of the island as the furthest outpost of Priam's kingdom, Hom. *Il.* XXIV. 544–6.' More extensively in Latacz 1997*b*: 31 f.—Spencer had also pointed out that Lesbos was one of the few places in later Greece named in *Hittite* texts: 275 and note 24.
44. Deger-Jalkotzy 1991: 148 f.
45. Mountjoy 1993.
46. Latacz 1994.
47. Hölkeskamp 2000: 27.
48. Weiler 2001: 57 f. (without knowledge of Latacz 1994).
49. See e.g. Korfmann 1999*a* and cf. p. 206 with note 4.

THE TALE OF TROY AND HISTORY

1. Mountjoy 1998. The earliest Mycenaean ceramics so far discovered at Hisarlık derive from Troy VI d (= LH II A. *c.*1500–1460): Mountjoy 1997: 276 f.
2. '(it was a question) of a city... the name of which is no longer legible. Forrer inserted Wiluša at that point... a very doubtful amendment upon which no historical finding should be based....': Heinhold-Krahmer 1977: 176.
3. Parker 1999.
4. Preliminary report: Aravantinos, Godart, and Sacconi 1995. Reference: TH Gp 164 (Godart and Sacconi 1999: 541).
5. Starke 1997: 456.

THE RESULT: THERE PROBABLY WAS A WAR OVER TROY

1. Bryce 1998: 392–404.
2. Bryce 1998: 399 f.
3. Bryce 2002: 267. 'The tradition of a Trojan war very possibly has a basis in historical fact. But if so, it almost certainly represents a conflation of events, beginning perhaps a century or more before the alleged dates of the war in Greek literature and continuing beyond the end of the Bronze Age.' However, according to the preface, this was written before August 2001 and evidently still without knowledge of the latest research on Troy (Starke, Niemeier, Mountjoy, *et al.*)
4. Niemeier 1999: 154.
5. Page 1959: 32, note 42.
6. See *Antike Welt*, 5/2000: 525.
7. Peschlow-Bindokat and Herbordt 2002. The author sees this new inscription as confirmation both of the geographical estimations of Starke 1997 and Hawkins 1999 (from south to north: Mira—Seha—Wilusa) and of Luwian as the language of western Anatolia in the second millennium BC.
8. Niemeier 2003*a* (forthcoming): 351, note 153a.
9. Note the very similar judgement of the eminent American ancient historian Kurt Raaflaub: 'In conclusion, I have presented both the reasons that—still or again—make faith in the historicity of at least a core tradition on an historical Trojan War possible, and the reasons that militate against such a belief. *In fact the two views may not be as incompatible as it seems*' (my italics, JL). This view was presented in February 1997 (at the Colloquium 'The World of Troy: Homer, Schliemann, and the Treasures of Priam' held by the Society for the Preservation of the Greek Heritage, Smithsonian Institute, Washington,

DC, 21–2 Feb. 1997), to an audience with general interests, without going into an exhaustive treatment of the extensive scholarly research and without the benefit of greatly intensified research into Troy and Asia Minor which has taken place since 1997. As this book has demonstrated, by 2003, the state of the research field had developed and diversified.

BIBLIOGRAPHY

Allen, Th. W. (1921), *The Homeric Catalogue of Ships* (Oxford).

Andrikou, E. (1999), 'The Pottery from the Destruction Layer of the Linear B Archive in Pelopidou Street, Thebes: A Preliminary Report', in Deger-Jalkotzy *et al.*, eds. (1999), *I*, 79–102.

Aravantinos, V. (1999), 'Mycenaean Texts and Contexts at Thebes: The Discovery of New Linear B Archives on the Kadmeia', in Deger-Jalkotzy *et al.*, eds. (1999), *I*, 45–78.

——, Godart, L. and Sacconi, A. (1995), 'Sui nuovi testi del palazzo di Cadmo a Tebe', *Atti della Accademia Nazionale dei Lincei*, 1–37.

——, ——, and —— (eds.) (2001), *Thèbes. Fouilles de la Cadmée. I: Les Tablettes en Linéaire B de la 'Odos Pelopidou'. Édition et Commentaire* (Pisa and Rome).

Bartoněk, A. (1991), 'Die Erforschung des Verhältnisses des mykenischen Griechisch zur homerischen Sprachform', in Latacz (1991), 289–310.

Becker, H., and Jansen, H. G. (1994), 'Magnetische Prospektion 1993 in der Unterstadt von Troia und Ilion', *Studia Troica*, 4, 105–14.

——, Fassbinder, J., and Jansen, H. G. (1993), 'Magnetische Prospektion in der Untersiedlung von Troia 1992', *Studia Troica*, 3, 117–34.

Bennet, J. (1995), 'Space through Time: Diachronic Perspectives on the Spatial Organization of the Pylian State', *Aegaeum*, 12, 587–601.

—— (1997), 'Homer and the Bronze Age', in Morris and Powell (1997), 511–34.

Beye, C. R. (1961), 'A New Meaning of *ναυς* in the Catalogue', *American Journal of Philology*, 82, 370–8.

Bittel, K. (1969), 'Bericht über die Ausgrabungen in Boğazköy im Jahre 1968', *Mitteilungen der Deutschen Orient-Gesellschaft*, 101.

Blegen, C. W. (1963), *Troy and the Trojans* (London).

—— *et al.* (1953), *Troy III: The Sixth Settlement* (Princeton).

Blome, P. (1991), 'Die dunklen Jahrhunderte', in Latacz (1991), 45–60.

Borchardt, J. (1997), 'Helme', in H.-G. Buchholz and J. Wiesner (eds.), *Archaeologica Homerica. Kriegswesen, Teil I: Schutzwaffen und Wehrbauten* (Göttingen), E 57–E 74.

Bowra, C. (1952), *Heroic Poetry* (London).

Bryce, T. (1998), *The Kingdom of the Hittites* (Oxford).

—— (2002), *Life and Society in the Hittite World* (Oxford).

Burkert, W. (1975), 'Apellai und Apollon', in *Rheinisches Museum für Philologie*, 118, 1–21.

——(1984), *Die orientalisierende Epoche in der griechischen Religion und Literatur* (Heidelberg).

Burr, V. (1944), *ΝΕΩΝ ΚΑΤΑΛΟΓΟΣ* (Leipzig).

Carpenter, R. (1956), *Folk Tale, Fiction and Saga in the Homeric Epics*, 2nd edn. (Berkeley).

Chadwick, J. (1959), *The Decipherment of Linear B* (Cambridge).

——(1969), *The Mycenaean World* (London).

Chantraine, P. (1986–8), *Grammaire homérique*, 6th edn. (Paris).

Cline, E. H. (1987), 'Amenhotep III and the Aegean: A Reassessment of Egypto-Aegean Relations in the 14th Century BC', *Orientalia*, 56, 1–36.

——(1994), *Sailing the Wine-Dark Sea: International Trade in the Late Bronze Age Aegean*, BAR International Series 591 (Oxford).

Cobet, J. (1994), 'Gab es den Trojanischen Krieg?', *Antike Welt*, no. 4, 1983, reprinted in no. 25, 1994 (special issue), 3–22.

——(1997), *Heinrich Schliemann: Archäologe und Abenteurer* (Munich).

——, von Graeve, V., Niemeier, W.-D., and Zimmermann, K. (eds.) (2003), *Frühes Ionien. Ein Bestandsaufnahme. Akten des internationalen Kolloquiums zum einhundertjährigen Jubiläum der Ausgrabung in Milet, Panionion/Güzelçamli 26.09–1.10.1999.*

Cook, J. M. (1975), 'Greek Settlement in the Eastern Aegean and Asia Minor', in *The Cambridge Ancient History II*, 3rd edn. (Cambridge), ch. XXXVIII.

Deger-Jalkotzy, S. (1991), 'Die Erforschung des Zusammenbruchs der sogenannten mykenischen Kultur und der sogenannten dunklen Jahrhunderte', in Latacz (1991), 127–54.

——, Hiller, S., and Panagl, O. (eds.) (1999), *Floreant Studia Mycenaea. Akten des X. Internationalen Mykenologischen Colloquiums in Salzburg vom 1.–5. Mai 1995*, Vols. I, II (Vienna).

Der Neue Pauly: Enzyklopädie der Antike (1996–), ed. H. Cancik and H. Schneider, (Stuttgart and Weimar).

Dickie, M. (1995), 'The Geography of Homer's World', in Ø. Andersen and M. Dickie (eds.), *Homer's World: Fiction, Tradition, Reality* (Bergen), 29–56.

Doblhofer, E. (1993), *Die Entzifferung alter Schriften und Sprachen* (Stuttgart).

Dörpfeld, W. (1894), *Troja 1893* (Leipzig).

——(1902), *Troja und Ilion: Ergebnisse der Ausgrabungen in den vorhistorischen und historischen Schichten von Ilion 1870–1894* (Athens).

Düntzer, H. (1979), 'Über den Einfluss des Metrums auf den Homerischen Ausdruck', *Jahrbücher für classische Philologie*, 10, 673–94; excerpts reprinted in Latacz (1979), 88–108.

Easton, D. F. (1992), 'Schliemanns Ausgrabungen in Troia', in J. Cobet and B. Patzek (eds.), *Archäologie und historische Erinnerung* (Essen), 51–72.

——(1994), 'Schliemann Did Admit the Mycenaean Date of Troia VI', *Studia Troica*, 4, 173–5.

——, Hawkins, J. D., Sherratt, A. G., and Sherratt, E. S. (2002), 'Troy in Recent Perspective', *Anatolian Studies*, 52 [published February 2003], 75–109.

Edel, E. (1996), *Die Ortsnamenliste aus dem Totentempel Amenophis*, iii (Bonn).

Fehrentz, V. (1993), 'Der antike Agyieus', *Jahrbuch des Deutschen Archäologischen Instituts*, 108, 123–96.

Floreant Studia Mycenaea see Deger-Jalkotzy *et al.* (eds.) (1999).

Forrer, E. (1924), 'Vorhomerische Griechen in den Keilschrifttexten von Bogazköi', *Mitteilungen der deutschen Orient-Gesellschaft*, 63, 1–24.

——(1924*a*), 'Die Griechen in den Boghazköi-Texten', *Orientalische Literaturzeitung*, 27, 113–25.

Friedrich, J. (1930), *Staatsverträge des Ḫatti-Reiches in hethitischer Sprache*, Part 2 (Leipzig).

Frühes Ionien see Cobet *et al.* (eds.) (2003).

Fuhrmann, M. (1994), review of Christa Wolf's 'Kassandra', *Arbitrium*, 1, 209–15.

Garstang, J., and Gurney, O. (1959), *The Geography of the Hittite Empire* (London).

Genette, G. (1982), *Palimpsestes: La Littérature au second degré* (Paris).

——(1994), *Die Erzählung* (Munich).

Giovannini, A. (1969), *Étude historique sur les origines du Catalogue des Vaisseaux* (Berne).

Godart, L. (1994*a*), 'La scrittura di Troia', *Atti della Accademia Nazionale dei Lincei*, 457–60.

——(1994*b*), 'Les Écritures crétoises et le bassin méditerranéen', *Académie des Inscriptions et Belles-Lettres. Comptes Rendus des Séances de l'Année*, 707–31.

—— and Sacconi, A. (1996), 'Les Dieux Thébains dans les Archives Mycéniennes', *Académie des Inscriptions et Belles-Lettres. Comptes Rendus des Séances de l'Année*, Jan.–Mar. (Paris), 99–113.

—— and ——(1996*a*), 'La Triade Tebana nei documenti in Lineare B del palazzo di Cadmo', *Atti della Accademia Nazionale dei Lincei*, 283–5.

—— and —— (1998), 'Les Archives de Thèbes et le Monde Mycénien', *Académie des Inscriptions et Belles-Lettres. Comptes Rendus des Séances de l'Année*, July–Oct. (Paris), 889–906.

—— and —— (1999), 'La Géographie des États mycéniens', *Académie des Inscriptions et Belles-Lettres. Comptes Rendus des Séances de l'Année*, Apr.–June (published 2001), (Paris), 527–46.

Gorny, R. L. (1993), 'The Biconvex Seals of Alişar Höyük', *Anatolian Studies*, 43, 163–91.

Gurney, O. R. (1952), *The Hittites* (London; rev. edn. 1990).

—— (1992), 'Hittite Geography: Thirty Years After', in H. Otten, E. Akurgal, H. Ertem, and A. Süel (eds.), *Hittite and Other Anatolian and Near Eastern Studies in Honour of Sedat Alp* (Ankara), 213–21.

Güterbock, H. G. (1986), 'Troy in the Hittite Texts', in Mellink, ed. (1986), 33–44.

—— (1990), 'Wer war Tawagalawa?', *Orientalia*, 59, 157–65.

——, Bittel, E., *et al.* (eds.) (1975), *Boğazköy V* (Berlin).

Hagenbuchner, A. (1989), *Die Korrespondenz der Hethiter*, 2 Parts (Heidelberg).

Haider, P. W. (1988), *Griechenland-Nordafrika: Ihre Beziehungen zwischen 1600 und 600 v. Chr.* (Darmstadt).

Hampl, F. (1962), 'Der Ilias ist kein Geschichtsbuch', *Seria Philologica Aenipontana*, 7/8, 37–63.

Hawkins, J. D. (1998), 'Tarkasnawa King of Mira: "Tarkondemos", Boğazköy Sealings and Karabel', *Anatolian Studies*, 48 (published 2000), 1–31.

—— (1999), 'Karabel, "Tarkondemos", and the Land of Mira: New Evidence on the Hittite Empire Period in Western Anatolia', *Würzburger Jahrbücher für die Altertumswissenschaft*, 23, 7–14 (abstract of a conference paper delivered in Würzburg, December 1998).

——, and Easton, D. F. (1996), 'A Hieroglyphic Seal from Troia', *Studia Troica*, 6, 111–18.

——, and Morpurgo Davies, A. (1998), 'Of Donkeys, Mules and Tarkondemos', in J. Jasanoff, Craig Melchert, and L. Oliver (eds.), *MÍR CURAD: Studies in Honor of Calvert Watkins* (Innsbruck), 243–60.

Heinhold-Krahmer, S. (1977), *Arzawa: Untersuchungen zu seiner Geschichte nach den hethitischen Quellen* (Heidelberg).

Helck, W. (1979), *Die Beziehungen Ägyptens und Vorderasiens zur Ägäis bis ins 7. Jahrhundert v. Chr.*, 2nd edn. (Darmstadt).

Heubeck, A. (1979), 'Schrift', *Archaeologia Homerica*, ch. 10 (Göttingen).

Hiller, S. (1999), 'Homerische und mykenische Phrasen', in Deger-Jalkotzy *et al.*, eds. (1999), *I*, 289–98.

Hoffner, Jr., H. A. (1982), 'The Milawata Letter Augmented and Reinterpreted', *Archiv für Orientforschung*, No. 19, 130–1.

Hölkeskamp, K.-J. (2000), 'Von Palast zur Polis—die griechische Frühgeschichte als Epoche', in H.-J. Gehrke and H. Schneider (eds.), *Geschichte der Antike: Ein Studienbuch* (Stuttgart and Weimar), 17–44.

Hope Simpson, R., and Lazenby, F. (1970), *The Homeric Catalogue of Ships* (Oxford).

Horrocks, G. (1997), 'Homer's Dialect', in Morris and Powell, eds. (1997), 193–217.

Houwink ten Cate, P. H. J. (1983–4), 'Sidelights on the Ahhiyawa Question from Hittite Vassal and Royal Correspondence', *Jaarbericht van het Vooraziatisch-Egyptisch Genootschap 'Ex Oriente Lux'*, 28, 33–79.

Iakovides, S. (1977), 'Vormykenische und mykenische Wehrbauten', *Archaeologica Homerica*, E 1 (Göttingen), 161–221.

—— (1983), *Late Helladic Citadels on Mainland Greece* (Leiden).

Jablonka, P. (1994), 'Ein Verteidigungsgraben in der Unterstadt von Troia VI: Grabungsbericht 1993', *Studia Troica*, 4, 51–66.

—— (1996), 'Ausgrabungen im Süd der Unterstadt von Troia im Bereich des Troia VI-Verteidigungsgrabens. Grabungsbericht 1995', *Studia Troica*, 6, 65–96.

Janko, R. (1992), 'The Origins and Evolution of the Epic Diction', in G. S. Kirk, *The Iliad: A Commentary*. Vol. IV: Books 13–16 (Cambridge), 8–19.

Kakridis, J. Th. (1949), *Homeric Researches* (Lund).

von Kamptz, H. (1982), *Homerische Personennamen* (Göttingen; dissertation, Jena, 1958).

Kirk, G. S. (1960), 'Objective Dating Criteria in Homer', *Museum Helveticum*, 17, 189–205.

—— (1985), *The Iliad: A Commentary*. Vol. I: Books 1–4 (Cambridge).

Klengel, H. (1979), *Handel und Händler im alten Orient* (Vienna, Cologne, and Graz).

—— (1989), *Kulturgeschichte des alten Vorderasien* (Berlin).

Kolb, F. (1984), *Die Stadt im Altertum* (Munich).

—— (2002), 'Ein neuer Troia-Mythos? Traum und Wirklichkeit auf dem Grabungshügel von Hisarlık', in H.-J. Behr, G. Biegel, and H. Castritius (eds.), *Troia: Mythos in Geschichte und Rezeption* (Braunschweig).

Koppenhöffer, D. (1997), 'TROIA VII—Versuch einer Zusammenschau einschliesslich des Jahres 1995', *Studia Troica*, 7, 293–353.

Korfmann, M. (1986), 'Troy: Topography and Navigation', in Mellink, ed. (1986), 1–16.

—— (1991), 'Troia—Reinigungs- und Dokumentationsarbeiten 1987. Ausgrabungen 1988 und 1989', *Studia Troica*, 1, 17–34.

—— (1991*a*), 'Der gegenwartige Stand der neuen archäologischen Arbeiten in Hisarlık (Troia)', in Latacz (1991), 89–102.

——(1992), 'TROIA—Ausgrabungen 1990 und 1991', *Studia Troica*, 2, 1–41.

——(1992*a*), 'Die prähistorische Besiedlung südlich der Burg Troia VI/VII', *Studia Troica*, 2, 123–46.

——(1993), 'TROIA—Ausgrabungen 1992', *Studia Troica*, 3, 1–37.

——(1994), 'TROIA—Ausgrabungen 1993', *Studia Troica*, 4, 1–50.

——(1995), 'TROIA—Ausgrabungen 1994', *Studia Troica*, 5, 1–40.

——(1995*a*), 'Troia: A Residential and Trading City at the Dardanelles', in R. Laffineur and W.-D. Niemeier (eds.), *Politeia: Society and State in the Aegean Bronze Age* (=*Aegaeum*, 12), 173–83 and Plates XXIII–XXXIII.

——(1996), 'TROIA—Ausgrabungen 1995', *Studia Troica*, 6, 1–63.

——(1997), 'TROIA—Ausgrabungen 1996', *Studia Troica*, 7, 1–71.

——(1997*a*), 'Hisarlık und das Troia Homers—Ein Beispiel zur kontroversen Einschätzung der Möglichkeiten der Archäologie', in B. Pongratz-Leisten, H. Kühne, and P. Xella (eds.), *Ana šadî Labnāni lū allik. Beiträge zu altorientalischen und mittelmeerischen Kulturen. Festschrift Wolfgang Röllig* (Kevelaer and Neukirchen-Vluyn), 171–84.

——(1998*a*), 'Troia, an Ancient Anatolian Palatial and Trading Center: Archaeological Evidence for the Period of Troia VI/VII', *The Classical World*, 91, 369–85 (reproduced with minimal change from D. Boedeker (ed.), *The World of Troy: Homer, Schliemann, and the Treasures of Priam* (Seminar at the Smithsonian Institution, 21–2 Feb. 1997), Washington, 1997).

——(1998*b*), 'Homers Troia aus der Sicht eines Ausgräbers', in W. Baum (ed.), *Perspektiven eines zeitgemässen Humanismus: Protokolle der 'Ersten Klagenfurter Humanismus-Gespräche'* (Klagenfurt), 103–25 (authorized text of lecture).

——(1998*c*), 'Stelen vor den Toren Troias: Apaliunas-Apollon in Truisa/Wilusa?', in G. Arsebük, M. J. Mellink, and W. Schirmer (eds.), *Light on Top of the Black Hill: Studies Presented to Halet Çambel* (Istanbul), 471–88.

——(1999), 'TROIA—Ausgrabungen 1998', *Studia Troica*, 9, 1–34.

——(1999*a*), *TROIA—Ausgrabungen 1999, Bericht vom 18 Aug. 1999* (typescript).

——(1999*b*), Zusammenfassung des Kolloquiumsbeitrages und des Vortrages [von Manfred Korfmann] 'Homer als Zeitzeuge für die Ruinen von Troia im 8. Jahrhundert v. u. Z.', *Würzburger Jahrbücher für die Altertumswissenschaft*, 23, 35–41.

——(2000), 'Homers Troia: Griechischer Aussenposten oder hethitischer Vasall?', *Spektrum der Wissenschaft*, 7, 64–70.

——(2000*a*), Rundbrief an die 'Freunde von Troia', 20 Aug. 2000.

Korfmann, M. (2001), 'Wilusa/(W)Ilios ca. 1200 v. Chr.—Ilion ca. 700 v. Chr. Befundberichte aus der Archäologie', in *Troia. Traum und Wirklichkeit. Wissenschaftlicher Begleitband zur Troia-Ausstellung* (Stuttgart, Braunschweig, and Bonn).

——, and Becks, R. (1999), Persönlicher Rundbrief an die 'Freunde von Troia', 19 Aug. 1999.

——, and Mannsperger, D. (1998), *TROIA: Ein historischer Überblick und Rundgang* (Stuttgart). In English as *Guide to Troy* (2003).

——, *et al.* (1998), 'TROIA—Ausgrabungen 1997 mit einem topographischen Plan zu "Troia und Unterstadt"', *Studia Troica*, 8, 1–70.

Kretschmer, P. (1924), 'Alakšanduš, König von Viluša', *Glotta*, 13, 205–13.

Kullmann, W. (1960), *Die Quellen der Ilias* (Wiesbaden).

——(1992), *Homerische Motive* (Stuttgart).

——(1993), 'Festgehaltene Kenntnisse im Schiffskatalog und im Troerkatalog der Ilias', *ScriptOralia*, 61 (Tübingen), 129–47.

——(1995), 'Homers Zeit und das Bild des Dichters von den Menschen der mykenischen Kultur', in Ø. Andersen and M. Dickie (eds.), *Homer's World: Fiction, Tradition, Reality* (Bergen), 57–75.

——(1999), 'Homer and Historical Memory', in E. A. Mackay (ed.), *Signs of Orality: The Oral Tradition and its Influence in the Greek and Roman World* (Leiden etc.), 95–113.

——(1999*a*), 'Homer und Kleinasien', in J. N. Kazazis and A. Rengakos (eds.), *Euphrosyne: Studies in Ancient Epic and its Legacy in Honor of Dimitris N. Maronitis* (Stuttgart), 189–201.

Latacz, J. (1979), *Homer: Tradition und Neuerung* (Darmstadt; Wege der Forschung, Vol. 463).

——(1988), 'Neue von Troja', *Gymnasium*, 95, 385–413.

——(ed.) (1991), *Zweihundert Jahre Homer-Forschung: Rückblick and Ausblick*, Colloquia Raurica, Vol. 2, (Stuttgart and Leipzig).

——(1991*a*), 'Hauptfunktionen des antiken Epos in Antike und Moderne', *Der altsprachliche Unterricht*, 34/3, 8–17.

——(1994), 'Between Troy and Homer: The So-Called Dark Ages in Greece', in *Storia, Poesia e Pensiero nel mondo antico: Studi in onore di Marcello Gigante* (Naples), 347–63.

——(1995), *Achilleus: Wandlungen eines europäischen Heldenbildes*, 2nd edn. (Stuttgart and Leipzig).

——(1997), *Homer: Der erste Dichter des Abendlands* (Munich and Zurich, 1985; 3rd edn. Düsseldorf and Zurich).

——(1997*a*), 'Epischer Zyklus', in *Der Neue Pauly*, Vol. 3, cols. 1154–6.

——(1997*b*), 'Troia und Homer', in H. D. Galter (ed.), *Troia: Mythen und Archäologie* (= H. D. Galter and B. Scholz (eds.), *Grazer Morgenländische Studien*, Vol. 4), (Graz), 1–37.

——(1998), *Die griechische Literatur in Text und Darstellung, Band 1: Archaische Periode*, 2nd edn. (Stuttgart).

——(1998*a*), 'Epos. II. Klassische Antike', in *Der Neue Pauly*, Vol. 4, 12–22.

——(2000), *Homers Ilias: Gesamtkommentar (Prolegomena: I. 1: Text und Übersetzung; I. 2: Kommentar)*, (Munich and Leipzig).

——(2001), *Troia—Wilios—Wilusa. Drei Namen für ein Territorium* (Basel; 2nd edn. 2002).

——(2002*a*), 'Troia—Wilios—Wilusa. Drei Namen für ein Territorium', in *Mauerschau, Festschrift für Manfred Korfmann*, Vol. 3, Remshalden-Grunbach, 1103–21.

——(2003), 'Frühgriechische Epik und Lyrik in Ionien', in Cobet *et al.*, eds. (2003).

Leaf, W. (1915), *Homer and History* (London).

Lehmann, G. A. (1985), *Die mykenisch-frühgriechische Welt und der östliche Mittelmeerraum in der Zeit der 'Seevölker'-Invasionen um 1200 v. Chr.* (Opladen) (= Rheinisch-Westfälische Akademie der Wissenschaften. Geisteswissenschaften. Vorträge. G 276).

Lehmann, G. A. (1991), 'Die "politisch-historische" Beziehungen der Ägäis-Welt des 15.-13. Jh.s v. Chr. zu Ägypten und Vorderasien: einige Hinweise', in Latacz 1991: 105–26.

Lehmann, G. A. (1996), 'Umbrüche und Zäsuren im östlichen Mittelmeerraum und Vorderasien zur Zeit der "Seevölker"-Invasionen um und nach 1200 v. Chr. Neue Quellenzeugnisse und Befunde', *Historische Zeitschrift*, 262, 1–38.

Lesky, A. (1968), 'Homeros', in *Realencyclopädie der classischen Altertumswisssenschaft, Supplement-Band XI* (Stuttgart), cols. 687–846.

Linsmeier, K.-D. (2003), 'Troia—umkämpfter Wächter über die Dardanellen', *Spektrum der Wissenschaft* (October), 22–5.

Mannsperger, B. (1995), 'Die Funktion des Grabens am Schiffslager der Achäer', *Studia Troica*, 5, 343–56.

Meier-Brügger, M. (1992), *Griechische Sprachwissenschaft, 2 Bde.* (Berlin and New York).

Meier-Brügger, M. (2000), *Indogermanische Sprachwissenschaft*, 7th edn. (Berlin).

Mellink, M. J. (ed.) (1986), *Troy and the Trojan War: A Symposium Held at Bryn Mawr College, October 1984* (Bryn Mawr).

Morris, I., and Powell, B. (eds.) (1997), *A New Companion to Homer* (Leiden).

Mountjoy, P. A. (1993), *Mycenaean Pottery: An Introduction* (Oxford).

——(1997), 'Troia Phase VIf and Phase VIg: The Mycenaean Pottery', *Studia Troica*, 7, 275–94.

Mountjoy, P. A. (1998), 'The East Aegean–West Anatolian Interface in the Late Bronze Age: Mycenaeans and the Kingdom of Ahhiyawa', *Anatolian Studies*, 48 (published 2000), 33–67.

Müller, K. (1930), *Tiryns III: Die Architektur der Burg und des Palastes* (Augsburg).

Naumann, R. (1971), *Architektur Kleinasiens von ihren Anfängen bis zum Ende der hethitischen Zeit*, 2nd edn. (Tübingen).

Neumann, G. (1975), 'Makedonia', in *Der Kleine Pauly* (Munich), cols. 910–19.

——(1975*a*), 'Thrake', in *Der Kleine Pauly* (Munich), cols. 777–83.

——(1992), 'System und Ausbau der hethitischen Hieroglyphenschrift', *Nachrichten der Akademie der Wissenschaften in Göttingen*, 4, 23–48.

——(1993), 'Zu den epichorsichen Sprachen Kleinasiens', in G. Dobesch and G. Rehrenböck (eds.), *Hundert Jahre Kleinasiatische Kommission der Österreichischen Akademie der Wissenschaften* (Vienna), 289–96.

——(1999), 'Wie haben die Troer in 13. Jahrhundert gesprochen', *Würzburger Jahrbücher für die Altertumswissenschaft*, 23, 15–23.

Niemeier, W.-D. (1998), 'The Mycenaeans in Western Anatolia and the Problem of the Origins of the Sea Peoples', in S. Gitin, A. Mazar, and E. Stern (eds.), *Mediterranean Peoples in Transition: Thirteenth to Early Tenth Centuries* BCE *(Symposion Jerusalem, 3–7 April 1995)*, (Jerusalem), 17–65.

——(1999), 'Mycenaeans and Hittites in War in Western Asia Minor', *Aegaeum*, 19, 141–55 (+ Plate XV).

——(2001), in M. Akurgal, M. Kerschner, H. Mommsen, and W.-D. Niemeier (eds.), *Töpferzentren der Ostägäis: Archäometrische Untersuchungen zur mykenischen, geometrischen und archaischen Keramik aus Fundorten in Westkleinasien (3. Ergänzungsheft der Österreichischen Jahreshefte)*, (Vienna).

——(2003*a*), 'Milet von den Anfängen bis ans Ende der Bronzezeit', in Cobet *et al.*, eds. (2003).

——(2003*b*), 'Hethitische Quellen und spätbronzezeitliche Topographie und Geschichte des westlichen Kleinasien', in Cobet *et al.*, eds. (2003).

Niese, B. (1873), *Der homerische Schiffskatalog als historische Quelle betrachtet*, Dissertation (Kiel).

Nilsson, M. P. (1967), *Geschichte der griechischen Religion I*, 3rd edn. (Munich).

Olivier, J.-P. (1999), 'Rapport 1991–1995 sur les textes en écriture hiéroglyphique crétoise, en Linéaire A et en Linéaire B', in Deger-Jalkotzy *et al.*, eds. (1999), II, 419–35.

Otten, H. (1966), 'Hethiter, Ḫurriter und Mitanni', in *Fischer Weltgeschichte, Band 3: Die altorientalischen Reiche II. Das Ende des 2. Jahrtausends* (Frankfurt am Main), 102–76.

——(1988), *Die Bronzetafel aus Boğazköy: Ein Staatsvertrag Tutḫalijas* IV (Studien zu den Boğazköy-Texten. Beiheft 1), (Wiesbaden).

Page, Denys (1959), *History and the Homeric Iliad* (Berkeley and Los Angeles).

Parker, V. (1999), 'Die Aktivitäten der Mykenäer in der Ost-Ägäis im Lichte der Linear B-Tafeln', in Deger-Jalkotzy *et al.*, eds. (1999), *II*, 495–502.

Parry, A. (ed.) (1971), *The Making of Homeric Verse: The Collected Papers of M. Parry* (Oxford).

Parry, M. (1928), *L'Epithète traditionelle dans Homère* (Paris).

Peschlow-Bindokat, A., and Herbordt, S. (2002), 'Die Hethiter im Latmos: Eine hethitisch-luwische Hieroglyphen-Inschrift am Suratkaya (Besparmak, Westtürkei), *Antike Welt*, 33/2, 211–15.

Pestalozzi, H. (1945), *Die Achilleis als Quelle der Ilias*, Dissertation (Zürich).

Pfeiffer, R. (1982), *Die Klassische Philologie von Petrarca bis Mommsen* (Munich).

Raaflaub, K. (1998), 'Homer, the Trojan War, and History', *Classical World*, 91, 386–403.

Rawlinson, Major H. C. (1850), 'A Commentary on the Cuneiform Inscriptions of Babylonia and Assyria, including Readings of the Inscription on the Nimrud Obelisk, and a brief notice of the Ancient Kings of Nineveh and Babylon', read before the Royal Asiatic Society by Major H. C. Rawlinson (London).

Richter, W. (1992), *Heinrich Schliemann: Dokumente seines Lebens* (Leipzig).

Riemschneider, M. (1954), *Die Welt der Hethiter* (Stuttgart).

Sakellariou, M. B. (1958), *La Migration grecque en Ionie* (Athens).

Schachermeyr, F. (1983), *Die griechische Rückerinnerung im Lichte neuer Forschungen* (Vienna).

——(1986), *Mykene und das Hethiterreich* (Vienna).

Schliemann, H. (1874), *Trojanische Alterthümer: Bericht über die Ausgrabungen in Troja* (Leipzig). (Reprinted with preface by M. Korfmann, Munich and Zurich, 1990.)

——(1884), *Troja: Ergebnisse meiner neuesten Ausgrabungen auf der Baustelle von Troja . . . im Jahre 1882* (Leipzig).

——(1891), *Bericht über die Ausgrabungen in Troja im Jahre 1890* (Leipzig).

Sieber, M. (1990), *Troia—Homer—Schliemann: Mythos und Wahrheit* (Mainz).

Sommer, F. (1932), *Die Aḫḫijavā*-Urkunden (Munich).

Spencer, N. (1995), 'Early Lesbos between East and West: A "Grey Area" of Aegean Archaeology', *The Annual of the British School at Athens*, 90, 269–306.

Sperling, J. (1991), 'The Last Phase of Troy VI and Mycenean Expansion', *Studia Troica*, 1, 151–8.

Starke, F. (1990), *Untersuchungen zur Stammbildung des keilschrift-luwischen Nomens* (Wiesbaden).

——(1995), *Ausbildung und Training von Streitwagenpferden: Eine hippologisch orientierte Interpretation des Kikkuli-Textes* (Wiesbaden), Studien zu den Boğazköy-Texten, 41.

——(1997), 'Troia im Kontext des historisch-politischen und sprachlichen Umfeldes Kleinasiens im 2. Jahrtausend', *Studia Troica*, 7, 447–87.

——(1998), 'Ḫattusa', *Der Neue Pauly*, Vol. 5, cols. 185–98.

——(1998*a*), 'Hethitisch', *Der Neue Pauly*, Vol. 5, cols. 521–3.

——(1998b), 'Kleinasien. C. Hethitische Nachfolgestaaten', *Der Neue Pauly*, Vol. 6, cols. 518–33.

——(1999), 'Luwisch', *Der Neue Pauly*, Vol. 7, cols. 528–34.

——(2000), 'Mira', *Der Neue Pauly*, Vol. 8, cols. 250–5.

——(2001), 'Troia im Machtgefüge des 2. Jahrtausends v. Chr.', in *TROIA. Wissenschaftlicher Begleitband zur Troia-Ausstellung 2001/2002* (Stuttgart), 34–45.

Stein-Hölkeskamp, E. (2000), 'Die Welten des Homer', in H. J. Gehrke and H. Schneider (eds.), *Geschichte der Antike: Ein Studienbuch* (Stuttgart and Weimar), 44–58.

Stoevesandt, M. (2000), 'Figuren-Index', in Latacz (2000), Prolegomena, 173–207.

Strabo, *The Geography of Strabo: With an English Translation by H. L. Jones*, vols. I–VIII (London and New York, 1917–32).

Thucydides: History of the Peloponnesian War (1954), translated with an introduction by Rex Warner (Harmondsworth).

Troy and the Trojan War see Mellink, ed. (1986).

Tsountas, C., and Manatt, J. I. (1897), *The Mycenaean Age* (London).

Ulf, C. (ed.) (2003), *Der neue Streit um Troia: Eine Bilanz* (Munich).

Vansina, J. (1985), *Oral Tradition as History* (London).

Ventris, M., and Chadwick, J. (1973), *Documents in Mycenaean Greek* (Cambridge 1956; 2nd edn. 1973).

Visser, E. (1997), *Homers Katalog der Schiffe* (Stuttgart and Leipzig).

——(1998), 'Formale Typologien im Schiffskatalog der Ilias: Befunde und Konsequenzen', in H. L. C. Tristram (ed.), *New Methods in the Research of Epic* (Tübingen), 25–44.

Wachter, R. (2000), 'Grammatik der homerischen Sprache', in Latacz (2000), Prolegomena, 61–108.

Watkins, C. (1986), 'The Language of the Trojans', in Mellink, ed. (1986), 45–62.

Webster, T. B. L. (1958), *From Mycenae to Homer* (London).

Weiler, G. (2001), *Domos Theiou Basileos: Herrschaftsformen und Herrschafts-Architektur in den Siedlungen der Dark Ages* (Munich and Leipzig).

Weltatlas (1958), *Grosser historischer Weltatlas*. Bayerischer Schulbuch-Verlag, Part I: Vorgeschichte und Altertum, 3rd edn. (Munich).

West, M. L. (1988), 'The Rise of the Greek Epic', *Journal of Hellenic Studies*, 108, 151–72.

——(1997), 'Homer's Meter', in Morris and Powell, eds. (1997), 218–37.

——(1997*a*), *The East Face of Helicon: West Asiatic Elements in Greek Poetry and Art* (Oxford).

——(2000), *Homerus. Ilias*. Recensuit Martin L. West, Vol. II (Munich and Leipzig).

——(2001), 'Atreus and Attarassiyas', *Glotta*, 77 [published 2003], 262–6.

Wilamowitz-Moellendorff, U. von (1903), 'Apollon', *Hermes*, 38, 575–86.

Willcock, M. M. (1978–84), *Homer: Iliad*, ed. with Introduction and Commentary by M.M.W., 2 vols. (London).

INDEX

Illustrations are indicated by page numbers in **bold**. Page numbers followed by *n* indicate a chapter note: 288*n*3. Titles of papers etc. are shown in single quotation marks and ignore the definite article for filing purposes. Titles of books are shown in italics; titles beginning with the definite or indefinite article are entered under the next word; *Hittites, The* (O. R. Gurney, 1952); *Stadt im Altertum, Die* ('The City in Antiquity', 1984).